Aesthetic Anxiety

141

Internationale Forschungen zur Allgemeinen und Vergleichenden Literaturwissenschaft

herausgegeben von

Alberto Martino
(Universität Wien)

Redaktion: Paul Ferstl und Rudolf Pölzer

Anschrift der Redaktion:
Institut für Vergleichende Literaturwissenschaft, Berggasse 11/5, A-1090 Wien

Aesthetic Anxiety
Uncanny Symptoms in German Literature and Culture

Laurie Ruth Johnson

Rodopi

Amsterdam - New York, NY 2010

Cover photo: Scott Liddell

Cover design: Pier Post

Le papier sur lequel le présent ouvrage est imprimé remplit les prescriptions de "ISO 9706:1994, Information et documentation - Papier pour documents - Prescriptions pour la permanence".

The paper on which this book is printed meets the requirements of " ISO 9706:1994, Information and documentation - Paper for documents - Requirements for permanence".

Die Reihe "Internationale Forschungen zur Allgemeinen und Vergleichenden Literaturwissenschaft" wird ab dem Jahr 2005 gemeinsam von Editions Rodopi, Amsterdam – New York und dem Weidler Buchverlag, Berlin herausgegeben. Die Veröffentlichungen in deutscher Sprache erscheinen im Weidler Buchverlag, alle anderen bei Editions Rodopi.

From 2005 onward, the series "Internationale Forschungen zur Allgemeinen und Vergleichenden Literaturwissenschaft" will appear as a joint publication by Editions Rodopi, Amsterdam – New York and Weidler Buchverlag, Berlin. The German editions will be published by Weidler Buchverlag, all other publications by Editions Rodopi.

ISBN: 978-90-420-3113-5
E-Book ISBN: 978-90-420-3114-2

Printed in The Netherlands

Acknowledgments

The Campus Research Board at the University of Illinois at Urbana-Champaign provided release time and financial assistance during the initial stages of this project, and a sabbatical leave granted by the University was also crucial.

I was fortunate to find Margaret Flynn and am extremely grateful for her careful and insightful copy edit. I also very much appreciate the work done by Esther Roth and Marieke Schilling at Rodopi. Bart Rossmann and Tim Cunningham at the University of Illinois provided important help with final editing.

John McCarthy is an intellectual role model whose ideas and encouragement inspired this book and much of my career as well. Mara Wade's help and confidence in my work made an enormous difference when it really mattered. Azade Seyhan's writing motivated me to study German Romanticism, and the significance of her pathbreaking scholarship is matched by her generosity and warmth. I am grateful to my parents, David and Karen Johnson, and to my sister, Victoria Johnson, for decades of support. I also am privileged to know and to have learned from many friends and colleagues who have discussed this book with me or contributed ideas or support at crucial junctures, including Amanda Boyd, Georg Braungart, Corinne Crane, Susan Curtis, Stefani Engelstein, Michael Finke, Joshua Gold, Andrea Goulet, Jeffrey Grossman, Jon Hamilton, Wail Hassan, Stephanie Hilger, Gregg Horowitz, Stephanie Jaeger, Stephen Jaeger, Robert Jenkins, Brett Kaplan, Karen Kelly, Lutz Koepnick, Jill Anne Kowalik, Angela Lin, Paul Michael Lützeler, Peter McIsaac, Elizabeth Oyler, Brad Prager, Kathy Richards, Howard Roback, Gertrud Roesch, Michael Rothberg, Hania Siebenpfeiffer, Daniel Simons, Christian Sinn, Helmut Walser Smith, Jörn Steigerwald, Lynne Tatlock, Holly Tucker, Meike Werner, and Yasemin Yildiz.

My deepest gratitude belongs to Carl Niekerk, an optimistic and patient exemplar of enlightenment who makes everything work every single day, who sees reality always, and who gently and tirelessly shapes it into form and sense. I dedicate the book to our lively and loving daughters, Naomi and Maaike.

Parts of chapters 1 and 2, in revised form, are forthcoming in *Image and Narrative*. Part of chapter 3 was published in *Women in German Yearbook* 23 (2007) 10-33. An earlier version of part of chapter 5 was published in *Kleists Erzählungen und Dramen. Neue Studien*, eds. Paul Michael Lützeler and David Pan (Würzburg: Königshausen und Neumann, 2001) 121-133.

Contents

Preface 9

Chapter 1
Aesthetic Anxiety and the Uncanny 21
Freud on the Acropolis
The Uncanny Beyond Repetition and the Return of the Repressed

Chapter 2
The Uncanny Before Freud: Psychological and Philosophical Aspects 47
Uncanny Anxiety and Sublime Awe
Philosophical Psychology, Mental Physicalism, and the Pre-Freudian Unconscious
Estranged Knowledge: "Anxious" Texts by Kant and Schelling

Chapter 3
Beautiful Breakdowns: Uncanny Symptoms and the Aestheticization of Illness 95
Magnetism as an Aesthetic and Scientific Practice in the Early Nineteenth Century
The Case Studies of Moritz and Schlegel

Chapter 4
Conspiracy Theories: The Melancholy and Manipulated Male Subject 143
The Curse of Enthusiasm
Male Hysteria and the Uncanny in Tieck and Schiller

Chapter 5
Too Much Memory: Uncanny Love 185
The Anxious Revolution Continues
Disturbers of Love: Uncanny Displacement in Kleist and Hoffmann
Uncanny Love and the Aesthetics of Healing in Lang and Schnitzler

Chapter 6
Conclusion: Childish Anxiety, Wish, Belief 235

Bibliography 243

Preface

…our unconscious has as little use now as it ever had for the idea of its own mortality.
[…unser Unbewußtes hat jetzt so wenig Raum wie vormals für die Vorstellung der eigenen Sterblichkeit.]
Sigmund Freud, *The Uncanny [Das Unheimliche]*

This book is about a rebellious, even revolutionary, and always anxious aspect of texts that appeared between the late eighteenth and early twentieth centuries, a time that can be described as both Romantic and modern. *Aesthetic Anxiety* argues that moments in these texts can be identified when Romanticism, with all of its anti-modern or reactionary traits, confronts its own indebtedness to the Enlightenment, to the modern and to the progressive—when, in a sense, Romanticism acknowledges what it has tried to repress. In these moments, the text's protagonist experiences an uncanny feeling of dislocation, even dissociation, and fear. This anxiety often takes the form of physical symptoms. I use analyses of these "sick" moments to argue that a kind of psychosomatic illness underlies Western modernity; its symptoms make more than casual intermittent appearances and date back to well before 1880-1933, the so-called "age of nervousness."[1] Uncanny anxiety also characterizes texts and movements beyond the German-speaking world, but it is in cultural products of that world that the clash of traditionalist and progressive impulses is compulsively and blatantly repeated and theorized; the uncanny reveals itself in the arc of that tradition as well as within its individual texts.

And yet the uncanny (*das Unheimliche*), an experience of frightening disorientation that is repetitive and reminds us of repetition itself (as well as of the repetitive tendencies of certain psychic mechanisms), traditionally has been understood to function in precisely the opposite way within Western intellectual history since the Enlightenment. According to this view, the uncanny emerges when a dark, irrational, essentially Romantic trait within the self or within a society comes to "light," invades rational space, and refuses to be assimilated into a comprehensible, enlightened agenda. While that understanding is often correct and has been helpful in revealing the "dark side" of the Enlightenment agenda, I argue that the revolutionary possibilities inherent in anxious, frightening, uncanny experiences are clearest when traditionalist, nostalgic impulses meet modernity. This apparent clash happens in literary texts in which, for instance, a character's memories may

---

Note: Throughout the book, translations not attributed to others are my own.
[1] Joachim Radkau, *Das Zeitalter der Nervosität: Deutschland zwischen Bismarck und Hitler* (Munich: Carl Hanser, 1998).

be roused by a completely new experience, or when the forces of cultural change inspire a melancholic, nostalgia-driven desire to slow down to an earlier era's pace. But rational and irrational, progressive and regressive motivations also often appear simultaneously in psychological case studies, studies that preceded Freud by at least a century and that either influenced Romanticism or were part of it. Recurrent psychosomatic symptoms of anxiety were of particular interest to early psychologists, who were at a loss to explain the origins of symptoms that could no longer be attributed to magical, demonic sources.

There remains an exciting potential in looking back to Romanticism and to the cultural movements that precede and follow it, including philosophical Idealism and empirical psychology in the eighteenth century, literary Realism and early psychiatry in the nineteenth, and Expressionism and psychoanalysis in the twentieth. German Romanticism in particular, which lasted roughly from the 1790s to the 1830s, was a movement whose influence on philosophy, aesthetic theory, literature, and psychology cannot be underestimated. The Idealism of the 1790s, which attempted to work with the best of Enlightenment thought in order to produce a model for a rational but not overly rationalized community, gives way, once the effects of the French Revolution have been more fully felt and analyzed, to an inward turn in German-speaking culture that prefigures later depth psychology and ultimately the work of Sigmund Freud. However, it is precisely during this Romantic period and in the German-speaking context that the uncanny, which is to a certain extent an extremely exaggerated manifestation of inwardness, estranges subjects from themselves and forces a turn outward.

Recent cultural theory has emphasized the need for a sense of estrangement in order to enable the tolerance of difference that builds a new form of community in a postmodern (or "trans-modern") age.[2] "Community" is now often understood in global, transcontinental terms that emphasize looking outward, beyond national boundaries and certainly beyond the individual psyche. However, in the late eighteenth and nineteenth centuries, in some of the most introspective of texts, an idea of cosmopolitan community is already indicated, and this idea is a direct forebear of today's critical understandings of responsible world citizenship.[3] But the process of

---

[2] See, for instance, Paul Gilroy's thinking on the need for a stance of "cosmopolitan attachment" characterized in part by "a degree of estrangement from one's own culture and history," in *Postcolonial Melancholia* (New York: Columbia University Press, 2005), 67.

[3] Gilroy argues that Montesquieu's *Lettres persanes* (*Persian Letters*) of 1721 was one of the first works to posit the necessity of estrangement, disorientation, and in fact of disloyalty, to one's own past and culture in order to interact with others on humane terms. "The cosmopolitan position from which Montesquieu wrote suggests that imagining oneself as a stranger in a limited and creative sense might instructively be linked to actually becoming estranged from the cultural habits one is born to. This alienation was not for him a disadvantage; it is his anthropological and indeed ethical method." See *Postcolonial Melancholia* 70-71.

creating such a community is frequently depicted in Romantic texts as neither pleasant nor beautiful, but as horrifying, repulsive, difficult, and ultimately more true to lived experience.

All of the literary, philosophical, theoretical, and psychological texts examined in this book contain one or more of the characteristics or that Freud says distinguish the uncanny from the merely frightening: "animism, magic and sorcery, the omnipotence of thoughts, man's attitude to death, involuntary repetition and the castration complex" ("...Animismus, der Magie und Zauberei, der Allmacht der Gedanken, der Beziehung zum Tode, der unbeabsichtigten Wiederholung und dem Kastrationskomplex").[4] However, while I rely on Freud's 1919 essay on "The Uncanny," a piece emblematic of many of the crucial trends of the middle phase of Freud's career, my interpretations and arguments are not strictly psychoanalytic. Rather, I reference Freud regularly (and particularly his middle- and late-career theories of hysteria, anxiety, and the origin of the self and of civilization, as well as his understanding of the uncanny) in order to enrich a broader approach to texts produced well before the discovery of psychoanalysis and before the naming and exploration of the unconscious. Rather than reading Freud back into Romanticism, then, I examine connections between early German psychology and psychiatry and the literary and philosophical discourses of that time in order to construct a cultural history of the uncanny as well as of the experience of an anxiety that is in part produced by the very aesthetic forms that attempt to bring it under control.

Rather than tracing the historical appearances of the word "uncanny," I attempt to show that the experience that Freud renders fairly monolithic—an encounter with something strangely familiar—had a rich and multivalent past, although Freud's essential understanding of the uncanny is already present in Romantic texts (such as Friedrich Schelling's *Philosophy of Mythology* of 1842, from which Freud derives his initial definition of the term). I wish to demonstrate the potential of that history for a new interpretation of the vexed constellation involving the Enlightenment, Romanticism, and modernity. I thus rethink the aesthetic notion of the uncanny before Freud in order to revisit critical aspects of German cultural history and to provide a more complete picture of the interaction between literature and psychology before the emergence of psychoanalysis.

---

[4] Sigmund Freud, "Das Unheimliche," *Gesammelte Werke* 12 (Frankfurt am Main: Fischer, 1999) 256. This edition is abbreviated henceforth as GW. The translation is James Strachey's in Freud, "The Uncanny," *The Standard Edition of the Complete Psychological Works of Sigmund Freud*, vol. 17 (London: Hogarth, 1953-1974), 243. This edition is abbreviated henceforth as SE.

Although only one book-length study has been devoted to the uncanny as of this writing,[5] the term is seminal in German cultural and literary history as well as in psychoanalytic theory. *Aesthetic Anxiety* produces a new narrative about the importance of aesthetics in discourses beyond literature and philosophy, about object relations and power dynamics, about the search for origin, and about the nature of the self in modernity's formative era. This narrative emerges from a close examination of various uses of uncanny repetition in various fields, namely literature, psychology, philosophy, and film. I reconsider Freud's contention that the experience of uncanniness can be a sign of illness but also signals the return of the repressed, and use this as a springboard for more in-depth readings of German texts. To be sure, the tension between modernity and tradition and between progressive and reactionary tendencies is particularly interesting in the context of German Romanticism, a movement that has been blamed for instigating a separation between the political and the philosophical or aesthetic, a separation that later functioned to legitimate intellectuals' participation in the Third Reich. I want to argue that that tension is not completely specific to German Romanticism, and, in a related vein, that the aesthetic has not been completely divorceable from the scientific since the modern age began.

I hope to illuminate the places where, in part through the aesthetic deployment of horror, anxiety, and disorientation, German texts attempted to show what was going wrong and what was going right with modern culture, and to unify aesthetic principles with various real-life practices. However, although the aesthetics of fear and the subcategory of horrifying uncanny repetition can function as part of a progressive critique of the reactionary aspects of Romanticism, the morbid fascination that the uncanny evokes also may contribute to regressive nostalgia and to an aesthetic glorification of that nostalgia. Among other things, *Aesthetic Anxiety* attempts to separate these cases from one another and to arrive at a better understanding of the uncanny's regressive and progressive potential.

By examining texts of early psychology and psychiatry together with literature, aesthetic theory, and philosophy (occasionally texts written by the same authors), I pull the notion of uncanniness away from the purely psychoanalytic or the philosophical-aesthetic context in which it has often been understood (for instance, as a complement to or opposite of the sublime, although I do consider the relationship between the uncanny and the sublime

---

[5] Nicholas Royle, *The Uncanny: An Introduction* (New York: Routledge, 2003). A number of other significant scholarly works foreground the uncanny (and I refer to them throughout this study), including Terry Castle's *The Female Thermometer: Eighteenth-Century Culture and the Invention of the Uncanny* (Oxford: Oxford UP, 1995) and Joachim von der Thüsen's *Het verlangen naar huivering. Over het sublieme, het wrede en het unheimliche* (Amsterdam: Querido, 1997). An issue of the journal *Paradoxa: Studies in World Literary Genres* is entirely devoted to essays on the uncanny: vol. 3.3-4, 1997.

in Chapter Two) and push it toward the more innovative and, I believe, more productive context of psychological symptomology, and in particular of anxiety. The repetitive, often horrible, but sometimes simultaneously desired experience of anxiety can be an aesthetic mode as well as a psychological state, and I go a step further to contend that portrayals of anxiety reveal the complicity of psychology with aesthetics.

It is in the context of a literary analysis (of E.T.A. Hoffmann's tale *The Sandman*) that Freud states that "every affect belonging to an emotional impulse, whatever its kind, is transformed, if it is repressed, into anxiety" ("jeder Affekt einer Gefühlsregung, gleichgültig von welcher Art, [wird] durch die Verdrängung in Angst verwandelt").[6] That repressed affect, that anxiety, will eventually return, dissociated from the initial emotional impulse that produced it; the dissociation between impulse and affect produces an uncanny symptom, and that symptom often takes an aesthetic form. *Aesthetic Anxiety* attempts to reconstruct the story that these uncanny symptoms tell within texts, but also within broader discourses about illness and health from the late eighteenth to the early twentieth centuries. Specifically, I argue that, in German modernity, the uncanny serves at once to relegate frightening material to the realm of the sick and unnatural *and* to bring such material into the mainstream domain of the self. The experience and representation of the uncanny has functioned to critique and redefine what that "self" precisely is since the Enlightenment, which is the temporal and conceptual home of subject philosophy. It is exactly at the moment in cultural history in which the transcendental self is being most fully defined and most solidly buttressed against the threats of the body and of nature that modern intellectuals are questioning its reliability; the appearance of the uncanny is a form of such questioning.

Aesthetic Anxiety's introductory chapter begins with Freud's intensely personal description of his own uncanny experience on the Acropolis, and then travels back to the Romantic philosopher (and medical student) Friedrich Schelling and his contention that the very earliest cultural narratives are already uncanny. I explore the thesis that uncanny repetition is a means of preserving what Schelling calls "the principle of the past:" it provides a way of living through and with inevitable loss, on an individual as well as cultural level. In Chapter One I also summarize philosophical, psychological, and literary thinking about the uncanny and related aesthetic concepts to date, and make the new argument that the uncanny does not represent the persistence of the anti-modern *within* modernity as much as it represents the deeply ambiguous nature of modernity itself. To be sure, uncanny repetition of repressed material is symptomatic of a state of melancholy, of nostalgia for a lost home (when one is experiencing "das Unheimliche," one yearns for "das Heimliche"). But I argue here and

[6] Freud, GW 12: 254/SE 17: 241.

throughout the book that the uncanny is a deeply modern experience not only because the demons of the pre-modern world have been "repressed," but because nostalgia is part of the condition of modernity. The rejection of fundamentalism and dogma, the embrace of the new, the mortal, the enthusiastic, and the complex go hand-in-hand with a not-always-reactionary, melancholic yearning for a lost unity that, as the modern subject knows all too well, never existed.

Chapters Two and Three provide evidence supporting the above argument through their focus on early texts of German psychology and psychiatry; in these chapters, I emphasize the close connections between those disciplines and the literature and philosophy of the same period. The Enlightenment was an inherently interdisciplinary time; it is not surprising that the authors of the texts considered herein would be heirs to the same traditions and familiar with the same canon. However, the link between psychology and literature in the eighteenth century is particularly strong; psychologists were often literary authors as well, and essays on mental disturbances borrowed freely from contemporary treatises on aesthetic theory. In light of the historical connections between these fields, I seek to demonstrate that early psychology and psychiatry have an aesthetic component right from the beginning. The novelist, aesthetic theorist, and empirical psychologist Karl Philipp Moritz, for instance, envisions his psychological experiments as a form of art, one particularly well-suited for analyzing and depicting the relationship between mind and body, and especially the places where that relationship derails or dissociates. Well before Freud, psychologists focus on uncanny experience as a way to understand inexplicable psychosomatic symptoms; the uncanny is already seen as a way into the unconscious, even before the unconscious is theorized as such. The uncanny, in Moritz's journal of empirical psychology and in the texts it inspires, already reminds us of something we would rather forget; it does not permit us to remain in denial. Uncanny experiences therefore can function as symptoms of reality, and ultimately can point the way to psychic health.

However, this path is a circuitous one. In Chapter Two, I use the concept of "philosophical psychology" to sketch the early history of the uncanny as a term that operates in aesthetic theory as well as in medical discourse. I contend that aesthetic concepts related to judgments of taste, such as sublimity, beauty, horror, dread, and repetition, were related in the late eighteenth and early nineteenth centuries to psychological categories such as enthusiasm, hysteria, and melancholy. This conceptual intertwining is particularly evident in texts that foreground the "victim/expert relationship," a pairing that Ian Hacking has called historically necessary for any definition and understanding of mental illness.[7] Philosophers and authors such as Schelling and Friedrich Schlegel, for instance, borrow from faculty psychology for their intense examinations of "clairvoyant" women whose visions promise their male doctors, priests, and other authorities access to a mysterious and highly uncanny subuniverse. While it seems clear from a present-day perspective that these women suffered from neuroses related to past trauma, Romantic psychologists and intellectuals attributed their hallucinations and psychosomatic infirmities to an ability to see into the future. The aestheticization of illness that emerges at around 1800 is thus intertwined with Romantic understandings of temporality and with the desire to deny mortality by redefining a melancholic yearning for the past as an extraordinary, but natural, power to see the future.

Chapter Three further explores the aesthetic aspects of Romantic medicine and seeks to demonstrate the common ground shared by Enlightenment thought and pseudoscience. The beginnings of empirical psychology in Germany were characterized by an interest in what today might be called the occult, and the earliest investigations were conducted not only by the editors of psychology journals and writers of case studies, but by third parties who then reported their findings anecdotally to those editors and psychologists. The case studies in Moritz's *Journal of Empirical Psychology (*1783-1793), a text that exemplifies the transition from Enlightened to Romantic thought, bring repressed content to light—hysterical pregnancies, live burials, and nocturnal panic attacks all feature prominently—but the journal is itself uncanny insofar as it magnifies and repeats the subjects' uncanny experiences: reports of psychosomatic complaints that are themselves repetitive are compiled in lists whose internal similarities provoke the unnerving sensation that this has all been read before. Freud will later say that the process of psychoanalytic therapy itself can evoke a similar unease, precisely because it performs the uncanny function of revealing and re-presenting "hidden forces" ("geheime[] Kräfte") within the psyche.[8]

Chapters Four and Five examine uncanny phenomena in literary texts and psychological discourses from the late Enlightenment through Romanticism up to the advent of psychoanalysis and Expressionism. Chapter Four looks in particular at two novels about secret societies ("Geheimbundromane") that are little-examined in scholarship on German literature but that were hugely influential in the development of Gothic fiction: Friedrich Schiller's *The Ghost-Seer* (1787/1789) and Ludwig Tieck's *William Lovell* (1795/1796). My readings juxtapose the "hysterical" sufferings of the male characters in these novels—sufferings involving numerous uncanny symptoms—with the clairvoyant female patients of the

---

[7] Ian Hacking, *Mad Travelers: Reflections on the Reality of Transient Mental Illnesses* (Charlottesville and London: UP of Virginia, 1998), 2.

[8] Freud, GW 12: 257/SE 17: 243.

psychological and philosophical-aesthetic texts of chapters Two and Three. Like the hallucinations of the women who so fascinated Moritz, Schelling, and Schlegel, the paranoia, panic, and sexual obsessions of the men in these novels reveal an uncanny melancholy. One of the core arguments of this section of *Aesthetic Anxiety* is that this melancholy is not only a symptom of being "stuck" in the past, but can also function as a way of living through a threatening and violent modernity; the melancholy affect that accompanies an uncanny experience enables the protagonist and/or reader to internalize otherwise deadly outside forces and to assimilate otherwise malign memories.[9]

In Chapter Five, I focus first on the psychological impact of nineteenth-century technological and industrial developments, an impact often revealed in uncanny symptoms. I locate an "ego-disturbance," similar to the one Freud identifies as central to the uncanny effect of E.T.A. Hoffmann's fiction, in texts by Heinrich von Kleist; this concept is a springboard for a more sustained exploration and questioning of the popular thesis that uncanny phenomena in literature and culture represent the dark side of Enlightenment or of reason. In Romantic and Realist literature, written by authors who explored the forward-looking as well as the frightening aspects of rapid and radical technological developments in what were often still feudally-organized societies, the uncanny opens up a space between fundamentalism or traditionalism and the often instrumental reason of modern life. Tzvetan Todorov differentiates the uncanny from the marvelous when he explains that uncanny phenomena "may be readily accounted for by the laws of reason" although they "are, in one way or another, incredible, extraordinary, shocking, singular, disturbing or unexpected."[10] When secrets, memories, or repressed information that should remain hidden nevertheless come to light and are re-represented in a form dissociated from their prior contexts, literary protagonists and readers alike are forced to live with an awareness of an inability to transcend the modern present. It is precisely the often-fantastic melding of technology, spirituality, and blood relations in these nineteenth-

---

[9] My argumentation about melancholy relies on Judith Butler's redefinition of the psychoanalytic term; in *Antigone's Claim* (New York: Columbia UP, 2000), for instance, in the context of a discussion of the incest taboo and families that persist with and through it, Butler describes a kind of "melancholia that attends living and loving outside the livable and outside the field of love," (78). I discuss this definition of melancholy and its potential to aid our understanding of certain uncanny phenomena in literature and culture in greater detail in Chapter Four.

[10] Tzvetan Todorov, *The Fantastic: A Structural Approach to a Literary Genre*, trans. Richard Howard (Ithaca: Cornell UP, 1975), 46. Todorov actually identifies different kinds of uncanniness in literature, which occur along a spectrum stretching from the "pure uncanny" to the "fantastic-uncanny;" the fantastic is the "frontier between two adjacent realms," namely the uncanny and the marvelous. While "new laws of nature must be entertained to account for the phenomena" of the "fantastic-marvelous," and in the "pure marvelous" the supernatural is simply accepted, in the "fantastic-uncanny," "events that seem supernatural throughout a story receive a rational explanation at its end," 43-44.

century texts that both represents and prompts uncanny anxieties, trapping the reader in a real, present awareness of alienation and of loss.

Chapter Five also returns to Freud and his essay on "The Uncanny," and examines seminal cultural products of the early twentieth century in the context of nascent psychoanalysis. Here the themes central to the previous chapters recur: intersections between science and pseudoscience (particularly in the fields of early psychology and psychiatry), understandings of psychosomatic illnesses from the Enlightenment through the nineteenth century, the tendency to aestheticize those illnesses, and the conflict between modernity and premodern impulses. Now, however, I integrate these themes with what I call the "uncanny love" central to the psychoanalytic therapy that promises to heal or at least help the modern subject understand his uncanny ailments. This love is evident in texts by one quintessentially modern writer and one filmmaker: Arthur Schnitzler and Fritz Lang. Friedrich Nietzsche's injunction in *On the Genealogy of Morals* to "forget actively," along with Freud's notion of repression, help develop my argument that the uncanny, in these texts and in this period, functions as a key component of a highly modern memory model that acknowledges, blatantly and repeatedly, the inherent instability and unreliability of memory. Even as a frightening and repressed memory comes back again and again in uncanny form, it changes, is itself subject to forgetting and re-repression, dissociates from the original experiential context, and is therefore a far-from-reliable indicator of what actually happened in the past. I analyze the recent re-release of *Metropolis*, in which the love relationship between Freder and Maria is revealed as truly uncanny—Maria is the re-embodiment, and the uncanny re-membering, of Freder's dead mother, Hel. I extend this interpretation to the completely modern and distressingly ancient love relationships in Schnitzler's *Dream Story*.

Uncanny phenomena in German culture just prior to 1933 seem indicative of a frightening regress into an aesthetic realm—that is, the reappearance of repressed memory reveals the inability to escape simulations of the past rather than the ability to move on. However, in the concluding chapter of *Aesthetic Anxiety*, I argue that the uncanny can accomplish more than one thing at a time. It can, by reminding us of things we would rather forget, by keeping *in* things we have tried to push *out*, force us to be part of a larger and increasingly centrifugal (or, what recent scholarship has called a "transmodern,"[11] or supermodern) world. Unlike the sublime, the uncanny does not permit any refuge, no matter how brief, in a feeling of transcendence. The anxiety generated by uncanny fear also motivates an aesthetically-charged revolution that has been underway since at least the late eighteenth century: a revolution against mythical and real power structures, institutions, and fathers that nevertheless acknowledges the inevitable and even indispensable nature of those repressive figures.

The uncanny is a model for a modern, embodied memory and for alternative, non-normative forms of desire. It therefore enables a different type of critique of practical, Enlightened reason and of modernity than, say, Nietzsche or Sade who, according to Theodor Adorno and Max Horkheimer, push "the scientific principle into destructiveness" and display "intellectual joy in regression…(in) the desire to beat civilization with its own weapons."[12] When puppets and other machines seem to have souls, portraits are terrifyingly lifelike, minds are read and thoughts are all-powerful, healthy limbs fall off and breathing people are buried, then seemingly irrational, non-intellectual means are used to question the tenets of modern rationality. And yet these methods, these depictions of seemingly inexplicable phenomena, Todorov and Freud remind us, ultimately *can* be explained logically, can be understood intellectually. Uncanny symptoms of a pervasive and persistently aesthetic anxiety (an anxiety revealed in aesthetic forms, but also itself aestheticized) thus appeal to an alternative space within the intellect and within modernity, a space where alterity is acknowledged and the past is both lost and present, rather than encouraging irrational nostalgia.

In his essay on "The Uncanny," Freud states that the modern unconscious, like the premodern person of faith, wishes to deny mortality. It therefore appears that the unconscious mind, where the memories that provoke uncanny experience reside, is resolutely anti-modern, since a key component of the modern mentality is the awareness of the boundedness of our own finite existence.[13] And indeed, while Freud acknowledges that the unconscious mind is to some extent primitive, I argue that the uncanny—

---

[11] Gilroy, *Postcolonial Melancholia* 44, 72; Gilroy cites Enrique Dussel's use of the term in *The Invention of the Americas*, trans. Michael D. Barber (New York: Continuum, 1995). Gilroy uses "transmodern" to describe "an amended history of modernity…a geopolitical project with a longer reach and more profound consequences than is customarily appreciated" (44); what he calls "transmodern dissidence is increasingly connected to the emergence of an anticapitalist culture that aims to make resistance to neoliberalism as global as capital has become" (72). I link the uncanny to this notion of transmodern resistance and to what I call a "transmodern aesthetic" in Chapter Six.

[12] Theodor Adorno and Max Horkheimer, *Dialektik der Aufklärung* (Frankfurt am Main: Fischer, 1988), 101-102.

[13] See also Gregg M. Horowitz's discussion of the emergence of modern aesthetics from "a perception of the finitude of sensuous life" and his assertion of the "fateful centrality of this perception to the development of aesthetic theory" in *Sustaining Loss: Art and Mournful Life* (Stanford: Stanford UP, 2001), 3, et al.

where denial and acknowledgment of mortality meet in the realm of the strangely familiar—is truly modern. Distorted, dissociated, even seemingly supernatural and, above all, compulsively repeated uncanny memories are the cause and the effect of looking around and realizing complicity in one's own downfall, one's own anxiety, one's own modernity. The uncanny moment is finite but repeated, usually in a form that can be called aesthetic. To experience and examine the uncanny is to experience a way of knowing while not knowing, of living with the awareness of mortality while simultaneously suspending that awareness; this paradox of consciousness does not paralyze, but makes action in the present possible.

Chapter 1

Aesthetic Anxiety and the Uncanny

...(uncanny is what one calls everything that should remain secret, hidden, and latent, but has come to light)
[...(unheimlich nennt man alles, was im Geheimniß, im Verborgnen, in der Latenz bleiben sollte und hervorgetreten ist)]
Schelling, *Philosophy of Mythology [Philosophie der Mythologie]*

...the whole psychical situation, which seems so confused and is so difficult to describe, can be satisfactorily cleared up by assuming that at the time I had (or might have had) a momentary feeling: *'What I see there is not real.'* Such a feeling is known as a 'feeling of derealization.'
[...die ganze anscheinend verworrene und schwer darstellbare psychische Situation löst sich glatt durch die Annahme, daß ich damals auf der Akropolis einen Moment lang das Gefühl hatte—oder hätte haben können: was ich da sehe, ist nicht wirklich. Man nennt das ein 'Entfremdungsgefühl'.]
Freud, *A Disturbance of Memory on the Acropolis [Eine Erinnerungsstörung auf der Akropolis]*

1. Freud on the Acropolis

In 1904, at the age of forty-eight, Sigmund Freud visited the Acropolis and had an experience that might be described as an "art attack."[1] Having reached the site somewhat by accident—he and his brother originally had intended to visit Corfu—Freud could not quite believe that he was actually at the famous place he had learned of in school, many years before. While attempting to synchronize his memories of the Acropolis's description with the view before him, Freud had a profound sense of derealization: "what I see there is not real" ("was ich da sehe, ist nicht wirklich"). In *The Future of an Illusion (Die Zukunft einer Illusion,* 1927), he recalls the moment as follows:

> A feeling of astonishment mingled with my joy. It seemed to say: 'So it really *is* true, just as we learnt at school!' How shallow and weak must have been the belief I then acquired in the real truth of what I heard, if I could be so astonished now!
> (In meine Beglückung mengte sich ein Gefühl von Erstaunen, das mir die Deutung eingab: 'Also ist das wirklich so, wie wir's in der Schule gelernt hatten!' Was für

[1] The Italian psychoanalyst Graziella Magherini has studied neurotic reactions specifically in viewers of great works of art; some results are described in "The Unconscious and Art: The Aesthetic Uncanny and the Function of the Selected Fact," talk given at The Third New Style European Psychoanalytical Federation Annual Conference in Helsinki, Finland, 15-18 April, 2004.

> seichten und kraftlosen Glauben an die reale Wahrheit des Gehörten muß ich damals erworben haben, wenn ich heute so erstaunt sein kann!)[2]

This combination of surprise and disbelief in the presence of overwhelming beauty recalls the experience of the sublime. But Freud's open letter to his friend Romain Rolland, written in 1936, analyzes the moment quite differently and, unsurprisingly, in psychological rather than in philosophical terms. While he continues to focus on the psychic dislocation created by the inability to reconcile simulation, or re-representation (the "reality" of the Acropolis as he learned it in school via reproductions of its images) and lived experience, Freud in 1936 emphasizes an aspect of this dislocation made visible by his own interim self-analysis. He understands the feeling of unreality at the Acropolis as originating within the self, in a conflict between body and mind, between sensory impressions and psychological convictions.[3] Rather than feeling overwhelmed and astonished because he sees something completely new, something unique—which would make this a sublime experience—Freud is astonished at the Acropolis by a sense of uncanny repetition. He has never done this before, and yet he remembers it. The "disturbance of memory" ("Erinnerungsstörung") that results is unsettling but ultimately productive. The disbelief that characterizes the uncanny experience —a disbelief lacking in the moment of the sublime—can be mobilized in the service of improved self-understanding, and of a psychic revolution. "This incredulity...this doubt of a piece of reality" ("Dieser Unglaube, dieser Zweifel an einem Stück der Realität")[4] can manifest as a skepticism that in turn encourages change.

Freud concludes that his sensation of disjuncture and unease, occasioned in the first instance by his inability to quite believe that the scene in front of him was the scene he learned of in school, has a deeper and older source. His father was never able to visit the Acropolis; at the same age as Freud, his income and autonomy were far more limited. But Freud does not feel guilty merely because he is able to do so much more than his father—rather, he feels guilty because his father never did, and never would have, even *desired* to travel to such a place. That is, Freud feels guilty, and thus also anxious and profoundly out of sync with his surroundings, because he has desires his father never had and feelings his father never felt. He has, in his own estimation—an estimation that continues to reassert itself, to repeat itself

[2] Sigmund Freud, *Die Zukunft einer Illusion*, in *Kulturtheoretische Schriften* (Frankfurt am Main: Fischer, 1974) 159. The translation is James Strachey's in *The Future of an Illusion, The Standard Edition of the Complete Psychological Works of Sigmund Freud*, vol. 21 (London: Hogarth, 1953-1974) 25. This edition is abbreviated henceforth as SE.

[3] Sigmund Freud, "Brief an Romain Rolland (Eine Erinnerungsstörung auf der Akropolis)" in *Gesammelte Werke* 16 (Frankfurt am Main: Fischer, 1999) 254. This edition is abbreviated henceforth as GW.

[4] Freud, GW 16: 254/ SE 22: 243.

over the course of his daily life in middle age—surpassed his father's interior life, and this creates guilt and anxiety as well as a shift in self-understanding. The "disturbance of memory" thus occurs on a second level: on the Acropolis, Freud's own mind forces him to remember his father in a way that makes him feel strange to himself, estranged from himself—he wishes, anxiously, that he did not have the feelings that make him fundamentally different from his father, and that therefore make him betray his father. This betrayal is a form of revolt, but a highly anxious one.

In 1919, between his trip to Greece and the letter to Rolland, Freud's essay "The Uncanny" ("Das Unheimliche") employs variations on another father-son relationship to develop a theory about a particular form of anxiety-inducing repetition. Nathanael, the protagonist of E.T.A. Hoffmann's romantic science-fiction nightmare, *The Sandman (Der Sandmann)* (1816), is haunted by the repressed memory of his father's death, for which he feels responsible. Familiar yet strange father figures surface throughout Nathanael's young adult life, and this haunting leads to mental illness and ultimately Nathanael's suicide. Freud uses a literary text to define the uncanny as "that class of the frightening which leads back to what is known of old and long familiar" ("jene Art des Schreckhaften, welche auf das Altbekannte, Längstvertraute zurückgeht").[5] He relies here on the *Dictionary of the German Language* (*Wörterbuch der deutschen Sprache)* of 1860, which in turn quotes a passage from Friedrich Schelling's *Philosophy of Mythology* (*Philosophie der Mythologie*, 1842) defining the uncanny as "everything that ought to have remained…secret and hidden but has come to light" ("Alles, was im Geheimnis, im Verborgenen…bleiben sollte und hervorgetreten ist").[6] And it does appear that Hoffmann's Nathanael would have been far better off had his own past been truly over, rather than persisting in the present as a haunting but insufficiently-understood remainder. While Freud's essay develops an argument about castration anxiety to explain the particular urgency of the uncanny, I wish for the moment to look briefly at *The Sandman* and to emphasize an aspect that Freud does not, though this aspect nevertheless relies on his understanding of the uncanny.

In Hoffmann's novella, Nathanael's failure to comprehend the significance of the frightening experiences that he in part creates, his inability to recognize and thus break free of his own servitude to the past, means that the only form of rebellion or protest available to him—and thus the only escape from an otherwise endless cycle of uncanny repetitions, of further hauntings—is death. His suicide is an uncanny form of murder, as Nathanael repeats a crime he himself actually never committed. By killing himself, and

[5] Freud, "Das Unheimliche," GW 12: 231/ "The Uncanny," SE 17: 220.

[6] Friedrich Schelling, *Philosophie der Mythologie*, in *Sämmtliche Werke* 2 (Stuttgart: Cotta, 1957) 649. Quoted here in Freud, GW 12: 235/SE 17: 224.

thus the memories of his father within him, he finally and truly kills his father as well. He also atones, in a way, for the crime of having chosen to participate in the experience of the uncanny by permitting himself to be frightened, again and again, by men who remind him of the dreaded "Sandman" who traumatized him as a child (and, again, at whose hands he in part willingly suffered). His suicide is the ultimate punishment for having desires that outlived and thus surpassed those of his father.

Schelling's *Philosophy of Mythology* does not seem, on the surface, to have much to do with haunting, with the kind of mental illness whose symptoms are perpetrated by the sufferer's failure to recognize their cause, or even with uncanniness more generally, although Freud's analysis primarily depends upon his definition. But Schelling also speaks of fathers—and specifically about the oldest traditions of thinking about patriarchal figures. He notes that in Hebrew,

> The word that…means 'father' is derived from a verb that means 'to desire, to long for;' that is, which contains the concept of need…. Accordingly, one could say that the word expresses a philosophical concept, in that the fatherly is the predecessor, the originator, that needs a successor.
> (das Wort, das…'Vater' bedeutet [ist] auf ein Verbum zurückzuführen, welches 'begehren, verlangen' ausdrückt, also zugleich den Begriff der Bedürftigkeit enthüllt…. Demgemäß, könnte man sagen, ist hier der philosophische Begriff ausgedrückt, da das Väterliche als Vorausgehendes, Anfangendes das eines Nachfolgenden Bedürftige ist).[7]

It is the father's need, the father's lack, the father's longing, to which the son responds, always insufficiently. The mythology formed from and around this thinking is, Schelling says, "the last of all mythologies and the end of the mythological process" ("die letzte aller Mythologien und das Ende des mythologischen Processes");[8] the myths of the fathers, myths of origin and of succession, contain their own ends and circumscribe their own demise.

But the world of Greek myth is far from dead, Schelling argues, since artists ever since have been repeating and reinscribing its themes and

---

[7] Friedrich Schelling, *Philosophie der Mythologie*, in *Schellingiana* 6, eds. Andreas Roser and Holger Schulten (Stuttgart-Bad Cannstatt: Frommann-Holzboog, 1996) 55. This edition is abbreviated henceforth as PM. My citations alternate between two versions of the *Philosophie der Mythologie*: the Munich lectures of 1841 (in the volume cited here) and the Berlin lectures of 1842, edited by Manfred Frank (as *Ausgewählte Schriften* 6, Frankfurt am Main: Suhrkamp, 1985). This edition is abbreviated henceforth as AS. The Berlin lectures are also cited from Manfred Schröter's edition of the *Einleitung in der Philosophie der Mythologie* 6 (Munich, 1927), which is available on a diskette included in the *Schellingiana* volume. The significance of the differences between the lectures of 1841 and of 1842 is a matter of some debate in Schelling scholarship; my decisions about which edition to cite are based primarily on which version provides a more stylistically smooth and accessible explanation of essentially the same philosophical or historical issue.

[8] Schelling, AS 6: 657.

forms—and its sense of loss, of demise—in their work.[9] Freud's letter to Rolland could be considered yet another working-through of the ancient, always-past, always-absent and -remembered rather than present, problematic of the father-son relationship. And Freud's essay on the uncanny, which unravels the deadly implications of Nathanael's misunderstanding of the circumstances of his father's death in *The Sandman*, echoes Schelling's contention that the foundational myths of Western culture are themselves based on a misunderstanding, a mistake, the "upholding of a principle that actually never should have been" ("Erhebung des eigentlich nicht seyn sollenden Princips"). Myth's reification as story, its increasingly obvious fictionality, means that its birth out of a mistake has been rectified. But the fact that we know that myth is an illusion does not render myth less important. Rather, mythology "becomes a truth of its own kind" ("wird zu einer Wahrheit eigener Art").[10]

Myth itself is uncanny—the thing that "should remain secret, hidden, and latent, but has come to light" ("im Geheimniß, im Verborgnen, in der Latenz bleiben sollte und hervorgetreten ist")[11]—and the ongoing attempts of art, theology, philosophy, and psychology to make sense out of myth's mistakes are, to an extent, repetitions or re-enactments of those mistakes (or of the false revelations that myth provides). And as Freud will later do, Schelling makes space for productive moments in all of this myth- and mistake-making. Myth and the subsequent attempts to come to terms with it (including rebellions against it) have a type of truth status: a relative truth, a "truth of its own kind." Efforts to interpret and analyze our myths, our art, and ourselves may be uncanny repetitions of foundational "mistakes," but they are simultaneously expressions of a desire to continue, and of a desire to live, as opposed to Nathanael's desire to die and thus end all repetition. Our rebellion against mythical fathers and texts may be propelled by the anxiety occasioned by uncanny experiences, but such experiences are also the foundation for revolution. The uncanny both traps and liberates, and it is the project of this study to identify the ways in which this happens in canonical and non-canonical products of German culture since the Enlightenment, and to propose that it is precisely the uncanny, a term that comes into broad usage

---

[9] Schelling, AS 6: 669.
[10] Ibid, 657.
[11] Ibid, 661.

at the same time that the modern cult of the self emerges,[12] that can point to alternate forms of thinking politically and to a new ethos of community and of self-other relations.

Freud's reading of his experience on the Acropolis would seem an excellent example of the productive aspect of uncanny experience: due to feeling estranged from himself and from his surroundings as a result of a sense of repetition, of something "strangely familiar," Freud comes to a better self-understanding as well as to a better understanding of his relationship to his father. But this remains one man's view of his own past, and while insightful, Freud's self-analysis does not really free him from his deeply problematic memories—or, specifically, from continuing to feel guilty that he is capable of more passion and insight than his father. Freud's letter to Rolland could also be criticized as propagating a highly poeticized or aestheticized view of a personal past: it is in the presence of great art that Freud is shaken and provoked to turn inward and backward, toward his own psyche and toward the past. But a personal revelation is nearly always required for political renewal; the psychological revolution that the uncanny can help enact can be the basis for social change.

How, though, can an experience characterized completely by repetition and anxiety be liberating? One way to understand this is to return to Freud's explication of the dissociation between emotion and affect, a disconnect created when affect is repressed.[13] Freud's theory of anxiety underwent substantial revision throughout his career, culminating in the book *Inhibitions, Symptoms and Anxiety* (*Hemmung, Symptom und Angst*, 1925), but we can condense the major mechanisms behind anxiety as it relates to the uncanny as follows. If I repress the expression of pain I feel when I think of someone or something I have lost,[14] then that pain will return as anxiety, but

---

[12] Manfred Frank asserts that self-consciousness was "such a theme of philosophical modernity that it could have characterized the entire epoch. (...) If philosophy summarizes itself conceptually, 'self-consciousness' has to be the magic word whereby modernity secures the foundations of its thought" ("so sehr ein Thema der philosophischen Moderne, dass es die ganze Epoche hat charakterisieren können. [...] Wenn Philosophie ihre Zeit in Gedanken erfasst, muss 'Selbstbewusstsein' als das Zauberwort gelten, mit dem die Moderne sich ihres Grundgedankens versichert"). In *Selbstgefühl. Eine historisch-systematische Erkundung* (Frankfurt am Main: Suhrkamp, 2002) 2, 7.

[13] This understanding of anxiety is taken from Freud's essay on "The Uncanny," which is relatively late, but does not yet reflect fully his thinking on the mechanisms producing and resulting from anxiety as expressed in *Inhibitions, Symptoms, and Anxiety (Hemmung, Symptom und Angst*, 1925). I treat the changes in Freud's thinking on anxiety as they relate to understanding the uncanny in more detail in Chapters Two and Four.

[14] James Strachey summarizes the main losses we can experience (according to Freud's later as well as earlier theories of anxiety)—losses all "liable to precipitate a traumatic situation at different times of life," as "birth [initial loss of unity with the mother], loss of the mother as an object, loss of the penis, loss of the object's love, loss of the super-ego's love." Editor's Introduction to Freud, *Inhibitions, Symptoms, and Anxiety* (New York: W.W. Norton & Company, 1959) 8.

detached, or liberated, from the sensation that created it. That experience of free-floating, "liberated" anxiety is uncanny. It may be triggered by, for instance, viewing a painting or standing at the Acropolis; that is, there is a symbolic and aesthetic register to this experience. The aesthetic representation of something perhaps only vaguely associated with my original, repressed loss expands the possibilities for aesthetic representation's significance—that is, for the significance of art itself—in political as well as in psychological realms.

An anxiety reaction induced by an artwork can initiate the liberating potential of the uncanny. When a person viewing an artwork has an anxiety reaction, he or she is nearly always focusing on a "selected fact" in the piece, such as a leg or knee in a portrait.[15] This image is a condensed representation of the viewer's own memories, and yet it is something new; it is also chosen actively by the viewer, not necessarily emphasized by the artist. The "selected fact" precipitates the return of a repressed affect, one now no longer attached to the emotion that produced it. While the neurotic reaction that the spectator experiences is uncomfortable and frightening, this essentially "sick" reaction is compatible with a standard psychoanalytic view of art's power to re-represent and ultimately shape psychic struggles, by bringing previously repressed psychic depth to the surface and thus making that depth accessible and communicable.[16] While the experience of uncanny anxiety when viewing art does not have to lead to meaningful change in the life of the subject—who can remain stuck in his or her suffering and even have psychotic episodes—the epistemological value of studying the experience is significant beyond the psychoanalyst's office. Uncanny anxiety can help render art psychologically meaningful beyond the discrete representation of certain individually significant issues, and beyond its ability to present something that resonates by chance with an individual viewer's history and psychological makeup.

An uncanny sense of disturbance and disorientation can function as a literal liberation when it creates an intersection of pain and pleasure. The anxiety created by an encounter with something strangely familiar may also produce a kind of pleasure, because an unconscious investment has been revealed, brought to consciousness. Uncanny repetition can force me to acknowledge my own investment in and involvement with a selected fact or a particular image, for instance. This reminds me of my relationship to objects in the world, and while this uncanny reminding is uncomfortable rather than reassuring, it is not necessarily completely unpleasant. It is at the intersection of feelings of pain and pleasure that psychoanalysis locates the individual's chance to work through conflicts (a process that Freud eventually extends to entire cultures as well). In a usually late stage of successful psychoanalytic

---

[15] Magherini, "The Unconscious and Art: The Aesthetic Uncanny and the Function of the Selected Fact" 4.

[16] Ibid, 4.

psychotherapy, the patient remembers earlier pain and experiences the feeling of freedom, analogous to pleasure, that comes of the awareness of the distance between past suffering and present "working-through" of conflicts created by that suffering. This stage can occur only when the patient has overcome his or her resistance to the therapy and to uncovering his or her real memories. What Freud calls the "compulsion to repeat" repressed content is a necessary precondition for the eventual "impulsion to remember" that brings about insight and healing.[17]

The repetition inherent to the uncanny—the return of repressed content—is a way of revealing what the subject knows, but does not realize or admit that he or she knows. Freud's indirect and aestheticized reliving on the Acropolis of earlier conflicts with his father brings those conflicts to light, and ultimately undermines their power to continue to trap him in frustration and helpless feelings. In that sense, then, his experience of derealization and dissociation liberates him from a negative psychological state while—and through—repeating the core elements of that state. The dissociated affect Freud experiences on the Acropolis (his feeling of depersonalization there has been detached from the earlier sensation of separation or difference from his father) prompts him to remember his father, and this remembering keeps alive the difficult feelings of loss and alienation he associates with his father. At the same time, Freud is reminded that he and his father are similar, related, yet different; that is, they are not identical repetitions of one another.

Uncanny experiences may manifest anywhere along a spectrum of affect from Freud's astonished derealization at the Acropolis to extremely unpleasant and even horrifying feelings, but they all have the power to force us to move beyond the individual psychological realm and to participate in a diverse community of true others. Unlike the sublime, a singular experience of awe that detaches us from the world (and which I discuss in more detail in Chapter Two), the uncanny reminds us that we are tethered to the past and ultimately to one another. The literary, psychological, and philosophical texts that I examine often depict uncanny experiences as happening in domestic spaces and in encounters with other people, a clear contrast to the solitary and and grand moment of the sublime.[18]

While it is perhaps destructive on a personal level, as we will see in some of the texts explored throughout this study, uncanny repetition can be a positive force deployed within the larger realm of culture. The dissociation, or liberation, of affect from sensation and the resulting feeling of derealization

---

[17] See for instance Freud, "Erinnern, Widerholen und Durcharbeiten," GW 10: 126-136/ "Remembering, Repeating and Working-Through," SE 12: 147-156.

[18] In his study of the uncanny in architecture, Anthony Vidler maintains that the uncanny for Freud is "a peculiar kind of fear, positioned between real terror and faint anxiety....Aesthetically an outgrowth of the Burkean sublime, a domesticated version of absolute terror, (the uncanny was) to be experienced in the comfort of the home." See *The Architectural Uncanny: Essays in the Modern Unhomely* (Cambridge, MA: MIT Press, 1992) 3

can expand our understanding of the relationship between a representation and its referent, between present and past, and between subjects and objects —or, between members of an estranged community, whether that community is understood as a family or as global society.

The uncanny can bear witness to the fact that we no longer reside in the world of the nation-state; while Paul Gilroy refers in this context to Britain in the early twenty-first century, the uncanny and the general anxiety it represents has always offered this option of bearing witness, at least since the Enlightenment.[19] The uncanny does not permit us to take shelter in the "defensive gesture" of trying to eliminate difference; or, to "seek consolation in the private and intimate places where romantic love and fidelity could offset the worst effects of warfare, turbulence, and vanished certitude."[20] And yet that defensive inward gesture is a precondition of the turn back to reality, to the acknowledgment of difference and the impossibility of imposing unity on diversity. Schelling, perhaps the most influential initiator of the Romantic inward turn, also defines most seminally the initially psychological, but ultimately social and outward-directed moment that is the uncanny. Schelling depicts the modern separation from desirous, longing, ancient fathers as a separation bought at the price of the experience of uncanny repetition, an experience replete with anxiety about the separation and the tragic but necessary, and in fact ethically justifiable, loss it entails.

Uncanny encounters, which occur when something strangely familiar evokes a repressed affect and provokes anxiety, remind us of something lost; we thus re-experience the loss. This re-experience, or repetition, while disruptive to our momentary well-being, also can serve the longer-term goal of individual and cultural progress. Following Nietzsche, Gilles Deleuze emphasizes the need to employ "techniques of social alienation" as "revolutionary means of exploration."[21] The alienating, dissociative sense of the uncanny and our subsequent attempts to understand it can be part of this exploration, at least incrementally and momentarily. Uncanny repetition can help us perform a crucial ethical act in a "disenchanted" world: it can contribute to our greater health by helping us "sustain loss."[22] This can be loss of all kinds—loss of the father, of the past, of a love object—but all of this is fundamentally loss of one kind, the enactment of inevitable separation and individuation that is singular and yet common to everyone.

All repetition is not uncanny: when Novalis calls love an "endless repetition" ("die Liebe ist eine endlose Wiederholung"), he invokes a sense of

---

[19] Paul Gilroy, *Postcolonial Melancholia* (New York: Columbia UP, 2005) 89.

[20] Ibid, 91.

[21] Gilles Deleuze, *The Logic of Sense*, trans. March Lester and Charles Stivale, ed. Constantin V. Boundas (New York: Columbia UP, 1990) 160-161.

[22] Gregg Horowitz, *Sustaining Loss: Art and Mournful Life* (Stanford: Stanford University Press, 2001).

yearning for a comforting and consciously fictionalized ideal.[23] The reaction provoked by the uncanny is very different from this kind of yearning. Uncanny repetition does not take us back to a previous experience, even if only as aesthetic re-representation; it disconnects us from that experience, although it is of course associated (via repression) with it. As a form of memory, the uncanny (*das Unheimliche*, the "un-homely") does remind us of home, and the word in fact contains the name for home (*das Heimliche*, the "home-ly"). But the return "home" implied by uncanny yearning is a dissociated, disoriented shifting of the very meaning of "home" in consciousness rather than a fictionalization of a universal Paradise.

The uncanny is a psychological and philosophical gesture whose aesthetic representation holds much promise for a reconsideration of the continuing value of Romanticism and its cultural heirs. It is time to return to Romanticism in order to stretch our understanding of uncanniness beyond repetition and the return of the repressed. In the following pages as well as in the chapters to come, I pursue the hypothesis that the experience of the uncanny is a melancholic reminder of loss and is therefore loss-sustaining. I attempt to show that this hypothesis is vital to an understanding of practical, lived community in an age that has rejected the sublime and other concepts that promise unique, metaphysical escape from repetitive, material entrapment. Throughout the close readings in the chapters that follow, I argue for the epistemological value and revolutionary promise of the concept "uncanny" by pursuing the following theses:

1. Centuries before Freud, the uncanny is operative in literature and philosophy, but also in the nascent disciplines of psychology and psychiatry. The discourse of German faculty psychology, in the late eighteenth century in particular, helps normalize neurotic symptoms by opening up the possibility that essentially anyone at any time may fall prey to uncanny memory.

2. The essentially private and domestic experience of uncanny repetition as neurotic illness can provoke a move into the public and political sphere. Whether in therapy, in love relationships, or in business dealings, the intense anxiety caused by uncanny phenomena drives insight and change. This

---

[23] Alice Kuzniar argues that Romantics such as Novalis and Friedrich Hölderlin consciously fictionalize a past universal Paradise in order to construct a regulatory idea for love and other relationships in their fiction and philosophy. She quotes the phrase "Die Liebe ist eine endlose Wiederholung," uttered by Heinrich to Mathilde in Novalis's *Heinrich von Ofterdingen* (1: 338), and continues: "When Novalis wrote, 'Wo gehen wir denn hin? Immer nach Hause' (1: 373), he suggested that one desires a return to the same, to a (universal) home with its Edenic implications. The longing may be unending and the goal forever beyond our reach. As Kundera says, we still long for Paradise, for time for us does not turn in a circle. But to long means to hold to the promise of happiness," in "A Higher Language: Novalis on Communication With Animals," *The German Quarterly* 76.4 (2003) 438.

happens through the experience of "uncanny melancholy," a mode that makes it possible to tolerate otherwise unbearable memory.

3. Literature is, most fundamentally, the communicative mode that brings together manifestations of and ruminations about uncanny experience most completely,[24] from the late eighteenth through early twentieth centuries. While psychology and psychiatry as well as philosophy are continually preoccupied with the problem of the uncanny, it is in literary texts that the dynamic tension between concepts such as illness and health, self and other, power and powerlessness, regress and progress—concepts that the uncanny helps bring into simultaneous existence—is most fully revealed.

4. While the uncanny may indeed represent the "dark side" of the Enlightenment, of reason, and of the sublime, it also opens up the possibility of a "third space"[25] beyond that dialectic. Broadly speaking, the space of the uncanny can be thought of as being analogous to the space of religion or belief, and this is not necessarily a purely irrational space. The "third space" is a realm of understanding and an attitude that is neither completely irrational nor completely instrumental. The uncanny is not synonymous with the unconscious, but it is analogous to the unconscious in key respects (Chapters Three, Four, and Five explore these similarities most fully). Neither fully modern nor persistently demonic, the uncanny is where the domains of reality and unreality intersect.

5. At the same time, the uncanny helps us resist the pull of the purely metaphysical by reminding us of real others. Unlike the sublime, the uncanny can help us refuse refuge in the transcendental and hence in the logocentric. This is largely due to the manifestation of uncanny phenomena in undeniably material, corporeal experiences of illness and anxiety as well as in the forms

---

[24] Nicholas Royle points out the Russian formalists' (and particularly Viktor Shklovsky's) role in calling to attention and using "the power of literature (especially poetry) to make strange, to defamiliarize, to make unfamiliar all sorts of familiar perceptions and beliefs." *The Uncanny: An Introduction* (New York: Routledge, 2003) 5.

[25] The idea of a "third space," used most prominently by Homi Bhabha, has been enunciated by other scholars as well in the service of linguistic and cultural-materialist interpretations that attempt to stretch the possibilities of representation; essays in the volume *Figuren der/des Dritten. Erkundungen kultureller Zwischenräume* (eds. Claudia Breger and Tobias Döring; Amsterdam and Atlanta: Rodopi, 1998) present a spectrum of understandings of the term. In *The Gift of Death* (trans. David Wills [Chicago and London: University of Chicago Press, 1995]), Jacques Derrida outlines the contours of such a space when he refers to the "origin and essence of the religious" in the thought of Jan Patocka. For Patocka, says Derrida, "religion exists once the secret of the sacred, orgiastic, or demonic mystery has been, if not destroyed, at least integrated, and finally subjected to the sphere of responsibility…Religion is responsibility or it is nothing at all," 2. For the understanding of the uncanny as analogous to the unconscious, I rely principally on Sebastian Gardner's explications of the unconscious in *Irrationality and the Philosophy of Psychoanalysis* (Cambridge: Cambridge University Press, 1993).

of technologically driven Doppelgänger and other machines. The portrayals of others who are really different, yet strangely familiar—from the mentally ill to the robotic—in German literary, psychological, and philosophical texts from the late eighteenth to early twentieth centuries point the way to release from the "menial illnesses" inherent in relationships between hero and heroine, therapist and patient, father and son, and toward relationships more truly intersubjective and thus more just.

The next section of this chapter takes as its starting point the embodied, material nature of uncanny experience as represented in texts of the late Enlightenment and beyond.[26] I argue that our understanding of the uncanny as an individual psychosomatic event can be transformed into a concept that illuminates and re-emphasizes something basic about modern time—namely, its dialectical nature. Finally, I argue that new readings of uncanny episodes, in texts from roughly 1780 to 1930, can rely on Freud's and other seminal definitions while producing a new understanding of uncanny, aesthetic anxiety as representative and constructive of "memory beyond mind": as an outward-directed, difference-sustaining move that, while seemingly so self-centered, ultimately helps create a state of "relatedness" among different, but equal, others.

2. The Uncanny Beyond Repetition and the Return of the Repressed

2.1. Uncanny Anxiety and the Embodied Mind

Forty years before the publication of Schelling's *Philosophy of Mythology*, Ludwig Tieck's sprawling novel *William Lovell* (1795-96) reads in part as an extended display of uncanny encounters figured at once as psychosomatic disorders and as aesthetic revelations. In *Lovell*, which imitates English fiction but also responds to anxieties specific to the German late Enlightenment, uncanny experience is grounded in the body and in illness. William's conviction that "the slower or faster circulation of blood [...] basically determines the differences in a person's inclinations" ("die langsamere oder schnellere Zirkulation des Blutes [...] im Grunde die Verschiedenheit in den Gesinnungen des Menschen aus[macht]")[27] influences

[26] Wolfgang Albrecht identifies the late Enlightenment ("Spätaufklärung") as beginning in the 1780s and lasting into the early decades of the nineteenth century; during this time, leading assumptions of the Enlightenment were already being consistently critiqued and revised. See "Die Literatur im Ensemble der deutschen Spätaufklärung. Eine einleitende Problemskizze," in *Das Angenehme und das Nützliche. Fallstudien zur literarischen Spätaufklärung in Deutschland* (Tübingen: Max Niemeyer, 1997), esp. 1-2.

[27] Ludwig Tieck, *William Lovell* (Stuttgart: Reclam, 1999) 256.

his perception of his own moods and problems. As the novel progresses, William loses all his love objects—mistresses, friends, mentors, father—and the memory of each loss returns as an uncanny symptom that is invariably part of a psychosomatic ailment: a confluence of blood circulation and psychological orientation, of nerves (or "Ganglien") and imagination, of vision and memory. Tieck uses representations of the embodiedness of mind to remind his readers that loss is not just a transcendental concept but a material phenomenon.

In fiction from the late eighteenth century on, the uncanny dissociations between sensation and affect that occur in the presence of the strangely familiar emphasize something wrong with the interdependent relationship between body and mind; they surface in novels like *Lovell* as part of an aestheticized portrayal of illness. When William encounters a man who bears an eerie resemblance to a portrait hanging in his father's home, a horribly burned woman who reminds him of a past mistress, or a friend whose panic attacks confront William with his own instability, the literary tools of symbol, metaphor, and allegory are used to explore hypotheses posited in contemporary psychology as well as in aesthetic theory.[28]

Using aesthetic experience as a way into the psyche and as a way to explore the mind's dependence on the mortal body, rather than as an escape from that mortality, is not limited to late eighteenth- and early nineteenth-century fiction. Related notions are explored in prominent philosophical texts of the time, with the *Philosophy of Mythology* coming rather late to the discussion (in 1841 and 1842), but summarizing and elaborating earlier thought on the subject. Sections of Kant's "precritical" writings, including the *Classification of Disturbances of the Mind* (*Versuch über die Krankheiten des Kopfes*, 1764) weave recent insights about psychology (such as the conviction that there is an important distinction between mental "weakness" and mental "disturbance") with tenets of the emerging critical philosophy. Schelling, Schiller, and Friedrich Schlegel all are preoccupied with the inescapability of corporeality, and with the impediments that a disturbed mind can present to the body; that is, they are concerned with more than just the entrapment of an active mind within a mortal frame. By the 1820s, a resurgence of interest in magnetism and mesmerism re-emphasizes the conviction of many psychiatrists, some of whom were fairly mainstream practitioners, that mental disorders, revealed in physical symptoms, may relate to past trauma.

This trajectory of thinking about relationships between psychosomatic symptoms and philosophical or psychological concepts (as well as in

---

[28] Chapters Two and Three elucidate literature's dependence in this period on psychological discourse (and particularly on the discourse of empirical psychology, or "Erfahrungsseelenkunde") in more detail. I rely in part on Lawrence Rothfield's argument that clinical medicine served as a model for the form and content of fictional narratives prior to the advent of classical modernism; see *Vital Signs: Medical Realism in Nineteenth-Century Fiction* (Princeton: Princeton University Press, 1992).

thinking about philosophical concepts in terms of psychosomatic illness) continues into the twentieth century, when Heidegger relies and expands on Freud's work in order to define an uncanny experience as one of an essentially primal anxiety, inseparable from the body and symptomatic of nervous illness.[29] Part of the "structure of uncanniness," according to Heidegger, is "*being's flight from itself*" ("die *Flucht des Daseins vor ihm selbst*").[30] But it is the awareness of the impossibility of escaping one's own being, and of the mind's entrapment in the body, that creates uncanny anxiety. Heidegger here synthesizes and resituates, within the context of phenomenological philosophy, what was already clear to authors around 1800: *The Sandman*'s Nathanael, along with William Lovell and the subjects of any number of the case studies in Moritz's journal, all suffer from this desire to "be no more" ("nicht mehr seyn," as Moritz puts it).[31] The aesthetic experiences in which these protagonists and patients attempt to take solace end up returning them to, worsening, or even precipitating the very anxiety they are so desperate to flee.

By the late eighteenth century, in other words, a preoccupation coalesces around ideas about psychosomatic problems as linked to the *desire for* aesthetic transcendence—rather than on aesthetic transcendence itself as a way out of psychological dilemmas. The nascent field of psychiatry is a disseminator of these ideas, along with literature and aesthetic theory. By the 1820s, when German psychiatry reaches a preliminary apex,[32] its influence on and mirroring of ideas prevalent in literature and philosophy is conspicuous, as a virtual catalogue of anxious symptoms with philosophical and aesthetic repercussions appears in texts across disciplines: Jakob Fries's medical perspective on what he calls "fever fantasy" and "fever intoxication" ("Fieberphantasie" and "-rausch,")[33] Karl Philipp Moritz's contributions in his journal of empirical psychology to contemporary thinking on the etiology of panic and anxiety attacks, or Friedrich Schlegel's aesthetic-philosophical approach to the multiple neuroses of his intimate friend the Countess Lesniowska.[34] Before elucidating further the argument that the

---

[29] Martin Heidegger, *Prolegomena zur Geschichte des Zeitbegriffs*, 1925, in *Gesamtausgabe* 20 (Frankfurt am Main: Vittorio Klostermann, 1979) 391.

[30] Ibid, 391.

[31] Karl Philipp Moritz, ed., *Gnothi Sauton, oder Magazin zur Erfahrungsseelenkunde als ein Lesebuch für Gelehrte und Ungelehrte*, vol. 4, eds. Petra and Uwe Nettelbeck (Nördlingen: Franz Greno, 1986) 24.

[32] Otto M. Marx, "The Beginning of Psychiatric Historiography in Nineteenth-Century Germany," *Discovering the History of Psychiatry*, eds. Mark S. Micale and Roy Porter (New York and Oxford: Oxford University Press, 1994) 39ff.

[33] Jakob Friedrich Fries, *Handbuch der Psychischen Anthropologie oder der Lehre von der Natur des menschlichen Geistes* (Jena: Croker, 1820-21) 86.

[34] Friedrich Schlegel, *Tagebuch [über die magnetische Behandlung der Gräfin Lesniowska], 1820-1826. Kritische-Friedrich-Schlegel-Ausgabe*, ed. Ernst Behler (Munich: Schöningh, 1958-) vol. 35. This edition is referred to henceforth as KA.

uncanny as a concept manifests the connection between psychological and aesthetic experience, and thus signifies more than a coming to light of repressed content, I will look at some recent thinking about the uncanny in literary and cultural scholarship. This thinking foregrounds my contention that the uncanny, understood as an interdisciplinary gesture as well as the return of an individual's repressed memory, is a form of memory beyond mind—not an illusorily transcendental moment enabled by a flight into aestheticism, but rather a fully corporeal, delimited, repetitive, modern gesture.

2.2. Using the Uncanny to Reframe the Dialectic of Enlightenment

It is generally agreed that the uncanny was first conceptualized in-depth in the late eighteenth century. When the Enlightenment banished demons and magic, the belief in such phenomena went underground, and this repressed belief resurfaced in individual psychology and in certain forms of cultural or collective experience.[35] For instance, epilepsy was understood as a form of demonic possession in the Middle Ages;[36] by 1800, it could no longer be blamed on real external entities, and so was considered a result of diseased relationships between body, mind, and soul. These relationships obtain when irrational and unwished-for content (desires, longings, sensations) is repressed, pushed inward, denied.

The uncanny is thus a "toxic side effect of the Enlightenment."[37] The toxicity stems from the frightening knowledge that the post-Enlightenment mind must itself be the origin and the home of apparititions and hallucinations previously attributed to a supernatural realm. Rationalists dispense with the traditional supernatural, but a new problem occurs as the Romantic interest in self-observation and self-exploration grows: the realization that our minds produce the things that frighten us and, and that our minds may even be capable of making us sick, leads to an increasing

---

[35] Terry Castle, *The Female Thermometer: Eighteenth-Century Culture and the Invention of the Uncanny* (Oxford: Oxford University Press, 1995) 8.

[36] Eliade, Mircea. *Shamanism: Archaic Techniques of Ecstacy*, trans. Willard R. Trask (New York: Pantheon Books, 1964).

[37] Castle, *The Female Thermometer* 8. She argues "that the eighteenth century in a sense 'invented the uncanny': that the very psychic and cultural transformations that led to the subsequent glorification of the period as an age of reason or enlightenment—the aggressively rationalist imperatives of the epoch—also produced, like a kind of toxic side effect, a new human experience of strangeness, anxiety, bafflement, and intellectual impasse. The distinctively eighteenth-century impulse to systematize and regulate, to bureaucratize the world of knowledge by identifying what Locke called the 'horizon...which sets the bounds between the enlightened and dark parts of things,' was itself responsible, in other words, for that 'estranging of the real'—and impinging uncanniness—which is so integral a part of modernity," 8-9.

internalization and "spectralization" of other people and even of the external world.[38]

When the Romantic reaction to Enlightened rationality turns others into pure images, the aforementioned desire to "be no more" can be understood as a simultaneous desire to *continue* to be after we are no more—that is, to survive our own deaths via phantasmagoric projection.[39] There is an irrevocably modern component to this seemingly anti-modern Romantic thought, since an acknowledgment of mortality is indeed built into even the most abstracted fantasy worlds, at least when those fantasies occur within the confines of psychosomatic disorders.

This compelling way of thinking about the uncanny in the Enlightenment and post-Enlightenment age references by-now standard critiques of the Enlightenment and its veneration of unstoppable, linear modern progress. Scholars working in the field of English and American literature and cultural studies rely particularly strongly on Max Horkheimer and Theodor Adorno's *Dialectic of Enlightenment (Dialektik der Aufklärung*, 1947): irrationality and rationality are always intimately related, and an excess of one will produce a reflexive move by the other. The "spectralization," or hallucination, of others belongs in the realm of the irrational, of the Romantic—but depends completely on the rational and the Enlightened.

Uncanny anxiety, particularly when it appears in aesthetic representations of psychosomatic symptoms (or as aestheticized symptom), then, is a full-fledged participant in the process of modernization, a process Adorno and Horkheimer claim is synonymous with the "Enlightenment's process of self-destruction" ("Selbstzerstörungsprozess der Aufklärung").[40] The pressure of living in a regime of instrumental rationality provokes repressed memory to return in uncanny form, and this very remembering, this flight into phantasmatic projection and spectralization of the world, in a sense keeps us firmly locked into the inexorable pull towards the extreme individualism, even atomization, that characterizes modernization. Rather than looking for real solutions to the dilemmas posed by modernization, we retreat into image-worlds—even if involuntarily, when faced with the strangely familiar.

---

[38] See on this point Elisabeth Bronfen's reading and expansion of Terry Castle's work, in *The Knotted Subject: Hysteria and its Discontents* (Princeton: Princeton University Press, 1998) 140.

[39] Bronfen revises this argument somewhat in her own focus on hysterics in the same period, saying that "at least with hysteric performances, spectralization may well also have embraced mortal contingency by restaging the phantasmatic objects—precisely at the site of the body." See *The Knotted Subject* 141.

[40] Max Horkheimer and Theodor Adorno, *Dialektik der Aufklärung*, quoted here in Willem van Reijen, "Die Dialektik der Aufklärung gelesen als Allegorie," in Willem van Reijen and Gunzelin Schmid Noerr, eds., *Vierzig Jahre Flaschenpost: 'Dialektik der Aufklärung' 1947 bis 1987* (Frankfurt am Main: Fischer Taschenbuch, 1987) 193.

The model of the dialectic of Enlightenment is still highly revealing and productive for an understanding of the basic move of the uncanny in Enlightened culture, but I would caution against using it as an all-encompassing explanation of, or substitution for an explanation of, the significance of uncanny phenomena in an Enlightened world. If we use Adorno and Horkheimer's dialectic of Enlightenment as an explanatory model, we *must* see the uncanny as illustrating a "sick" response to that which is too instrumental, and therefore as signaling modern self-destruction. This understanding, however, may overlook the progressive possibilities of the uncanny, of anxiety, and in fact of modernity. It also tends to favor the construction of a seamless theoretical argument over the investigation of the uncanny's potential to illuminate historical and conceptual connections among the fields of philosophy, psychology, literature, and aesthetic theory beginning in the eighteenth century.

Jürgen Habermas argues that the *Dialectic of Enlightenment* overstates the entwined nature ("Verschlingung") of myth and Enlightenment.[41] Modern differentiation between the spheres of morality, science, and art resists a return to mythic or spectral structures, he says, even if the ways in which power is deployed within these spheres can and should be questioned.[42] The involuntary repetition and eerie phantasmagoria that characterize anxious uncanny symptoms do not represent unconscious attempts to re-entwine these spheres so much as they stake out a different space altogether, one in which reality is not so much denied as shifted, estranged,[43] and therefore open to critique and reform.

Writers working in the late eighteenth and early nineteenth centuries, such as Schelling, were not attempting to re-sanctify myth in order to keep the primitive in the modern so much as they were seeking a way to keep tradition compatible with progress, feeling and reflex aligned with reason and premeditation, and memory reconcilable with imagination. In so doing, they continued an ancient discussion about what can be known of the past and how it should be preserved. Aeschylus' *Oresteia*, for instance, is preoccupied with the consequences of reified myth—with what happens when old explanations and traditions harden into unquestioned justifications for present-day

---

[41] For more on the limits of Adorno and Horkheimer's model for understanding the progressive potential of modernity in particular, see Jürgen Habermas, "Die Verschlingung von Mythos und Aufklärung: Horkheimer und Adorno," in *Der philosophische Diskurs der Moderne. Zwölf Vorlesungen* (Frankfurt am Main: Suhrkamp, 1985) 130-157.

[42] Willem van Reijen expands on Habermas's critique of the *Dialectic of Enlightenment* in more detail in "Die Dialektik der Aufklärung gelesen als Allegorie," *Vierzig Jahre Flaschenpost: 'Dialektik der Aufklärung' 1947 bis 1987* 193-196.

[43] John Locke refers to "estranging of the real" as a necessary consequence of Enlightened reason in *An Essay Concerning Human Understanding*, ed. A. D. Woozley (London: Collins, 1964), Book I, "Introduction," Sec. 7. Cited here in Castle, *The Female Thermometer: Eighteenth-Century Culture and the Invention of the Uncanny* 9.

violence. Aeschylus proposes a progressive solution to these problems: the Athenians of the Oresteia permit the Furies to live among them; these goddesses of anger and rebellion are living, physical reminders of repressed feelings.[44] The proper integration of those feelings into civilization keeps the culture functional and its individuals interrelated.

Dialectically motivated arguments about how the uncanny functions in the post-Enlightenment world are not opposed to the notion that repressed content can become an accepted and even popular part of overt cultural expression; an Aeschyleian dynamic may be at work today when we realize that the fantastic and grotesque not only have always been with us, but have in fact been crucial components of mainstream modern culture and have served as quite rational expressions of irrational desires.[45] This coexistence of irrationality and rationality does not reflect a collapse, or destructive "entwining," of the two so much as a mutually sustaining reciprocity reflected in all levels and spheres of modern cultural production.

Schelling describes an imagination that is more than the manufacturer of spectres (and thus more than the converter of real others into spectral images) when he says that mystery, "the actual religious principle" ("das eigentliche religiöse Princip") must be "hidden within" reason ("im Innern geborgen").[46] This unification of reason and religion is not incompatible with uncanny repetition; in fact:

> This is exactly why Greece has a Homer, because it has mysteries; that is, because Greece was able to defeat the principle of the past completely, a principle that was still dominant and external in oriental systems, and was able to push that principle inside; that is, into the secret, into the mystery from which it after all originally came. (Gerade darum hat Griechenland einen Homer, weil es Mysterien hat, d.h. weil es ihm gelungen ist, jenes Princip der Vergangenheit, das in den orientalischen Systemen noch herrschend und äußerlich war, völlig zu besiegen und ins Innere, d.h. ins Geheimniß, ins Mysterium [aus dem es ja ursprünglich hervorgetreten war] zurückzusetzen).[47]

For Schelling, "defeating the principle of the past" does not mean erasing the past, but rather something quite like Freud's much later notion of repressing it. This repression enables a Homer to emerge, but Schelling's *Philosophy of Mythology* also acknowledges that the principle of the past will resurface as uncanny experience (it will "come to light"); this is a dialectical move. However, the dialectical move of the uncanny in our modernity, for Schelling, is not from irrationality to rationality and back again, but rather reflective of a reciprocity between and co-existence of sensation (or perception) and

---

[44] Aeschylus, *The Oresteia*, trans. Richmond Lattimore (Chicago: U of Chicago P, 1953).
[45] See Victoria Nelson, *The Secret Life of Puppets* (Cambridge and London: Harvard UP, 2001), esp. 1-23.
[46] Schelling, AS 6: 661.
[47] Ibid, 661.

reaction (or affect), and between forgetting (repressing) and remembering (repetition, return). The principle of the past (rather than real events in the historical past), a principle represented by the "false, mistaken religion" of myth that nevertheless "becomes a truth of its own kind,"[48] is not entwined with, but fully different from the modern and differentiated world. Attempts to "defeat" the mythical past by pushing it back into the inscrutable mystery from whence it came are necessary for the ultimate re-emergence of the past *as* representation and its integration into the modern present. This integration is not a collapse between present and past, but rather a working-together, through analysis and interpretation, that acknowledges the unbridgeable difference between the mythical and the modern.

A "principle of the past" very much like Schelling's was of interest to Freud as well. In the therapeutic context, he focused on patients' present re-representations of their memories of the past rather than on attempting to reconstruct precisely what had happened in the real past. And, in the context of his work as an amateur anthropologist and collector of artifacts from ancient cultures, he was motivated to collect and interpret representations of an idea of the past rather than to engage in precise historical reconstruction. His passion for collecting reflected an "ahistorical fantasy structure inherent in the process of miniaturization and collection."[49] The approximately two thousand objects in Freud's collection, primarily from ancient Greece, Rome, Egypt, and China, were of course real pieces created in the real past. As displayed in his offices in Vienna (and eventually London), however, and as artifacts he interacted with, spoke to, touched, and even ate with, they were "dead but unburied....ghosts":[50] uncanny reminders, nostalgic re-presentations of a whole impossible to reconstruct, of a past truly over. These "selected facts" from the past represented for Freud not the reality of the past, but its principle, its past-ness. As reminders of death and hence creators of an "eerie temporal discoordination of the past, present, and future,"[51] Freud's objects preserved, or sustained, death, the irrevocable loss of the past, and the difference between past and present rather than promising immortality or devolving into pure image.

---

[48] Schelling, AS 6: 657.

[49] Helen Deutsch, "Doctor Johnson's Autopsy, or Anecdotal Immortality," *The Eighteenth Century: Theory and Interpretation* 40.2 (1999) 124. Deutsch here employs the theory of collecting developed in Susan Stewart's *On Longing: Narratives of the Miniature, the Gigantic, the Souvenir, the Collection* (Durham and London: Duke UP, 1993).

[50] Gregg Horowitz uses the formulation "dead but unburied...ghosts" and writes that "Freud lived and thought in intimate contact with his collection. He spoke to and addressed his artifacts and sometimes took whichever one was most inspiring to him at the moment to the breakfast table," *Sustaining Loss: Art and Mournful Life* 130; Horowitz relies on testimony from *Sigmund Freud and Art: His Personal Collection of Antiquities*, eds. Lynn Gamwell and Richard Wells (Binghamton: State University of New York, and the Freud Museum, London, 1989).

[51] Horowitz, *Sustaining Loss: Art and Mournful Life* 130.

Freud's fascination with collecting and with the "simultaneity of the noncontemporaneous,"[52] the ability of re-representations of the past to demand present attention, was also a fascination with a kind of repetition. His "ghosts" repeat an idea of the past as they "haunt" his present. He is compelled to collect and display these objects, compelled to re-represent the past to himself, repetitively. In the essay on "The Uncanny," Freud writes that "whatever reminds us of this inner 'compulsion to repeat' is perceived as uncanny" ("Wir sind durch alle vorstehenden Erörterungen darauf vorbereitet, daß dasjenige als unheimlich verspürt werden wird, was an diesen inneren Wiederholungszwang mahnen kann").[53] His objects are uncanny because they are reminders as well as enacters of repetition. It is the emphasis on memory as a form of haunting that both traps us in the past and, by provoking fear and anxiety, propels us forward, that in part makes Freud's essay so compelling. This is the reframing of the dialectic of Enlightenment that the uncanny can provoke: the recurrence of ghostly representations of the past (or, "the principle of the past") demonstrates the simultaneity of, and reciprocity between, pastness and present, between the "ghost" and the living, mortal collector-viewer, between oblivion and memories of memories (being reminded of repetition itself).

Uncanny repetition offers an opportunity, not always realized by protagonists and patients, but to us, to the interpreters of the modern texts and case studies in which the uncanny figures prominently, to act on our desire to simultaneously push inward and to understand the "principle of the past," to tolerate our desire for aesthetic redemption together with the realization of its impossibility. And, as Freud extended his understanding of temporality within an individual consciousness to an entire civilization, so we will find that this modern dialectic does not and cannot happen merely within our own minds. The estrangement of past perception from present affect that occurs when something repressed, hidden, comes to light is a transformation of memory, but also an extension of memory—what the phenomenologist Edward Casey calls "the outreach of memories into the surrounding world of the remembering subject."[54] When Nathanael encounters Coppola, the uncanny double of his childhood tormentor, the Sandman (Coppelius), he remembers the Sandman and his father's death, but also "re-members" that past, reshapes it in a way that influences his entire present and the real others who populate it. Nathanael ultimately cannot tolerate the irreconcilability of his desire to escape his past (pursued in part through his obsession with the beautiful doll Olimpia) and his real present, into which that past always intrudes. But the

---

[52] This is part of Carl E. Schorske's description of Freud's view of civilization and the psyche, in "Freud: The Psychoarcheology of Civilizations," *Cambridge Companion to Freud*, ed. Jerome Neu (Cambridge: Cambridge UP, 1998) 9.

[53] Freud, GW 12: 251/SE 17: 238.

[54] Edward Casey, *Remembering: A Phenomenological Study* (Bloomington and Indianapolis: Indiana UP, 1987) 288.

uncanny phenomena he encounters and the intolerable anxiety they provoke, the psychosomatic disorders they create, force him quite literally down to earth (in his jump from the tower at the story's end); uncanny experiences force "transcending the mind as a container of memories"[55] and returning to the body, returning to earth.

All memory is not uncanny, and memory does of course reside in the mind of the remembering subject; memory is "my own,"[56] located in me, as well as centrifugal, outward-directed. But uncanny memories, I argue, have a particular way of "reaching out" to the world outside, as Casey would say. Uncanny memories and the aesthetically charged anxiety they sustain create a marginal, or "liminal," state of "no-longer and not-yet"[57] that imbricates us intimately with others. Freud's uncanny collection of ghostly, "dead but unburied" objects is representative of such liminality, but examples of more modest scope appear in literature, philosophy, and psychology from the late eighteenth century onward. In every case, the form of memory that transpires when something external, yet strangely familiar, to the remembering subject appears, is embodied (felt in and expressed through the body) and interrelated (requiring the existence of real others, who may be represented as images to and within the self, but who are nevertheless different from the self). And in every case, the appearance of an uncanny symptom represents a stage in a modern dialectic of remembering and forgetting: uncanny memory requires the repression of a past perception or sensation that is dissociated from emotional affect. Through this process, the experience of the uncanny, whether in daily life or as portrayed aesthetically, can point the way back to a renewed involvement with real others, by ultimately expanding memory beyond the individual mind.

---

[55] Casey, *Remembering: A Phenomenological Study* 288.

[56] Casey explains that while memory has a "density of involvement" with the world beyond the self, an involvement that to a great extent can "depersonalize" the self, we should still pay attention to the "many personal features of remembering," which belong to the individual self's *Jemeinigkeit* (here he cites Heidegger's *Sein und Zeit* [*Being and Time*, trans. J. Macquarrie and E. Robinson {New York: Harper and Row, 1962} 67-69]). *Remembering: A Phenomenological Study* 289 and 289n2.

[57] Casey here cites Victor Turner's assertion of a "relationship between the marginal phase or 'liminality' and community. As something 'essentially unstructured (which is at once destructured and prestructured), liminality in Turner's view resists facile unifications by virtue of its paradoxical combination of the no-longer and the not-yet, the living and the dead," *Remembering: A Phenomenological Study* 236. Turner is cited in *The Forest of Symbols: Aspects of Ndembu Ritual* (Ithaca: Cornell UP, 1967) 98.

2.3. The Uncanny as a Bridge to Relatedness and as a Form of Memory Beyond Mind

The notion that memory can be a tool for creating relationships between self and other, as opposed to only forming images of others within an eternally lonely self, is a preoccupation for philosophers, psychologists, and authors at precisely the same time that the world threatens to become, for Romantics, a sheer effect of the mind. In response to Johann Gottlieb Fichte's radical argument that the ego posits itself and all else, Friedrich Schlegel, the pre-eminent philosopher of the Romantic movement, develops an incomplete theory about the necessity of difference between self and world and the ways in which the recognition of that difference is encoded in memory traces. In a meditation on love, Schlegel argues that there is, outside of our own minds, outside of the "I" ("Ich") a "live, counter-engaged *you*" ("ein lebendiges, gegenwirkendes *Du*"). When "I" and "you" recognize (or remember, as memory trace) one another, we share "an actual inner bond between different, but similar spirits" ("eine eigentliche innerliche Verbindung geschiedener, aber ähnlicher Geister").[58] Recognition and remembering then act reciprocally between self and other, between self and world, as well as within the image-world created by the individual self. Schlegel acknowledges, however, that this recognition and remembering never will suffice to bring the other or the world into the self; that is, an awareness of separation and loss is always part of the process of remembering that maintains our always-incomplete relationship to others. Loss and anxiety about loss are inevitable components of being with others in the world; memory in Schlegel's philosophy acknowledges and maintains, or sustains, that loss.[59]

More than a century later, R.D. Laing's examination of anxiety and neurosis offers a psychologically motivated parallel to Schlegel's thinking:

> The analytic theory of object-relations is based on the finding that the recognition of our own separate existence, and the separate existence of the other person, is gained only slowly and often painfully....Anxiety remains an ultimate risk even in mature

---

[58] Schlegel, KA 12: 350-351.

[59] Elsewhere Schlegel addresses memory and loss in more detail, in the context of thinking about the nature of what he calls "world consciousness," or the "Welt-Ich": "Das Welt-Ich hatte seinen Ursprung vergessen: es findet ihn wieder. Dieses Wiederfinden ist die *Erinnerung*: diese Erinnerung aber muß mit *Schmerz* und *Reue* verbunden sein, über den *wo nicht gänzlichen*, doch *teilweisen Verlust* der ursprünglichen Einheit, über den innern Zwiespalt und Kampf, der das Wesen des Welt-Ichs ganz zu zerrütten droht" ("World-consciousness had forgotten its origin: it finds it once more. This finding-again is *memory*: this memory, however, must be bound up with *pain* and *regret* about the *loss* [*if not complete*, then at least *partial* loss] of original unity, about the inner division and struggle that threatens to completely destroy world-consciousness"), KA 12: 435. I have addressed German Romantic thinking on reciprocity and alterity in more detail in "Dorothea Veit's *Florentin* and the Early Romantic Model of Alterity," *Monatshefte* 97.1 (2005) 33-62.

> object-relations, since there is no escape from the tragic paradox that whereas our relatedness to others is part of us, the real other person is not.[60]

Our similarity and sympathy with the other is real, as is the bond with, or love for, the other that ensues. But we can never subsume the real other into ourselves. This realization of loss and difference occurs over and over for Schlegel and the Early Romantic[61] group of which he was a part. The Early Romantic philosophy of reciprocity ("Wechselwirkung") between concepts and images within self-consciousness and among different consciousnesses, and the notion of loss that is always part of these interactions, is reflected in the contemporary psychology of Karl Philipp Moritz, Friedrich August Carus, Carl Gustav Carus, and Gotthilf Heinrich von Schubert, all of whom are interested in the ways in which the mind is affected by the world and in how the mind portrays the world to itself. However, psychologists of the era shift the focus from the mechanisms of self-consciousness to observable experience, and their studies often privilege repetitive—in fact uncannily repetitive—phenomena. Like Romantic reciprocity, which is a repetitive back-and-forth between concepts (such as remembering and imagining, knowing and believing, thinking and feeling), uncanny repetition helps constitute relationships between self and world, in this case via memories that are dissociated from their origins. More than the hysterical creation of spectres in a mind that is merely a phantom zone, uncanny memory forces self-consciousness outward; it is a kind of memory beyond mind. The uncanny is a return to memory, after forgetting, and this return is inherently strange, estranged. While John Locke asserts that a sense of estrangement from one's own past and self is a condition of being in the world after the Enlightenment,[62] Schelling argues that such estrangement is as old as myth. Uncanny experiences are generated by the unconscious mind, which is itself as old as myth, but only fully theorized in the modern era, most completely of course by Freud (I address pre-Freudian concepts of the unconscious and their relationship to depictions of the uncanny in Chapter Two).

Where Friedrich Schlegel and the Romantics turn to reciprocity to establish a philosophy of relatedness between self and world, Freud (strongly influenced by Romanticism) turns to repetition. Samuel Weber points out that repetition is at the foundation of Freud's thinking on binding ("Bindung") between self and other, and of Eros: "in order to conceptualize the notion of

---

[60] R.D. Laing, "An Examination of Tillich's Theory of Anxiety and Neurosis." *British Journal of Medical Psychology* 30 (1957) 88-91.

[61] "Early" or "Jena" Romantic group members included Friedrich and August Wilhelm Schlegel, Friedrich Schelling, Dorothea Veit (later Schlegel, after her marriage to Friedrich in 1804), Novalis, Ludwig Tieck, Caroline Schlegel-Schelling, and Friedrich Schleiermacher; the period spans 1796-1801.

[62] John Locke, *An Essay Concerning Human Understanding*, ed. A. D. Woozley (London: Collins, 1964), Book I, "Introduction," Sec. 7.

binding, Freud cannot avoid resorting to that of *repetition*: as a temporal process, binding is inconceivable except as a form of repetition."[63] Weber says that reverting to repetition forces Freud to establish a reciprocal relationship in his thinking between love and loss, and between the pleasure principle and the death drive. This back-and-forth movement, like Schlegel's conceptual reciprocity, and like Laing's notion of object relations, is anxious —suspended, no-longer and not-yet—and revealing of what Casey calls memory's "'thick autonomy'—a density of involvement (with the world) that...inheres in recollection itself." By "autonomy," Casey means that memory can be liberated from not only the initial perception or sensation that created it, but from the individual remembering subject as well. Uncanny memory, which is a repetition of repressed content but also something new, and which is the liberation of sensation from affect, thus goes "beyond mind" and appears in bodies (often within the context of psychosomatic disorders), in significant places (of commemoration, or of evocation)—it appears out in the world, in aestheticized and anxious form.

On the one hand, uncanny memories reveal "the typical narcissistic problem of a lack of belief in the continuity and substantiality of the self and in the continuity of the process of being alive."[64] The subject's "momentary depersonalizations or derealizations, symptomatic of the failure of defenses against aggressive or exhibitionistic wishes" may transpire only within his own mind, and only briefly.[65] In other words, uncanny experience is a highly individualistic and temporary sensation. A focus on a private and psychological uncanny can impede our ability to assess a text's political value, because such a focus tempts us to read only from a psychological standpoint; modern European fiction generally tends to "privatize" political impulses, to drive them into the inner realm of the "mysterious" to which Schelling refers.[66] But the uncanny can be dragged out of the private realm and situated in a social context; uncanny memories even can be transmitted intersubjectively and intergenerationally. This happens when an encounter with something strangely familiar evokes memories of social trauma.[67] The transsubjective space in which social violence occurs is also the space of common memory formation, and a space to experience the relatedness

---

63 Samuel Weber, *The Legend of Freud* (Stanford: Stanford UP, 2000) 122-123.

64 Sheldon Bach, "Narcissism, Continuity and the Uncanny," *The International Journal of Psycho-Analysis* 56 (1975) 78.

65 Ibid, 78.

66 Richard T. Gray, "The Hermeneut(r)ic(k) of the Psychic Narrative: Freud's 'Das Unheimliche' and Hofmannsthal's *Reitergeschichte*," *The German Quarterly* 62.4 (1989) 473-488.

67 Yolanda Gampel, "The Interminable Uncanniness," *Psychoanalysis at the Political Border: Essays in Honor of Rafael Moses* (Madison, CT: International Universities Press, 1996) 85. Cornelia Blasberg provides a model for thinking about transsubjective and intergenerational memory in "Geschichte als Palimpsest. Schreiben und Lesen über die 'Kinder der Täter,'" *Deutsche Vierteljahrsschrift für Literaturwissenschaft und Geistesgeschichte* (2003) 464-495.

between different but similar subjects through re-representing those memories. The modern differentiation between private and public spheres can lead to a conversion of political goals into psychological concerns. The uncanny, however, as an aesthetic concept but also as a form of lived experience (that takes place in intersubjective spaces as well as within the confines of psychosomatic illness), can exist in several spheres at once.

Uncanniness can in fact now be found in urban and public spaces, according to Anthony Vidler's architectural analysis: "the labyrinthine spaces of the modern city have been construed as the sources of modern anxiety... the theme of the uncanny serves to join architectural speculation on the peculiarly unstable nature of 'house and home' to more general reflection on the questions of social and individual estrangement, alienation, exile, and homelessness."[68] "Private" memories of loss and separation have, when brought into modern urban space, political implications; a sense of estrangement is present in the design of recent Holocaust memorials as well. James E. Young relies on Vidler's thinking to construct a connection between such memorials and "the memory of loss," particularly in Libeskind's Jewish Museum in Berlin.[69] Such structures bring representations of the past into the present while reminding of the eternal estrangement between past and present, self and other. They provoke reflection on social questions and sustain loss, thereby answering the desire to live, without promising redemption or healing, and certainly without promising fusion. Uncanny repetition of aspects of the past, relived as dread and fear and as a type of illness, can be a working-through, not just an acting-out, of repressed dilemmas. The uncanny can be a form of memorializing rather than just of perpetuating trauma; in uncanny spaces within and outside of the mind, trauma continues, but in mutated form, on levels psychological, social, and potentially political as well.

In the only book-length study of the uncanny to date, Nicholas Royle writes that uncanny astonishment, dread, or even horror has the potential to remind us of others, and therefore to bring us back "home,"[70] with all of the ambiguity that Freud says the word "home" entails.[71] This "coming home," which Friedrich Schlegel says is a remembering, replete with "*pain* and

68 Vidler, *The Architectural Uncanny: Essays in the Modern Unhomely* ix.

69 James E. Young, "Against Redemption: The Arts of Countermemory in Germany Today," *Symbolic Loss: The Ambiguity of Mourning and Memory at Century's End*, ed. Peter Homans (Charlottesville: The UP of Virginia, 2000) 126-144.

70 Royle, *The Uncanny: An Introduction* 2.

71 Freud writes: "Wir werden überhaupt daran gemahnt, daß dies Wort heimlich nicht eindeutig ist, sondern zwei Vorstellungskreisen zugehört, die, ohne gegensätzlich zu sein, einander doch recht fremd sind, dem des Vertrauten, Behaglichen und dem des Versteckten, Verborgengehaltenen," GW 17: 235 ("In general we are reminded that the word '*heimlich*' is not unambiguous, but belongs to two sets of ideas, which, without being contradictory, are yet very different: on the one hand it means what is familiar and agreeable, and on the other, what is concealed and kept out of sight," SE 12: 224-225).

regret" about loss or separation ("diese Erinnerung aber muß mit *Schmerz* und *Reue* verbunden sein, über den *wo nicht gänzlichen*, doch *teilweisen Verlust* der ursprünglichen Einheit"),[72] does not imply a reversal of history or a return to any kind of origin, but rather a process of recognizing ourselves better via recognizing different (yet familiar) others. When we do this, and when we experience the *de*-realization or *de*-personalization that "memory beyond mind" precipitates, we have the possibility to enter a non-mystical, real space of relatedness with others. That dimension depends on the existence of the principle of the past, of the mythical mistakes that are the prerequisite for all history to come.

In the next chapter, I examine texts of philosophy and early psychology, including Kant's *Dreams of a Spirit-Seer* (*Träume eines Geistersehers*, 1766) and Schelling's *Clara: Or, On Nature's Connection to the Spirit World* (*Clara, oder Zusammenhang der Natur mit der Geisterwelt*, written between 1810-1811), in order to demonstrate that the pervasive presence of an aesthetic component—of an aesthetic anxiety—in Enlightenment and Romantic explorations of psychosomatic disorders helps bring a philosophy of difference and relatedness into modern consciousness, precisely when these texts focus on dilemmas that challenge the stability of that consciousness.

[72] Schlegel, KA 12: 435; see longer passage in Note 59 of this chapter.

Chapter 2

The Uncanny Before Freud: Psychological and Philosophical Aspects

For it is possible to recognize the dominance in the unconscious mind of a 'compulsion to repeat' proceeding from the instinctual impulses and probably inherent in the very nature of the instincts—a compulsion powerful enough to overrule the pleasure principle, lending to certain aspects of the mind their daemonic character, and still very clearly expressed in the impulses of small children; a compulsion, too, which is responsible for a part of the course taken by the analyses of neurotic patients. All these considerations prepare us for the discovery that whatever reminds us of this inner 'compulsion to repeat' is perceived as uncanny.
[Im seelisch Unbewußten läßt sich nämlich die Herrschaft eines von den Triebregungen ausgehenden Wiederholungszwanges erkennen, der wahrscheinlich von der innersten Natur der Triebe selbst abhängt, stark genug ist, sich über das Lustprinzip hinauszusetzen, gewissen Seiten des Seelenlebens den dämonischen Charakter verleiht, sich in den Strebungen des kleinen Kindes noch sehr deutlich äußert und ein Stück vom Ablauf der Psychoanalyse des Neurotikers beherrscht. Wir sind durch alle vorstehenden Erörterungen darauf vorbereitet, daß dasjenige als unheimlich verspürt werden wird, was an diesen inneren Wiederholungszwang mahnen kann.]
Freud, *The Uncanny [Das Unheimliche]*

1. Uncanny Anxiety and Sublime Awe

Acknowledged or otherwise, anxiety courses through the history of modern aesthetics. In an early treatise on classical art entitled *On the Imitation of the Greeks* (*Gedancken über die Nachahmung der Griechischen Werke in der Mahlerey und Bildhauer-Kunst*, 1755), Johann Joachim Winckelmann chooses, of all sculptures, the Laocoön, a depiction of agonizing death, to exemplify "noble simplicity and still grandeur" ("edle Einfalt und stille Grosse"). In the wake of Alexander Gottlieb Baumgarten's attempt to unite the science of sense perception with transcendental judgment in the *Aesthetica* of 1750-1758, the number of texts devoted to aesthetic theory increases, and their focus on beauty is attended frequently by a fear of decay. This fear intensifies and increasingly is acknowledged (rather than denied, as in the case of Winckelmann) concurrent with the rise of secularism and the awareness of finitude. This awareness dominates and even helps to organize modern aesthetic theory and cultural production;[1] Kant's *Critique of Judgment* (*Kritik der Urteilskraft*, 1790) demands that the artist must be absent from the artwork—or, at least symbolically, die—for art to be truly

[1] Gregg Horowitz makes this argument in *Sustaining Loss: Art and Mournful Life* (Stanford: Stanford University Press, 2001) 3, et al.

beautiful. At the same time, thinking about art can only occur in the context of thinking about natural, historical (and therefore transitory) beauty.[2] Well before Kant's final critique, Winckelmann's influential *History of the Art of Antiquity* (*Geschichte der Kunst des Alterthums*, 1764) contends that beauty depends on corporeal violence: as Winckelmann scholar Alex Potts notes, "the imperatives of ideal beauty lead ineluctably to the image of the hermaphrodite or castrated figure…the most radical destruction conceivable of bodily signs of manliness."[3] The intentional juxtaposition and acknowledgment of beauty's interdependence with ruin are also an expression of and response to anxiety relating to mortality and decay.

In the brief essay "On Transience" ("Vergänglichkeit," 1916), Freud eases this kind of anxiety by constructing an apparently soothing view of mortality attenuated by repetition. On a summer walk before the outbreak of the First World War, Freud listens as one of his companions, a "young but already famous poet" ("jung[er], bereits rühmlich bekannt[er] Dichter[]") laments that "all this beauty was fated to extinction, that it would vanish when winter came, like all human beauty and all the beauty and splendour that men have created or may create" ("daß all diese Schönheit dem Vergehen geweiht war, daß sie im Winter dahingeschwunden sein werde, aber ebenso jede menschliche Schönheit und alles Schöne und Edle, was Menschen geschaffen haben und schaffen könnten").[4] Freud responds that our own mortality permits us to enjoy and value the cyclical rhythms of natural beauty: "As regards the beauty of Nature, each time it is destroyed by winter it comes again next year, so that in relation to the length of our lives it can in fact be regarded as eternal" ("Was die Schönheit der Natur betrifft, so kommt sie nach jeder Zerstörung durch den Winter im nächsten Jahre wieder, und diese Wiederkehr darf im Verhältnis zu unserem Lebensdauer als eine ewige bezeichnet werden"). Human beauty is like a "flower that blossoms only for a single night" ("eine Blume…welche nur eine einzige Nacht blüht"), but that only increases its worth.

---

[2] Immanuel Kant, *Critique of Judgment*, trans. Werner S. Pluhar (Indianapolis: Hackett Publishing, 1987) 45: 174; Gregg Horowitz uses aspects of this section of the third critique in his larger argument that Kant "discovers aesthetic modernism," *Sustaining Loss: Art and Mournful Life* 26, et al.

[3] Alex Potts, *Flesh and the Ideal: Winckelmann and the Origins of Art History* (New Haven and London: Yale University Press, 1994) 166; he addresses Johann Joachim Winckelmann's *Geschichte der Kunst des Alterthums* (Dresden, 1764) 160-161. Potts also explains that when Winckelmann transfers his aesthetic theory to real statues, he shifts his understanding of the sublime from a "primary category"—that which comes before the experience of beauty, foregrounds it—to a posterior, intimated category; when we view actual statues, we intimate the sublime through the beautiful. See Potts, p. 113.

[4] Sigmund Freud, "Vergänglichkeit" in *Gesammelte Werke* 10 (Frankfurt am Main: Fischer, 1999) 358. This edition is abbreviated henceforth as GW. The translation is James Strachey's in "On Transience" in *The Standard Edition of the Complete Psychological Works of Sigmund Freud* 14 (London: Hogarth, 1953-1974) 305. This edition is abbreviated henceforth as SE.

The essay unsurprisingly invites the reader to identify with Freud's position, particularly after he persuasively concludes that a "revolt…against mourning" ("die seelische Auflehnung gegen die Trauer")[5] is at work in the young poet's mind. The desire to diminish the value of beautiful objects in nature is linked to the desire to deny the pain that comes from the inevitable "detachment of libido from its objects"—to deny the pain of loss, and thus to disallow mourning. The poet's denial of mourning lands him in a state of unproductive melancholy. In a passage considerably more optimistic than those in his later writings about culture, Freud encourages us to acknowledge mourning rather than to rebel against it, since

> (m)ourning, as we know, however painful it may be, comes to a spontaneous end. When it has renounced everything that has been lost, then it has consumed itself, and our libido is once more free (in so far as we are still young and active) to replace the lost objects by fresh ones equally or still more precious. It is to be hoped that the same will be true of the losses caused by this war. When once the mourning is over, it will be found that our high opinion of the riches of civilization has lost nothing from our discovery of their fragility.
> (Wir wissen, die Trauer, so schmerzhaft sie sein mag, läuft spontan ab. Wenn sie auf alles Verlorene verzichtet hat, hat sie sich auch selbst aufgezehrt, und dann wird unsere Libido wiederum frei, um sich, insofern wir noch jung und lebenskräftig sind, die verlorenen Objekte durch möglichst gleich kostbare oder kostbarere neue zu ersetzen. Es steht zu hoffen, daß es mit den Verlusten dieses Krieges nicht anders gehen wird. Wenn erst die Trauer überwunden ist, wird es sich zeigen, daß unsere Hochschätzung der Kulturgüter unter der Erfahrung von der Gebrechlichkeit nicht gelitten hat.)[6]

What Freud's postwar writings on culture (perhaps most notably *Civilization and its Discontents*) reveal, however, is an admission that mourning itself, although preferable to the poet's cynicism, can be a repetitive process that continually re-reveals anxiety about loss and decay, particularly when we and our culture are no longer "young and active." That is, since lost loved objects are replaced by new ones which also inevitably will be lost, mourning comes increasingly to resemble melancholy. The "normal affect of mourning" ("Normalaffekt der Trauer"), if repeated continually, is no longer so different from the "disruption of self-consciousness" ("Störung des Selbstgefühls")[7] that marks melancholy suffering.

In "On Transience," Freud's poet friend echoes a little-known piece by Friedrich Schelling from 1810-1811 entitled *Clara: Or, On Nature's Connection to the Spirit World (Clara: oder Zusammenhang der Natur mit der Geisterwelt*). This text, left as a fragment, was intended as a prelude to *The Ages of the World*, which was written between 1811-1815. In *Clara*, the

[5] Freud, GW 10: 359/SE 14: 305.
[6] Ibid, 361/307.
[7] Freud, "Trauer und Melancholie," GW 10: 428-429/ "Mourning and Melancholia," SE 14: 244.

heroine wonders fearfully about decay in nature and about the nature of decay.

> (Nature) seems to have a secret consuming poison within herself; but why does she transmit it to her children, so that they too are consumed? …Whence this universal, never-ending force of death?
> (Sie [die Natur] scheint selbst ein geheimes verzehrendes Gift in sich zu haben; aber warum theilt sie es ihren Kindern mit, daß auch sie davon verzehrt werden?…Woher diese allgemeine, nie aufhörende Gewalt des Todes?)[8]

Poisonous, killing her own children, nature is the ultimate bad mother. But Clara recognizes the potential for beauty precisely in this threatening situation —in the process of repetitive decay. Turning the juxtaposition of "nature" and "mother" in a still-anxious but more personal and less murderous direction, Clara says:

> If children had been given to me and then they were all taken away, I could never consider it as chance or a temporary fortune to have been the mother of these souls; I would feel—yes, I would know—that they belong to me eternally and I to them and that no power on Earth or in heaven could take them from me or me from them.
> (Wären mir Kinder geschenkt und alle Kinder genommen, so könnte ich es nie für Zufall oder ein vorübergehendes Geschick halten, die Mutter dieser Seele zu seyn; ich fühlte, ja ich wüßte, daß sie ewig zu mir gehören, ich zu ihnen, und daß sie mir, ich ihnen, durch seine Gewalt der Erde, noch selbst des Himmels genommen werden können.)[9]

Clara here describes a response to the loss of love objects that could be called eternal mourning—the permanent attachment of libido to something permanently lost.

Clara seems concerned more directly with our ability to live with loss by asserting the possibility of life after death than it is with aesthetic theory per se, but it revolves around the question of the nature and reliability of sense perception, which is at the foundation of aesthetics. Its discussion of frightening phenomena within the framework of sense perception anticipates Freud's overt admission of the topic of the frightening to aesthetic inquiry in the essay on "The Uncanny" of 1919.

However, long before Freud acknowledges the repulsive and the frightening as legitimate categories of aesthetic investigation, there is an aesthetics *of* fear in Western thought and in the German tradition. This aesthetics of fear and dread ("Schreckens-" and "Schauerästhetik") often is

---

[8] Friedrich Schelling, *Clara, oder Zusammenhang der Natur mit der Geisterwelt, Sämmtliche Werke*, ed. K.F.A. Schelling, vol. 9 (Stuttgart and Augsburg: Cotta, 1861) 29, 30. This edition is referred to henceforth as SW. The translation is Fiona Steinkamp's in *Clara, or On Nature's Connection to the Spirit World* (Albany: State University of New York Press, 2002) 22. This volume is referred to henceforth as Steinkamp.
[9] Ibid, 19/14.

linked not to uncanny repetition but to sublime awe. As Steven Cresap states, the "pleasure of aesthetic horror is connected with the expansion of awareness believed to occur in the experience of the sublime."[10] The sublime is supposedly a unique, singular experience, whereas the uncanny is characterized by repetition. And yet the expansion of awareness that the sublime promises is also afforded by its dark aesthetic twin, the uncanny, and the uncanny may provide a better instrument for accessing the pain and pleasure of aesthetic horror, especially when, as is so often the case, that horror is linked to the awareness of decay and death. In turn, this awareness often manifests in the symptoms of psychological illness; studies of mental disorders beginning in the mid-eighteenth century are rife with speculation that the symptoms of these disorders are symbols not just of organic imbalances, but of emotional states, such as fear.

Superficially, the aesthetics of fear in the eighteenth century has much to do with the visible—depictions of feelings of horror, symbolic renderings of fright reactions and of perceptions of decay and death (as in the Laocoön). Such reactions were attributed generally to immediate, equally visible causes. Carsten Zelle explains that the basic definition of a fright reaction (or the affect of fright) as revealing a "high degree of fear" (ein hoher Grad der Furcht") was tied specifically to something surprising; one reacts with an expression of fright to an "unexpected ill or to an unsuspected danger" ("Schrecken ist eine plötzlich erregte Fucht vor einem unerwarteten Übel oder einer unvermuteten Gefahr").[11] Fear could be mastered by anticipating danger; or so runs the thinking in mid-century texts by authors such as Wolff and Kant. This mastery is important not just for personal comfort but for the survival of the Enlightened social order.[12]

Starting in the middle decades of the eighteenth century, however, fright and fear are depicted as reactions and emotions that no longer necessarily have to be avoided. At about the same time that the concept of the uncanny appears in psychology, literature, and aesthetic theory, fear begins to be portrayed as a standard component of experience, and as part of a normal subjectivity Psychologist Johann Sulzer's notions of different types of fright, including "empty," "sublime," and "healing" ("leerer," "erhabener," and "heilsamer") represent an increasingly common understanding of fear as something potentially admissible into the world of the rational subject, as long as it is redeemed and restrained by aesthetically acceptable portrayal.[13] In *Laocoön* (*Laokoon*, 1766), Gotthold Ephraim Lessing returns to the statue whose depiction of fear Winckelmann essentially denied, and develops a

---

10 Steven Cresap, "Sublime Politics: On the Uses of an Aesthetics of Terror," *Clio* 19.2 (1990) 111.

11 Carsten Zelle, *Angenehmes Grauen. Literaturhistorische Beiträge zur Ästhetik des Schrecklichen im achtzehnten Jahrhundert* (Hamburg: F. Meiner, 1987) 28.

12 Ibid, 28.

13 Ibid, 385.

concept of "pleasurable dread" ("angenehmes Grauen") that is an important component of "subjective self-perception" ("subjektives Selbstgefühl").[14]

Pleasurable dread, however, is only available to viewers of aesthetically portrayed pain; it is an estranged experience, a fear at one remove. In 1782, Karl Philipp Moritz acknowledges this vicarious pleasure when he writes that we in fact really enjoy the sight of another's fear; this pleasure in the pain of another "shakes and elevates" ("erschüttert und erhebt") our souls.[15] Moritz cites the example of pain and death on an enormous scale: "When thousands fall to the sword on one day, that is really something *great*. And the *great* is what we want; our souls desire expansion, our imagination wants to encompass *a lot*" ("Wenn Tausende an einem Tage vor dem Schwertstreich fallen, das ist doch etwas *Großes*. Und das *Große* wollen wir ja; unsre Seele will ja erweitert sein, unsre Einbildungskraft will *viel* umspannen").[16]

One focus within the aesthetics of fear by the 1780s, then, is on evaluating our perceptions when we observe another's suffering. This extends the understanding of fear reactions beyond that of a sudden response to a surprise shock. Moritz's involvement with empirical psychology during the same years that he wrote most of his aesthetic theory (the 1780s and early 1790s) reveals an interest in exploring connections between present fright and past experience, or in admitting the possibility that the thing that is surprising and therefore frightening may represent the return, or repetition, of something forgotten. While Moritz and other empirical (or faculty) psychologists of the eighteenth and early nineteenth centuries do not develop a coherent theory of trauma, repression, and affect as related events, the very emergence of psychology ("Seelenkunde") as a discipline during the Enlightenment represents an acknowledgment of the role of memory and the ways in which it can malfunction. One way such a malfunction can occur is in an uncanny disconnect between something problematic in the past and something frightening in the present.

Well before Ernst Jentsch explicitly theorizes the uncanny in his 1906 essay entitled "On the Psychology of the Uncanny" ("Zur Psychologie

---

[14] Gotthold Ephraim Lessing, *Sämtliche Schriften*, ed. Karl Lachmann (Stuttgart: G. J. Goschen, 1893) 9: 20; paraphrased in Zelle, *Angenehmes Grauen. Literaturhistorische Beiträge zur Ästhetik des Schrecklichen im achtzehnten Jahrhundert* 412.

[15] Karl Philipp Moritz, *Fragmente aus dem Tagebuche eines Geistersehers*, in *Werke*, ed. Horst Günther (Frankfurt am Main: Insel, 1981) 3: 302. James Trainer points out that this kind of pleasure in the pain of another does not indicate sadistic enjoyment, but "rather the acceptance of fear as an 'agreeable sensation.'" He examines essays on aesthetic theory written in nineteenth-century England, such as Anne Laetitia Barbauld's *On the Pleasure Derived From Objects of Terror* and *An Enquiry Into the Kinds of Distress Which Excite Agreeable Sensations* (1825), in order to analyze a Gothic aesthetics of fear already, in my view, anticipated by German philosophers and psychologists a few decades prior. See Trainer, *Ludwig Tieck: From Gothic to Romantic* (London, The Hague, and Paris: Mouton & Co., 1964) 11-25.

[16] Moritz, *Werke* 3: 301.

des Unheimlichen"),[17] and before Freud famously responds to that same essay, the uncanny is a substantial component of the aesthetics of fear. In the 1770s and 1780s (the first documented use of the word is in 1773), "uncanny" means "not quite safe to trust" or "dangerous, unsafe"[18]—its meaning in this period is thus considerably broader than Schelling's definition of 1841-1842, which Freud later borrows. In 1784, William Beckford uses "uncanny" repeatedly in his novel *Vathek*, where it refers to the exotic, uncategorizable other, in this case something or someone Oriental, who arouses fear and unease.[19] During the same decade, either the word "uncanny" or synonyms for it surface in aesthetic theory and philosophy concerned with repulsion, fear, and mental disorders; "uncanny" indicates a dissociative, repetitive, anxious experience related to, but quite different from, the experience of the sublime.

The sublime has been conceptualized in various ways since antiquity, but virtually every thinker who has addressed it since Longinus has considered it a unique moment of awe. For Longinus,[20] the sublime is a category of rhetoric representing the height, or climax, of a speech. The nature of the person speaking also matters, because the "sublime is the echo of a great soul."[21] The association between mental exceptionalism and sublimity continues into the eighteenth century, but Edmund Burke's *A Philosophical Enquiry Into the Origins of Our Ideas of the Sublime and Beautiful* of 1759 separates the sublime from the beautiful, saying that sublimity is an experience of "delightful horror" rather than of the contemplative pleasure that results from encountering beauty.[22] Attempting to understand sublimity through the science of sense perception, Burke contends that "sublime terror" is the highly physical response of a threatened subject fighting for survival: "Having thus ran through the causes of the sublime with reference to all the senses, my first observation...will be found very nearly true; that the sublime is an idea belonging to self-preservation. [...] its

---

[17] It is this essay to which Freud primarily responds in his own piece on "The Uncanny." Jentsch's essay appears in two parts, in the *Psychiatrisch-Neurologische Wochenschrift* 22 (1906) 196-198, and in 23 (1906) 203-205.

[18] *Oxford English Dictionary*, quoted here by Rosemary Jackson in *Fantasy: The Literature of Subversion* (London and New York: Methuen, 1981) 63-64.

[19] This discovery of the possible first use of the term "uncanny" in fiction belongs to Jorge Luis Borges, who documents it in *Otrás Inquisiciones* (Buenos Aires, 1960) 191; cited here in Jackson, *Fantasy: The Literature of Subversion* 64.

[20] Or: the unknown scholar who penned *On the Sublime* in the first century A.D., usually attributed to Longinus.

[21] Longinus, *On the Sublime*, quoted here in Günter Dammann's afterword to Carl Grosse's *Der Genius* (Frankfurt am Main: Zweitausendeins, 1982) 750.

[22] Edmund Burke, *A Philosophical Enquiry Into the Origins of Our Ideas of the Sublime and Beautiful*, 1757 (Oxford: Oxford University Press, 1990) 36.

strongest emotion is an emotion of distress, and…no pleasure from a positive cause belongs to it."[23]

While Kant disagrees with Burke's contention that the sublime is solely a distressing experience, he acknowledges (in *Observations on the Feeling of the Beautiful and Sublime,* 1763) a subcategory of sublimity called the "terrifying sublime" (as opposed to the "noble" and "splendid" sublime). This subset involves "a certain dread, or melancholy."[24] But it has nothing directly to do with memory—the sublime is an unrepeatable moment that in fact forbids re-representation. In a famous passage from the *Critique of Judgment*, he calls the commandment forbidding graven images—forbidding idolatrous representations—"the most sublime passage in the Jewish Law."[25]

The uncanny, on the other hand, is anything but unique; it is nothing but re-presentation (of something which, for a time, was not present to consciousness), and re-representation. Anneleen Maaschelein says that a "continually repeated movement of revealing meaning and then withdrawing it, constitutes the working of the uncanny in discourse;" this is also how the uncanny operates within the psyche itself.[26] Unlike sublime awe, uncanny anxiety has characteristics of mourning and of melancholy—it is a repetitive forgetting-and-acknowledging of decay, of transience, and of what Schelling's Clara calls the "never-ending" deadly violence of nature. While the experience of the sublime transports us out of time and makes us feel immortal—if only briefly—the uncanny makes us feel mortal, and feel the danger of decay, again and again. The sublime in eighteenth-century aesthetic theory is characterized by what Alex Potts calls "elevated inhumanity"—we may feel sublime awe, for instance, when we view sculptures representing violently damaged beautiful bodies—in fact, says Potts, the "sublime figure…can only exist by way of a categorical, often violent denial of its subjectivity and desire."[27] The uncanny figure asserts the subjectivity that has been denied—or, rather, asserts the denial itself, and speaks desire from the space of ruin, of laceration or castration, and of misrecognition.

It is perhaps not surprising that, although the word "uncanny" surfaces in the 1770s, its real emergence as a concept and phenomenon in psychology and literature is contemporaneous with the rise of Romanticism, a movement in which the experience of depersonalization and disorientation in

---

23 Edmund Burke, *A Philosophical Enquiry Into the Origins of Our Ideas of the Sublime and Beautiful*, second edition, 1759 (New York: Garland Publishing, 1971) 160.

24 Immanuel Kant, *Über das Gefühl des Schönen und Erhabenen, Vorkritische Schriften bis 1768*, in *Werke in zwölf Bänden*, ed. Wilhelm Weischedel, volume 2 (Frankfurt am Main: Suhrkamp, 1996) 825-829. The translation is John T. Goldthwait's in *Observations on the Feeling of the Beautiful and Sublime* (Berkeley: University of California Press, 1991) 47-48.

25 Ibid, 828/47-48.

26 Anneleen Maaschelein, "Double Reading/Reading Double: Psychoanalytic Poetics at Work," *Paradoxa: Studies in World Literary Genres* 3.3-4 (1997) 395.

27 Potts, *Flesh and the Ideal: Winckelmann and the Origins of Art History* 113.

the face of the unexpected, frightening other is both feared and explicitly desired.[28] The challenge that Romanticism (and specifically Early Romantic philosophy) poses to the relatively stable and coherent subject of critical philosophy emerges not only from Romantic skepticism about critical philosophy's positing of a synthetic unity of consciousness, but also as a result of what Richard Terdiman calls the "memory crisis" of post-revolutionary Europe. Terdiman argues that Europeans experienced this crisis in the form of an "insecurity of their culture's involvement with its past, the perturbation of the link to their own inheritance...a sense that their past had somehow evaded memory, that recollection had ceased to integrate with consciousness."[29]

In its ability to destabilize a sense of coherent self-identity, to disorient the self-positing subject, even if only momentarily, the uncanny does stand in conceptual proximity to the sublime.[30] However, rather than mimicking or re-representing sublime awe, uncanny encounters with frightening others (or with the otherness, the strangeness, of oneself) bring back something past, yet in altered form. Like the sublime, the uncanny involves an encounter with otherness; a sublation between subject and object takes place. But while the sublime entails the awareness of one's own lack of understanding,[31] the uncanny is a moment of understanding all too well, a mistake or malfunction of memory that simultaneously reveals something real. In the broadest sense, it demonstrates that no matter how alienated or

---

28 Rolf-Peter Janz, Fabian Stoermer, and Andreas Hiepko portray the shift from a more clinically detached aesthetics of fear in the eighteenth century to a more involved, welcoming view of the aesthetic possibilities of fear and of uncanny experience in the nineteenth in the introduction to their edited volume entitled *Schwindelerfahrungen: Zur kulturhistorischen Diagnose eines vieldeutigen Symptoms* (Amsterdam and New York: Rodopi, 2003) 9-10. Writing primarily about the function of the sublime in English Romanticism, David Simpson says that the "romantics' interest in the grand and threatening objects of nature went along with their general obsession with categories of otherness. Even when their poems and writings image the subsumption or displacement of this otherness, as they sometimes do, the terms of the dialectic are at least still there to be recovered and thought through. Wordsworth's misunderstanding someone always reminds us that there *is* someone there." "Commentary: Updating the Sublime," in *Studies in Romanticism* 26.2 (1987) 258-259.

29 Richard Terdiman, *Present Past: Modernity and the Memory Crisis* (Ithaca: Cornell University Press, 1993) 3-4.

30 Nicholas Royle says that the uncanny can "be a matter of something strangely beautiful, bordering on ecstasy.... It can involve a feeling of something beautiful but at the same time frightening.... It comes above all, perhaps, in the uncertainties of silence, solitude and darkness" (*The Uncanny: An Introduction* [New York and London: Routledge, 2003] 2). David Ellison reminds us that the eighteenth-century sublime and the uncanny are both "hybrid notions in that they are built upon the complex mixture and interplay of the aesthetic and the ethical" (*Ethics and Aesthetics in European Modernist Literature: From the Sublime to the Uncanny* [Cambridge: Cambridge University Press, 2001] ix).

31 As explained by Andrew Smith, in *Gothic Radicalism: Literature, Philosophy and Psychoanalysis in the Nineteenth Century* (Houndmills, England and New York: Macmillan-St. Martin's, 2000) 149.

dissociated we may feel from the past, from others, and from our own selves, these entities all belong to us and we to them, as Clara and her fantasized absent children belong to one another.

Anxious and frightening experiences that are re-represented in consciousness and then externally, in aesthetic form, can also be intersubjective experiences, attempts to reach out, and to pull the outside in. Hegel echoes this understanding of the psychological experience and aesthetic representation of fear when he says that we desire repetition, even if unpleasant, for it connects us to community, to other "conscious beings" who are the real objects of our "desiring minds."[32] Schelling's *Philosophy of Mythology* affirms that this desire for repetition also applies to the frightening resurfacing of things long hidden. The repetition of something familiar but long forgotten fuels the desire for other minds that is at the foundation of our self-consciousness[33] in that it connects us to community—to the community of the past as well as to the present. Uncanny repetition is a form of re-involvement with the world in an age characterized by disinterest and detachment.[34] Although it can disrupt communication and harmonious community with others, uncanny experience also reinforces a sense of not-aloneness and therefore a sense of self.

Philosophical texts such as Kant's *Dreams of a Spirit-Seer* and Schelling's *Clara*, psychological treatises including Gotthilf Heinrich von Schubert's *Diseases and Disturbances of the Human Soul* and Moritz's *Journal of Empirical Psychology*, and literature such as Schiller's *Ghost-Seer* consistently represent or discuss uncanny experiences in dialogic or epistolary form, or in the form of speeches intended for others. As such, they reinforce the notion that uncanny encounters do not merely involve a sensing of another's presence; they are also attempts to interact with and possibly to internalize the other. Before examining the understanding of self/other

---

32 Julian Roberts explains Georg Wilhelm Friedrich Hegel's stance on the operation of repetition in self-consciousness in *German Philosophy: An Introduction* (Atlantic Highlands, NJ: Humanities Press International, Inc.) 97. He cites Hegel in *Phänomenologie des Geistes, Theorie-Werkausgabe*, Eds. Eva Moldenhauer and Karl Markus Michel (Frankfurt am Main: Suhrkamp, 1969-1971) 3: 143-145. The translation is A.V. Miller's in *Phenomenology of Spirit* (Oxford: Oxford University Press, 1977) 109-111.

33 Hegel, *Phänomenologie des Geistes* 146-147/*Phenomenology of Spirit* 111-112. Roberts paraphrases Hegel's understanding of the role of desire in self-constitution thus: "Self-consciousness only comes to itself in another self-consciousness. In mutual recognition selves recognize one another as generic beings, i.e. as reproductive identities. When one self comes across another it sees not only another, but also itself (because both selves have the same generic identity). Because of the principle of desire, the self has to try to negate the other. In doing so it ends up negating not only the other (and thus affirming itself), but also itself (because of the generic identity). Thus the principle of negation both restores the self to itself, and also affirms the identity of the *other*....The result, in effect, is that, "They recognize themselves as mutually recognizing one another,"" *German Philosophy: An Introduction* 98.

34 I borrow here from Norbert Elias's argument about the development of knowledge in the West in *Involvement and Detachment*, trans. Edmund Jephcott (Oxford: Basil Blackwell, 1987).

relations that emerges from uncanny disorders and encounters, I briefly recall some important shifts in eighteenth-century psychology, movements that permit the ascent of a notion of the unconscious before Freud, and hence also the ascent of the uncanny.

2. Philosophical Psychology, Mental Physicalism, and the Pre-Freudian Unconscious

The sublime and the uncanny are of interest to philosophers in part because they are extreme moments in consciousness, capable of disabling coherent judgment and affecting future judgments; understanding them helps to define the parameters of consciousness. But it is the importance of feeling in these experiences that makes them of interest to psychologists, whose focus on psychosomatic disorders is also a way of exploring questions about consciousness. The nature of these questions changes, however, during the course of the late eighteenth century. From approximately 1700 on, German psychologists generally worked within a dualistic framework, whose ongoing indebtedness to a Cartesian model of the self meant that German psychology diverged strongly from the French and English traditions prior to approximately 1770. While philosophers such as Locke rejected the sense of certainty and confidence about the self that came in the wake of Descartes's contention that consciousness, or the *res cogitans*, is the reliable repository of reason, German psychologists often continued to separate the operations of consciousness from emotional states, which were attributed to the passions of the body.[35]

By the 1770s, however, there is a shift towards a "mental physicalism," which included a view of emotional states as natural and which gradually replaced the Cartesian-influenced model that had dominated the German-language tradition since the seventeenth century. This shift was not a complete rejection of philosophical psychology; rather, mental physicalists borrowed aspects of the thinking of Leibniz and Wolff, who had already revised Descartes on the point of the uniqueness of consciousness. Leibniz acknowledges that mental activity depends on the body—the body is no mere machine, and mental activity can happen independently of conscious thought. Wolff amends Descartes' restriction of consciousness to the thinking subject alone, arguing that consciousness is only constituted in relations between subject and object. Like Leibniz, Wolff distinguishes between initial physical

[35] My paraphrase of this development in German psychology relies largely on Matthew Bell's summary of thinking about consciousness, mental activity, and the body from Descartes onward in *The German Tradition of Psychology in Literature and Thought, 1700-1840* (Cambridge: Cambridge University Press, 2005) 16-20.

sense perception, or sensation, and apperception, or the awareness that one is perceiving something.[36]

This two-stage theory of perception will continue into German psychology's transition into "mental physicalism," which asserts the embodiedness of mind, but has no difficulty accepting a separation between physical sensation and mental perception (or apperception).[37] Albrecht von Haller, Moritz, C.F. Pockels, and Johann Gottfried Herder, Johann Caspar Lavater, and others mobilize theories dating back to antiquity about the embodiedness of mind to argue that mental functions correspond to various locations in the body. Imagination is part of that mind, and increasingly its functions are seen as organic and of scientific interest.

Later in the eighteenth century, imagination regains some of the status it had enjoyed in the Renaissance, when it was considered a force powerful enough to have physical effects on the imaginer and his surroundings. Lodovico Antonio Muratori's influential *On the Power of the Human Imagination* (*Della Forza della Fantasia Umana*, 1745) states that the imagination (based at least initially on perceptions of physical sensations) can produce not only dreams but visions, hallucinations, phobias, and somnabulistic states.[38] These manifestations in turn reveal the workings of a realm acknowledged by Leibniz and later by mental physicalists that lies beyond consciousness, an area of the mind that functions without our assistance or intention.

Plotinus gives us the earliest documented explicit thinking about the unconscious, which reveals itself in two situations: while we are performing habitual acts, and while we are focused completely on an external object, thus becoming at least briefly unaware of our own existence. We reach this state, then, when we are not anxious at all—when we are engaged in "noble activities…which at the time in no way compel our consciousness."[39] Our awareness that it is possible to temporarily lack self-consciousness reveals that we can function without always thinking about our functioning—mental activity must be possible without self-consciousness. It is precisely the awareness *of* the existence of this incessant, automatic mental activity that, I will argue, makes subsequent modern thinkers so anxious about the unconscious realm. Consciousness of the unconscious is one of the foundations of anxiety.

The unconscious begins to be conceptualized as a source of problems and associated with uncertainty and even fear in the Renaissance,

---

[36] Bell, *The German Tradition of Psychology in Literature and Thought, 1700-1840* 20-21.

[37] Ibid, 59.

[38] Lodovico Antonio Muratori, *On the Power of the Human Imagination (Della Forza della Fantasia Umana)* 1745. Cited here in Henri F. Ellenberger, *The Discovery of the Unconscious: The History and Evolution of Dynamic Psychiatry* (New York: Basic Books, 1970) 112.

[39] Plotinus, *The Enneads* 1.4: 10.21-33; trans. Stephen MacKenna (London: Faber, 1956) 49. Cited here in Bell, *The German Tradition of Psychology in Literature and Thought, 1700-1840* 8.

when it was considered a unitary realm of "dark ideas;" this description persists for many years. Enlightenment thinkers dispute our ability to access that realm: Wolff contends that dark ideas are beyond reason, while Baumgarten assigns them a status "lower" than that of conscious knowledge, but says they are open to examination through reason.[40] Once Enlightened medicine has introduced the concept of "mental hygiene" to modern psychology, a sort of confidence arises about the power of conscious will over unconscious passions and disorders whose origin is "dark." On the one hand, studies of mental disorders and speculation about their roots in the unconscious mind proliferate during the latter half of the eighteenth century; on the other, proponents of mental hygiene propose relatively undifferentiated "solutions" to psychosomatic problems. One such contribution is Kant's, in the essay entitled "Of the Power of the Mind to Be Master of One's Morbid Feelings Through Simple Decision" ("Von der Macht des Gemüths, durch den blossen Vorsatz seiner krankhaften Gefühle Meister zu sein"). Here Kant provides advice about diet, balanced work and relaxation, and healthy breathing that he developed from his own experience with "hypochondriasis," or a range of physical complaints with no clearly ascertainable cause.[41]

By the early decades of the nineteenth century, practitioners of German psychiatry attempt to apply the insights of mental physicalism to the unconscious, seeking a physiological basis for the unconscious mind.[42] Gotthilf Heinrich von Schubert suggests that dreams reveal the workings of the unconscious, which resides in the "ganglious system" ("Gangliensystem").[43] Karl Gustav Carus also connects the unconscious to the body, but adds a symbolic dimension: by viewing the body and its motions, we learn about mental processes unknown to the viewed person himself. Organic entities—that is, bodies— "betray" unconscious activity.[44] Although we can fix representations of such activity by viewing the body, by "reading" the body of the other symbolically, Carus reminds us that the unconscious itself cannot be fixed in time—it is constantly active, never at rest.[45]

The efforts of Romantic psychologists and psychiatrists to locate unconscious mental processes in the body do not seem to have alleviated

---

[40] Bell, *The German Tradition of Psychology in Literature and Thought, 1700-1840* 29.

[41] Immanuel Kant, "Von der Macht des Gemüths, durch den blossen Vorsatz seiner krankhaften Gefühle Meister zu sein," *Werke*, ed. Ernst Cassirer, volume 7 (Berlin: Bruno Cassirer, 1916) 411-431. Cited here in Ellenberger, *The Discovery of the Unconscious: The History and Evolution of Dynamic Psychiatry* 197.

[42] Bell, *The German Tradition of Psychology in Literature and Thought, 1700-1840* 208ff.

[43] Gotthilf Heinrich von Schubert, *Die Symbolik des Traumes*, 1814 (Heidelberg: Lambert Schneider, 1968) 1-3.

[44] Karl Gustav Carus, *Symbolik der menschlichen Gestalt. Ein Handbuch zur Menschenkenntnis* (Hildesheim: Olms, 1977) 11.

[45] Ellenberger, *The Discovery of the Unconscious: The History and Evolution of Dynamic Psychiatry* 207-208. See also Rita Wöbkemeier, *Erzählte Krankheit. Medizinische und literarische Phantasien um 1800* (Stuttgart: Metzler, 1990) 97-99.

anxiety about the "dark," or "night," side of science and of nature, since it is in this same Romantic period that the flexible boundaries between waking and dream life and between consciousness and unconsciousness are traversed frequently in psychology and in literary texts. Authors such as E.T.A. Hoffmann and Heinrich von Kleist explore the possibility that the realm of "dark ideas" is frightening not because what emanates from it is unknown and mysterious, but because it somehow *is* known—"dark" knowledge comes from within us and from within our own pasts, and it has collective power. Schelling's nature philosophy fortifies this thinking by asserting that nature and consciousness were originally unified; nature and the "nature of the self" were identical, and the realm of dark ideas connects us to that original unity even now.[46]

Eduard von Hartmann's 1869 *Philosophy of the Unconscious* (*Philosophie des Unbewußten*) finally names the unconscious as such. Like Schelling, Schubert, and other nature philosophers before him, Hartmann conceives of the unconscious as a universal and absolute force underlying all of existence. That force, however, is only one of three forms that the unconscious takes: the others are a physiological unconscious and a relative, or psychological, unconscious. The three forms together create a coherent framework for discussing the nature of individual perception and personality but also of cultural history and fate, and this framework will go on to influence Freud's conviction that individual and cultural development proceed similarly.[47]

Despite attempts to medicalize or rationalize the unconscious, or to give it the status of a synthesizing, coherent universal force, there is substantial anxiety about it before Freud showcases it as the source of the most profound psychic distress. In the eighteenth and nineteenth centuries, the unconscious is a unifying realm of will and a physiological entity, but it is also the locus of mental/physical disorders brought on by too much imagination, and by too much thinking in general. This anxiety pervades literature in which characters' actions seem inexplicable and at the whim of some unseen force, but it is also present in early philosophical thinking about mental realms beyond consciousness. Hegel proposes a category called "the nonexisting" ("das Nichtseiende"), a realm in which wrong is done unknowingly, and in which all claims made to redress such wrongs are unjustified—the claims themselves are based in guilt, a guilt that is felt for

---

[46] Friedrich Wilhelm Joseph von Schelling, *Zur Geschichte der neueren Philosophie* (Münchener Vorlesungen) (Darmstadt: Wissenschaftliche Buchgesellschaft, 1953) 3: 335. These ideas are prevalent throughout Schelling's nature philosophy and also in the philosophy of mythology.

[47] See Ellenberger, *The Discovery of the Unconscious: The History and Evolution of Dynamic Psychiatry* 209-210.

crimes unconsciously committed.[48] In associating crime, guilt, and (unjustified, guilty) redress with the non-conscious, and in calling that non-conscious "the nonexisting," Hegel mobilizes the Oedipus myth; like Schelling in the *Philosophy of Mythology*, Hegel associates the unconscious with past mistakes and loss. Here the unconscious seems to escape from its prison in the "ganglious system" and become a truly ghostly object.

From the early days of German psychology through the nineteenth century, from the prevalence of philosophical psychology and mental physicalism and into the "psychophysics" of the mid-nineteenth century,[49] the relationship between mind and body is elusive, but it is clear that the uncanny and the desirous fear that emerges within it come from that relationship rather than from external demons.[50] The stronger the perceived link between an emotion, or passion, and the body, the more frightening that emotion is deemed to be—not because the body is somehow possessed by external evil, but because it is in danger of disintegrating from within.[51]

The following readings examine uncanny occurrences, or thinking about what will later be called "the uncanny," in texts written either on the cusp of or just after the shift between Cartesian and mental physicalist understandings of mind in early German psychology. The uncanny occurrences all fall into one of two categories: 1) perceptions of dissociation between body and mind, either within the context of mental illness (or, in Kant's phrase, a "disturbance of the mind") or of clairvoyance (the exhibition of paranormal powers; in this case, the dissociation is not just between mind and body but between present and future); 2) perceptions of something external to the self that is frightening—something that provokes a

---

[48] Hegel, *Phänomenologie des Geistes* 347/*Phenomenology of Spirit* 282-283. Judith Butler discusses this passage in Hegel in *Antigone's Claim: Kinship Between Life and Death* (New York: Columbia University Press, 2000) 29-33.

[49] Katherine Arens reproduces Gustav Theodor Fechner's definition of psychophysics of 1859: it must be "based on experience and on mathematical connections of facts of experience, which requires measurement of that offered by experience; and, to the degree which it does not yet stand available, this measurement must be sought. After the measurement is then given in terms of physical quantities, the first and primary task of this book will be the determination of measurements in terms of mental quantities, where it has been lacked heretofore; the second, the exploration of the applications and effects which are attached to them." Fechner is quoted in *Elemente der Psychophysik* (Leipzig: Breitkopf & Härtel, 1907) vii. Arens explains that Fechner differs from strict empiricists in that he wishes to examine the psychology of an entire group rather than of just one mind (as indicated in the second task he describes above). *Structures of Knowing: Psychologies of the Nineteenth Century* (Dordrecht, Boston, and London: Kluwer Academic Publishers, 1989) 107-108.

[50] Roy Porter notes that a contradiction of supernatural accounts of mental disorders is present as early as the Hippocratic corpus of the fourth century B.C. *Flesh in the Age of Reason* (New York and London: W.W. Norton, 2003) 45.

[51] As Hans-Müller Braunschweig explains in "Der unheimliche Körper," *Psychotherapie, Psychosomatik, medizinische Psychologie* 42.1 (1992) 16.

dissociation between sensation and perception (the dissociation then is the uncanny symptom).

These two categories correspond to symptoms Freud will call uncanny in his essay of 1919, namely: omnipotence of thoughts (clairvoyance) and things associated with animism (frightening visions that seem supernatural, but that actually can be explained logically). Both categories circumscribe thinking *about* the unconscious in some way—an awareness of a level of activity that is not present to or always subject to intention. While Matthew Bell is right to warn against reading early psychology "as if it were merely unconceptualised psychoanalysis,"[52] the latter is a discipline that synthesizes much previous work, and the multiple appearances of the often competing claims of Enlightenment and Romantic psychology and aesthetic theory in Freud's thought demand closer study of at least a few of those claims.

3. Estranged Knowledge: "Anxious" Texts by Kant and Schelling

The questions that Immanuel Kant (1724-1804) and Friedrich Schelling (1775-1854) pose about clairvoyance and life after death are so out of place in their respective œuvres that the texts in which these questions appear generally are ignored. And yet, such questions were not considered strange in the mid-eighteenth to early nineteenth centuries, a time in which paranormal phenomena were taken seriously.[53] Increasingly, as faculty psychologists working in the wake of Wolff and advocates of mental physicalism such as Herder attest, paranormal occurrences are suspected to originate within the self, or in the interactions between self-consciousness and other minds. Ghostly visions are indeed all in our heads, but this does not rule out the existence of what Daniel Tiffany calls a realm both imaginary and material: a "material occult."[54] As Tiffany explains, a "basic inclination of materialism" is "to make the intangible tangible."[55] Representations of uncanny experience in Kant and Schelling in part reflect the desire to make the intangible tangible by exploring the possibility of a material, body-based occult realm. Anxious questions about life after death and contact with ghosts pose a problem for modern, detached (or, disinterested) philosophers and psychologists; Kant and Schelling address the anxiety right at its source by

---

[52] Bell, *The German Tradition of Psychology in Literature and Thought, 1700-1840* 1-2.
[53] Karin Schutjer, *Narrating Community After Kant: Schiller, Goethe, and Hölderlin* (Detroit: Wayne State University Press, 2001) 34.
[54] Daniel Tiffany, *Toy Medium: Materialism and Modern Lyric* (Berkeley: University of California Press, 2000) 3.
[55] Ibid, 5.

relocating the spirit world *within* the body, thus making it tangible—but this creates new dilemmas.

Kant and Schelling attempt to defend their views of the project of metaphysics against assaults not only from seers and esotericists, but from the threats to coherent subject philosophy posed by the mind itself, and particularly by its malfunctions. Like literary authors and psychologists of the same period, Kant and Schelling locate mental illness in moments when the split between the transcendental and the nontranscendental is most apparent —or, when relationships between body and mind break down. This breakdown often makes itself known through melancholy or anxious symptoms—through signs that point to an inability to escape repetitions of past trauma. It is exactly at the cultural moment in which the transcendental self is being most fully defined and most solidly buttressed against the threat of the body and of nature that modern intellectuals question its reliability.

In Kant's case, this questioning is most apparent before he writes the critiques, in the "precritical" period of the 1760s. That period is characterized by what Paul Geyer calls the "demolition of rationalism"[56] and by Kant's attempts, largely unsuccessful during this phase, to establish a stronger role for sense perception in the constitution of knowledge. The ways of knowing that emerge in two largely overlooked texts from this decade, texts that address ghostly visions and mental disorders, are ways of knowing based neither on the coherent principles of reason nor on reliable sense perceptions, but on a basic estrangement within the self. These early Kantian texts establish a philosophical basis for understanding uncanny experience as such, and for understanding it as a part of mainstream modern subjectivity.

3.1. Kant, *Dreams of a Spirit-Seer* (*Träume eines Geistersehers, erläutert durch Träume der Metaphysik*)

Kant's *Dreams of a Spirit-Seer* (1766) is one of the first philosophical treatments of what will later be known as the uncanny, although the word "uncanny" does not appear on its pages. The piece was inspired by the Swedish theologian and mystic Emanuel Swedenborg, whose report of clairvoyant and other out-of-body experiences entitled *Arcana Coelestia* (1747-1758) offered Kant the chance to attack arguments that rationalists such as Wolff had made in favor of the soul's immortality and immateriality. In *Dreams*, Kant asserts that rationalist philosophers and esoteric mystics alike have little proof of an immaterial and immortal soul. He aims to demonstrate that the intense desire to see and to communicate with a ghostly

[56] Paul Guyer, ed., *The Cambridge Companion to Kant* (Cambridge: Cambridge University Press, 1992) 7.

world originates in the desire to believe that good moral actions performed in this life will be rewarded in the next, and that this belief is not only unfounded, but unnecessary. Virtuous actions should be their own reward; it is precisely the knowledge that this life *is* the only life that enables truly moral behavior—morality that exists without expectation of compensation in an afterlife. But before he can assert this, Kant must prove, in somewhat Byzantine fashion, that ghosts do not exist.

The experience of phenomena that will later be called uncanny—in this case, of intimations or visions of ghosts—is neither mystical nor incomprehensible, but rather completely explicable:[57] such phenomena are, says Kant, the mental products of "dreamers of sensation" ("Träumer der Empfindung"), whose visions of a spirit world at first appear similar to what he calls the visions of a world of ideas, divorced from experience, produced by rationalists, or "dreamers of reason" ("Träumer der Vernunft").[58] It is appropriate to call individuals in both categories "dreamers," since the "alleged visions" in both cases, whether of ideas or of spirits, are "mere delusions of the mind" ("die gedachte[n] Erscheinungen [laufen auf] bloße Hirngespenster aus").[59]

The "dreamers of reason" are "dream castle builders...each of them living peacefully in his own world of thought, to the exclusion of everything else" ("Luftbaumeister der mancherlei Gedankenwelten...deren jeglicher die seinige mit Ausschließung anderer ruhig bewohnt"),[60] while the "dreamers of perception" are "those who claim to have occasional intercourse with spirits" ("diejenige, so bisweilen mit Geistern zu tun haben").[61] Both types of dreamers, the metaphysicians and the mystics, make the crucial mistake of believing their ideas or visions to be unique, and of thinking that they therefore possess a specialness of experience—they commit the error of asserting that they know or see a reality accessible to no one else. This is bad for philosophy in general; the rationalists' lack of acknowledgment of other minds means that their achievements cannot compete in the "common world" ("gemeinschaftliche Welt") in which quantitative scientists ("Größenlehrer") are very much at home.[62]

However, while Kant begins his attack on the possibility of the soul's immortality with a comparison between rationalism and spirit-seeing,

---

[57] As Tzvetan Todorov eventually will argue in his formalist study of aesthetic modes, when he differentiates the uncanny from the marvelous and the fantastic using this very criterion. See *The Fantastic: A Structural Approach to a Literary Genre*, trans. Richard Howard (Ithaca: Cornell University Press, 1975) 43-46; also, see Note 10 in the Preface to this study.

[58] Immanuel Kant, *Träume eines Geistersehers, erläutert durch Träume der Metaphysik* (Stuttgart: Reclam, 1976) 40-41 (A58-62).

[59] Ibid, 40 (A58-60).

[60] Ibid, 39 (A57-58).

[61] Ibid, 40 (A58-60).

[62] Ibid, 40 (A58-60).

he then separates the two.[63] While the deluded philosopher, the "day-dreamer," is able to "reckon() his delusions as products of his own activity" ("zu Wirkungen seiner eigenen Tätigkeit ...zählet"),[64] the spirit-seer by contrast, even while fully awake, and in possession of perfectly healthy physical powers of perception, nevertheless perceives imaginary objects to be external— "as if they were truly placed amongst the objects which he really perceives through his senses" ("was er von außen empfängt und erleidet").[65] Like Lodovico Moratori (whose work on the imagination appears just two decades before *Dreams*), Kant grants that imagination is a force powerful enough to convince us that products of our own fantasy are external objects. But Kant uses a specifically dualistic understanding of mind and body to contend that the imagination that engages in this type of projection is not just powerful, but sick. He asserts that

> all representations of our imagination are accompanied by certain motions in the nerve tissues or the vital spirit in the brain called *ideae materiales,* i.e., perhaps by concussions or vibrations of the subtle element secreted by the nerve tissues; which, however, resemble the motions which could be produced by the sense impressions of which these nerve vibrations are copies.
> (alle Vorstellungen der Einbildungskraft zugleich mit gewissen Bewegungen in dem Nervenewebe oder Nervengeiste des Gehirnes begleitet sind, welche man *ideas materiales* nennt, d.i. vielleicht mit der Erschütterung oder Bebung des feinen Elements, welches von ihnen abgesondert wird, und die derjenigen Bewegung ähnlich ist, welche der sinnliche Eindruck machen könnte, wovon er die Kopie ist.)[66]

In the "nerve vibrations of fantasies" (as opposed to the vibrations that come from physical sense impressions), the "direction lines of motion intersect one another within the brain" ("die Richtungslinien der Bewegungen [schneiden] sich innerhalb dem Gehirne") meaning that the subject cannot "distinguish his mental delusions from real perceptions received from outside through his senses" ("die Einbildungen als meine eigene[] Hirngespinste von dem Eindruck der Sinne zu unterscheiden").[67] This lack of differentiation is at the heart of the "type of mental derangement" ("diejenige Art von Störung des Gemüts") that leads a "confused victim" ("der verworrene Mensch") to project objects of fantasy outside of himself.[68]

Kant thus ascribes the ghostly visions of Swedenborg and others to a mental confusion (based, again, on a disturbed relationship between perception and nervous vibrations) so intense that it approximates a disease

---

[63] Philosophers differ from spirit-seers "not only in degree but in kind" ("nicht bloß dem Grade, sondern der Art nach gänzlich unterschieden." Kant, *Träume eines Geistersehers, erläutert durch Träume der Metaphysik* 41-42 (A60-63).
[64] Ibid, 41 (A60-62).
[65] Ibid, 41 (A60-62).
[66] Ibid, 44 (A65-66).
[67] Ibid, 44 (A65-66).
[68] Ibid, 44-45 (A65-67).

ranging in severity from neurosis to madness.[69] Disturbingly, this problem is not limited to individuals; by 1790 at the latest, Kant sees the popularity of Swedenborg and other mystics as a phenomenon representing a veritable "wave of hysteria in the country" ("Welle der Hysterie im Lande"), an "evil" ("Übel") resembling a contagious epidemic—but one that likely will be of limited duration. In a letter to Ludwig Borowski written that same year, he says:

> The doctors of the soul will no doubt have as difficult a task to fight this epidemic, as the doctors of the body had a few years ago when the Russian flu spread overnight from Vienna to all the countries in the world. Nevertheless, the flu epidemic ceased as suddenly as it had started.
> (Die Seelenärzte werden zweifellos die allergrössesthe Mühe haben, diese Epidemie zu bekämpfen, wie die Leibärzte vor etlichen Jahren als die russische Grippe plötzlich von Wien aus in alle Länder der Welt sich verbreitete. Trotzdem hat diese Grippenepidemie aufgehört, und das genau so schnell wie sie began.)[70]

The dilemma would seem to be solved. Kant has fenced off spirit-seeing from other types of "day-dreaming" by referring to the last ground of sense perception, a foundation for knowledge that, in the particular case of ghostly visions, is disrupted due to organic defect (a problem of communication between nerves and imagination). And yet Moses Mendelssohn, in his review of *Dreams of a Spirit-Seer*, identifies a basic ambiguity in the text:

> The joking earnestness with which this work is written leaves the reader now and again in doubt as to whether Mr. *Kant* wanted to make metaphysics ridiculous or spirit-seeing believable. It contains the seeds of important observations that deserve more serious development, some new thoughts about the nature of the soul as well as several asides against the accepted systems.
> (Der scherzende Tiefsinn, mit welchem dieses Werkchen geschrieben ist, läßt den Leser zuweilen in Zweifel, ob Herr *Kant* die Metaphysik hat lächerlich, oder die Geisterseherey glaubhaft machen wollen. Indessen enthält es den Samen zu wichtigen Betrachtungen, einige neue Gedanken über die Natur der Seele, so wie einige Einwürfe wider die bekannten Systeme, die eine ernsthaftere Ausführung verdienen.)[71]

The ambiguity to which Mendelssohn refers points to more than inconsistencies or incompleteness in Kant's argument. There is also a sinister subtext in *Dreams* about the nature of consciousness: Not only do I really not know the thoughts of another, but I may not even reliably know my own

---

69 Kant, *Träume eines Geistersehers, erläutert durch Träume der Metaphysik* 44-45 (A65-67).

70 "Krankheit" includes a spectrum of problems from "Wahnsinn" (neurosis) to "Verrückung" (madness). From a letter written by Kant to Ludwig Ernst Borowski in 1790, cited here in *Dreams of a Spirit-Seer and Other Related Writings*, trans. John Manolesco (New York: Vantage Press, 1969) 159.

71 Moses Mendelssohn, "Rezension der *Träume*," *Allgemeine deutsche Bibliothek*, des vierten Bandes zweytes Stück (Berlin and Stettin: Friedrich Nicolai, 1767) 281.

thoughts. Before the explicit theorizing of the unconscious in nineteenth-century works such as von Hartmann's, Kant's piece demonstrates a disquieting sense that a realm is *there*, *within me* but somehow *not present* to me, not available to my sense perception. The misdirected nervous vibrations that lead to "sick" displacements of fantasy objects from the imagination to the external world reveal the mind's capacity for strangeness and for estrangement—not just from others, but from itself.

Although Kant separates the errors of the rationalists from those of the spirit-seers by relying on a way of understanding body and mind as both substantial and dual, this explanation is insufficient (as Mendelssohn implies) to do away with any need for a sense of something outside of ourselves that is nevertheless linked to our own imaginations—or, in this case, to do away with any yearning for a metaphysical belief system. Kant admits his own inclination "to assert the existence of immaterial natures in the world, and to put my own mind in the same category as these beings" ("das Dasein immaterieller Naturen in der Welt zu behaupten, und meine Seele selbst in die Klasse dieser Wesen zu versetzen").[72] The soul, in his understanding, is "as if bound to two worlds at once" ("als verknüpft mit zweien Welten zugleich")—the immaterial and the material world.[73] This does not mean that ghosts really exist. Rather, the soul is the locus where the material and immaterial world coexist. The immaterial world resembles a predecessor of Freud's unconscious rather than a realm independent of us where the dead really do live on. And this is a world that is part of all of us, not only of the sick or the mad.

The "dreamers of reason," who do not make sufficient contact with a community of others (a community he will later argue is constituted most fundamentally in the "common sense," or *sensus communis*[74]), may not be "sick" in precisely the way that spirit-seers are, but Kant's distinction between the two categories of dreamers is not completely neat. For one thing, the rationalists and the spirit-seers are both prey to the "flattering hope for a continued existence after death" ("der schmeichelhaften Hoffnung…daß man noch auf irgend eine Art nach dem Tode übrig sei") which contemporary philosophers of various persuasions have made part of their systems.[75] Rather than be completely critical of this hope, Kant admits that his own

> lack of knowledge is also responsible for the fact that I did not dare to deny completely the truth of the various ghost tales; on the contrary, I have always

---

[72] Immanuel Kant, *Träume eines Geistersehers, erläutert durch Träume der Metaphysik*, in *Werke* 2: 934 (A25). References to this edition are given henceforth as TGS.

[73] Ibid, 936-937 (A30-31).

[74] The theory of the *sensus communis* is elaborated most fully in 1790 in the *Kritik der Urteilskraft* §21, 5: 293-296.

[75] Kant, *Träume eines Geistersehers, erläutert durch Träume der Metaphysik* 51 (A76-78).

maintained a certain reserve and a sense of wonder towards them, doubting each story individually, but attributing some truthfulness to all of them put together.
(Eben dieselbe Unwissenheit macht auch, daß ich mich nicht unterstehe, so gänzlich alle Wahrheit an den mancherlei Geistererzählungen abzuleugnen, doch mit dem gewöhnlichen obgleich wunderlichen Vorbehalt, eine jede einzelne derselben in Zweifel zu ziehen, allen zusammen genommen aber einigen Glauben beizumessen.[76]

The uncertainty that underlies Kant's attitude toward ghost stories as a whole points to a possible acceptance of their greater, communal "truthfulness;" namely, their ability to represent a need to imagine different modes of existence that nevertheless do not fit into any particular belief system. If vibrations in the nervous tissues communicate a perception represented in the imagination, then ghostly visions must be based on something past. Like the imaginative re-representation of actual external objects, ghostly visions are based on a memory of a perception of past experience. And yet that past is disconnected from our present re-representation of it, in the case of both ghostly visions *and* the representation of real sensations within our imagination.

This is another area in which Kant's distinction between misguided philosophers and ghost-seers is not quite sufficient to do away altogether with intuitions of another realm, beyond the bedrock realm of sense perception. The split between past mind and present mind that marks neurotic delusions hails from empiricist thinking such as Locke's in the *Essay Concerning Human Understanding* (1690), which lays the foundation for the later Idealist development of a concept of inner perception, or "reflections" (perceptions of the life of the soul) as opposed to "sensations" (perceptions of the external world). Both are sensory—consciousness is not "non-sensual" ("unsinnlich") —but they are fundamentally dissociated.[77] The same problem that other minds pose for our self-understanding (a problem that Kant's notion of the *sensus communis* cannot fully dispense with) is posed by our *own* minds—our past mind is in a sense "other" to our present mind. The doubt that this implied understanding of the imagination raises in *Dreams* anticipates Wittgenstein's challenge to the Cartesian concept of the mind as an inner theater,[78] in which the possessor of that mind knows its contents uniquely and reliably.

In the *Arcana Coelestia,* Swedenborg addresses the topic of "What It Means to Be Outside of the Body, and to Be Carried by the Spirit to Another Place" ("Was es heiße, außer dem Körper zu sein, und vom Geist an einen

---

[76] Kant, *Träume eines Geistersehers, erläutert durch Träume der Metaphysik* 52 (A78-79).
[77] Manfred Frank, *Selbstgefühl. Eine historisch-systematische Erkundung* (Frankfurt am Main: Suhrkamp, 2002) 93.
[78] Ludwig Wittgenstein, *Philosophical Investigations* §258, cited here in Simon Blackburn, *The Oxford Dictionary of Philosophy* (Oxford: Oxford University Press, 1996) 303.

andern Ort getragen zu werden").[79] While this title may be evocative of fantasies of alien abduction, it also re-presents the sense of disorientation that is the uncanny. Swedenborg recalls his own experience of this feeling:

> While wandering through the alleys of a city, and through fields, and at the same time in conversation with spirits, I thought I was as alert and perceptive as at other times… but after I had walked in this way for several hours, I suddenly could see my body, and I was aware that I was in a different place, which astonished me greatly. I realized that I was in the same condition as those, of whom it is said that they are "mentally taken to another place," because as long as this lasts, you do not even think of the path, even if it encompasses several miles, hours, or days. You feel no weariness; you are led along paths unknown to you, up to a certain place. This happened so that I might know that man can be led by the Lord, without knowing whence and where.
> (Durch die Gassen einer Stadt, und durch die Gefilde wandelnd, und zugleich auch im Gespräch mit Geistern, wußte ich nicht anders, als daß ich so wach und sehend sei wie zu andern Zeiten,…nachdem ich aber so etliche Stunden gewandelt, war ich auf einmal im Sehen des Körpers, und wurde gewahr, daß ich an einem andern Orte sei, worüber ich sehr erstaunt war, und merkte, daß ich in demselben Zustand gewesen war, in dem jene, von denen es heißt, sie seien "*im Geist an einen andern Ort weggeführt worden*," denn so lang er währt, denkt man gar nicht an den Weg, und wenn dieser auch mehrere Meilen betragen würde; Stunden oder Tage ausmachen würde; auch spürt man keinerlei Ermüdung; man wird alsdann auf Wegen geführt, die man selbst nicht kennt, bis an den bestimmten Ort. Dies geschah, damit ich auch wissen möchte, daß der Mensch vom Herrn geführt werden kann, ohne daß er weiß, woher und wohin.)[80]

This passage, which resembles a description of a fugue state (albeit with theological overtones), explains in part the fascination that Swedenborg held for Kant. In *Classifications of Mental Disorders* (*Versuch über die Krankheiten des Kopfes*), which appeared initially in 1764 and was republished in 1798 (but without taking the intervening critiques into serious consideration[81]), Kant challenges the ancient concept that "disease occurs when the soul—spontaneously or by accident—leaves the body or is stolen by ghosts or sorcerers…(and that the) healer searches for the lost soul, brings it back, and restores it to the body to which it belongs."[82] Both *Classifications* and *Dreams* attempt to do the work of that ancient and discredited healer, but in an Enlightened and modern context: The act of representing and attempting

---

[79] From the excerpts from Swedenborg's *Arcana Coelestia* in Kant, *Träume eines Geistersehers, erläutert durch Träume der Metaphysik* 97.
[80] Ibid, 98.
[81] Immanuel Kant, *The Classification of Mental Disorders*, trans. and ed. Charles T. Sullivan (Doylestown, PA: The Doylestown Foundation, 1964) vi. The *Classification* offers a model for mental illness not unlike a spectrum model of today's psychiatry: illnesses happen in stages, and manifest, at varying levels of intensity, the same basic underlying problems. This implies that we could all be vulnerable, or could demonstrate these traits in various levels at various times in our lives.
[82] Ellenberger, *The Discovery of the Unconscious: The History and Evolution of Dynamic Psychiatry* 6.

to understand mental disorder is an attempt to search for and retrieve the lost soul.

Kant is aware, however, that he cannot complete this work; this awareness is represented in a much-quoted letter to Charlotte von Knoblauch of 1763, which contains Kant's admission that, while he "found it unnecessary in the past to worry much about (spirits) or to allow myself to shiver and be scared by the dead in the darkness of a cemetery," reading Swedenborg's tales has given him pause ("daß ich, der ich mir überhaupt nicht gerne Ungelegenheit mache, nicht vor rathsam hielt, mir deswegen auf Kirchhöfen oder in einer Finsterniß bange werden zu lassen...bis die Geschichte des Herrn Swedenborg mir bekannt gemacht wurde")—it is difficult to "raise any serious objections to (their) truth and credibility" ("Was kann man wider die Glaubwürdigkeit dieser Begebenheit anführen?"); finally, Kant concludes, the "portrait (of Swedenborg) is very strange" ("Dieses Portrait ist seltsam").[83] But Kant's fascination is not with the possibility of the soul's immortality or the ability of certain individuals to communicate with spirits; this simply does not "conform to the rules of sound reason" to which he always submits such accounts ("ich [habe] doch jederzeit der Regel der gesunden Vernunft...erachtet").[84] His interest is in the difficulty Swedenborg presents for a coherent understanding of time and space—for instance, when Swedenborg inexplicably knows about a fire burning fifty miles from his present location—and his fascination is with the uncanny sense of displacement represented by that anecdote, as well as in Swedenborg's own account of disorientation in passages from the *Arcana Coelestia* such as the one cited above.

For Kant, the only afterlife we can know anything about takes place in the finite, mortal, present and remembering soul. Spirit-seeing ("Geistersehen") and clairvoyance ("Hellsehen") appear in Kant's precritical writings as a manifestation of a desire that is not unlike what Freud will later call repetition compulsion. This desire for repetition, Freud says, "lend(s) to certain aspects of the mind their daemonic character, and (is) still very clearly expressed in the impulses of small children;" it is "a compulsion, too, which is responsible for a part of the course taken by the analyses of neurotic patients" ("[der Wiederholungszwang verleiht] gewissen Seiten des Seelenlebens den dämonischen Charakter [...], [äußert] sich in den Strebungen des kleinen Kindes noch sehr deutlich [...] und [beherrscht] ein Stück vom Ablauf der Psychoanalyse des Neurotikers").[85]

Clairvoyance is also a phenomenon that reminds us *of* the compulsion *to* repeat: "All these considerations prepare us for the discovery

---

[83] From Kant's letter to Charlotte von Knoblauch of August 10, 1763; quoted here in *Träume eines Geistersehers, erläutert durch Träume der Metaphysik* 100-101, 105.
[84] Ibid, 100.
[85] Freud, "Das Unheimliche," GW 12: 251/ "The Uncanny," SE 17: 238.

that whatever reminds us of this inner 'compulsion to repeat' is perceived as uncanny" ("Wir sind durch alle vorstehenden Erörterungen darauf vorbereitet, daß dasjenige als unheimlich verspürt werden wird, was an diesen inneren Wiederholungszwang mahnen kann").[86] Kant's *Dreams*, in spite of its argument and because of its content, acknowledges that the spirit-seer or clairvoyant transposes onto the future what is already, in the present, a basic and universal sense of estrangement: I *can* only think *of* myself as an object. Non-mediated reflection about anything is not possible, let alone about consciousness—I "cannot *enter into* the thinking of myself as a spirit" ("[ich *komme*] in die Vorstellung meiner selbst als eines Geistes gar nicht *hinein*").[87] The only way to imagine myself is as the kind of externalized object fantasized by the spirit-seer. Kant's attempt to divorce the organically based delusions of spirit-seers from the willfully created illusions of rationalists ultimately helps to demonstrate that the rationalist Wolff's assertion (itself repeated any number of times in the history of the philosophy of consciousness) that consciousness "requires both a subject and an object"[88] applies not only to both types of projection but to most everyday thinking as well.

Metaphysics is really just a "science of the *borders of human reason*" ("Wissenschaft von den *Grenzen der menschlichen Vernunft*").[89] And it is an uncanny "uncertainty" or lack of knowledge ("Unwissenheit") that marks those borders. On the one hand, metaphysics allows us to use reason to see things otherwise hidden; on the other, it opens the way to even more uncertainty. Consciousness philosophy permits us to identify and pursue what Kant calls "the real task" ("die eigentliche Aufgabe") of modern thought: that of making

> the unity of consciousness (which is part of understanding) visible to itself, in the context of the relationships of the *soul* to the organs of the brain (which belong to the external senses), and to make the *seat* of the soul, as its *local* present, visible.
> (die Einheit des Bewußtseins seiner selbst [vorstellig] [welche dem Verstande angehört], im Raumes Verhältnisse der *Seele* zu den Organen des Gehirns [welches zum äußeren Sinne gehört], mithin den *Sitz* der Seele, als ihre *lokale* Gegenwart, vorstellig zu machen….)[90]

But while metaphysics allows us to see this problem of the relationship between body and mind and between mind and mind (making "the unity of consciousness visible to itself") in the first place, it cannot provide the answers: "This not only an unsolvable problem for metaphysics, but also in

[86] Freud, GW 12: 251/SE 17: 238.
[87] Kant, TGS 947 (A49). Emphasis mine.
[88] Cited here in Bell, *The German Tradition of Psychology in Literature and Thought, 1700-1840* 20.
[89] Kant, *Träume eines Geistersehers, erläutert durch Träume der Metaphysik* 76-77 (A115).
[90] Kant, "Über das Organ der Seele," *Werke* 11: 259.

and of itself contradictory" ("welches eine Aufgabe für die Metaphysik, für diese aber nicht allein unauflöslich, sondern auch an sich widersprechend ist").[91] Modern thinkers know that personhood emanates from the top down; the location of the soul's "seat" has moved from the intestines to the brain.[92] But this shift of the center of thought from the "abdominal brain" ("Unterleibsgehirn")[93] to the head has not done away with the phenomena of dissociation, disorientation, and the need for a sense of connection to other selves, other consciousnesses, that Swedenborg expresses so urgently and confidently in writings that were immensely popular.

The attribution of hallucinations and clairvoyant visions to disordered nerve vibrations does not alleviate a fundamental anxiety of and about transcendental philosophy: namely, the fact that that philosophy leaves the relationship between the subject's constitution of the world of appearances and the real existence of objects "undecided" or "floating" ("in der Schwebe").[94] Kant's ambiguity about the distinction between metaphysics and spirit-seeing leads indirectly to the unsettling realization that perhaps anyone could fall prey to fantastic delusions, despite the claims of rationalists and mystics alike that they have special access to an immaterial realm.

Kant's use of Swedenborg's claim to have seen spirits in order to demonstrate the lack of basis for a rationalist belief in the soul's immortality is consistent with his attempts, during this same period, to prove that perception is the only reliable source of knowledge about the self and the world, and that our perceptions may be communally validated. In a letter to Moses Mendelssohn of April 8, 1766, Kant states that metaphysics in the form practiced by the rationalists is already delusional, a "dreamed-up science" ("erträumte Wissenschaft").[95] When he eventually does found his own project of metaphysics in the critiques of the 1780s, Kant differentiates the aims of empirical psychology from those of transcendental philosophy, saying that the knowledge we gain from observation cannot justify the

---

[91] Kant, "Über das Organ der Seele," *Werke* 11: 259.

[92] By the Renaissance, as Roy Porter explains: "No longer were the viscera or 'vitals' where the essential self lay. The new centre of symbolic gravity lay up in the head, the brain and the nerves." *Flesh in the Age of Reason* 60.

[93] Magnetists in the late eighteenth and nineteenth centuries such as Dietrich Georg Kieser (1779-1862) resuscitated the notion of the "Unterleibsgehirn," which Kieser described as encompassing the "Gangliensystem und dessen Centralgebilde" (in *Über thierischen Magnetismus und Somnambulismus*, 1846; cited here in Heike Scheuerbrandt, "Die Stimme der Natur. Dietrich Georg Kiesers Auffassung vom tierischen Magnetismus," *Athenäum. Jahrbuch für Romantik* [1999] 236).

[94] Rolf-Peter Janz, Fabian Stoermer, and Andreas Hiepko here cite Herbert Herring's *Das Problem der Affektion bei Kant* in *Schwindelerfahrungen. Zur kulturhistorischen Diagnose eines vieldeutigen Symptoms*, eds. Rolf-Peter Janz, Fabian Stoermer and Andreas Hiepko (Amsterdam and New York: Rodopi, 2003) 19n34.

[95] From Kant's letter to Moses Mendelssohn of April 8, 1766; cited here in Kant, *Träume eines Geistersehers, erläutert durch Träume der Metaphysik* 114.

deduction of the categories of thought, or the "principle of right" ("Prinzip des Rechts"). But the principle of right, even in Kant's transcendental philosophy, remains unthinkable without what he calls a "coherent self-feeling" ("kohärentes Selbstgefühl"); this "subjective consciousness is, however, a violent condition. It is an observation turned on itself; it is not discursive, but rather intuitive" ("Das subjective Bewußtseyn ist aber ein gewaltsamer Zustand. Es ist ein auf sich selbst gekehrtes Beobachten; es ist nicht discursiv, sondern intuitiv").[96] This intense, intuitive, pre-conscious state precedes reflection in every single mind, those that produce proofs of reason based on perception as well as those that imagine bizarre visions. Kant compares the hallucinations of spirit-seers to the monstrosities ("Mißgeburten") that a collector of natural objects must possess in his cabinet along with his perfect specimens, and includes an analogy to repression here as well: the collector of natural and healthy objects must possess deformed objects, but must be "careful not to let everyone see them and not to let them be seen too clearly" ("so muß er doch behutsam sein, sie nicht jedermann und nicht gar zu deutlich sehen zu lassen").[97] The metaphor of the natural history cabinet is another indicator of what Monique David-Ménard has called the "proximity between thought and madness" throughout Kant's philosophy.[98]

After the completion of *Dreams*, Kant never again addresses this dilemma or Swedenborg in depth (though his letter of 1790 to Borowski as well as a letter of 1795 to S.T. Sommering, in which he criticizes the con artist Caliogstro as well as the practices of Franz Anton Mesmer, do refer to the popularity of the paranormal). The translator of *Dreams*, John Manolesco, ruminates:

> The name Swedenborg does not appear once in all the three Critiques, whilst relatively obscure names which exerted some influence on his pre-critical development abound throughout his critical works...Was Kant trying to forget him? Or the circumstances which led to the writing of the *Spirit Seer*? Did he ever worry secretly about a possible confrontation with the arch-spirit seer, the worst of all madmen, in the Noumenal World?[99]

What we do know is that Kant ends *Dreams* by saying "Human reason was not meant to try and part the highest clouds in heaven or lift from our eyes the curtains in order to reveal to us the secrets of another world" ("Es war auch die menschliche Vernunft nicht gnugsam dazu beflügelt, daß sie so hohe Wolken teilen sollte, die uns die Geheimnisse der anderen Welt aus den

---

[96] Kant, lecture on *Metaphysik L1*, cited here in Manfred Frank, *Selbstgefühl. Eine historisch-systematische Erkundung* 94. Frank points out that this view is strongly influenced by Leibniz, in that it describes an unconscious process as preceding the act of conscious reflection.

[97] Kant, TGS 981 (A113-114).

[98] Monique David-Ménard, "Kant's 'An Essay on the Maladies of the Mind' and *Observations on the Feeling of the Beautiful and the Sublime*," trans. Alison Ross, *Hypatia* 15.4 (2000) 83.

[99] Kant, *Dreams of a Spirit-Seer and Other Related Writings* 28.

Augen ziehen").[100] Even in this somewhat dismissive conclusion, an intuition of another mode of existence, one that cannot be subsumed into a belief system (whether philosophical, psychological, or theological) is present despite *Dreams*' denials of the uncanny stories that make us aware *of* that intuition in the first place.

The uncertainty or ambiguity in Kant's text, which follows from the fact that he is discussing uncanny experiences, but which also creates a feeling of uncanniness, points *back* to the thinking of Spinoza, who contends that our emotions, which are body-based, intuit something beyond the self (a self he understands as being something akin to an embodied mind). But Kant's thinking, unlike Spinoza's, takes place in an estranged and Enlightened context. Friedrich Schlegel will later help lead a revival of Spinozist thought in Germany, but he uses this thinking to pursue esoteric and theologically tinged interests. Fundamentally, Schlegel and Kant both need metaphysical systems where Spinoza did not. In a sense, the Enlightenment breaks with the integrated view of body and mind that was possible in earlier times and creates a need in thinkers like Kant and Schlegel to reach out for systems.

By focusing on mental disorders—and in particular on uncanny disorders such as clairvoyance, where body/mind come unhinged and the synthetic identity of consciousness is questioned—Kant does not so much reject uncanny experience as help render it mainstream. In *Dreams*, he asserts that clairvoyance cannot function as proof of the existence of an immaterial, immortal soul, and that there is no such proof. Rather, clairvoyance and mental illness serve as forms of proof that we desire transcendence, a space presently unavailable to us—we desire other forms of relatedness and of community. That is, these examples of displacement (of objects of the imagination to the external world, as in the case of spirit-seeing) and of dissociation (between body and mind, as in the case of mental illness) prove something about our minds, something within us, rather than proving that the thing we imagine (fearful experience, illness, ghosts) exists.

Kant anticipates Freud's view that "in insanity there hides a piece of forgotten truth" ("in der Wahnidee ein Stück vergessener Wahrheit steckt")[101] —that is, something basic about reality surfaces in the symptoms of illness, and in particular the tendency of the past to return in some form. Kant's precritical writings do indicate a need to somehow link present mental disorders with past experience, along with a need to find present explanations for inexplicable past events. This look to the past is repeated by the texts themselves; Kant's reference to "melancholy juice" in the *Classifications*, for instance, repeats an aspect of traditional biomedicine's theory of the humours. But Kant did not actually subscribe to that theory; rather, by re-mobilizing

[100] Kant, *Träume eines Geistersehers, erläutert durch Träume der Metaphysik* 84 (A126-128).
[101] Freud, *Der Mann Moses*, GW 16: 191.

terms from ancient medicine, Kant evokes the principle of the past at a time when there really was no satisfactory explanation for the malfunctions of the mind.

In a sense, the uncertainties about the project of metaphysics that Kant ambiguously addresses, and then "forgets" during the critical period, come back in the work of Friedrich Schelling, who treats similar issues in a way much closer to that of Spinoza and without a demonstrable need for a totalizing system. His fragment *Clara: Or, On Nature's Connection to the Spirit World* displays an openness, not toward the possibility that ghosts actually exist, but toward the possibility that our intuition allows us to imagine other forms of existence.

3.2. Schelling, *Clara: Or, On Nature's Connection to the Spirit World (Clara, oder Zusammenhang der Natur mit der Geisterwelt)*

In simultaneously defending and deconstructing the importance of myth, and in his philosophy in general, Schelling employs a style of strict rational deduction that evinces his indebtedness to an empiricist and rationalist tradition.[102] But that style is interrupted consistently by his attempts to mix spirituality and biology, to acknowledge a metaphysical aspect to illness, and to rationalize concepts that might otherwise belong in the realm of sentiment. These interruptions contribute to a philosophy that ultimately is a mix of rationalism and what Rita Wöbkemeier calls a "speech that pushes into the metaphorical; one that brings in metaphysics, religion, and melancholy where otherwise biological relationships are thematized, in formulations that border on the mathematical" ("...ins Metaphorische drängende Rede, die Metaphysik, Religion, Melancholie ins Spiel bringt, wo ansonsten biologische Verhältnisse des Organismus in ans Mathematische grenzenden Formulierungen thematisiert werde").[103] Here Schelling's considerably more extensive philosophies of myth and of nature resemble texts of Romantic psychiatry such as Gotthilf Heinrich von Schubert's *Diseases and Disorders of the Human Soul* (*Krankheiten und Störungen der menschlichen Seele*, 1845); both attempt to synchronize the claims of aspects of the discourses of traditional biological medicine with the claims of metaphysics.

Manfred Frank describes Schelling's resurrection of myth in the nineteenth century as not at all reactionary, but rather as a "universal mythology of the human that supports a true 'public sphere'" ("[eine] wahre

[102] Wöbkemeier, *Erzählte Krankheit. Medizinische und literarische Phantasien um 1800* 20.
[103] Ibid, 20.

'Öffentlichkeit' stiftender, universalistischer Menschheits-Mythologie").[104] It is in this context that *Clara: Or, On Nature's Connection to the Spirit World* (1810-1811), a philosophical fragment by Schelling often deemed reactionary or esoteric, can be reevaluated. *Clara* can be read as a legitimate part of Schelling's philosophical and psychological production rather than as a bizarre fringe piece.

In *Clara*, Schelling addresses topics similar to those in his lectures on the *Philosophy of Mythology*, which he also expected would be greeted with skepticism. In the introduction to the lectures given in Munich in 1841, Schelling grants:

> Especially for these lectures, I have chosen a subject that seems to lie far from everything that is aimed at immediate usefulness, and nevertheless, if you follow my presentations with perseverance, you soon will see yourself set in the middle of questions whose answer, depending on how it turns out, is of decisive meaning for life and its current conditions.
> (Ich habe insbesondere für die diessmaligen Vorträge einen Gegenstand gewählt, der weit abzuliegen scheint von allem, was auf einen unmittelbaren Nutzen gerichtet ist, und dennoch, wenn Sie meinen Vorträgen mit Ausdauer folgen, werden Sie sich bald in die Mitte von Fragen versetzt sehen, deren Beantwortung, je nachdem sie ausfällt, selbst für das Leben und seine gegenwärtigen Zustände von entscheidender Bedeutung ist.)[105]

In both the *Philosophy of Mythology* and in *Clara*, Schelling speaks to the Romantic need or desire, a desire that Freud will rearticulate repeatedly, to understand an idea of a forgotten (or repressed) origin—an origin which is only imagined as a singular, unique past moment. In reality, both Schelling and Freud will contend, origin is a moment of re-representation that repeats itself. Origin exists only in memory and in memories of those memories.[106] The beginning for which the Romantics yearn is already a re-presentation, a repetition. Like Freud and Nietzsche, Schelling attempts to construct a conceptual archaeology of the archaic (rather than attempting to write a history of archaic times and peoples); this style of thinking permits a continuity between the primitive and today, between the mythological (which, as we saw in Chapter One, is a series of explanatory "mistakes") and the

---

[104] Manfred Frank, "Wie reaktionär war eigentlich die Frühromantik? (Elemente zur Aufstörung der Meinungsbildung)," *Athenäum. Jahrbuch für Romantik* (1997) 146.

[105] Friedrich Schelling, *Philosophie der Mythologie* (Munich lectures of 1841), in *Schellingiana* 6, eds. Andreas Roser and Holger Schulten (Stuttgart-Bad Cannstatt: Frommann-Holzboog, 1996) 11. This edition is abbreviated henceforth as PM.

[106] Writing about Ruth Klüger's representations of her memories of life in Auschwitz, Michael Rothberg notes that "'origin' is at once located at the moment of the memoir's enunciation and in the open wounds of the memories that it probes" That is, origin only exists in memory, and in meta-memory (or, in memories of memories). Imagery (in this case, barbed wire in Auschwitz) is linked via memory to an idea of "origin." See *Traumatic Realism: The Demands of Holocaust Representation* (Minneapolis: University of Minnesota Press, 2000) 131.

modern (which repeats but also distances itself from those mythological mistakes). By focusing on the "principle of the past" rather than on precise reconstruction of historical events, Schelling, Nietzsche, and Freud are in fact focusing on how the past is represented in the present. This is an estranged way of approaching, or knowing, the past. But it is not necessarily completely abstract. The works of all of these thinkers, even Schelling's supposedly esoteric *Clara*, demonstrate a desire to understand real present suffering in part by determining the role that contemporary evocations of ancient myths play in that suffering.

By foregrounding conversations between four characters about the relationship between death and immortality, and by focusing on an All Souls' Day celebration, *Clara* seems concerned primarily with the possibility of life after death. It references contemporary discussions about the soul's immortality, and reframes well-rehearsed debates between empiricists and rationalists on this topic. But Schelling's fragment is also a rumination on mourning and melancholy, and it anticipates other Freudian concepts as well. In *Clara*, Schelling deploys several themes that Freud will identify as uncanny—including animism, omnipotence of thoughts, and man's attitude toward death—in order to answer an uncanny problem of modernity.

Contemporary culture, Schelling says, is marked by the "dissolution of the peaceful unity, in which not too long ago the sciences coexisted" ("Auflösung der friedlichen Eintracht, in welcher vor nicht allzu langer Zeit die Wissenschaften zusammenlebten").[107] Now that modern philosophy has severed its bond with the natural world, and philosophy has divorced itself also from the concerns of psychology, we are estranged from nature and from our own bodies. The consequence is that philosophy has become its own uncanny substitute: "instead of the real spirit (of knowledge) there is a surrogate of the same, that is supposed to be to a certain extent more spiritual than the spirit" ("statt des eigentlichen Geistes [der Erkenntnis besteht] ein Surrogat desselben, das gewissermaßen noch Geistiger als der Geist seyn soll").[108] Estranged modern philosophy has become an echo chamber, reminding itself of something now hidden. With *Clara*, in which he introduces the "soul" as a binding force between nature and spirit, Schelling does not advocate a return to hermetic views of nature, nor to primitive belief systems. Rather, he attempts to move the alienated and reified modern subject philosophy represented, in his view, by Fichte into a new dialectical phase, and he attempts to do this in a way superior to Hegel's. In *Clara*, Schelling responds to what he sees as the negative, cold uncanniness of post-Fichtean philosophy with another, more progressive and certainly mournful understanding of estrangement, thus moving subjectivity and the dialectical time in which it moves into a new, truly critical space for the next phase of

---

[107] Schelling, SW 9: 3.
[108] Ibid, 4.

reason. *Clara* displays an openness toward the possibility that our intuition is essentially unreliable, but at the same time allows us to imagine other modes of existence. In the following, I wish to show the significance of *Clara* for Schelling's philosophy, but also for a Romantic "melancholy realism" that constitutes a critical Romanticism that, in turn, is Freud's real heritage.

In *Clara*, Schelling addresses topics similar to those in his lectures on the *Philosophy of Mythology*, about which he also expected skepticism. In the introduction to the lectures given in Munich in 1841, Schelling acknowledges:

> Especially for these lectures, I have chosen a subject that seems to lie far from everything that is aimed at immediate usefulness, and nevertheless, if you follow my presentations with perserverance, you soon will see yourself set in the middle of questions whose answer, depending on how it turns out, is of decisive meaning for life and its current conditions.
> (Ich habe insbesondere für die diessmaligen Vorträge einen Gegenstand gewählt, der weit abzuliegen scheint von allem, was auf einen unmittelbaren Nutzen gerichtet ist, und dennoch, wenn Sie meinen Vorträgen mit Ausdauer folgen, werden Sie sich bald in die Mitte von Fragen versetzt sehen, deren Beantwortung, je nachdem sie ausfällt, selbst für das Leben und seine gegenwärtigen Zustände von entscheidender Bedeutung ist.)[109]

Despite the fact that it also focuses on questions whose meaning for life is decisive, *Clara* is an unfinished piece that Schelling rarely spoke about and never intended to publish. The scant scholarship that exists on the text expresses the consensus that Schelling conceived of its themes and arguments not long after the unexpected death of his wife, Caroline Schlegel-Schelling, in 1809 (they were married in 1803). *Clara* is most obviously a discussion of the possibility of life after death and of the necessary bond between nature and body created by the soul. Although the focus on a "spirit world" and on the presence of the dead in this world seems to indicate that *Clara* does not really fit into Schelling's rational ouevre, Alexander Grau has argued persuasively that *Clara* really should be situated within main tendencies of Schelling's thought, even if the fragment does also mark a departure from the thrust of his writings before Caroline's death. For instance, the *Stuttgarter Privatvorlesungen* of 1810-1811, the first major philosophical writings Schelling produced after the tragedy, contain many of the same themes as *Clara*. Grau notes that after Caroline's death Schelling essentially shifts his philosophical focus from freedom (his last text before her death is the *Philosophical Exploration of the Nature of Human Freedom*) to death; the primary theme of his work shifts, but the critical structure is essentially the same. If this is right, then *Clara* indeed deserves more attention than scholarship has paid it thus far, and my contention here (informed by Grau's

---

[109] Schelling, PM 11.

larger argument) is that the uncanny themes in this text are consistent with the main tenets of Schelling's philosophy of mythology and of nature.

Clara has three primary interlocutors: a priest (who narrates), a doctor, and Clara herself, a young widow living in a convent outside of town. They conduct discussions, primarily about the possibility of communication between the world of the living and the world of the dead, that begin on All Souls' Day and end "at the boundary of winter and spring" ("noch auf der Grenze von Winter und Frühling").[110] The priest represents arguments in favor of the mind or spirit, the doctor speaks on behalf of nature and the corporeal, and Clara is personality or the soul. A clergyman, who appears near the beginning of the text, represents Immanuel Kant. In the initial discussion, the priest consoles Clara about her husband Albert's death, saying that perhaps this world offers us only a limited view of reality. Perhaps there is a higher spirit capable of uniting us with the dead, who really never stop "living" with us.[111] Although the priest here wishes to reassure Clara about the possibility of real life after death, he expresses that wish by saying that the dead still "live" here, in us.

At this point a clergyman, representing Kant, enters and states that all we have of the dead are our memories of them. The acts of memorialization that we perform are a ritualistic, repetitive calling-back of memories of the dead that simultaneously help us to remember that our life is here and now, on earth; these acts of remembering the dead, when performed properly, prevent us from forgetting our own finitude. The frequent acknowledgment of mortality, he says, keeps us focused on the present and helps us live better lives. We must not, however, use such commemorations to fool ourselves into believing "that we can be connected to the inhabitants of that other world" ("daß wir mit den Bewohnern jener andern Welt in Verbindung stehen können") but rather to remind ourselves that we cannot:

> We who are living are allocated to this world only once; here we should do as much good as we can, we should show our every love and trust to those to whom we are close and we should do so for as long as we remain with them on their path. And we would certainly fulfill this duty to each other far more closely and conscientiously if we were continually to remind ourselves of their mortality....We have within us a single point that is open and through which heaven shines in. This is our heart or, to be more precise, our conscience. In the latter we find one law and one purpose, a purpose that cannot be from this world, for more often than not it is in conflict with it. Thus, for us it serves as a pledge from a higher world and it raises him who has learned to follow it to the comforting thought of immortality.
> (Wir Lebende sind einmal auf diese Welt angewiesen; hier sollen wir das mögliche Gute thun und den mit uns Verbundenen jede Liebe und Treue beweisen, solange wir noch mit ihnen auf dem Wege sind, und gewiß würden wir diese Pflicht gegeneinander weit genauer und gewissenhafter erfüllen, wenn wir uns stets erinnerten, daß sie sterblich sind....Wir haben in uns einen einzigen offnen Punkt,

[110] Schelling, SW 9: 92.
[111] Ibid, 16.

> durch den der Himmel hereinscheint. Dieser ist unser Herz oder, richtiger zu reden, unser Gewissen. Wir finden in diesem ein Gesetz und eine Bestimmung, die nicht von dieser Welt seyn kann, mit der sie vielmehr gewühnlich im Kampf ist, und so dient es uns zu dem Unterpfand einer höheren Welt, und erhebt den, der ihm folgen gelernt hat, zu dem trostreichen Gedanken der Unsterblichkeit.)[112]

Here Schelling refers to Kant's position, in his Dreams of a Spirit-Seer, on the existence of an immaterial world—as a world that can exist only as a thought produced by a materially housed mind.

None of the very small number of scholars who have devoted any attention to *Clara* grant the Kant figure much significance. He does only appear relatively briefly in the text. And yet, an essay Schelling published in the *Fränkliche Staats- und Gelehrten-Zeitung* in 1804, a few years before he wrote *Clara*, may provide more encouragement to see the Kant figure as in fact the leading philosophical instance in the fragment, as the character whose words should shape our view of the positions in the dialogue that then takes place in the remainder of the text among the more prominent characters. In the essay of 1804 entitled "Immanuel Kant," Schelling writes that Kant, who died at an advanced age, outlived some of his "most fervent enemies… physically, but (outlived them) all morally, and the fire of progress served only to distinguish the pure gold of his philosophy from the other ingredients of his time, and to portray it in clear brilliance" ("Seine heftigsten Gegner hat er zum Theile physisch, alle aber moralisch überdauert, und das Feuer der weiter Fortschreitenden hat nur gedient das reine Gold seiner Philosophie von den Zuthaten der Zeit zu scheiden und in reinem Glanze darzustellen").[113] Kant's philosophical genius has been "misunderstood" ("verkannt"); in particular, his ability to unify speculative thinking about society with insights from the natural sciences has been underestimated.[114] And, by investigating the nature of art in a scientific manner, Kant has helped place the study of the past in "indirect relationship to everything in the future" ("indirekte[m] Verhältnis zu allem Späteren"), although Kant himself did not necessarily intend this.[115] By virtue not of intention but of his actions, Kant has attained a kind of immortality in the history of philosophy as science.

Clara, the doctor, and the priest immediately challenge the clergyman's view that the thought of immortality is merely something that comforts us: Clara in particular finds his words "cold" and asserts her own "ardent longing" ("heiße[] Sehnsucht") for a greater meaning than can be found in this life alone.[116]

---

112 Friedrich Schelling, "Über den Zusammenhang der Natur mit der Geisterwelt," *Ausgewählte Schriften*, ed. Manfred Frank (Frankfurt am Main: Suhrkamp, 1985) 4: 113. This edition is abbreviated henceforth as AS. The translation is in Steinkamp, 12, 13.

113 Schelling, AS 3: 11.

114 Ibid, 16-17.

115 Ibid, 19.

116 Ibid, AS 4: 115/13.

However, while the form of a dialogue among four individuals provides a space in Clara for the possibility of other views about communication with spirits and life after death, nothing in the text that follows the clergyman's exit refutes his standpoint on mortality and on the rituals that should, at their best, remind us of mortality, for this will permit us to lead better lives. Rather, the remainder of the fragment is concerned consistently with the role of memory—which is not so much the return of the past or of the dead into the present and the living, but rather an attitude of the living toward the dead, the loving toward the now invisible beloved, an attitude within the discrete present moment toward the principle of the past. This memory can occur involuntarily or in the form of ritual. So while the topic and mood of this fragment seem melancholic, the importance of the Kant figure and the subsequent discourse on memory within it moves our attention toward mourning.

After the clergyman's exit, the two remaining men (the priest and the doctor) reassure Clara about the possibility of life after death in part not because they really think this is true, but because they are concerned that her memories are bad for her health, and that focusing on the possibility of reuniting with her husband in the future will help her live better in the present. They encourage her interest in clairvoyant visions (clairvoyance is a kind of repetition in the present of the future).[117] Over numerous pages, the priest and doctor worry about the unhealthy implications of Clara's memories of her dead husband and her victimized ancestors (Clara asserts that robbers have desecrated the graves of her "fathers"[118]). At the All Souls' Day ritual at the town graveyard, the priest also is affected by depressing thoughts of transience: "We sat sunk in silent melancholy. How many of those who were now walking on the graves would be lying beneath them in the following

[117] I would argue that here the text also represents a "victim/expert relationship" that I noted in the Preface and which Ian Hacking has shown characterizes the history of the study of mental illness (see Mad Travelers: Reflections on the Reality of Transient Mental Illnesses [Charlottesville and London: UP of Virginia, 1998]). The doctor and the priest are completely preoccupied with Clara's moods and well-being, and their conversations are determined almost solely by their determination, from moment to moment, day to day, and season to season, of her psychosomatic status. The constellation of doctor, priest, and a woman who is prone to morbidity and melancholy and obsessed with clairvoyance also replicates the standard composition of players in magnetic treatments. Schelling was fascinated with magnetism and mesmerism, and in particular with his close friend Gotthilf Heinrich von Schubert's conviction that, during the laying-on of hands that occurs in magnetic therapy, there arises an "extraordinary sympathy between the magnetizer and the patient…the patient's will becomes one with that of the magnetizer." Ansichten von der Nachtseite der Naturwissenschaft (Dresden: Arnoldische Buchhandlung, 1808) 345; cited here in Steinkamp 93n6. In Clara, the repeated attempts of the priest and the doctor to engage the young widow in a Socratic-style dialogue (in which Clara, as respondent, essentially only answers with monosyllabic questions that prompt her instructors to expand upon their ideas, or with brief affirmatives ["How?" "Without a doubt," "Certainly," etc.]) are verbal enactments of the laying-on of hands that characterized magnetic treatments.

[118] Schelling AS 4: 111/Steinkamp 11-12.

year?" ("Wir saßen in stille Wehmuth versunken. Wie viele, die hier über diese Gräber wandeln, werden übers Jahr selbst da unten liegen?")[119] In the scene that follows, Clara's appearance is a reminder of transience as well, but this reminder comes involuntarily. When she walks into the room where the priest and doctor wait for her, her resemblance to works of art—to the portraits of her dead ancestors that fill the cloister—is so uncanny that the doctor and priest are frightened.[120] Clara is a walking reminder of the fact that the past is over, and yet her ancestors clearly persist in her—or, rather, they do not: it is their loss, and the crimes committed against them (the grave desecrations and property theft), that are memorialized in part by her shocking physical resemblance to their portraits. As the doctor says while looking at the portraits of Clara's family, now stored for safekeeping in the cloister: "It seems to me that the difference between our times and the previous ones becomes no more apparent than in such a collection of portraits" ("Der Unterschied unserer und der vorigen Zeiten scheint mir durch nichts anschaulicher zu werden als durch eine solche Sammlung von Bildnissen"). The priest then recounts: "At that very moment Clara entered the room in the highest of spirits, and only now did the resemblance become so frighteningly apparent that we all had to stop ourselves from betraying what we were feeling" ("In dem Augenblicke trat Clara äußerst heiter herein, und die Aehnlichkeit wurde nun erst bis zum Erschrecken auffallend, daß wir alle uns zusammennehmen mußten, die Empfindung zu verbergen").[121] Later, Clara again memorializes the past and re-invokes its loss (and emphasizes the difference between past and present) when she visits the priest and acts, for just one day, as a "replacement" ("Ersatz") for his children's dead mother. While the doctor and priest worry that too much remembering can be unhealthy, the fragment on the whole (mainly through Clara and the clergyman) presents memory, whether in the form of involuntary recall or of ritualistic commemoration, as a necessity for living ethically in a modern world in which we no longer can take comfort in visions of spirits.

The name Clara indicates "clarity," but is also related to "clairvoyance" ("clear seeing," or "Klarsehen," as well as the power to see the future). The character of Clara is likely based on the historical Clara of Assisi, a noblewoman born in 1193 or 1194 who became an abbess, led the convent community of San Damiano, and was canonized in 1255, only two years after her death. The moment of clearest knowledge, of absolute intuition about truth, of clearest "sight," must come, says the doctor, at the moment of death, when the dying person is "completely released from the sensible world" ("ganz von der Sinnenwelt entbunden") and "the highest,

[119] Schelling, AS 4: 108/Steinkamp 10.
[120] Ibid, 109/11.
[121] Ibid, 110, 111/11.

inner life is revealed" ("dann wird das höchste innerliche Leben enthüllt").[122] At that moment of "highest clairvoyance," the doctor says, the person is deeper in memory than ever: "Far from their memory being lost, the past from far back becomes clear to them, as does the future, and often the remote future at that" ("Weit entfernt die Erinnerung zu verlieren, wird ihnen weit zurück die Vergangenheit helle, wie die Zukunft oft in nicht unbeträchtlicher Ferne").[123] This state of heightened consciousness is not dissimilar to Schelling's portrayal of the ideal relation between past and present in *The Ages of the World (Die Weltalter)*:

> How few people truly know the past! Without a powerful present, which emerges by separating from itself, there can be no past. He who cannot confront his own past has none; or rather he never gets out of it, he lives in it permanently.
> (Wie wenige kennen eigentliche Vergangenheit! Ohne kräftige, durch Scheidung von sich selbst entstandene Gegenwart gibt es keine. Der Mensch, der sich seiner Vergangenheit nicht entgegenzusetzen fähig ist, hat keine, oder vielmehr kommt er nie aus ihr heraus, lebt beständig in ihr.) [124]

The way out of an unproductive, uncritical and unrealistic melancholic state, of being trapped in the past, is through a highly self-aware separation from one's own present—or, through attaining the insight into the present that comes from viewing it at a distance. This successful state of consciousness is perhaps symbolized best by the experience of clairvoyance.

Clara very likely reflects Schelling's own interest in clairvoyance, which was encouraged in part by Gotthilf Heinrich von Schubert. Like Schubert, Schelling visited a "seeress," a houseguest of their mutual acquaintance Justinus Kerner and the inspiration for Kerner's book *The Seeress of Prevorst (Die Seherin von Prevorst)*.[125] Schelling's notes on the fragment include the observation that in clairvoyance everything is sensed and felt immediately, with no mediating representation ("everything is immediate, nothing mediate" ["alles unmittelbar, nichts mittelbar"]); the clairvoyant has "no memory of things as absent. No past" ("keine Erinnerung der Dinge als abwesend. Keine Vergangenheit").[126] In the experience of clairvoyance, which is perhaps as close as we can get to communication with anything like a spirit world, the decay and death we worry about is gone, at least momentarily; everything is present and immediate. And yet the clairvoyance that Schelling contends is "no memory of things as absent" is not really a lack of memory at all, but rather precisely an *effect* of uncanny memory; that is, a consequence of the estrangement and distance between a

---

122 Schelling AS 4: 162/Steinkamp 48, 49.
123 Ibid, 163/49.
124 *Die Weltalter. Fragmente*, ed. Manfred Schröter (Munich, 1979) 11.
125 Ellenberger, *The Discovery of the Unconscious: The History and Evolution of Dynamic Psychiatry* 79-81.
126 Schelling, AS 4: 212/Steinkamp 83.

past perception and the present affect that represents that past perception in altered form.

When Clara insists that she longs "ardently" for a death that "assembles (consciousness) rather than disperses" ("Denn mir schien der Tod immer eher sammelnd als zerstreuend") and that "promotes depth and not superficiality" ("verinnigend, nicht veräußernd"),[127] she expresses a desire for a reunification with her dead husband and dead fathers; this desire can only come from an experience of loss and melancholy, and even of repulsion (Clara is "sunk in thoughts led by melancholy" ["versunken in ihre von Trauer geleiteten Gedanken"] and "feels an obvious disgust and abhorrence for everything of this world" ["verspürt offenbar Ekel und Abscheu vor allem Diesseitigen"]).[128] While she is in this mood state, Clara's memories are not gone; rather, they are completely present and extend into the world around her.[129] This is a state akin to what the phenomenologist Edward Casey terms "multi-modal remembering": several sensory modes, visual, verbal, and tactile, are experienced as simultaneous, which yields a momentary illusion of the past, or something like the past, as present. And yet this is only an illusion, and Clara knows it. She longs for death because then the estrangement of the present from the past will be definitively over; but more than this, her constant preoccupation with the past and with the dead will be over as well. That is, the *proximity* of present to past, which is at the same time an estrangement, will be no more.

The "multi-modal remembering" of clairvoyance in *Clara* is similar to the Romantic ideal of *devotio moderna*, a form of life developed by the order of the Carthusians in the eleventh century. In the first section of the fragment, the doctor calls this order the "only one I wish to be maintained, one that appears to me to fill a need in human society" ("Von allen möglichen Orden wünsche ich nur, daß Einer erhalten erde, der mir eine Nothwendigkeit für die menschliche Gesellschaft zu haben scheint").[130] The Carthusians wished to structure and perform medieval devotion as an alternative to the instrumental aspects of modern life. They advocated a personal relationship to God, introspection, and contemplation; in a sense, this was a very modern response to medieval Church dogma, somewhat ahead of its time, and yet in the centuries that followed, the Carthusians remained the order perhaps truest to medieval worship practices.[131] In the attitude of *devotio moderna*

---

[127] Schelling, AS 4: 163/Steinkamp 49.

[128] Ibid, 124/21.

[129] Edward Casey describes this type of "the outreach of memories into the surrounding world of the remembering subject" in *Remembering: A Phenomenological Study* (Bloomington and Indianapolis: Indiana University Press, 1987) 288. I discussed this form of "memory beyond mind" in Chapter One, Section 2.2.

[130] Schelling, AS 4: 121/Steinkamp 18.

[131] Alexander Grau, "Clara. Über Schellings gleichnamiges Fragment," *Zeitschrift für philosophische Forschung* 51.4 (1997) 599.

privileged by Romantics who wished to present a glorified view of medieval life as a "modern" ideal, uncanny experience can arise. That is, it is in this extremely artificial, aestheticized, and Romantic attitude that one is vulnerable to spirit-seeing, to the fantastic visions of one's own imagination, and to melancholy. And yet all of these experiences also acknowledge something very real and Enlightened—the inescapable transience of life and the permanence of mourning. The figure of Clara exemplifies the *devotio moderna*'s unification of longing for the past (whether medieval, ancestral, or personal) and for the future (of a death that "assembles" consciousness and "promotes depth") with a life lived completely in the corporeal and mortal present.

In the cloister in which she lives, which is arguably a kind of tomb, kind of a symbolic burial site, outside of the town, Clara is literally surrounded by possessions and portraits of dead family members; directly outside are the graves and the commemorative rituals. But none of this living entombment will bring the past back, will make it visible again. And despite the attentions of her interlocutors: the doctor, who wants to use reason to save Clara from her memories, and the priest, who argues for the possibility of communication with spirits, their "therapy" with Clara does not work. Clara dies, in the cloister. The words of the clergyman, who does not participate in the extended dialogues (or, in Clara's "treatments") persist long after he has left the scene.

In the fragment, an empty space represents Clara's last thoughts. Schelling perhaps intended to insert a section here based on, or directly quoting, handwritten notes by his late wife Caroline. These notes are entitled "Be mindful of death!" ("Gedenke an den Tod!").[132] They depict Caroline's own memories of a lily-filled meadow, a place of nature's continual decay and renewal. Schelling sets *Clara*'s All Souls' Day ceremony in a similar meadow; the fragment as a whole is about commemoration and about the representations of the dead that are encountered and remembered by the living, and not really about the possibility of the soul's immortality. The fact that the doctor and the priest cannot "heal" Clara by discussing at length what the clergyman (Kant) has called the "comforting thought of immortality" points to the probability that Schelling thought the clergyman was right: death is a definite and singular phenomenon, while memory is an ever-changing, communicative, living process.

The components in Schelling's fragment that can be called uncanny —the discussions of clairvoyance, of decay, and of frightening verisimilitude —all of which occur within the framework of a three- or four-way conversation, help reveal an interpersonal dynamic in *Clara* that reflects a very contemporary view of relatedness and interaction between men and women. Romantics such as Friedrich Schlegel envisioned women as equal

---

132 Steinkamp 91n1.

dialogue partners, and in *Clara* this is at least occasionally the case; Clara is, in any event, the absolute focus of her interlocutors. Schelling's text releases something akin to what Cristina Mazzoni, in her work on hysteria, calls a "repressed feminine element" in modern European culture, a voice that, among other things, acknowledges the omnipresent horror and anxiety about transience.[133] That element is also released, or liberated, in eighteenth- and nineteenth-century writings on mental disorders. This release is an Enlightened act; or, something Enlightened within Romanticism, and something modern amidst the multiple reactions against modernity that were taking place in the years when Schelling wrote *Clara* as well as the essay on Kant. A text about clairvoyance is a text about something anti-modern. But Clara's position as a discussant as well as a kind of patient is modern, and this is a position that attained through the uncanny experiences and discussions of uncanny material, a position constructed in and through the form of a dialogue with men representative of major societal positions of the time (doctor, priest, clergyman). Keeping Schelling's very positive view of Kant's philosophy in mind (a view he stresses in the essay entitled "Immanuel Kant") helps us interpret *Clara* as an envisioning of visions and ruminations about the afterlife as ways of living with loss in modern times. This envisioning is a modern act, or an act of clarity, that is at the same time anxious and always mindful of mortality and of decay. Clara says that the obvious connection between man and mortal nature terrifies her:

> I am often terrified…of the thought that everything is related to man. Indeed, if another power within me didn't balance out this horror of nature, I would die from the thought of this eternal night and retreat of light, of this eternally struggling beingness that never actually is"
> (Mir kann vor diesen Verbindungen oft grauen…vor dem Gedanken, wie alles Bezug hat auf den Menschen. Ja hielte diesen Schauern der Natur nicht eine andere Macht in mir das Gleichgewicht, ich müßte vergehen im Gedanken an diese ewige Nacht und Flucht des Lichts, dieß ewig ringende, nie seyende Sein.)[134]

In his philosophy of nature, Schelling contends that nature follows spiritual as well as mechanical laws, and that all matter was produced by a world soul. Nature is the "past of the self" ("die Vergangenheit des Ichs"),[135] and a fundamental unity underlies everything grounded in that past.[136] But an

---

[133] Cristina Mazzoni, *Saint Hysteria: Neurosis, Mysticism, and Gender in European Culture* (Ithaca and London: Cornell University Press, 1996) 1, et al.

[134] Schelling, AS 4: 27/Steinkamp 19.

[135] See Dieter Jähnig's discussion of the aesthetic dimension of Schelling's nature philosophy, as expressed through a retelling of natural history as cultural and psychological history, in *Schelling. Die Kunst in der Philosophie*, vol. 1 (Pfüllingen: Günther Neske, 1966) 133.

[136] Schelling explicates this understanding of nature in, among other texts, *Von der Weltseele. Eine Hypothese der höheren Physik zur Erklärung des allgemeinen Organismus* (Hamburg: Friedrich Perther, 1798). Ellenberger reads the nature philosophy in a psychological context in *The Discovery of the Unconscious: The History and Evolution of Dynamic Psychiatry* 202-203.

uncanniness is part of this unity. In the *Philosophy of Mythology*, Schelling says that a possible origin of religious belief systems is in the "instinctual fear of something uncanny in nature" ("die gedankenlose Scheu vor irgend einem unheimlichen in der Natur").[137] This fear is purely instinctual, not rational, and it precedes the construction of a belief system. That is, anxiety about something "unhomely" in one's natural "home" is itself completely natural. The religion or "cult" ("Kultus"[138]) that springs up to assuage the anxiety is perhaps the first of the series of fundamental mistakes, the myths that will be repeated and re-represented throughout the history of nature and of consciousness. These mythical narratives represent and aestheticize the original anxiety as well as address or assuage it; the history of anxiety thus is imbricated by the history of its mistaken, yet necessary, aesthetic treatment.

In another passage from the lectures on the *Philosophy of Mythology*, Schelling posits a distinction between a decaying modern present and a glorious cultural past that is reminiscent of Friedrich Schiller's thinking about "sentimental" versus "naïve" cultural production. Schelling depicts a supposedly pure past, an "age of cheerful poetry" ("Weltalter heiterer Poesie") that he envisions as "free of (the) religious terrors and all of those uncanny feelings, which oppress later (modern) humanity" ("frei von religiösen Schrecken und allen jenen unheimlichen Gefühlen…,von denen die spätere Menschheit gedrückt wurde").[139] But he then reminds us that this lost past never existed; it has always only been a representation of an idea. Schelling draws the distinction between this imagined past, when a "happy and guilt-free atheism" ("glücklich[er] und schuldlos[er] Atheismus") reigned, and the "barbarism" ("Barbarismus") of later times in order to remind us that we live squarely in a modernity whose myths and terrors must be reckoned and lived with.

The hopes of finding a naïve and happy primitive people even today, perhaps "on distant islands" is, Schelling admits, difficult to resist (he asks: "Who has not gladly thought (of this fantasy)?" ["Wer dächte sich {das} nicht gerne ein…?"]). But rather than look to this easy, "well-known and beloved way of thinking" ("bekannte[] und beliebte[] Denkweise"),[140] Schelling encourages us to accept that we have always been modern—we are products of the torturous and anxious explanations for a past that was never a state of cheerful innocence, but rather initially and always marked by intense fear and a sense of the uncanny. Before the anxiety about culturally produced paranoia and technologically enhanced doppelganger, there was anxiety about the uncanniness of nature itself. The father figures erected to relieve that anxiety then aroused even more uncanny fear, as these creations are seen as and in

137 Schelling, PM 55.

138 Ibid, 95.

139 Schelling, AS 6: 25.

140 Ibid, 25.

fact become demanding, desiring creators.[141] They are figures of uncanny love who replace the father in monotheistic belief systems, who is, Schelling writes in *The Ages of the World*, a "psychotic" ("psychotischer") God who is a lonely "wild madness, tearing itself apart" ("wilder Wahnsinn, der sich selber zerreißt").[142]

Schelling reminds us, though, that the father-creators who dominate belief systems from prehistory to modernity remain constructions of the "son," without whom no access to the father is possible; this son is himself a creation of the constructed explanatory belief system, from which, as we will see below "all reality" has been "removed." There is nevertheless a truthfulness to this system, or at least to the yearning for it, that Schelling also addresses in this passage:

> But all reality was removed from Christianity along with the rejected paganism. Christianity is in admittedly the relationship to the father and the worship of the same in spirit and in truth, everything heathen disappears in this result; that is, everything that is not in relationship to God in his truth; but this result has, without his laws, no empirical truth. Who sees me sees the father, Christ says, but he adds: I am the way, and: No one comes to the father except through me.
> (Aber eben mit dem ausgestoßenen Heidnischen wäre auch alle Realität aus dem Christenthum hinweggenommen. Das Letzte ist allerdings das Verhältnis zum Vater und Anbetung desselben im Geist und in der Wahrheit, in diesem Resultat verschwindet alles Heidnische, d. h. alles was nicht im Verhältnis zu Gott in seiner Wahrheit ist; aber dieses Resultat hat ohne seine Voraussetzungen selbst keine empirische Wahrheit. Wer mich siehet, siehet den Vater, sagt Christus, aber er setzt hinzu: Ich bin der Weg, und: Niemand kommt zum Vater als durch mich.)[143]

The "father" is also not accessible at any one place, but is rather a figure of uncanny displacement: Abraham, the "arch-father" ("Erzvater"), was a wanderer, a nomad, estranged and a stranger (Schelling links the name "Abraham" to "Aberhaupt," signifying everywhere and nowhere at once):

> Abraham of the Hebrews means therefore: Abraham, who belongs to those who are passing through, who are not bound to any domicile, who live as nomads, as the arch-father in Canaan also always is called the stranger, because he who remains nowhere is everywhere only a stranger, a wanderer.
> (Abraham der Ibri heißt also: Abraham, der zu den Durchziehenden, an keinen festen Wohnsitz Gebundenen, nomadischen Lebenden gehört, wie der Erzvater in Kanaan auch stets der Fremdling heißt, denn der nirgends Weilende ist überall nur ein Fremdling, ein Wanderer.)[144]

---

[141] Schelling, PM 55.
[142] Schelling, SW 8: 43.
[143] Schelling, PM 250.
[144] Schelling, PM 160.

The condition Schelling describes above is impossible to realize. *Clara* is an attempt to reach some clarity from within the irrevocably modern and in fact inescapable state of being oppressed by uncanny feelings.

Schelling and Freud arguably display (at least at times) a way of thinking that could be described as "melancholy realism." Ian Baucom uses this term in a book entitled *Specters of the Atlantic: Finance Capital, Slavery, and the Philosophy of History* (2005). Baucom argues that an experiential and epistemological mode of "melancholy realism" helps define the long nineteenth century. He argues that the

> fantasy of Freudian melancholy…is that melancholy is a fundamentally pastoral practice, that it serves to preserve, safeguard, or protect the dead by offering them an unsurrenderable, interminable, commemorative lodging within the social, political, and psychical imagination of the living.[145]

Baucom goes on to say that really it is the other way around. Melancholy

> manifests itself not as the result of the traumas that have happened to us but as a way of making ourselves happen within the space of the traumatic, not as a way of lodging the past within the present but as a way of lodging the present (and ourselves) in the deathly afterlife of past historical situations…(this is) a type of romantic historicism. The melancholy spectator not only invests in the dead, but also seeks to enter into the historical situation that led to their death.[146]

The dead are not preserved in us; rather, we enter into them, into their past, via our memories of them. In this type of melancholy, the decathexis between memory and object that characterizes mourning does not happen. Unlike Kant's Enlightened disinterested spectator, the Romantic melancholy realist is involved, and attempts to make visible, to see again, and thus to remain together with, the past, with the dead, with the things we can no longer see. For the Romantic melancholy realist knowledge and love come together. The melancholy realist is not so much oriented toward longing for the lost past, but rather toward knowledge of what we cannot yet see. The phenomenon of clairvoyance incorporates and manifests this multi-temporal kind of knowledge: a knowledge of the loss of the past, of the transience of everything present, and of the loss even of the future perfect—of what we will have had, but do not yet know. This is a state of melancholy realism (as opposed to the unproductive trap of "living constantly in the past" that Schelling outlines in the passage from *The Ages of the World* cited above). Schelling's *Clara*, about a young woman grieving for her dead husband by discussing his death with three other men in her dead husband's home, surrounded by his portraits and belongings, would seem to be all about

[145] Ian Baucom, *Specters of the Atlantic: Finance Capital, Slavery, and the Philosophy of History* (Durham: Duke UP, 2005) 258.
[146] Ibid, 259.

making the invisible visible, and, in its lengthy discourses on the possibility of life after death, it would seem to be very much concerned with making visible, or intelligible, what we do not yet know and therefore cannot yet see.

But, into this melancholic meditation comes Kant. Or, that is, a figure who represents Kant, and who intervenes in Clara's melancholy by reminding the other characters in the text of the fact that the past actually is over, that all we "have" is its traces, the "principle of the past" rather than the past itself. This notion of the "principle of the past" resonates with other passages in Schelling's philosophy, and makes plausible the argument that *Clara* (the fragment) is not so much a collection of musings on life after death as a contribution to a modern and mournful understanding of loss. Clara's frighteningly uncanny resemblance to the portraits of the dead, her live burial in the convent, remind us that the lost object is actually forever invisible, entombed, decathected. Schelling perhaps does not go quite so far as to make his heroine, Clara, into a re-embodiment of Antigone, the one who finally buries the dead. But he does indicate a desire, long before Freud, to confront the Oedipal psychodrama, and to present a different narrative of relating past to present than either that of Kant's disinterested spectatorship or of an overinvolved Romantic melancholy.

It is at the intersection of feelings of entrapment and liberation, and of pain and pleasure, that psychoanalysis will later locate the individual's chance to work through conflicts. In a usually late stage of a successful psychoanalytic psychotherapy, the individual remembers earlier pain and experiences the feeling of freedom, analogous to pleasure, that comes of the awareness of the distance between past suffering and present "working-through" of conflicts created by that suffering. This stage can occur only when the patient has overcome his resistance to the therapy and to uncovering his real memories. What Freud calls the "compulsion to repeat" repressed content is a necessary precondition for the eventual "impulsion to remember" that can bring about insight and healing.[147] A kind of melancholy, a sort of stuckness, is essential for eventual decathexis and mourning. An uncanny dissociation that occurs when the familiar becomes strange—again and again—prompts us to remember, and this remembering keeps the difficult feelings of loss and alienation that we associate with separation from dead loved ones alive. At the same time, as with the uncanny similarity between Clara and the portraits of her dead ancestors, we are reminded that we are related to, yet different from, the dead. We need the experience of uncanny repetition, an experience of the strangely familiar that ultimately reminds us of difference, to let them go.

In a sense Freud's later work in particular is haunted by the principle of the past coming back (or, by the past's pastness rather than actual past events), and this haunting is preceded by Schelling's concern with uncanny

[147] Freud, SE 12: 147-156.

repetition. The uncanny, anxious, compulsively repetitive love of the son for the dead father in the *Philosophy of Mythology* is similar to Clara's love for her dead husband: this love, through which Clara "makes herself happen within the space of the traumatic," is a mode of remembering characteristic of a modernity that is not yet over.

Anthony Vidler notes that for the Romantics in general, the uncanny was

> a psychological and an aesthetic phenomenon, (that) both established and destabilized at the same time....Something was not...merely haunted, but rather revisited by a power that was thought long dead. To such a force the romantic psyche and the romantic aesthetic sensibility were profoundly open; at any moment what seemed on the surface homely and comforting, secure and clear of superstition, might be reappropriated by something that should have remained secret but that nevertheless, through some chink in the shutters of progress, had returned.[148]

Schelling, perhaps more so than other German Romantics, recognized the revolutionary, freeing potential in the experience of the return of things that should have remained hidden, but come back nevertheless. The awareness of this return, this uncanny feeling, is an indispensable part of the experience of the "abyss of freedom."[149] Schelling acknowledges that the origin of myth is false, and hence implies that myths of origin are false at their origins. He thereby helps opens up a path to psychoanalysis (which, like Romanticism, is already a sort of theoretical echo chamber, itself uncanny), its interest in soliciting representations of the past in the present as the way to insight, and its shift from a search for one stable origin to a focus on the principle of the past.

Conclusion

The following chapter continues to integrate philosophical and psychological aspects of the uncanny from the late eighteenth century and into the nineteenth, but shifts focus to the aestheticization of illness in particular, and to the continuing simultaneously liberating and repressive function of the uncanny, in texts by Karl Philipp Moritz and Friedrich Schlegel. In psychological and pseudopsychiatric explorations and case studies that rely on methods ranging from "pure" observation to magnetic treatments, these two men, transitional figures between Enlightenment and Romanticism as well as between empiricism and idealism, use uncanny phenomena in an attempt to continue the project of philosophical psychology.

---

[148] Anthony Vidler, *The Architectural Uncanny: Essays in the Modern Unhomely* (Cambridge, MA: MIT Press, 1992) 26-27.

[149] This is the term used by Slavoj Zizek in *The Abyss of Freedom/Ages of the World*, an essay by Zizek with the text of Schelling's *Die Weltalter* (second draft, 1813) in English translation by Judith Norman (Ann Arbor: University of Michigan Press, 1997).

Schlegel's late phase, during the 1820s, coincides with one peak of the movement called "Romantic medicine"[150] whose practitioners included psychiatrist and aesthetic theorist Gotthilf Heinrich von Schubert (1780-1860). Schubert's writings on dreams and mental disorders represent a psychologically informed response to and dialogue with the philosophical-aesthetic view of uncanny anxiety and sublime awe sketched out in Section 1 of this chapter. Like Schlegel and other Romantic psychiatrists, Schubert's focus, whether in his dream theory or in his studies of mental disorders, is on challenges to the stability of consciousness and on the "uncertainties of silence, solitude, and darkness" where, Nicholas Royle contends, the uncanny originates;[151] these uncertainties represent a lack of origin and a lack of a fixed place. As for so many Romantics, but also already for Kant in the precritical writings, for Schubert it is when the supposed stability or fixedness of consciousness is challenged that philosophies of consciousness are most interesting. Representations of mental disorders can be beautiful, but they can also yield a productive understanding of reality.

The way that practitioners of Romantic medicine use the Western esoteric tradition relies on, rather than rejects, Enlightenment faculty psychology. Schubert cites Karl Philipp Moritz's *Journal of Empirical Psychology* (*Magazin zur Erfahrungsseelenkunde*) as an inspiration and source for his own work,[152] and, like Schelling, Schubert visited the "seeress" Fredericke Hauffe.[153] Schubert and Schlegel espouse the idea that we may perceive things more accurately when ill or when in "magnetic sleep"—then we are in touch with what Friedrich Schlegel will later call "inner esoteric world history."[154] This does not quite mean that the world is reduced to a mental effect, but rather that the relationship between self and world is revisioned from Aristotle's view in *De anima*, which was the major model of mind from antiquity through the nineteenth century.[155]

Schubert believed that man and nature had disconnected due to man's "self-addiction" ("Ich-Sucht"); he also believed, however, that man would eventually be reunited with nature and with the "world soul" from which all matter comes. For Schubert, a longing for love and longing for death are both expressions of a desire for this return, for a return home. That

---

150 See August J. D'Alessandro's discussion of Schubert's *Symbolik des Traumes* as representative of "Romantic medicine" in "A Historical Review of *Die Symbolik des Traumes*," *Psychiatric Quarterly Supplement* 42.2 (1968) 337-343; for more on "Romantic medicine," see also Wöbkemeier, *Erzählte Krankheit. Medizinische und literarische Phantasien um 1800* 22ff.

151 Royle, *The Uncanny: An Introduction* 10.

152 D'Alessandro, "A Historical Review of *Die Symbolik des Traumes*" 339.

153 Ellenberger, *The Discovery of the Unconscious: The History and Evolution of Dynamic Psychiatry* 81.

154 Friedrich Schlegel, *Kritische Ausgabe*, ed. Ernst Behler (Munich: Schöningh, 1958-) 35: xxxvii. This edition is abbreviated henceforth as KA.

155 Bell, *The German Tradition of Psychology in Literature and Thought, 1700-1840* 4, et al.

longing expresses itself in uncanny ways, including in dreams, which have their own poetic language.[156] Body and soul are related, but within each person there is an individual soul and an element of the world soul. It is in moments in which we become aware of the world soul—of the consciousness of others, of those beyond our minds—that we experience what Schubert calls "cosmic moments" ("kosmische Momente").[157] Dreams are such moments, uncanny experiences in which we ourselves are also another, one who is and is not us.

Like Kant, Schelling, and Schubert, Moritz and Schlegel acknowledge that the turn to transcendentalism does not free us from finitude; we are inescapably embodied and mortal, transient. But even when they themselves are at their most self-involved (Moritz is the author of the woefully introspective *Anton Reiser*; Schlegel's late philosophy verges on solipsism), their work reflects a desire to re-unite the self with the world, and to maintain the link between what Schlegel will call "self-consciousness" and "world-consciousness."[158] In studies of extreme psychosomatic disturbances rife with uncanny occurrences, Moritz and Schlegel test and forge that link.

---

[156] Ellenberger, *The Discovery of the Unconscious: The History and Evolution of Dynamic Psychiatry* 205-206.
[157] Ibid, 729.
[158] Friedrich Schlegel, KA 12: 435.

Chapter 3

Beautiful Breakdowns: Uncanny Symptoms and the Aestheticization of Illness

The uncanny effect of epilepsy and of madness has the same origin.…The Middle Ages quite consistently ascribed all such maladies to the influence of demons, and in this their psychology was almost correct. Indeed, I should not be surprised to hear that psycho-analysis, which is concerned with laying bare these hidden forces, has itself become uncanny to many people for that very reason.
[Das Unheimliche der Fallsucht, des Wahnsinns, hat denselben Ursprung. …Das Mittelalter hatte konsequenterweise und psychologisch beinahe korrekt alle diese Krankheitsäußerungen der Wirkung von Dämonen zugeschrieben. Ja, ich würde mich nicht verwundern zu hören, daß die Psychoanalyse, die sich mit der Aufdeckung dieser geheimen Kräfte beschäftigt, vielen Menschen darum selbst unheimlich geworden ist.]
Freud, *The Uncanny [Das Unheimliche]*

1. Magnetism as an Aesthetic and Scientific Practice in the Early Nineteenth Century

I argued in Chapter Two that the uncanny helps reveal not only an aesthetic component within psychology and psychiatry, but also a dynamic of subject-object relations within those disciplines. At the same time, those relationships work through aesthetic forms. In this chapter, I am interested in how practitioners of early psychology and of esoteric psychiatry examine and, to a certain degree, mobilize uncanny symptoms in their patients in order to wield power and to create a particular kind of "beautiful" experience; however, this experience can and often does elude the practitioners' complete control.

In 1818, Friedrich Schlegel (1772-1829) expressed his excitement about the contemporary revival of the psychiatric practice of "animal magnetism" ("animalischer" or "tierischer Magnetismus"). The "animal" of animal magnetism refers to the soul, the *anima*. This practice, which usually included the laying on of hands in order to properly direct ethereal magnetic fluids, promised to bridge for good the twin chasms separating philosophy from psychology and idealism from empiricism. In a series of fragments that never coalesced into a planned systematic study of magnetism, Schlegel wrote the following:

> This so-called animal magnetism (…) announces itself as an epoch-making event in inner esoteric world history. Until now we had only *material* knowledge (physical-mathematical—or philological-historical) and dialectical, or *ideal* knowledge. But now a new magnetic and magical knowledge appears, a knowledge of the spirit; but it

> is not conceived of as ideal, rather as completely factual. With regard to the truth or falsehood of its character, it *still* has a completely undecided, or rather ambivalent and double nature; it can be demonically abused and can serve religion in a godly manner. But as a preliminary *word of the spirit*, it is the first stirring of the new age, and the actual turning point of the present historical development.
> [Der sogenannte animalische Magnetismus [...] kündigt sich vollkommen an, wie eine Epoche machende Begebenheit der innern esoterischen Weltgeschichte. Wir hatten bis jetzt nur ein *materielles* Wissen (physisch-mathematisches—oder philologisch-historisches) und ein dialektisches oder *ideelles*. Hier tritt nun ein neues magnetisches und magisches Wissen auf, ein Geisterwissen; aber kein ideell erdachtes, sondern ein ganz factisches. *Noch* ist es in Hinsicht seines Charakters der Aechtheit oder Falschheit von ganz unentschiedner, oder vielmehr zwiefacher und doppelter Natur; kann dämonisch mißbraucht werden und göttlich der Religion dienen. Als beginnendes *Geisterwort* aber ist es die erste Regung der neuen Zeit, und der eigentliche Wendepunkt der gegenwärtigen Entwicklung.][1]

There is no question that Schlegel's fascination with magnetism in the later part of his career went hand in hand with his idealization of a resurgent Catholic church as the locus of a new, beautiful body politic. He envisioned the patient's body as a site where inexplicable, transcendent phenomena became, if only briefly, visible and palpable; in his later fragments, the church becomes a place where aesthetic forms are conduits for otherwise abstract political expressions.

Schlegel's interest in magnetic treatments arose neither from a desire to actually heal the sick nor from his wish to unify the goals and claims of philosophy and psychology. Rather he was intrigued, particularly after converting in 1808 to Catholicism (but also as early as the seminal Early Romantic years in Jena in the 1790s), with the fluid boundary between science and art, and with how the knowledge gained from empirical observation could be transformed into metaphor. That metaphorical knowledge ideally would continue to shape the "inner esoteric world history" that, for Schlegel as for his earlier Romantic contemporary Novalis, was the truest history—not a mere retelling of events, but expressing the course and flow of ideas that emanated from not entirely explicable sources The fine fluid of "animal spirit" had been posited by Galen in the second century[2] and revised by Franz Anton Mesmer at the end of the eighteenth century into the material at the basis of the theory of animal magnetism. It was not only analogous to this ideational flow, but also would help to construct it. Properly directed magnetic fluid would lead not only to the proper functioning of the

---

[1] Friedrich Schlegel, *Kritische Ausgabe*, ed. Ernst Behler (Munich: Schöningh, 1958-) 35: xxxvii. This edition is abbreviated henceforth as KA.

[2] Galen follows Aristotle's argument (from *De anima*) that the soul has a biological basis, as well as his doctrine that form and matter are separate but interdependent.

individual human body, but of the body politic as well.[3]

Practicing the laying-on of hands—and sometimes also literally of magnets, whose shape should be "convenient...for application" to the body—began in earnest in Mesmer's Paris practice in 1778.[4] The goal was to manipulate the flow of a patient's "magnetic fluid," thereby relieving symptoms ranging from weakness to hallucinations, primarily in female patients. Treatments usually involved inducing a hypnotic-like state of "magnetic sleep," a "twilight" condition in which the subject was most open to what Gotthilf Heinrich von Schubert in 1808 called "the intervention of the future, higher existence in our present less complete existence."[5] In the state of magnetic sleep, the patient could essentially travel through time and thus be freed temporarily from physical constraints.

Magnetic and mesmeristic therapies were used only when symptoms recurred frequently, and the therapies themselves were often repeated. Mesmer's account of the case that helped him found the practice of magnetism typifies the repetitive nature of symptoms and treatment alike:

> In the years 1773 and 1774, I undertook the treatment of a young lady. She was twenty-nine at the time and was named Oesterline. For several years, she had been subject to a convulsive malady, the most troublesome symptoms being that the blood rushed to her head and brought about a most cruel toothache as well as an extreme pain in the ears. This was followed by delirium, rage, vomiting and fainting. This offered a highly favorable circumstance to me for observing accurately the ebb and flow to which *Animal Magnetism* subjects the human body. The patient often had beneficial periods, followed by a remarkable degree of alleviation; however, the comfort was always momentary and imperfect.
>
> The desire to ascertain the cause of this imperfection and my own uninterrupted observations brought me again and again to the point of recognizing Nature's handiwork and of penetrating it sufficiently to forecast and affirm, without hesitation, the different stages of the illness.[6]

---

[3] Robert Darnton asserts that, in 1780s France, "although it originally had no relevance whatsoever to politics, (magnetism) became, in the hands of radical mesmerists like Nicolas Bergasse and Jacques-Pierre Brissot, a camouflaged political theory very much like Rousseau's, [...] providing radical writers with a cause that would hold their readers' attention without awakening that of the censors." While this is part of a "prerevolutionary radical mentality," it bears some similarities to Schlegel's later German Romantic postrevolutionary reactionism and his deployment of magnetism as part of a plea to reconstruct a beautiful simulation of a medieval Catholic monarchy. See *Mesmerism and the End of the Enlightenment in France* (Cambridge: Harvard University Press, 1968) 3.

[4] Matthew Bell, *The German Tradition of Psychology in Literature and Thought, 1700-1840* (Cambridge: Cambridge University Press, 2005) 173. Mesmer lived from 1734-1815. The notion that magnets should conform to the shape of the body is found in Franz Anton Mesmer, *Mesmerism: The Discovery of Animal Magnetism*, trans. Joseph Bouleur (Edmonds, WA: Holmes Publishing Group, 1998) 9.

[5] Ibid, 173.

[6] Mesmer, *Mesmerism: The Discovery of Animal Magnetism* 9.

Oesterline's symptoms are classic signs of "epilepsy;" at the time, the term designated a catch-all disorder whose breadth and lack of clear cause helped earn it the title of "the uncanny disease."[7] Epileptics traditionally have been distinguished from shamans and other visionaries in that their epileptic episodes are involuntary. The point of Mesmer's magnetic treatments was in part not to make the disorder disappear, but to elicit convulsions and other symptoms repeatedly and deliberately and to reduce their spontaneous, unpredictable appearances. The controlled eliciting of symptoms made it possible for Mesmer to observe the patient and her recurring distress nearly constantly, so that he could "again and again" penetrate "Nature's handiwork." The "convulsive malady" that plagued Oesterline for years was for Mesmer a "highly favorable circumstance" for his own ability to understand nature as well as for the scientific development of medical treatment.

In the early nineteenth century, as magnetism devolved increasingly from an accepted medical practice into a parlor game, certain new elements, such as chamomile or milk baths and breathing exercises, were introduced.[8] But the basic characteristic of repetition remained in the treatment's ritualistic deployment, whether it involved laying on of hands, bathing, deep breathing, or actual magnets, as well as in the symptoms to be treated. Doctors, patients, and observers attempted repeatedly to use the practice to bring the self outside of itself as a form of communication with nature and other people. In the 1890s Freud addresses this communicative aspect of magnetism when he asserts, with Josef Breuer, that the practice has "communicative powers," and that the unconscious forces revealed by magnetism or hypnotism prove the existence of a world in which ideas circulate in a completely different manner than in the conscious mind.[9] The "communicative powers" of magnetism do not force reason upon the unconscious mind, but rather render the unconscious knowable by bringing therapist and patient closer together precisely in the realm of illness. In the practice of magnetism, the therapist enters, or penetrates, a disordered psyche and simultaneously deploys and gains, as Schlegel puts it decades before Freud, "magical knowledge…a

---

[7] More on the uncanny characteristics of epilepsy can be found in Hans-Joachim Görres, "Hinter einer Mauer des Schweigens. Epilepsie—die unheimliche Krankheit" (*Universitas* 6 [1988] 659-667) and in Mircea Eliade, *Shamanism: Archaic Techniques of Ecstacy*, trans. Willard R. Trask (New York: Pantheon Books, 1964). Lauren Slater presents a rich view of epilepsy as a liminal phenomenon in *Lying: A Metaphorical Memoir* (New York: Random House, 2000), informed by contemporary psychiatry and psychopharmacology.

[8] See Heike Scheuerbrandt, "Die Stimme der Natur. Dietrich Georg Kiesers Auffassung vom tierischen Magnetismus" (*Athenäum. Jahrbuch für Romantik* [1999]) 238-243.

[9] Sigmund Freud, *Gesammelte Werke*, vol. 1 (Frankfurt am Main: Fischer, 1999) 13. This edition is abbreviated henceforth as GW. The translation is James Strachey's in Freud, *The Standard Edition of the Complete Psychological Works of Sigmund Freud*, vol. 2 (London: Hogarth, 1953-1974), 12. This edition is abbreviated henceforth as SE.

knowledge of the spirit" ["magisches Wissen...ein Geisteswissen"].[10] For Mesmer as well as for Schlegel, one of the primary characteristics of this knowledge gained through doctor-patient communication was its repetitive and ritualistic nature.

While German and Viennese psychiatrists did revive magnetic practice briefly in the 1820s,[11] magnetism nevertheless was acknowledged widely before and during that time to be of dubious scientific value. Discussions about whether natural or supernatural explanations of phenomena should be given more weight peaked in the late eighteenth and early nineteenth centuries, although it was widely agreed that the supernatural did not exist. In the years between the rise of empirical psychology (in the 1770s in particular) and that of psychiatry (which was established firmly as a discipline in the German-speaking territories by 1820), animal magnetism changed from an experimental but somewhat accepted medical practice to a source of esoteric fascination. But the association of animal magnetism with a specifically Romantic kind of medicine did not merely mark a flight from Enlightened rationality and the pressures of political and economic-industrial modernization. By continuing to focus on animal magnetism into the mid-nineteenth century, Schlegel and Romantic psychiatrists such as Gotthilf Heinrich von Schubert accomplished something more complex than might first appear to be the case. Magnetism offered the Romantics a chance to unite aesthetics with science. On the one hand this bolstered a vision of the aesthetic as a separate, and somehow elevated, sphere of reality (as opposed to Kant's depiction of the aesthetic as a way of experiencing reality), but on the other hand magnetism relied on older empiricist convictions about how reality is known.

Even if an unabashedly esoteric and even fantastic agenda lay on the surface of Schlegel's writings on magnetism, science, and philosophy during these years, his compulsive returning to and re-eliciting of psychosomatic symptoms in magnetic treatment reveals persistent empirical principles within Romanticism. Magnetism and materializations (or séances) were ways of accessing these forces. In a sense this "play" was very real, with experiments in an unconventional setting, yet carried out in a highly conventionalized and stylized way. The social fascination with psychological disorders and their mysteries brought psychological problems out into the world and helped to normalize psychosomatic disease. A fascination with the paranormal or parapsychological extended beyond parlors and literature into the "high" science of empirical faculty psychology of the late eighteenth century (as we

---

[10] Schlegel, KA 35: xxxviii.

[11] Erna Lesky documents the work of the practitioners who continued to use magnetism in the early nineteenth century and states that the "activities of Anton Mesmer had never been completely forgotten in Vienna." *The Vienna Medical School of the Nineteenth Century* (Baltimore and London: Johns Hopkins University Press, 1976) 31.

will see shortly in Karl Philipp Moritz's *Magazin zur Erfahrungsseelenkunde*, 1783-1793) as well as in Schlegel's Romantic-era protocols forty years later.

Romantic medicine inherited Enlightenment thinking about psychology in several ways. What came to be called "Romantic medicine" during the nineteenth century was indebted directly to the "dynamic-vitalistic wing of Enlightenment medicine."[12] Romantic medicine united rationalist and esoteric traits, especially when it turned to the study of psychiatric disorders. Psychologists of the late Enlightenment had already espoused "mental physicalism," which included the notion that the mind was itself organic.[13] Emotions, then, were seen "increasingly…as natural states of the psyche."[14] Working at the crossroads of Enlightenment and Romanticism, magnetists saw their patients' problems as being natural and organically based but also capable of producing visionary abilities. They viewed these problems as proof that something existed beyond materialism and rational empiricism.

Fascination with observing psychosomatic symptoms was prevalent in both the empirical psychology of the eighteenth century and the Romantic medicine of the nineteenth century, extending into the twentieth century and psychoanalysis.[15] All of these modern movements exhibit uncanny traits in their focus on compulsively repetitive symptoms, which point to something not fully explicable. The symptoms that magnetists studied, as well as their own re-eliciting of those symptoms, belong to what Freud eventually calls the uncanny, "that class of the frightening which leads back to what is known of old and long familiar" ("jene Art des Schreckhaften, welche auf das Altbekannte, Längstvertraute zurückgeht").[16] Uncanny symptoms lead the therapist to material submerged in the patient's unconscious.

Freud did not base his theory of the unconscious on Mesmer's magnetism, but magnetism does help reveal what might be called an aesthetic aspect of the Freudian unconscious, and of psychoanalysis in general. Freud not only represents the return of Enlightenment ideas after the long nineteenth century of Romanticism, he also inherits the Romantic tendency to aestheticize illness. In writings ranging from studies of "neurotic" religious ceremonials, to descriptions of demonic possession in the modern age, to

---

[12] Lesky, *The Vienna Medical School of the Nineteenth Century* 31.

[13] See for instance John W. Yolton, *Thinking Matter: Materialism in Eighteenth-Century Britain* (Minneapolis: University of Minnesota Press, 1984).

[14] Bell, *The German Tradition of Psychology in Literature and Thought, 1700-1840* 59.

[15] Johann Christian August Heinroth mentions "Psychosomatik" in the *Lehrbuch der Störungen des Seelenlebens* 2: 43. Tobias Leibold cites this in a comprehensive study that also includes a summary and history of the term "psychosomatic." Leibold describes psychosomata as conceptualized at the beginning of the nineteenth century as an "Ensemble von evolvierenden Wissenssystemen […] im Prozess ihrer Abgrenzung von Psychophysik und traditioneller Psychologie." See *Enzyklopädische Anthropologien. Formierungen des Wissens vom Menschen im frühen 19. Jahrhundert bei G.H. Schubert, H. Steffens und G.E. Schulze* (Würzburg: Königshausen & Neumann, 2009) 285.

[16] Freud, GW 12: 231/SE 17: 220.

investigations of patients' fantasies about children being beaten, Freud draws out the sensual and aesthetic components of each experience. These aspects involve judgments of taste as well as "aesthetics" in its earliest incarnation, the study of sense perception. Such experiential components, in his patients and in himself, are part of his data. This data is generally compiled and re-presented in order to understand what a present sensation reveals about the patient's ability to live with his past. Most interesting for Freud, as for Mesmer and Schlegel, are those present sensations that indicate a clear dissociation within the mind or between mind and body. The neurotic symptoms observed in analysis, like the visions and convulsions elicited by magnetism, connect past to present, but symptoms are no longer bound explicitly and strictly to that past. Understanding the uncanny (compulsively repetitive, animistic, strangely familiar) aspects of animal magnetism helps explain why magnetism persisted, even if largely as a symbolic ritual, well into the modern era when the unconscious was discovered.

Magnetism is also uncanny in that it relates to what Freud calls "the old, animistic conception of the universe" of which the uncanny reminds us, with *anima* meaning the soul (as mentioned above).[17] Magnetists literally "animated" their patients into convulsions and confessions of hallucinations (usually interpreted as clairvoyant visions). Like Kant's use of the term "melancholy juice" in his precritical psychological writings of the 1760s, the theory and practice of animal magnetism re-invoked convictions from the Galenic past of traditional biomedicine. They reflect convictions that resurface in uncanny repetitions in a world not quite able to synthesize mechanistic with metaphysical explanations of mental processes.[18]

In his fragments on magnetism, Schlegel does relativize the practice's status and potential: its character is still unclear, and it can be deployed for purposes demonic or godly. Such a description is not limited to Schlegel's late philosophy; liminality and ambiguity characterize magnetism from its beginnings. Mesmer was a thinker indebted neither wholly to mechanistic nor to hermetic, magical traditions. As renewed interest in Mesmer since the 1980s indicates, overlapping mechanistic and esoteric thinking typifies some of the most progressive science of the modern era. Magnetism inhabits a liminal zone because it is no longer archaic medicine but not yet a fully realized modern practice. As Schlegel says, it represents the "first stirring" of a "new age" rather than a culmination.

Animal magnetism is therefore analogous to what I referred to in Chapter One as an uncanny "memory beyond mind." It is a repetitive, corporeal practice that binds doctor, patient, and observer in the process of manipulating symptoms (such as convulsions, fainting, babbling) long

---

[17] Freud, GW 12: 253/SE 17: 240.

[18] Roy Porter addresses such interminglings of mechanism and esotericism in *Flesh and the Age of Reason* (New York and London: W.W. Norton, 2003) 60.

detached from past perceptions or sensations. Those past perceptions are thus "lost," and this loss re-emerges whenever the magnetist re-elicits the patient's nervous symptoms. In the process, the uncanny symptoms of free-floating anxiety becomes freed from the individual patients who experience them as symbolizing much larger events. They predict the future and prompt a "reading" by the entire therapeutic community.

Magnetism is one form of early psychiatry that, when used to treat symptoms of psychosomatic illness revealing uncanny qualities, tends to enhance and exaggerate those qualities. In eliciting the patient's ongoing recollection of certain facts from her own fantasy life, animal magnetism participates in the aestheticization of illness by converting disease into metaphor. Magnetism lifts disease out of the realm of contingent, historically located suffering, determined in part by the sufferer's gender and class, and transfers it into the realm of the modern Romantic subject, who turns history into memory and narrative into fragment.

Nearly forty years before Schlegel's intense involvement with magnetism began, Karl Philipp Moritz (1756-1793) founded the *Journal of Empirical Psychology (*the complete title is *Gnothi Sauton, oder Magazin zur Erfahrungsseelenkunde als ein Lesebuch für Gelehrte und Ungelehrte*), the first journal of its kind in Germany. The often exhaustively detailed case studies and eye-witness or first-person accounts of psychological aberrations that fill the journal's ten volumes, and the relative paucity of editorial comment and analysis, enhances the impression of objectivity and makes the journal seem far removed from Schlegel's esoteric philosophy and aesthetic vision of magical treatments that inhabit a nebulous zone between observable phenomena and the world of ideas. And yet the cases chosen for inclusion in the *Journal* bear striking similarities to the symptoms suffered by the patients who interested Schlegel (the most prominent of whom I analyze later in this chapter). The fourth volume's presentation of "Confessions about the Ability to See Future Events, By Madam***" ("Geständnisse über das Vermögen künftige Dinge vorherzusehn, von Madam ***")[19] anticipates the clairvoyant visions of magnetism patients as well as of countless nineteenth-century hysterics.

In choosing case studies that emphasize the similarities between the foci of empirical psychology, of subject philosophy, and of aesthetic theory, Moritz participates in an aestheticization of illness similar to that presented by the Romantics. And indeed, the proximity between concepts of aesthetics and psychology dates back to at least the mid-eighteenth century and

---

[19] Karl Philipp Moritz, *Gnothi sauton oder Magazin zur Erfahrungsseelenkunde als ein Lesebuch für Gelehrte und Ungelehrte*, eds. Petra and Uwe Nettelbeck (Nördlingen: Franz Greno, 1986) vol. 4: 83ff. References to the *Erfahrungsseelenkunde*, translated as the *Journal of Empirical Psychology*, are cited henceforth as ES.

Alexander Gottlieb Baumgarten's treatise on the basis of aesthetics (1742).[20] Eleven years before the publication of the first volume of Moritz's *Journal*, Ernst Platner states that psychology and aesthetics are "one and the same" ("einerley").[21]

Both Schlegel and Moritz are preoccupied with the tradition in modern Western philosophy of conceiving of the "mind as a great mirror, containing various representations—some accurate, some not."[22] What brings the two men together for our purposes here is their fascination with inaccurate or distorted reflections or representations—distortions that may, both men suspect, actually reveal something very clear about mental life and its embodiment. Both focus on psychological case studies in which the relationship between "flesh and reason" goes awry. In these "mistakes" of the body and mind, moments marked by frightening dissociation, something emerges that is different from modern daily experience but also not collapsible into a "return" to primitive existence.

Moritz and Schlegel both combine elements of mainstream contemporary science with esoteric thought. Both employ an approach and style that ends up rendering their projects uncanny—the ten volumes of the *Journal* with lists upon lists of case studies enumerating repetitive symptoms; the almost numbing repetition of six years of protocols in Schlegel's magnetism notebook. Both have been called "transitional" figures around 1800[23]; their thought was often simultaneously Enlightened and Romantic; both believed that psychology was the way to bridge empiricism and metaphysics (that is, both were interested in the problem of philosophical psychology prevalent in psychological studies at the time); both considered the examination of psychosomatic illness (or, of disturbed relations between mind and body) to be an ideal starting point for building such a bridge. Seen from this perspective, the leap from early empirical psychology to animal magnetism, and from Moritz to Schlegel, is not as great as it might at first

---

[20] Carsten Zelle, "Experiment, Experience and Observation in Eighteenth-Century Anthropology and Psychology - The Examples of Krüger's Experimentalseelenlehre and Moritz' Erfahrungsseelenkunde," *Orbis Litterarum* 56.2 (2001) 94.

[21] Ernst Platner, *Anthropologie für Ärzte und Weltweise* (Leipzig, 1772) IV. Quoted here in Raimund Bezold, Popularphilosophie und Erfahrungsseelenkunde im Werk von Karl Philipp Moritz (Würzburg: Königshausen und Neumann, 1984) 122. By aligning psychology with aesthetics, Platner distinguishes psychology from anthropology, though the latter was a field to which Moritz's *Empirical Psychology* also was supposed to contribute. While Platner contends that psychology had to do with the mind alone, and anthropology treated mind and body as a holistic entity, for Moritz, "psychology" combined the aesthetic interests emphasize by Platner together with an acknowledgment of mind as embodied and a preoccupation with mind-body relations.

[22] Richard Rorty, *Philosophy and the Mirror of Nature* (Princeton: Princeton University Press, 1980) 12.

[23] Tzvetan Todorov, *Theories of the Symbol*, trans. Catherine Porter (Ithaca: Cornell University Press, 1982) 153, 165.

appear to be.

Schlegel and Moritz are, then, exemplary figures in the history of the persistence of a dark side of medical history within the Enlightened and post-Enlightenment era. Michel Foucault comments on the relationship between body and mind in the emerging discipline of psychiatry, saying that

> neither physiology nor therapeutics can become those absolute viewpoints from which the psychology of mental illness can be resolved or eliminated....And although the success of psychoanalytic intervention is one with the discovery of the 'truth' of the neurosis, it uncovers it only within the new psychological drama in which it is caught up.[24]

In the following analyses, we will see the extent to which the "psychological drama" of treatment itself constitutes an aestheticization of illness, one that in turn depends upon the experience of uncanny repetition.

2. The Case Studies of Moritz and Schlegel

2.1. Moritz, *Journal of Empirical Psychology (Magazin zur Erfahrungsseelenkunde)*

Germanists know Karl Phillip Moritz primarily as a novelist and aesthetic theorist; it is less widely known that the *Journal of Empirical Psychology* represents a substantial part of his life's work. The *Journal* appeared in ten volumes over ten years, between 1783 and 1793. Moritz and his fellow editors, C. F. Pockels and Salomon Maimon, collected and excerpted texts—including letters, reports, and autobiographies—from subjects who either reported their own experiences in the first person or whose narratives of their strange afflictions were paraphrased by the editors. Moritz's brief introductions and conclusions are usually descriptive and rarely interpretive, but many of the *Journal*'s case studies and brief analyses reflect an interest in psychosomatic phenomena with no apparent organic cause,

---

[24] Michel Foucault, *Mental Illness and Psychology*, trans. Alan Sheridan (Berkeley: University of California Press, 1987) 86-87. Daniela Watzke discusses the history of the "psychodrama" as a treatment method for psychiatric patients in "Hirnanatomische Grundlagen der Reizleitung und die 'bewusstlose Sensibilität' im Werk des Hallenser Klinikers Johann Christian Reil," in: *Reiz – Imagination – Aufmerksamkeit. Erregung und Steuerung von Einbildungskraft im klassischen Zeitalter (1680-1830)*, eds. Jörn Steigerwald and Daniela Watzke (Würzburg: Königshausen & Neumann, 2003) 262-265. In Reil's practice, Watzke explains, psychodrama was used to reveal a patient's identity to himself, as if in a mirror. "Durch die Verkörperung der Halluzinationen verlieren diese die Macht über den Patienten und der Betroffene ist in der Lage, Realität und Fiktion zu unterscheiden" (264).

phenomena similar to those that later fascinated depth psychologists and eventually Freud.

A significant number of the case studies in the *Journal of Empirical Psychology* can be grouped according to their subjects' manifestation of uncanny symptoms. Whether suffering from hysterical pregnancy symptoms, nocturnal panic attacks in which ghosts of dead relatives appear, or visions of resurrected friends, the subjects of Moritz's case studies experience forms of frightening repetition or doubling that seem undeniably related to past trauma or to feelings of guilt and anxiety related to the past. Thus the ten volumes of the *Journal* represent in part a sustained attempt to depict and explain uncanny (as well as other psychophysical) phenomena long before Freud redefines the term. Moritz's journal helps build the modern notion of the uncanny in the German tradition.

The uncanny symptoms that characterize numerous cases in the *Journal* can be used as a way to reveal and to organize thinking about an aesthetic component within early empirical psychology, a discipline whose early stages focused strongly on the observation of what will later be called neurotic or hysterical symptoms. In the *Journal*, but also in his aesthetic and literary writings, Moritz engages in an "art of observation," which is simultaneously observation as an art. The focus of his observation is the moment of derailing or dissociation of the body-mind relationship, and it is exactly where the mind-body relationship derails or dissociates that a new aesthetic unity within disunity emerges. On the one hand, Moritz's agenda in the *Journal* is similar to Kant's in the *Dreams of a Spirit-Seer*: he categorizes religious revelations and anxiety attacks together under "mental disorders" ("Seelenkrankheiten"), and his use of accepted medical categories to circumscribe and contain a wide variety of psychospiritual symptoms implies that these conditions run counter to the Enlightened social order.[25] But on the other hand, the collection of case studies is so large and varied that these categories are inevitably loose and imprecise, and the very objectivity and precision that the *Journal* aims to convey transmute into an often impressionistic and even sensational sort of storytelling. The *Journal* therefore is a form of aesthetic re-representation itself. But in addition, the cases within it emphasize a relationship between mind and body, and between disorder and symptom, that is analogous to the relationship Moritz establishes in his aesthetic theory between substance and surface, and between the thing signified and its sign.

The mix of materialism and moral philosophy that characterizes the *Journal* derives from various sources: English and French sense psychology and the relatively new science of anthropology (and the accompanying notion

[25] Martin L. Davies, *Identity or History? Marcus Herz and the End of the Enlightenment* (Detroit: Wayne State University Press, 1995) 20-21.

of "physiological psychology,"[26]) as well as from Rousseau, from Moses Mendelssohn, and not least, from Moritz's own Pietist background.[27] Each volume is divided into sections that reflect an emphasis on material mechanisms and the relationships between perceptions and symptoms, rather than on precisely why or how mind and body seem to relate the way they do. These sections include "the science of the soul" ("Seelennaturkunde"), "the study of mental disorders" ("Seelenkrankheitskunde"), "the study of mental signs" ("Seelenzeichenkunde"), "mental nutrition" ("Seelendiätetik"), and "soul medicine" ("Seelenheilkunde")—fields corresponding to similar categories in Marcus Herz's *Medical Encyclopedia* (*Medizinisches Enzyklopädie*) of 1782.[28]

By the time Moritz begins publishing the *Journal* in 1783, these key terms of faculty psychology have surfaced and are being used in roughly the same way by practitioners throughout the German-speaking territories.[29] Like Herz, Moritz situates his use of psychological and medical terminology at least implicitly in a context together with fundamental concepts of the emerging critical philosophy.[30] He views "soul" ("Seele") and "mind," or "spirit" ("Geist") as almost synonymous, and both are presumed to be embodied in some way. The body quite literally signifies what is happening in the mind—the body both signs and is itself a sign, and its signing or signifying can be decoded. The act of recording and publishing case studies is then part of the decoding process, part of "the study of mental signs" ("Seelenzeichenkunde"). In addition to the fact that he was part of the post-Wolffian trend in German faculty psychology towards mental physicalism, or the attempt to locate mental phenomena in specific places in the body, Moritz's thinking about the body doubtless owes a direct debt to Spinoza's contention that the body was the basis or ground for the action of the mind.[31]

---

[26] Hans Joachim Schrimpf, *Karl Philipp Moritz* (Stuttgart: Metzler, 1980) 36.

[27] Ibid, 36.

[28] Schrimpf, *Karl Philipp Moritz* 36.

[29] Matthew Bell notes that already by the time that Johann Heinrich Zedler's *Universal-Lexicon* was published, between 1732 and 1754, it was clear that "Germany's systematisation of psychology was ahead of France's and England's." *The German Tradition of Psychology in Literature and Thought, 1700-1840* 13. Zedler's early encyclopedia contains detailed definitions of *Seelen-Lehre*, *psychologia*, and *Psychologie*, and formed a basis for reference for Herz's later, more differentiated dictionary. See also Davies, *Identity or History? Marcus Herz and the End of the Enlightenment*, especially 89ff.

[30] Davies points out that Herz here was in company with other medical practitioners of his time, including Haller, Zimmermann, Weikard, and Platner; all considered themselves "philosophical doctors" ("*philosophische Ärzte*"): "Medicine and philosophy were, after all, complementary aspects of the only science that mattered, the science of Man." *Identity or History? Marcus Herz and the End of the Enlightenment* 89.

[31] Spinoza's positions are summarized in Moira Gatens, "Towards a Feminist Philosophy of the Body," in *Crossing Boundaries: Feminisms and the Critique of Knowledges*, ed. Barbara Caine, E.A. Grosz, and Marie de Lepervanche (Sydney: Allen & Unwin, 1988) 60.

Throughout the *Journal*, Moritz differentiates mental disorders such as vanity and laziness from "madness" ("Wahnwitz"). True madness, he says, is not and cannot be the focus of his psychology. In the following passage, he asserts that the success of the *Journal* rests on its focus on those psychosomatic disorders caused by (and healed by) imagination, disorders lacking an obvious organic cause.

> Madness is always, to a great extent, grounded in the body, and is often healed by treatments that work primarily on the body. –Madness cannot be the main subject of experiential psychology; rather, it depends on the nature of our imaginative power, the diversions (Abweichungen) and the proper manner of directing them, if this study is to be as useful as it really could be.
> (Der Wahnwitz ist doch immer größtentheils mit in dem Körper gegründet, und wird oft durch Mittel geheilet, die vorzüglich auf den Körper wirken. —Er kann also nicht der Hauptgegenstand der Erfahrungsseelenkunde seyn, sondern es kömmt vorzüglich auf die Natur unsrer vorstellenden Kraft, auf die Abweichungen und die gehörige Art des Einlenkens derselben an, wenn dieß Studium so nützlich seyn soll, als es doch wirklich seyn kann.)[32]

Mental disorders caused by and treated with the powers of the imagination are by no means divorceable from the body, however. In an intriguing passage, Moritz states that psychosomata can be contagious, and possibly also hereditary:

> The diseases of the soul can perhaps, just as the diseases of the body, be transmitted from parents to children, or can be hereditary in entire families. As some of the previous facts seem to prove.
> They can be dominant in a people or in a country.
> They can be contagious.
> They can be curable or incurable.
> (Die Krankheiten der Seele können vielleicht, eben so wie die körperlichen, von den Eltern auf die Kinder fortgepflanzt, oder in ganzen Familien erblich seyn. Wie dieses einige von den vorhergehenden Faktis zu beweisen scheinen.
> Sie können bei einem Volke oder in einem Lande vorzüglich herrschen.
> Sie können ansteckend seyn.
> Sie können heilbar oder unheilbar seyn.)[33]

In the late eighteenth century, contagious and hereditary diseases were clearly differentiated—for instance, contagious disease was signaled by fever, whereas hereditary disease was not.[34] And yet here Moritz brings the two together, a conflation that is probably not due to his incomplete understanding of contemporary medicine, but rather to his convictions about aesthetics and

---

[32] Moritz, ES 4: 12.

[33] Ibid, 31.

[34] See for instance the entry on "Fevers" by Leonard G. Wilson in the *Companion Encyclopedia of the History of Medicine*, vol. 1 (London and New York: Routledge, 1997) 382-411.

to the liminal nature of mental illness, both in reality and in its representation in medical, philosophical, and aesthetic texts.

When choosing texts for the *Journal*, Moritz intentionally selected extreme or bizarre reports (suicide notes written "immediately before the deed" ["unmittelbar vor der That"] or an account of a patricide are not atypical). These reports, however, come not from asylum patients but from Moritz's (or the other editors') acquaintances or their friends. The emphasis on the strange or even seemingly inexplicable stems partly from the conviction among empirical psychologists that one learned the most about the psyche by observing the most drastic types of psychological disturbances, and there is implicit emphasis placed on the fact that such disorders can and do occur in otherwise completely normal individuals. Moreover, an interest in aesthetics and in the strange attraction of the frightening is evident in the brief analyses or "suggestions" that follow the case studies; such an interest is also apparent in Moritz's introductory statements to various volumes. For instance, at the beginning of the fourth volume, he writes:

> It seems as if the diseases of the soul in and of themselves, like everything dreadful and horrible, arouse the most attention; even the shudder that they often precipitate is accompanied by a certain secret enjoyment that is located in the wish to be severely shaken.
> (Es scheinet, als ob die Krankheiten der Seele schon an und für sich selbst, so wie alles Fürchterliche und Grauenvolle, am meisten die Aufmerksamkeit erregen, und sogar bei dem Schauder, den sie oft erwecken, ein gewisses geheimes Vergnügen mit einfließen lassen, das in dem Wunsche, heftig erschüttert zu werden, seinen Grund hat.)[35]

Here Moritz's psychological observations reference his own aesthetic theory; in the *Fragments from the Diary of a Spirit-Seer* (*Fragmente aus dem Tagebuche eines Geistersehers*), he notes that observation of painful or frightening experiences "shakes and elevates" ("erschüttert und erhebt") the observer.[36] This enjoyment may seem passive, but it actually requires a degree of participation by our own imaginations, and thus a form of exertion of force upon the object observed (I return hereinafter to the notion of observation as involving imagination and force).

Moritz understands the imagination as an essentially unconscious mental activity (as the soul's "essence," and as something "habitual" in nature), but this is an activity that, with insight, can be guided. The imaginative power of the soul is responsible for both the creation of art and for mental illness. From the introduction to the *Journal*'s fourth volume again:

---

[35] Moritz, ES 4: 7.

[36] Karl Philipp Moritz, *Fragmente aus dem Tagebuche eines Geistersehers*, in *Werke*, ed. Horst Günther (Frankfurt am Main: Insel, 1981) 3: 302. This passage also was cited in Chapter Two.

> Since the essence of the soul consists primarily of its *imaginative power*, the origin of mental illnesses must be sought in some kind of purposeless, habitual expression of this power. For when I speak here, for instance, of *inertia*, I am not speaking of it inasmuch as it is in the body, but rather inasmuch as it is founded in the *imaginative power* of the soul, and therefore it can also be helped through a better steering of the same power.
> (Da nun das Wesen der Seele vorzüglich in ihrer *vorstellenden Kraft* besteht, so muß auch der Ursprung der Seelenkrankheiten, in irgend einer zur Gewohnheit gewordenen unzweckmäßigen Äußerung dieser Kraft zu suchen seyn. Denn wenn ich hier z.B. von der *Trägheit* rede, so rede ich nicht von ihr, in so fern sie im Körper, sondern in so fern sie in der *vorstellenden Kraft* der Seele gegründet ist, und also auch durch eine beßre Lenkung derselben ihr wieder abgeholfen werden kann.)[37]

The description of the imaginative power that is responsible for mental illness as "purposeless" echoes the argument Moritz makes for the autonomy of the artwork in On the Figurative Imitation of the Beautiful (Über die bildende Nachahmung des Schönen, 1788). Here he reads meaning into appearance, and substance into surface: in contemporary art, he says, "appearance and reality...have become the same" ("Die Erscheinung ist mit der Wirklichkeit...eins geworden").[38] For Moritz, it is the surface that enables any direct understanding of substance; and in fact, in the artwork whose signs refer "only to themselves" ("nur auf sich selber zeigen"), substance has become surface, and vice versa.[39] Moritz's theory of aesthetic autonomy (of signs that have no purpose beyond and signify nothing outside the work of art), and of "appearing sense" ("erscheinender Sinn"), or meaning in appearance, produced during the same period as his empirical psychology, constructs a relationship between depicted and depiction, substance and appearance, and between signified and signifier that resembles the relationship implied in the Journal's cases between disorder and symptom, and in fact between body and mind. The fact that the symptom is all we have, particularly in the case of "mental disorders" ("Seelenkrankheiten") whose origins are impossible to discern, makes that symptom the real repository of meaning, just as the appearance of the beautiful art work provides our only direct access to the essence of beauty. Ultimately, it is our active imaginative power that, whether in the context of illness or of aesthetic creation, will

---

[37] Moritz, ES 4: 12.

[38] Karl Philipp Moritz, *Über die bildende Nachahmung des Schönen*, in *Beiträge zur Ästhetik*, eds. Hans Joachim Schrimpf and Hans Adler (Mainz: Dieterichsche Verlagsbuchhandlung, 1989) 78.

[39] Georg Braungart explains that for Moritz the observation of an art work's surface is exactly what provides direct, unmediated access to the entire experience of the beautiful, and that this relationship is mirrored in that between mind and body: "Die Oberfläche des Kunstwerks, die Oberfläche des menschlichen Körpers - sie ermöglichen die *unmittelbare* Erfahrung des Schönen," in "'Intransitive Zeichen': 'Die Signatur des Schönen' im menschlichen Körper bei Karl Philipp Moritz," *Rhetorik*, eds. Joachim Dyck, Walter Jens, and Gert Ueding, 13 (Tübingen: Niemeyer, 1994) 3.

bring us beyond the past and beyond ourselves, precisely by repetitively imitating the "model" ("Vorbild") of the past, even as we forget it:

> I imitate my model; I try to reach it…My model extends my goal higher than I do. I must try to reach this goal according to my abilities and in my own way; finally I must forget my model and seek, if possible, to extend my goal even higher.
> (Ich ahme meinem Vorbild nach; ich strebe ihm nach…Durch mein Vorbild ist mir bloß das Ziel höher, als von mir selbst, hinaufgesteckt. Nach diesem Ziele muß ich nun, nach meinen Kräften, auf meine Weise, streben; zuletzt mein Vorbild selbst vergessen, und suchen, wenn es möglich wäre, das Ziel noch weiter hinaus zu stecken.)[40]

Several of the subjects of the *Journal*'s case studies perform just such imitative, yet ultimately forgetful acts of imagination in order to live with and through their psychosomatic disorders.

The first volume includes a case entitled "The Strength of Self-Consciousness" ("Stärke des Selbstbewußtseyns").[41] One of the more straightforward defenses in the entire *Journal* of the insight and willpower that can lead to a "better steering" of the imagination, this is the report of one Herr Fischer, who identifies himself as a "teacher at the grey monastery in Berlin" ("Lehrer am grauen Kloster in Berlin"). He tells of nightly panic attacks, which he began to experience at age seventeen. Fischer achieves insight into these attacks over time—he eventually realizes, when an attack begins, that he will not die, but rather that the feelings he has are simulations of real problems: "my throat is *as if* pressed together. My entire body is *as if* in chains, or imprisoned" ("die Kehle ist *wie* zugedrückt. Der ganze Körper ist *wie* gefesselt, oder eingekerkert").[42] Fischer in fact can control the duration of the attack by exerting his will and consciously moving a limb—usually his right hand: "then the entire illusion disappeared fairly quickly" ("dann verschwand das ganze Hirngespinst ziemlich bald").[43] He repeats this act each time attacks occur, and they eventually become far less frequent.

Fischer concludes that while clearly there are mechanical and material causes for the attacks and for their cure, at the same time, there is "something higher in the soul" that transcends the materially induced pain of the moment.

> Precisely these experiences prove so convincingly that there is something higher in the soul which always remains the same despite all of the brain's confusions and disorganizations. This activity can be hindered by unnatural sensations that stem from disorder in the brain, and it can be numbed, but it cannot be destroyed.

---

[40] Moritz, *Beiträge zur Ästhetik* 29.
[41] Moritz, ES 1: 38-42.
[42] Ibid, 38.
[43] Ibid, 40.

> ([E]ben dieselben Erfahrungen, beweisen eben so unleugbar, daß noch etwas höheres in der Seele ist, welches bei allen Verwirrungen und Unordnungen des Gehirns doch immer dasselbe bleibt, und dessen Thätigkeit zwar durch widernatürliche aus Unordnungen im Gehirn entspringende Empfindungen gehindert, und gleichsam betäubt, aber wohl nicht vernichtet werden kann.)[44]

To overcome the attacks, Fischer must repeat what the attacks themselves do: he must mimic or re-represent them, and thereby become alien to himself. He must objectify or externalize himself, and dissociate from himself. He must make the familiar strange. He thus can break the cycle of a given attack, but only in a repetitive way—he applies the same "cure" every time, and it is almost always his right hand that he is able to raise.

The inclusion of the Fischer case demonstrates Moritz's interest in this type of experience of dissociation and objectification between body and mind, but elsewhere Moritz gives a somewhat different account of the mind's actual power during such experiences. A passage in his autobiographical "psychological novel" of 1785, *Anton Reiser*, addresses the mind's uncanny power to remember its own mortality, always in an encounter with another. When Anton reads Goethe's novella *The Sorrows of Young Werther* (*Die Leiden des jungen Werther*), the love story at the book's core does not particularly impress him, "for a person who loved and was loved seemed to him a strange and totally different type of being, because it was for him impossible ever to imagine himself as the object of a woman's love" ("denn ein Mensch der liebte und geliebt ward, schien ihm ein fremdes ganz von ihm verschiedenes Wesen zu sein, weil es ihm unmöglich fiel, sich selbst jemals, als einen Gegenstand der Liebe von einem Frauenzimmer zu denken").[45] Trapped in his neurotic subjectivity, Anton cannot represent himself to himself as a love object. He cannot project himself meaningfully into relationships of real alterity, real dialogue, or so it would seem. However, Anton does identify with a different and particularly uncanny aspect of Goethe's novella:

> The passage in which Werther compares life to a marionette play, where the puppets are pulled by a string, and he himself plays along or rather is played with in the same manner, the passage in which he grips his neighbor by the wooden hand and suddenly shudders—this passage awoke in Reiser the memory of a similar feeling which he had had often upon giving someone his hand. Due to force of habit one forgets that one has a body, a body subject to all of the laws of destruction in the corporeal universe, like a piece of wood that we saw or cut, and that one must move according to the exact same laws that govern man-made machines.
> —We are only occasionally aware of this destructibility and physicality of our body, and we shock ourselves when we suddenly feel that we believe ourselves to be something we are not, and are instead something that we fear.—When one extends his hand to another, and only sees and touches the other's body but has no knowledge of

[44] Moritz, ES 1: 41.
[45] Karl Philipp Moritz, *Anton Reiser. Ein psychologischer Roman* (Stuttgart: Reclam, 1990) 292.

> his thoughts, an idea of corporeality becomes livelier than when we observe our own body...
> (Die Stelle, wo Werther das Leben mit einem Marionettenspiel vergleicht, wo die Puppen am Draht gezogen werden, und er selbst auf die Art mitspielt oder vielmehr mitgespielt wird, seinen Nachbar bei der hölzernen Hand ergreift, und zurückschaudert—erweckte bei Reisern die Erinnerung an ein ähnliches Gefühl, das er oft gehabt hatte, wenn er jemandem die Hand gab. Durch die tägliche Gewohnheit vergißt man am Ende, daß man einen Körper hat, der ebensowohl allen Gesetzen der Zerstörung in der Körperwelt unterworfen ist, als ein Stück Holz, das wir zersägen oder zerschneiden, und daß er sich nach eben den Gesetzen, wie jede andere von Menschen zusammengesetzte körperliche Maschine bewegt.—Diese Zerstörbarkeit und Körperlichkeit unsers Körpers wird uns nur bei gewissen Anlässen lebhaft—und macht daß wir vor uns selbst erschrecken, indem wir plötzlich fühlen, daß wir etwas zu sein glaubten, was wir wirklich nicht sind, und statt dessen etwas sind, was wir zu sein uns fürchten.—Indem man nun einem andern die Hand gibt, und bloß den Körper sieht und berührt, indem man von dessen Gedanken keine Vorstellung hat, so wird dadurch die Idee der Körperlichkeit lebhafter, als sie es bei der Betrachtung unseres eignen Körpers wird...)[46]

Anton's reading of *Werther* reminds him of being reminded, during those anxious and uncanny moments of contact with the machine-like body of another, that he too has a mortal, transient body. This is a frightening, but enlightening, knowledge that comes through the body and through the mind's power to recognize and re-member the decaying form in which it is housed. While this experience is dissociative and jarring, it is not isolated. It is in the process of reaching out to others that we really feel real; only when we touch the other's body, but have no idea whatsoever what he is thinking, do we have any notion of the true nature of our own existence.[47]

The separation in Anton Reiser's mind and life between passionate love and the detached puppetry of human existence, revealed in his reading of the quintessential novella of emotional involvement, Goethe's *Werther*, implies that for Moritz these things were also separate—that Moritz, too, may have envisioned a split between emotion and reason, and between a Romantic involvement with the passions and the cold world of instrumental reason. But the story of Philomela in Ovid's *Metamorphoses*, which Moritz retells in his aesthetic theory, reveals something different: a re-involvement with the past and with passion through the use of an uncanny reason in the present. Ovid's (and Moritz's) heroine Philomela cannot speak because her tongue has been

---

[46] Moritz, *Anton Reiser. Ein psychologischer Roman* 293. The reference to Goethe's *Werther* is taken from Werther's letter to Lotte of January 20, 1772: "'Ich stehe wie vor einem Raritätenkasten und sehe die Männchen und Gäulchen vor mir herumrücken und frage mich oft, ob es nicht optischer Betrug ist. Ich spiele mit, vielmehr, ich werde gespielt wei eine Marionette und fasse manchmal meinen Nachbar an der hölzernen Hand und schaudere zurück." Cited in *Anton Reiser* 293.

[47] Ernst-Peter Wieckenberg analyzes mind-body relations in Moritz in more detail in "Die Schwindsucht, der Körper und die Aufklärung bei Karl Philipp Moritz." *Text + Kritik* 118/119 (1993) 15-23.

cut out by Tereus, her rapist. Yet she narrates the story of this crime by weaving its description into a linen cloth. In Moritz's words, the "silent characters" ("stummen Charaktere") in this garment, which is a physical thing but removed from the wounded body that produced it, "spoke louder than sounds that shatter the ear, because their sheer *being* bore witness to the shameful crime that produced them. The description here became one with the thing described—the severed tongue spoke through the speaking cloth" ("sprachen lauter als Töne, die das Ohr erschüttern, weil schon ihr bloßes *Daseyn* von dem schändlichen Frevel zeugte, der sie veranlaßt hatte. Die Beschreibung war hier mit dem Beschriebenen eins geworden—die abgelößte Zunge sprach durch das redende Gewebe").[48]

Fischer "cures" himself thanks to the insight that his body and mind are separate yet related entities, yet he must then force body and mind to work together in order to end the attacks. Moritz notes that just such a forceful application of insight is necessary for healing; the "better steering" of the imagination that can end illness cannot be achieved through mere exhortation to improve. "Mental disorders" (the "Seelenkrankheiten," which included problems as varied as envy, vanity, laziness, a lack of "human understanding" ["Menschenverstande"], melancholy, and inertia) are understood similarly to organic illness in this respect:

> But just as little as it would help a lame person if I wanted to say to him: move!—I would have just as little effect on an inert person if I were to say to him: don't be inert, or if I were to try to prove to him that it is wrong to be inert.
> I really rather must be on the lookout for the cause of his inertia in some direction that his power of imagination is accustomed to taking, and try to work against this habit in an exemplary manner.
> But now I discover that what keeps me active is always the *thinking-together of cause and effect*; the latter is only possible if the former precedes it. I therefore conclude that the inactive or inert person's spirit has become unaccustomed to *thinking cause and effect together properly*. He thinks of
> pleasant effects without taking heed of cause or of the force at work, which are after all the only things that enable these effects.
> (Eben so wenig aber, wie es dem Lahmen etwas helfen würde, wenn ich ihm sagen wollte, bewege dich—eben so wenig würd' ich dadurch auf den Trägen wirken, wenn ich ihm sagte: sei nicht träge, oder wenn ich ihm auch zu beweisen suchte, daß es unrecht sey, träge zu seyn.
> Ich muß vielmehr der Ursach seiner Trägheit in irgend einer verwöhnten Richtung seiner vorstellenden Kraft nachspähen, und der vorzüglich entgegen zu arbeiten suchen.
> Nun finde ich aber, daß dasjenige, was mich in Thätigkeit erhält, immer das *Zusammendenken von Ursach und Wirkung ist*, indem ich mir die letztere nur möglich denke, wenn die erstere vorhergegangen ist.
> Ich schließe also, daß der Unthätige, der Träge seinen Geist verwöhnt hat, *Wirkung und Ursach gehörig zusammenzudenken*. Er denkt sich angenehme Wirkungen, ohne

[48] Moritz, *Beiträge zur Ästhetik* 79.

> auf die Ursach oder die thätige Kraft Rücksicht zu nehmen, wodurch sie allein möglich gemacht werden können.)[49]

To get well, we must re-connect what has become disconnected; we must bring the past together with the present, and find again that to which we have become "unaccustomed." But it is in the uncanny disconnect between sensation and affect, between signified and sign, that art emerges. In fact, this dissociation is necessary for the creation of art, and, implicitly, for healing.

In the *Journal*, Moritz extends his interest in (or perhaps obsession with) self-observation to encompass the observation of other selves—or, more accurately, he becomes an observer of other self-observers. In so doing, he intends ultimately to produce a "socially critical psychological anthropology."[50] But the Journal's scientific orientation does not exclude the judgments of taste and the kinds of evaluations of sensory perceptions normally thought of as belonging to the realm of aesthetics.

In arguing that there is a close proximity between aesthetic theory and key concepts of early psychology, one that dates at the latest to 1742 and Alexander Baumgarten's *Texts for the Foundation of Aesthetics* (*Texte zur Grundlegung der Ästhetik*), Carsten Zelle states that "one of the maxims of the Enlightenment can be regarded as being the transformation of the 'spirit of observation' into the 'art of observation', i.e., the strengthening of the capacity 'to take exact notice of the differences in what is perceived.'"[51] Specifically, practitioners of "Erfahrungsseelenkunde," or *empirical* psychology, also engage in techniques of "Experimentalseelenlehre," or *experimental* psychology, in which the expert not only observes but actually exerts force on his surroundings in order to change them and to become part of the perceptual experience—to engage actively with the object of study.

In 1759, Johann Sulzer unites the two approaches when he states that, like physical facts, psychological facts can and must be researched "through experience and experiment" ("durch Erfahrung und Experiment") as

---

49 Moritz, ES 4: 8-9. These introductory comments are included in a section Moritz added after the first three volumes were prepared, and are entitled "Revision der drei ersten Bände dieses Magazins."

50 Translated in part from Sybille Frickmann, "'Jeder Mensch nach dem ihm eignen Maaß' - Karl Philipp Moritz' Konzept einer 'Seelenkrankheitskunde,'" *The Germany Quarterly* 61.3 (1988) 387: "Durch die Sammlung psychologischer Fallgeschichten verschiedenster Ausrichtung [...] sollte bei gleichzeitigem Verzicht auf spekulative Theorienbildung das breite Spektrum menschlichen Verhaltens zunächst einmal gesammelt und gesichtet werden, um im Anschluß daran auf der Grundlage dieser empirischen 'Fakta' eine in ihren Ansätzen bereits gesellschaftskritische psychologische Anthropologie zu konzipieren."

51 Carsten Zelle, "Experiment, Experience, and Observation in Eighteenth-Century Anthropology and Psychology" 94.

well as through "observation" ("Beobachtung").[52] The practice of observing already places the object of observation "into a state in which it would otherwise not be," says Zelle, and thus observation is already a type of "force."[53] The practice of recording and thus representing one's observations only reinforces this dynamic, as even the most descriptive listing of facts involves, in the words of Johann Krüger's text on mood states ("Gemüthsbewegungen") of 1746, "forc(ing) nature to show us that which she had intended to conceal from our eyes" ("[die Natur] dazu zu zwingen, uns das zu zeigen, was sie von unseren Augen verbergen wollte").[54] Krüger, whose *Toward an Experimental Psychology* (*Versuch einer Experimental-Seelenlehre*) of 1756 was likely a substantial influence on Moritz's thinking about psychology,[55] wished to use his power of observation to unlock the "dark," and explicitly female, side of nature; he goes so far as to analogize experimental psychology to rape.[56]

Practitioners of experimental psychology in the mid-eighteenth century, including Krüger, debated the acceptability and value of the overt exertion of force upon the experimental object. For instance, Krüger initially deemed it acceptable to experiment on human criminals (he later retracts this), but not on animals. He also espoused the idea that pregnant women's thoughts could affect their fetuses, saying that a kind of external force is necessary to direct those thoughts positively and properly. In the passage below, he expresses this conviction by recommending beautiful art as a defense against fetal deformity.

> This is not the place to prove this; rather, I refer here only to experience, and maintain that the influence that one contends a mother's imagination has on the child is even greater than imagined. Accordingly, all mothers should properly assume, at the beginning of pregnancy, the calmness of mood and the satisfaction that come of innocence and virtue. It is said that the Chinese hang beautiful paintings in the rooms of pregnant women and sing for the women songs about virtue. I cannot deny that I approve of this habit, and that I agree with them in this matter.
> (Es ist hier der Ort nicht dieses zu beweisen, sondern ich berufe mich hierinnen allein auf die Erfahrung, und halte dafür, daß der Einfluß, welchen man von der Einbildungskraft der Mutter auf das Kind behauptet, noch grösser sey, als man ihn

52 Johann Georg Sulzer, *Kurzer Begriff aller Wißenschaften* (Leipzig, 1759) section 204. More on Sulzer can be found in Wolfgang Riedel's "Anthropologische Achsendrehung und Wende zur Ästhetik bei Johann Georg Sulzer," in Hans-Jürgen Schings, ed., *Der ganze Mensch. Anthropologie und Literatur im 18. Jahrhundert* (Stuttgart: Metzler, 1994) 410-439.

53 Zelle, "Experiment, Experience, and Observation in Eighteenth-Century Anthropology and Psychology" 95.

54 Johann Gottlob Krüger, *Neue Lehre von den Gemüthsbewegungen / mit einer Vorrede vom Gelde; begleitet von Herrn Johann Gottlob Krügern, Der Weltweisheit und Arzneygelährtheit Doctorn und Professorn auf der Königl. Preuszl. Friedrichs Universität* (Halle: C.H. Hemmerde, 1746) 15.

55 Zelle, "Experiment, Experience, and Observation in Eighteenth-Century Anthropology and Psychology" 99.

56 Ibid, 100.

> sich vorzustellen pflegt. Diesem zufolge sollten sich alle Mütter vornemlich im Anfange der Schwangerschaft der Gemüths-Ruhe und einem Vergnügen überlassen, das auf Unschuld und Tugend gegründet ist. Man sagt, daß die Chineser den schwangern Frauen schöne Gemählde in die Stuben hängen, und ihnen Lieder, welche von der Tugend handeln, vorsingen. Ich kann nicht leugnen, daß ich diese Gewohnheit billige, und also in diesem Glaubens-Artikel mit ihnen einig bin.)[57]

While the injunction to model beautiful, virtuous art for pregnant women in hopes that this will make them and their unborn children more virtuous may be reminiscent of Novalis's call for women to meditate on the portrait of the queen every night before going to bed,[58] the connection between mind and body implied in Krüger's statement expresses more than moralistic posturing. Krüger's appeal for the use of beauty to ward off a literally crippling, deforming fear is typical of the intersection of psychology and aesthetics prevalent in Moritz's thought as well.

The idea that "force" can be a legitimate part of observation is also apparent in the above passage: the stage-managed change of a woman's psyche via a change in her physical environment is in turn supposed to change her body for the better. Krüger here implicitly acknowledges that our perception of reality always depends to some extent on our own participation in external events. In other words, even when we are just thinking about an external object, we are enacting change; we are engaging with the object. In his "Prospectives for an Experimental Psychology" ("Aussichten zu einer Experimentalseelenlehre"), Moritz himself tends in this interpretive direction, saying that the types of observation we conduct of others must resemble—or, in a sense, repeat—our observation of ourselves.[59] All observation involves self-observation, and self-observation already entails looking "outward," in that we must externalize or instrumentalize parts of ourselves in order to be able to observe those parts. Unfortunately, says Moritz, this externalization and objectification can always only be partial:

> What has become of my intention to be an observer of man and an observer of myself? Who gives me the coldness and also the cheerfulness of the soul that I need in order to observe all that occurs as a play, and the people who trouble me as actors? Indeed, if one were not also caught up in this play oneself…
> (Wo ist aber mein Vorsatz geblieben, Beobachter des Menschen, Beobachter meiner selbst zu sein? Wer gibt mir Kälte und Heiterkeit der Seele dazu, alles was geschieht, so wie ein Schauspiel zu betrachten, und die Personen, die mich kränken, wie Schauspieler? Ja wenn man nur nicht selber mit im Spiele begriffen wäre…)[60]

---

[57] Johann Gottlob Krüger, *Gedanken von Erziehung der Kinder* (Halle: Carl Hermann Hemmerde, 1760) 18-19.
[58] Novalis, *Glauben und Liebe*, in *Werke*, ed. Gerhard Schulz (Munich: Beck, 1969).
[59] Zelle, "Experiment, Experience, and Observation in Eighteenth-Century Anthropology and Psychology" 103; Moritz, *Werke* vol. 3: *Erfahrung, Sprache, Denken* (1993) 93, 92.
[60] Karl Philipp Moritz, *Beiträge zur Philosophie des Lebens*, in *Werke* 3: 16.

We can, however, act as if we were not part of life's melodrama; this lifting of ourselves as observers out of daily drama and subsequent exaltation of ourselves to the status of "creator of the universe" ("Schöpfer des Weltalls")[61] is a simulation only, but the appearance of objectivity gives us something of its substance as well.

If we take a bit further Zelle's argument about the proximity between empiricism and experiment, and between psychological and aesthetic theory, while considering Krüger's thinking about the force inherent in observation, we can read the Journal as a text that exerts the kind of "force" that transformed mere observation into a type of art. On the one hand, Moritz emphasizes that his *Journal* merely presents information and provides a forum for its public consumption; yet his choice of cases such as the one below produces similar reactions in the reader as the novella Werther produced in *Anton Reiser*—these odd tales of dissociation between mind and body, between the sign and the thing signified, and between observer and object of observation evoke an "idea of corporeality" that is of a different order than that produced by everyday existence.

In the case entitled "A Physiological-Psychological Problem" ("Ein physiologisch-psychologisches Problem") contributed by Herr Tiemann, a city official from Minden, dissociation occurs on multiple levels in a situation characterized by bizarre repetition. Tiemann relates the story of a woman who, during each of her seven pregnancies (all of which resulted in healthy children), lost a finger. The loss of the finger in each instance was preceded by burning sensations (Fischer also mentions experiencing burning sensations during his nighttime attacks). With each pregnancy

> the digits fell off in the following order. During the first pregnancy the first section of the middle finger—during the second the first section of the index finger—during the third a section of the little finger—during the fourth a section of the thumb—during the fifth, on the right hand, the first section of the index finger—during the sixth part of the little finger—during the seventh part of the thumb. The woman indeed had preserved the fallen-off bones, and promised to give them to me already last year; but after exhaustive searching she could not find any, which I much regret.
> (sind die Glieder in folgender Ordnung abgefallen. Bei der ersten Schwangerschaft fiel an der linken Hand das erste Glied des Mittelfingers—bei der zweiten das erste Glied am Zeigefinger—bei der dritten das am kleinen oder Ohrfinger—bei der vierten am Daumen—bei der fünften an der rechten Hand das erste Glied des Zeigefingers—bei der sechsten am kleinen oder Ohrfinger—bei der siebenten am Daumen. Die Frau hatte zwar die herausgefallenen Knochen aufbewahrt, und versprach mir schon voriges Jahr diesselbe zu geben; allein nach allem möglichen Durchsuchen konnte sie keinen finden, welches ich sehr bedauerte.)[62]

The woman's children essentially are parts of her body walking around in the world; externalized parts of herself. They are gone, but not gone: like Freud's

[61] Moritz, *Werke* 3: 16.
[62] Moritz, ES 4: 224.

"ghostly" artifact collection, her bones are dead but unburied. The lost fingers, or rather her deformed hands with the places where the fingers were —the lack of fingers—is an uncanny reminder of the loss of self, the parts of the self that are now walking around in the world. Nicholas Royle's assertion that "(a)s a crisis of the proper and natural, it (the uncanny) disturbs any straightforward sense of what is inside and what is outside"[63] applies strikingly to this woman's "method" of commemorating her own anxiety and loss.

Losing fingers during anxiety attacks is an uncanny repetition of childbirth and symbolizes loss of self; that loss, that traumatic separation of self from self, is sustained by the continuing presence of the absence of fingers. The uncanny transformation of repeated childbirth into repeated self-mutilation culminates in the woman's reply to the question of how many children she has:

> instead of an answer the woman raised both hands and showed my friend that she had only three whole, undamaged fingers left, namely on the right hand the ring- and middle finger, on the left hand the ring finger.
> (statt der Antwort hob die Frau beide Hände in die Höhe und zeigte meinem Freund, daß sie nur noch drei ganze Finger, nämlich in der rechten Hand den Ring- und Mittelfinger, in der linken Hand den Ringfinger unverletzt übrig hatte.)[64]

The representation of anxiety about the loss of self symbolized by childbirth in this case is indeed a strange retelling, or rather pre-telling, of Freud's account of the loss of fingers or of the hand as representative of castration anxiety. In a 1924 essay entitled "Fausse Reconnaissance," Freud explains that the redirection of anxiety into the figure of the finger is a form of "false memory"—a confusion of recollections of intention and action; or, remembering doing something (something one *intended* to do) that one has actually never done.[65] The woman in Herr Tiemann's account remembers preserving her fallen-off fingers, but now cannot find them, and now has only their absence to "remind" her of the children she has "lost."

Like Freud, Moritz's interest is in the relationship of imagination (or of fantasy) to death (or loss). In a note appended to this case, Moritz speculates that this woman must have been able, through the power of imagination, to occasion the loss of her own fingers: "It will be difficult to uncover a physiological basis here" ("Ein physiologischer Grund möchte doch hier wohl schwerlich aufzufinden seyn").[66] In a sense, the woman is making an unconscious choice, choosing this uncanny form of rebellion

---

[63] Nicholas Royle, *The Uncanny: An Introduction* (New York and London: Routledge, 2003) 2.
[64] Moritz, ES 4: 226.
[65] Freud recounts here part of his work with the Wolf-Man, who remembers things he has never done, thus confusing his recollection of an intention to do a thing with the actual performance of the action. See "Fausse Reconnaissance (Déjà Raconté) in Psycho-Analysis," SE 13: 206.
[66] Moritz, ES 4: 226.

against an otherwise claustrophobic existence and thereby participating in an extremely non-normative expression of desire. The "silent characters" of Philomela's cloth are here more silent still—they have become absent fingers on mutilated hands—hands marked not only by the loss of digits, but by the ring finger that remains, symbolizing the marriage responsible for the entire situation.

This self-amputation is one of the more powerful examples of the "study of mental signs" ("Seelenzeichenkunde") in the *Journal*. Like Herr Fischer, the fingerless mother exerts a kind of will upon her own body, but she perpetuates the attacks on herself, while he stops his attacks though he cannot "cure" himself. Both experience a "dissociation between sensation and affect" that the neurologist Antonio Damasio has identified as uncanny (as a reminder of something we would rather forget, here a reminder of loss of self, of threats to the self, and potentially of seeing one's own children as threats). Both subjects experience this dissociation and they experience a basic disturbance in their "extended consciousness," or in what Damasio calls the "autobiographical self."[67]

Moritz is interested especially in the aesthetic appeal of exactly those types of disturbances. *Anton Reiser* was conceived originally as a fictionalization of a case study from one of the sections of the *Journal*.[68] Anton's life seems characterized by nothing but disturbances in self-consciousness. His melancholy, or what Moritz calls "weariness of life" ("Lebensüberdruß"), results from his personality type, which is "vain" (or "eitel"). And Moritz's notion of the kind of "vanity" that results in melancholy sounds very much like narcissism. Again, all observation is fundamentally an extension of, or repetition of, self-observation. Anton Reiser arrives at the depressing and frightening realization that he will never escape himself, that he is the entire world, the only self and all others at once. This excess of self is at the same time empty: Anton has, "from childhood on, *too little existence of his own*" ("von Kindheit auf *zu wenig eigene Existenz*").[69] He suffers from an uncanny split within himself; he has "fundamentally always a double, totally divorced inner and outer life" ("im Grunde immer ein doppeltes, ganz voneinander verschiedenes inneres und äußeres Leben").[70]

Another case in the *Journal*, the "Example of a Strange Powerlessness" ("Beyspiel einer sonderbaren Ohnmacht"), evinces more of this uncanny self-doubling. As in the previous cases, a subject experiences a dissociation, a self-externalization: "A young woman had long lain ill due to a

---

[67] Antonio Damasio, *The Feeling of What Happens: Body and Emotion in the Making of Consciousness* (San Diego, New York, and London: Harcourt, 1999) 75.
[68] Or "Seelennaturkunde;" see Schrimpf, *Karl Philipp Moritz* 35.
[69] Moritz, *Anton Reiser. Ein psychologischer Roman* 413-414.
[70] Ibid, 246.

serious weakness of the nerves, and finally she seemed to all appearances to be dead" ("Ein junges Frauenzimmer hatte an einer heftigen Nervenschwäche lange krank gelegen, und war endlich allem menschlichen Ansehen nach gestorben").[71] She is placed in a coffin, mourned, but on the day of her burial, she convulses back to life. Afterwards she reports a sense of overwhelming anxiety not unlike that reported by Herr Fischer—her body initially will not respond to her commands. Finally, it is the thought of being buried alive that gives her body the ability to reveal what's going on in her mind, and she convulses and screams. C.F. Pockels, one of Moritz's co-editors, then adds that this case is "a warning about how careful one must be in burying corpses, so that they are not buried too early" ("eine Warnung, wie vorsichtig man bey dem Begraben der Leichen verfahren muß, daß sie nicht zu früh begraben werden").[72] The use of the word "corpses" ("Leichen") is odd here, since the implication is that one can be buried accidentally when one is not actually yet a corpse. The case study's emphasis is on the representation or misrepresentation of reality rather than on reality itself.

Nicholas Royle states that being buried alive, or even the fear of live burial alone, is for many the quintessential uncanny; Jan Bondeson calls it "our most primal fear."[73] Live burial stands in converse relationship to the figure of uncanny "ghosts" who are dead but *un*buried and thus sustain their own loss, and sustain their collectors through the loss of the past they represent. In live burial, the undead are buried, and this is uncanny in a different way. The young woman in the "Example of a Strange Powerlessness" is in a sense simultaneously dead and alive; she feels as if she is having a dream in which she is dead. This representation of the dream is for all intents and purposes her reality during the time she is thought dead, and yet it is not true—she is actually also alive.

In *Flesh in the Age of Reason*, Roy Porter maintains that a "growing anxiety about premature burial" in the late eighteenth century coincided with a "new concern with ascertaining the true signs of death and snatching back the 'apparently dead.'"[74] He traces the prevalence of this fear to a paper that a Parisian anatomy professor named Jacques-Bénigne Winslow published in 1740, addressing the

> uncertainty of the signs of death: absence of pulse or breathing were not to be taken as definite marks—the onset of putrefaction alone was a reliable indicator of irreversible dissolution. 'Lifeless' patients who could not safely be declared dead should be subjected to resuscitation procedures: tickling the nose with a quill, shrieking into the

71 Moritz, ES 5: 3, 205.
72 Ibid, 207.
73 Royle, *The Uncanny: An Introduction* 142; Jan Bondeson, *Buried Alive: The Terrifying History of Our Most Primal Fear* (New York and London: W.W. Norton & Company, 2001).
74 Porter, *Flesh in the Age of Reason* 214.

> ears, cutting the soles of the feet with razors, inserting needles under the nails or thrusting a hot poker up the anus. Burial should be delayed.[75]

Despite the prevalent fears about live burial in the eighteenth and nineteenth centuries (Moritz's friend Salomon Maimon argued on behalf of Jews accused of burying their dead too early; by the early nineteenth century, bells were installed occasionally in coffins as a "safety" measure), it rarely actually happened. Anxiety about it in the nineteenth century arose roughly at the same time as did the popularity of Gothic fiction and of its predecessors in the German tradition (including Carl Grosse's *The Genius* of 1791).

In the essay on "The Uncanny," Freud interprets fears of live burial as representative of "the phantasy...of intra-uterine existence" ("der Phantasie vom Leben im Mutterleib").[76] The dead but unburied ghost who acts to remind of and thus sustain the loss of the past, is a representation of memory beyond the individual's mind and an acknowledgment of transience, mobility, and lack of return. Live burial, the burial of someone who is *as if* dead ("scheintot"), is a kind of fantasy of, or representation of, a "lascivious" ("lüstern") desire for return, and for redemption, since "life in the uterus" is a life before time and its mistakes. Live burial is, in the classic psychoanalytic view, a return of a repressed fantasy. This is an important reading and applies to many texts, but I also wish to argue that the uncanniness of live burial is more complex and multivalent than the reading of it as a return to an infantile fantasy might suggest.

I rely again on Gregg Horowitz's work to argue that there is an alternative way of viewing the uncanny power of live burial (or fear of it); he contends the following in a discussion of burial in general:

> Burial rituals are not for preventing decay but rather for preventing it from being witnessed. For the sake of the dead—or for memory's sake, as we say—such rituals hobble our vision....The dead have a claim on us the normative power of which is captured in the ritualized demand for entombment.[77]

Horowitz's argument is that the dead need our help rather than vice versa—it is not so much that we wish to be protected from the sight of decay and from reminders of our own inevitable deaths as that the dead are in danger from *us*, the living. Specifically, they are in danger of being instrumentalized by us, because they cannot speak for themselves. Therefore we must hide them *from* us, and we must honor "the claims of the dead" through rituals of grieving and remembering.[78] Burial is an acknowledgment by us that the dead can no

---

[75] Porter, *Flesh in the Age of Reason* 215.

[76] Freud, "Das Unheimliche," GW 12: 257/ "The Uncanny," SE 17: 244.

[77] Gregg Horowitz, *Sustaining Loss: Art and Mournful Life* (Stanford: Stanford University Press, 2001) 151.

[78] Horowitz, *Sustaining Loss: Art and Mournful Life* 152.

longer "press their own claims."[79] The display of corpses such as Lenin's is repulsive because, by displaying this body rather than hiding it, we act *as if* Lenin could still speak for himself.[80] Like the display of Lenin's dead-but-unburied body, live burial is wrong—it respects the claims neither of the dead nor of the living.

The argument can be shifted away from Horowitz's emphasis on claims and responsibilities, and yet related to his argument that burial of the dead is a ritual that "hobbles our vision"—that burial allows repression of our own acknowledgment of death to continue. By hobbling our vision, burial renders our vision fuzzy, causes loss of focus, allows repression to continue. But the uncanny moment of live burial, burial by mistake, brings the fuzziness into focus as we confront the repressed fear. At the same time, live burial is a tremendous violation of the claims not just of the living—it is a huge mistake, the person should not be buried because she still lives and speaks, can make claims for herself—but of the dead as well. The live buried person is literally not at home— she does not belong among the dead, where she violates their silence and violates the rituals the living have to respect the claims of the dead, rituals of grieving and remembering. Live burial turns the respectful memorial rituals of the living, rituals that are honoring of claims, into lies; it violates memory of self and of community. Although the trope of live burial does not appear in every text of the Romantic era, the fears that it induces, including claustrophobia, fear of suffocation, of being trapped, of being violated, of not being able to speak for or make claims for oneself—these are all indeed fears that contribute to the liminal state of uncanny melancholy.

In the *Journal*, Moritz and Pockels refrain from speculating about why this particular young woman, this chambermaid, would have this experience. But, like Herr Fischer and the fingerless mother, the chambermaid could be seen as suffering when she observes herself, when she tries to "force" her internal experience to coincide with her external reality. The uncanny part of the experience, and the horror, come not from being asleep or having children or having fainted (for a very long time), but from being aware that one is to a large degree at least temporarily powerless because body and mind are completely out of synch. The subjects of Moritz's case studies do not occupy the same space with themselves—they are at a remove from themselves, and the observer/psychologist (or, the reader of the journal) is at once in close proximity to them, intimate with them, knowing intimate details about them, and at an even further remove than they are from themselves. These case studies make the familiar strange, and the strange "strangely familiar."

---

[79] Horowitz, *Sustaining Loss: Art and Mournful Life* 153.
[80] Ibid, 153.

And again, while Moritz does not engage in interpretation of the chambermaid's symptoms, in the fourth volume of the *Journal*, he writes at some length about the "desire to die" ("Sterbensbegierde"), or a desire to "be no more" ("nicht mehr seyn"), which he considers synonymous with "weariness of life" ("Lebensüberdruß").[81] The desire to die, even if only for a while, is an excessive reaction to excessive feelings, and this desire is appealing. It appeals to what Moritz calls our "unhappy tendency towards theater" ("[unserem] unglücklichen Hang zum Theater"),[82] but also to our desire to engage more productively in the art of observation. Moritz realized the constructed nature of the empirical data that he was collecting, and realized his own part in that construction, as a self-observer observing other self-observations. The *Journal* as a whole thus participates in a form of aestheticization, a theatricalization (an "Inszenierung") of illness—by virtue of its very re-representation of cases characterized by uncanny repetition, and aided by Moritz's interest in aesthetic theory. It reverses the old relationship between aesthetics and science: cosmic law, a matter of science, once postulated that the universe and cosmic law must be characterized by harmony and order. But for Moritz, the psyche has become the cosmos, and psychic law is characterized by disharmony and disorder.

The *Journal of Empirical Psychology* exemplifies a tendency toward aestheticization in early psychology and psychiatry, and this tendency would only increase through the early decades of the nineteenth century—for instance, with the renewed popularity in the 1820s of magnetism and mesmerism. By giving pride of place to case studies that evince repetitive (or uncanny) neurotic symptoms, Moritz re-tells (or repeats) central elements of his own neuroses. Many of the journal's subjects suffer from problems similar to Moritz's own, including depression, "melancholy," and sexual dysfunction; they also have "an unhappy inclination to theater." The empirical psychology of the late eighteenth century did not concern itself with healing any of these problems, but it was preoccupied with the consequences of observation and of self-observation. As Carsten Zelle explains, for Moritz, the "incentive to get to know oneself brings about the opposite result. The self-observer becomes alien to himself. Reading Moritz' *Aussichten* or *Vorschlag* reveals a contrary state of affairs, namely, that self-observation leads to self-alienation."[83] The activity of one's own mind seems to be the activity of someone else. Moritz's case studies are records of observations, of people observing themselves and others. The following section takes up another instance of such meta-observation, in the six years of detailed notes left by Friedrich Schlegel about the psychological states of his friend and "patient," the Countess Lesniowska.

---

[81] Moritz, ES 4: 1, 24.

[82] Ibid, 66.

[83] Zelle, "Experiment, Experience and Observation in Eighteenth-Century Anthropology and Psychology" 103.

2.2. F. Schlegel, *Protocol of the Magnetic Treatment of the Countess Lesniowska* (*Tagebuch [über die magnetische Behandlung der Gräfin Lesniowska]*)

Although Schlegel's fragments on magnetism were composed late in his career, their emphasis on reciprocally related concepts (such as material and real, magnetic and magical) recalls the tone of many of his philosophical and historical writings, including those written before his conversion to Catholicism in 1808. But for six years (1820-1826) Schlegel turned metaphorical musings into real-life practice, when he recorded in minute detail the magnetic treatment of the Viennese countess Franziska Lesniowska. In turn, these treatments in effect transformed a real woman into a representation of Schlegel's view of the future: the Countess's attacks intensified, and she ultimately became a nun, thus joining what Schlegel envisioned as the "new age" of the Church on earth.

Schlegel's protocols of the Countess's treatments have been almost completely ignored; the notes were not discovered until 1967 in the private collection of the painter Ludwig Schnorr, who also attended the treatments and about whom I say more below.[84] However, these records of the therapy and of its consequences for Lesniowska's mental and physical state constitute significant documentation of an important phase of Romanticism and a vital moment in cultural history. The Romantic fascination with mesmerism, magnetism, the occult, and parapsychology has long been acknowledged as influential for later depth psychology and the development of psychotherapy, but that fascination also reveals much about intersections between psychiatric treatment and aesthetics. Specifically, Schlegel's Romantic preoccupation with esoteric psychiatry, and the connections he attempts to make between psychiatry and aesthetic theory, demonstrate that well before Freud a symptom of an illness could also be understood as an uncanny signifier of a returning memory.

This preoccupation is most evident in the late phase of Schlegel's career (lasting from roughly 1818 until his death in 1829), which was generally ignored by philosophers and literary critics during his lifetime. Their lack of interest arose partly from the fact that Schlegel spent much of his time during these years in government service as a liaison between Metternich's administration and the Catholic Church in Vienna, and partly from his more pronounced turn to the right and esoteric thought. Between 1820 and 1823 he worked for the reactionary Late Romantic journal *Concordia*, and in 1825 decided to remove his Early Romantic novel *Lucinde*, an erotic piece with progressive tendencies, from his collected works. He also alienated friends during this same period, including Ludwig Tieck, whose

[84] Ursula Behler's detailed introduction to Volume 35 of the *Kritische Ausgabe* is the most comprehensive text about the protocols.

baffled response to Schlegel's revelation of apocalyptic visions was "Man, do you really believe all of that?"[85]

However, Tieck offered a more ambiguous view of his friend's convictions after hearing Schlegel's final lectures in Dresden:

> He found no satisfaction in science or in art, also not in faith, in his Christianity. He had to build up something incomprehensible here as well, where no one would understand him, and he dismissed every layperson almost scornfully. He was more rebellious than any apostle.
> (Genüge fand er in keiner Wissenschaft und in keinem Kunstwerk, auch im Glauben, in seinem Christentum nicht. Er mußte auch hier etwas Unbegreifliches aufbauen, wo keiner ihn verstand, und wo er jeden Laien fast höhnisch abwies. Dreister als irgendein Apostel.)[86]

According to Ursula Behler, who edited the volume of the *Kritische Ausgabe* containing Schlegel's protocols of the Countess Lesniowska's magnetic treatments, much of *Zur Geschichte und Politik* (*On History and Politics*, 1820-1828) is "driven by an esoteric hypothesis…that, among other things, is based on an interpretation of the new 'magnetic and magic knowledge'" ("…von einer esoterischen Hypothese getragen…die u.a. auf einer Interpretation des neuen 'magnetischen und magischen Wissens' basiert").[87] Similarly, Norbert Miller has pointed out that Schlegel's late writings replace his earlier emphasis on reflexivity with a much more monolithic belief: what had been a dialogue between individuals becomes stylized as a relationship between "prophet and congregation."[88] At the same time, Miller resists seeing Schlegel's esoteric turn as negating the aims of Early Romantic philosophy, with its ironically self-aware and inherently skeptical attitude towards its own "desire for infinity" ("Sehnsucht nach dem Unendlichen").[89] Rather, in the decade before his death in 1829, Schlegel melds his philosophies of the self and history into a new objectivity, a "true" realism in which the individual's

---

[85] "Mensch, glaubst du denn wirklich das alles?" Dankwart Guratzsch, "Dreister als irgendein Apostel. Friedrich Schlegel gibt auch an seinem 200. Geburtstag seinen Biographen und Kritikern noch immer Rätsel auf," *Die Welt* 60 (March 11, 1972) IV.

[86] "Genüge fand er in keiner Wissenschaft und in keinem Kunstwerk, auch im Glauben, in seinem Christentum nicht. Er mußte auch hier etwas Unbegreifliches aufbauen, wo keiner ihn verstand, und wo er jeden Laien fast höhnisch abwies. Dreister als irgendein Apostel," Guratzsch IV.

[87] Schlegel, KA 35: vii-viii.

[88] Norbert Miller, "Sehnsucht nach dem Unendlichen. Vor 150 Jahren starb Friedrich Schlegel," *Süddeutsche Zeitung* 10 (January 13-14, 1979) 138.

[89] Ibid, 138.

relationship to God provides an alternative to empiricism as well as the ultimately unsatisfying constructions of idealism.[90]

To several people who had contact with Schlegel during these years, however, he simply was becoming harder to understand, and his religiosity stunned them. Some blamed Schlegel's wife, Dorothea Veit, with whom he was no longer actually living but whose influence was presumed to be profound. In just one example, Friedrich von Gentz, a propagandist for the Austrian Army, wrote in a letter to the Austrian politician Johann Philipp Freiherr von Wessenberg on May 18, 1816: "Schlegel was never suited for practical activities, and for several years a religious, or better yet, churchly fervor has made him a complete fool; his wife has a large part in this" ("Zu praktischen Geschäften war [Schlegel] nie tauglich; und seit einigen Jahren hat ihn die religiöse, oder besser kirchliche Wut vollends zum Narren gemacht, woran seine Frau großen Anteil hat").[91] While Dorothea indeed played a role in Schlegel's conversion to Catholicism in the very early years of the nineteenth century, by the time he was living in Vienna, other women were inspiring him and serving as concrete representations of his philosophical constructs. In addition to the countess Franziska Lesniowska, Schlegel studied during his Vienna years at least three other women who combined clairvoyant abilities with nervous symptoms, all of whom underwent lengthy magnetic treatments.[92] He saw these women as modern embodiments of medieval mystics; like the revived practice of magnetism itself, they represented what he referred to in the fragments on magnetism as the "stirring of the new age." In order to fulfill this role, each of these women, with their malfunctioning but prophetic bodies, needed one thing in particular: "men of intellect" ("Männer von Geist").[93]

For Schlegel, magnetism was a practice that presented rich possibilities for deploying his philosophical agenda, whose search for a "true realism" created an alternative to an overly instrumental materialism or an unworkable idealism. The "christliche Magnetotherapie"[94] that Schlegel favored involved the use of a small wooden box resembling an altar.[95]

---

90 Ernst Behler elaborates on Schlegel's use of God to effect a turn away from idealism as follows: "In scharfem Abrücken von dem idealistischen 'Abgrund des Absoluten' erarbeitet Schlegel eine Theorie des liebenden Gottes, der sich...dem sehnenden Ich als das allein befriedigende Objekt zu erkennen gibt und in dem die Einheit, wie auch die Selbständigkeit aller Lebens- und Geistesformen allein gesichert ist." In "Philosophie in Notizheften. Friedrich Schlegels Lehrjahre—Rechenschaft vor der Nachwelt," *Rheinischer Merkur* 9.1 (March 1963) 13.

91 Schlegel, KA VII: cxviii.

92 Two of these women are denoted in Schlegel's very fragmentary notebooks from this period as "Căcilia P." and "Marie A."; see KA 35.

93 Letter from Friedrich to Dorothea Schlegel on September 28, 1818, KA 35: xvi.

94 Ibid, xxxvii.

95 Scheuerbrandt, "Die Stimme der Natur. Dietrich Georg Kiesers Auffassung vom tierischen Magnetismus" 235.

Magnetic treatments simulated the performance of Christian rituals in more ways than one. Sessions often evoked the same language and aesthetic staging of suffering, redemption, illness, and erotic desire prevalent in Catholic services. As Cristina Mazzoni has noted, understanding a sufferer's "*hysterica passio*" as reenacting the "*Passio Christi*" persisted throughout the nineteenth century into decadent and symbolist literature,[96] movements influenced strongly by Romanticism.

The real Franziska Lesniowska (1781-1853) suffered from an enormous litany of psychosomatic symptoms, some of which may have been related to past psychic trauma. Countess Lesniowska's husband committed suicide in 1810, about ten years before she fell ill, and when her children were very small. Her sister killed herself in 1817. Both husband and sister jumped out of windows and died young. In early 1820, the ailing Lesniowska had her first clairvoyant vision. By late 1820, she was gravely ill with what her doctor diagnosed as "weakness and intensity of her nerves" ("Geschwächtheit und Heftigkeit ihrer Nerven").[97] Her symptoms included overwhelming sleepiness, joint pain, anxiety, gastrointestinal distress, nightmares, and visions often involving large male figures. No explanation was ever found for why she became so sick at this particular time and remained so, with periods of remission, until her death in 1853.

However, when Schlegel and Lesniowska first met via family connections in Frankfurt in 1818, her symptoms were not yet evident to him. He did feel strongly attracted to her, as he reported to his wife Dorothea:

> The countess pleased me very much, and I think I will see much of her in Vienna. (…) She appears to sacrifice herself very much for her children, but other than that she seems to have filled her soul completely with religion and to live within it. You can easily imagine, that I am already in my way counting her as one of my own: we got to know one another very quickly. (…) …she seeks and needs men of intellect….
> (Die Gräfin hat mir sehr gefallen, und ich denke sie viel zu sehen in Wien. […] Sie scheint sich sehr für ihre Kinder aufzuopfern, außerdem aber ihre Seele ganz von der Religion gefüllt zu haben und in dieser zu leben. Du kannst leicht denken, daß ich sie schon nach meiner Art unter die Meinigen zahle: wir wurden sehr schnell bekannt. […] …sie sucht und bedarf Männer von Geist….).[98]

When he returned to Vienna, Schlegel moved into a room in the same street as the Countess's city residence. She helped Schlegel edit his philosophical notebooks, he was a regular visitor at her country estate, and he even eventually assumed co-guardianship of her two young sons. In 1819, in another letter to Dorothea, Schlegel described his growing relationship with Lesniowska in terms of his relations with women in general:

---

[96] Cristina Mazzoni, *Saint Hysteria: Neurosis, Mysticism, and Gender in European Culture*, Ithaca: Cornell University Press, 1996) 81.
[97] Schlegel, KA 35: xvii.
[98] From the letter from Friedrich to Dorothea Schlegel on September 28, 1818; KA 35: xvi.

> For myself, I always derive the most life experience from contact with women. With men, on the other hand, I always repay it and give what I can right and left without paying attention to what I will get in return, if only that which is mine arrives at the right place and takes root.
> (Für mich selbst schöpfe ich nun einmal immer die meiste Lebenserfahrung aus dem Umgange mit Weibern. Bey den Männern dagegen vergelte ichs wieder und gebe, was ich vermag, rechts und links, ohne viel auf das zu sehen, was ich zurück empfange, wenn nur das Meine am rechten Ort trifft und Wurzel fasst.)[99]

Schlegel was about to spend several years, at times during daily visits, gaining a more intimate and illuminating "life experience" with this particular woman.

Lesniowska's appeal to Schlegel only grew once her symptoms became apparent and she began magnetic therapy under the supervision of Dr. Franz Röhrig in 1820. Her attractiveness stemmed not from the possibility that she could be healed, but rather in her potential to deliver a particular kind of experience. Schlegel's observations of her lengthy therapy reveal his view of this experience as partly, if not primarily, aesthetic. The fact that he invited a painter, Ludwig Schnorr, to be the customary second observer at Lesniowska's treatments suggests that Schlegel saw her visions as artistic performances, something to be experienced rather than cured.

In her early clairvoyant visions in 1820, Lesniowska repeatedly saw an image of a man whom Schlegel determined was Schnorr. Although Schlegel did not know the artist personally, he was familiar with Schnorr's belief that magnetic treatments could at once alleviate symptoms and inspire prophetic visions. Schnorr gladly accepted Schlegel's invitation to meet the Countess, and ultimately to view her treatments at the hands of Dr. Röhrig. He also intended to help out with the magnetic therapy, and after his first meeting with Schlegel and Lesniowska, Schnorr wrote excitedly:

> (A) prophetic vein appears powerfully bound up in my body and soul, which has already saved a person from the most awful cramps and from death through mere laying on of hands; I have (the meeting with Countess Lesniowska) to thank for the discovery of this immeasurable treasure, or at least the fact that I possess it in such a high degree.
> ([Eine] prophetische Ader scheint nun mit einer Kraft in meinem Körper und der Seele zusammenzuhängen, die durch bloßes Händeauflegen schon eine Person vom furchtbarsten Krampfe und vom Tode gerettet hat, und die Entdeckung dieses unermeßlichen Schatzes habe ich eben, wenigstens daß ich ihn in einem so hohen Grade besitze, [der Begegnung mit Gräfin Lesniowska] zu danken).[100]

Schnorr's passionate belief in his own healing powers and his eager desire to begin fulfilling Lesniowska's vision of him may have had some connection to tragedies in his own past. His two children, aged two years and three months,

---

[99] From a letter of January 16, 1819; KA 35: xviii.

[100] Schlegel, KA 35: xxii (Nachlass Schnorr).

both died in 1815, and his brother died in 1819. Unlike the Countess, however, Schnorr did not become ill after grieving; rather, his nascent interest in mesmerism and magnetism coalesced with an increasingly fervent Catholicism to make him both a more prolific painter and a sort of lay pseudo-psychiatrist.

During Lesniowska's magnetic treatment sessions, the three men interrogated her nearly constantly about her feelings and perceptions, and they noted down the appearance of virtually every known symptom of her condition, as well as details such as the temperatures of her milk baths. Dr. Röhrig subscribed to the "Strasbourg School" of mesmerism, according to which the doctor and the two attending observers all participated in transmitting their healthy, "universal" animal fluid to the patient via the laying on of hands. Again, that fluid supposedly existed in the entire cosmos as a binding, life-giving force. The patient also followed a strict course of rest, milk baths, and chamomile tea.

Mesmer himself, as well as the followers of the magnetic practice recommended by the Strasbourg School, believed that the treatment's success depended on the psychic health of the therapist. Ursula Behler writes that

> a lively belief in the success of the enterprise and a strong will during the treatments were necessary. In the magnetizer...a healthy and strong soul was demanded: firmness of character, mastery of affects and of passions, patience and stamina.
> (der lebendige Glaube an das Gelingen des Unternehmens und der feste Wille beim Agieren notwendig waren. Vom Magnetiseur wurde...eine gesunde und starke Seele gefordert: Charakterfestigkeit, Beherrschung der Affekte und Leidenschaften, Geduld und Ausdauer).[101]

While surely Röhrig, Schnorr, and Schlegel displayed these characteristics during the six years of treatments, no one addressed the fact that the patient might have also needed a considerable amount of "patience and stamina." Despite the attention paid to Lesniowska's moods and symptoms, it is clear from the protocols that Schlegel's primary concern was not to understand the symptoms per se, but rather his interest in the Countess's ability to be a clairvoyant (Hellseher or Geisterseher), and in his own function as manager of this "soul business" ("Seelengeschäft").[102] He strongly encouraged Lesniowska to enter a convent, where she could devote herself to her visions full-time, and shortly before her death she did so.

In his descriptive diary of Lesniowska's six-year treatment, Schlegel demonstrates an explicit interest only in the content of visions occurring in the present. These visions are provoked in part by the magnetic treatments themselves, which Schlegel calls "séances." Visions did not take place in every session, however. Often, Lesniowska fell into what her observers

---

[101] Schlegel, KA 35: xxxii.
[102] Ibid, 35.

characterized as a "magnetic sleep," and this happened occasionally and quite suddenly during other times of the day as well. While asleep, Lesniowska had dreams that Schlegel does not distinguish explicitly from the clairvoyant visions she experienced during treatments. The content of her dreams as well as of her visions could be pleasant, but was more often frightening:

> She told me a *dream*, (in which) she (received) a package, which was given her in a very friendly (deceitful) way, as a memento… It contained a small sack, a brush, and a sulfur thread; she was supposed to just light the sack with the sulfur. She did this, the brush was coated with tar, the sack was full of powder. There was a violent explosion, when it was ignited, from which she awoke *in horror*.
> (Sie erzählte mir einen *Traum*, [worin] sie ein Paket [bekam], welches ihr auf sehr freundliche {perfide} Art überbracht wurde, als ein Andenken…Es enthielt ein Säckchen, einen Pinsel, und einen Schwefelfaden; sie sollte das Säckchen nur mit dem Schwefelfaden {anzünden}. Sie that dieß, der Pinsel war mit Pech bestrichen, das Säckchen war voller Pulver. Es geschah ein gewaltiger Knall, als sich dieses entzündete, von dem sie *mit Schrecken* erwachte).[103]

Two days before this frightening dream of violent discharge, Lesniowska had attended mass. Schlegel recounts that while there, she "had…those intimate prayers and conversations with God, as often before, which she cannot later relate" ("…jene innerlichen Gebete und Gespräche mit Gott, wie schon oft, von denen sie nichts wieder erzählen kann").[104] Ineffable experiences were common among women undergoing magnetic treatment and they inevitably required the magnetizer to articulate the patient's "inner voice of nature" ("innere Stimme der Natur").[105] Schlegel apparently drew no conclusions about the source of Lesniowska's dream or the content of her conversations with God, but he did consider both events as evidence that she had access to a world "on the other side of the self" ("jenseits des Ichs"),[106] at once real and immaterial. Lesniowska's dreams and visions were modern-day versions of the ancient hieroglyphs that fascinated Schlegel. In a letter to his brother August Wilhelm of June 6, 1826, he writes: "I feel very attracted to this symbolic riddle-world, which touches many mysteries of the soul and of the spirit" ("Ich fühle mich sehr von dieser symbolischen Rätselwelt angezogen, die mit vielen Geheimnissen der Seele und des Geistes in Berührung steht").[107]

Schlegel makes no effort in the treatment protocols to explore why the Countess is able to re-represent memories of her nightmares and visions,

---

[103] Schlegel, KA 35: 101.

[104] Ibid, 101.

[105] Scheuerbrandt, "Die Stimme der Natur. Dietrich Georg Kiesers Auffassung vom tierischen Magnetismus" 236.

[106] See Ernst Behler, "Philosophie in Notizheften" 13.

[107] Oskar Walzel, ed., *Friedrich Schlegels Briefe an seinen Bruder August Wilhelm* (Berlin: Speyer & Peters, 1890) 647.

but not of her conversations with God. In other words, although Schlegel notes often that Lesniowska "speaks from memory" ("spricht aus der Erinnerung"), his descriptions often seem focused solely on the present. Nevertheless, the protocols do reflect a general understanding among nineteenth-century psychologists and artists of the mind-body relationship as of the mind translating the body's apprehension of past and present phenomena. The health or sickness of the body was considered by Schlegel and by the Strasbourg School of mesmerism as being partly dependent upon the mind's ability to translate bodily perceptions into culturally decodable representations. In Lesniowska's case, the visions emerging from her "magnetic sleep" depict her memories of past perceptions in a compulsively repetitive way that Schlegel describes as repulsive and frightening.[108]

Schlegel's diary teems with tedious recollections of Lesniowska in sleep, prayer, and minor physical pain, all the while observed by three men who alternately lay hands on her and discuss church history. He writes:

> From 7-9 she fell asleep numerous times...somewhat later she fell into a deeper sleep...when Schn[orr] was impatient and unwilling, she got a strong cramp in the foot, which in any event stopped immediately when I prayed...She told me three or four times, that I should pray...She fell asleep again...In the following period she slept little...In the afternoon, she fell asleep during the discussion about the Armenian Archimadrites and the Greek church.
> (Von 7-9 schlief sie mehrmale ein...etwas später trat ein tieferer Schlaf ein.... als Schn{orr} einen Augenblick ungeduldig und unwillig war, bekam sie einen heftigen Krampf in den Fuß, der jedoch auf mein Gebet sofort aufhörte....Sie sagte mir drey bis viermale, daß ich beten sollte...Sie schlief wieder ein. ...Sie würde in der nächsten Zeit selten schlafen... Sie schlief Nachmittags über dem Gespräch von dem armenischen Archimandriten und der griechischen Kirche ein).[109]

But Lesniowska's magnetic sessions were often designed explicitly to elicit trances that reproduced prior, often nightmarish, visions or additional repetitions of her psychosomata. In the psychoanalytic context, these recurrences of symptoms, which range from merely disorienting to horrifying, would be understood as the return of repressed mental content. In the nightmare that Lesniowska recounts to Schlegel, the brush that ignites a sack filled with explosive powder functions as an anxiety-inducing selected fact.[110] In addition to its resonance as a sexual metaphor, the overly potent brush could represent one aspect of a memory. Instead of paint, the brush is

---

108 Schlegel, KA 35: 114, et al.

109 Ibid, 100-115.

110 In Chapter One, I explicated the notion of the "selected fact" as a condensed representation of the subject's own memories. When the subject focuses on this fact, a repressed affect is re-experienced, but now as detached from the original past experience, and thus as uncanny. See also Graziella Magherini, "The Unconscious and Art: The Aesthetic Uncanny and the Function of the Selected Fact," talk given at The Third New Style European Psychoanalytical Federation Annual Conference in Helsinki, Finland, 15-18 April, 2004, p. 4.

dipped in tar, making it a catalyst for catastrophe rather than a tool to produce art, but the reference to art is not arbitrary. Much like her magnetic treatment sessions, Lesniowska's dreams manifest an aesthetic interruption, a highly stylized intervention in a daily life that was otherwise often filled with ennui and what we now would almost certainly call depression.

I do not mean to suggest that it was only Lesniowska's experience of personal tragedy, combined with the fact that her children were grown and she had little to do, that led to her extended outbreak of what was then called "nerves." She did, after all, participate industriously in editing Schlegel's notebooks and devote considerable effort to religious studies, also during her years of illness. Schlegel's understanding of her symptoms diverges in many respects from a contemporary view. The early nineteenth-century concept of "nerves" included organic diseases. Nervous disorders were considered potentially, if not necessarily, contagious. Symptoms that today would be considered psychiatric were interpreted as a result of tissue disorder or, again, of simply breathing air contaminated with unhealthy "fluid."[111] And, in a conceptual move particularly difficult for us to grasp today, for the Romantics restoring health did not necessarily demand the elimination of illness.

David Farrell Krell has pointed out that for Schlegel and his Romantic contemporaries, "ease and disease are discomfitingly close; illness is a myopic word for the good health of a spiriting and spirited life."[112] Here he refers in particular to the Romantic notion of an "absolute spirit" that manifests itself in nature and in bodily symptoms and functions, whether healthy or ill.[113] In this manner Schlegel's late thought resembles a conviction grounded in his early Romantic years. In the "Preliminary Studies" for his encyclopedia project of 1798, Novalis posits illness as the way to health, or in fact as a form of health—of illness as cure.[114] Freud's insistence in the essay on "The Uncanny" that the terms "unheimlich" and "heimlich" are not opposites but instead closely related emerged previously in Novalis's theory that a "local illness often cannot be cured except by means of a general illness, and vice versa."[115] Krell reminds us that Novalis found the proximity between life and death and between health and illness potentially beautiful and pleasurable, and not just in his written works; the young philosopher-poet

---

111 More on these issues can be found in the entries on "Contagion/Germ Theory/Specificity," "Fevers," and "Mental Diseases" in the *Companion Encyclopedia of the History of Medicine* Vol. 1, eds. W.F. Bynum and Roy Porter (London and New York: Routledge, 1997).

112 David Farrell Krell, *Contagion: Sexuality, Disease, and Death in German Idealism and Romanticism* (Bloomington: Indiana University Press, 1998) 66.

113 Ibid, 67.

114 This view is influenced in turn by the Scottish physician John Brown and his intentional obscuring of the distinction between health and disease, as elaborated most fully in his *Elementa medicinae* of 1780.

115 Novalis, *Werke* 706. Cited here in Krell, *Contagion: Sexuality, Disease, and Death in German Idealism and Romanticism* 49.

loved his ailing child fiancée Sophie, in his own words, "almost more due to her illness" ("Ich liebe sie fast mehr ihrer Krankheit wegen").[116] Schlegel visited the sick Sophie shortly before her death and remarked that she was "very beautiful and very attractive" ("sehr schön und sehr anziehend");[117] Goethe also stopped at her home and remarked that Sophie's intense pain was a sign of "healthy flesh" ("gesund Fleisch").[118] Each of these "men of intellect," as Schlegel characterizes himself in his letter to Dorothea quoted above, discern beauty in a girl's sick body. By 1820, Schlegel will have taken the Early Romantic philosophy of proximity between ease and disease to its logical conclusion when he participates in "healing" treatments that immobilized female patients in a somnambulistic, hallucinatory haze.

Schlegel's conviction that Lesniowska's visions essentially express a virtuous spirit, one that manifests itself most fully when housed in an ill body, is also apparent throughout the protocols. In other words, Schlegel concerns himself less with whether or not Lesniowska feels better in the conventional sense; instead he focuses on the magnetizer's ability to enhance her often beautiful and sometimes shocking visions. It is intriguing that Schlegel only explores this interest through the uncanny exemplification of uncanny symptoms. In a sense, Lesniowska becomes in Schlegel's diary an uncanny repetition of Clara, the clairvoyant heroine of Schelling's fragment of 1810-1811. As we saw in Chapter Two, Schelling draws Clara as a spiritual, contemplative, and relatively simple woman whose name probably alluded to Clara of Assisi, a real nun who was eventually sanctified.[119] But Schelling's portrayal of Clara's visions and musings contribute to his philosophy of nature, while Schlegel's record of Lesniowska's mutterings, dizziness, and cramps never transcend the context of pseudo-psychiatry.

Nevertheless, the real Franziska Lesniowska was a widow and mother who fled the claustrophobic "private" domestic space in which all of her eerily public treatments took place. She did so by turning both outward and inward—by bringing the outside world of doctors and painters and philosophers into her home and into contact with her body, while at the same time "retreating" into nervous illness. Nicholas Royle argues that "a sense of homeliness uprooted, the revelation of something unhomely at the heart of hearth and home," often characterizes the phenomenon of the uncanny.[120] Lesniowska's uncanny form of grieving, her melancholic symptoms, together with the repetitive magnetic treatments, may be a way of living with

---

[116] Novalis, *Schriften* 4: 156.

[117] Cited in Max Preitz, *Friedrich Schlegel und Novalis. Biographie einer Romantikerfreundschaft in ihren Briefen* (Darmstadt: H. Gentner, 1957) 29.

[118] Novalis, *Schriften. Die Werke Friedrich von Hardenbergs*, eds. Paul Kluckhohn and Richard Samuel, vol. 4 (Stuttgart: W. Kohlhammer, 1960-1988) 159.

[119] See Alexander Grau, "Clara. Über Schellings gleichnamiges Fragment," *Zeitschrift für philosophische Forschung* 51.4 (1997) 596n15.

[120] Royle, *The Uncanny: An Introduction* 1.

unbearable memories. This understanding of Lesniowska's symptoms enables post-psychoanalytic readers to adopt Freud's view of psychosomatic illness while acknowledging Romanticism's influence on Freud's thinking. Romanticism and, more narrowly, animal magnetism focused on the moment of the symptom's appearance and reappearance. For the magnetist, as for the psychoanalyst, a symptom's repetition during an extended course of treatments makes it worthy of therapeutic attention. As Mesmer enthusiastically noted, it was the "uninterrupted observation" of his patient's "delirium, rage, vomiting and fainting" that allowed him to fully describe her illness. But Mesmer attributed these symptoms to "Nature," and Schlegel ascribed Lesniowska's visions and ailments to "history," believing that she represented a modern form of medieval mysticism that would help usher in a new age of a Catholic monarchy and beautiful rituals. For Freud, the source of uncanny psychosomatic symptoms is a part of the mind itself and its unconscious. And the unconscious mind is perhaps the ultimate example of a retreat into to the interior that nevertheless always draws the outside in.

Although it is tempting to diagnose Lesniowska and her apparently willing participation in years of repetitive magnetic treatments as neurotic, Schlegel's diary of the Countess's therapy also illuminates the psychoanalytic literature on this topic. In 1907, Freud describes obsessive patients compelled to perform rituals that take the form of "neurotic ceremonials," which resemble religious performances in "...the qualms of conscience brought on by their neglect, in their complete isolation from all other actions [...]and in the conscientiousness with which they are carried out in every detail" ("...der Gewissensangst bei der Unterlassung, in der vollen Isolierung von allem anderen Tun [...] und in der Gewissenhaftigkeit der Ausführung im kleinen").[121]

Unlike religious rituals, neurotic ceremonials take place in private and vary from individual to individual. Additionally, "while the minutiæ of religious ceremonial are full of significance and have a symbolic meaning, those of neurotics seem foolish and senseless. In this respect an obsessional neurosis presents a travesty, half comic and half tragic, of a private religion" ("die kleinen Zutaten des religiösen Zeremoniells [sind] sinnvoll und symbolisch gemeint [...], während die des neurotischen läppisch und sinnlos erscheinen. Die Zwangsneurose liefert hier ein halb komisches, halb trauriges Zerrbild einer Privatreligion").[122] Lesniowska's treatments, which took place in her home but were observed by three men, and which were esoteric yet symbolic, fall into a liminal zone between religious ritual and neurotic ceremonial.

The uncanny depersonalization and derealization that characterized Lesniowska's clairvoyant hallucinatory experiences characterize what the

[121] Freud, GW 7: 131/SE 9: 119.
[122] Freud, GW 7: 132/SE 9: 119.

post-Freudian universe sees as symptomatic of an "altered ego state," whose victims have "difficulty in assessing and evaluating perceptions of the external world, together with disturbances of the sense of self." In the essay on "The Uncanny," Freud attributes "presentiments" with these characteristics to the obsessional neurotic in particular:

> ...every obsessional neurotic I have observed has been able to relate analogous experiences. They are never surprised at their invariably running up against someone they have just been thinking of, perhaps for the first time for a long while. If they say one day 'I haven't had any news of so-and-so for a long time', they will be sure to get a letter from him the next morning, and an accident or a death will rarely take place without having passed through their mind a little while before. They are in the habit of referring to this state of affairs in the most modest manner, saying that they have 'presentiments' which 'usually' come true.
> (...alle Zwangsneurotiker, die ich studiert habe, wußten Analoges von sich zu erzählen. Sie waren gar nicht überrascht, regelmäßig der Person zu begegnen, an die sie eben—vielleicht nach langer Pause—gedacht hatten; sie pflegten regelmäßig am Morgen einen Brief von einem Freund zu bekommen, wenn sie am Abend vorher geäußert hatten: Von dem hat man aber jetzt lange nichts gehört, und besonders Unglücks- oder Todesfälle ereigneten sich nur selten, ohne eine Weile vorher durch ihre Gedanken gehuscht zu sein. Sie pflegten diesem Sachverhalt in der bescheidensten Weise Ausdruck zu geben, indem sie behaupteten, 'Ahnungen' zu haben, die 'meistens' eintreffen.)[123]

Lesniowska's visions may have been grander than the obsessional neurotic's near-constant sense of coincidences and predictions that come true, but for Schlegel, they coalesced into a mystical message about at least one possible future: that of the new age of the Church on earth, and the conversion of "inner esoteric world history" into external reality.[124]

Lesniowska doubtlessly did suffer from a kind of psychosomatic distress that can be understood in psychoanalytic terms, and magnetism was a real forerunner of the hypnotic practices of the later nineteenth century which influenced the early phase of Freud's career. However, Schlegel's focus on the future, whether of world history or in his obsession with clairvoyant women, underscores one significant difference between Romantic psychology and Freudian psychoanalysis. The psychosomatic symptoms that Freud likely would have interpreted as signs of the past returning Schlegel saw as evidence of clairvoyant ability, as the future revealing itself. The same disordered mental states that scholars since Freud read as an inability to integrate memory into present reality, possibly as a form of melancholic yearning, were understood by Schlegel as an extraordinary but natural power to see the future.

Whether we read the Countess's dreams as testimony to the past or future, we only have Schlegel's account of treatments attended by a

---

[123] Ibid, 252/239-240.
[124] Schlegel, KA 35: xxxvii.

philosopher-author and an artist, both of whom interpreted a peculiarly aesthetically charged psychological state. Schlegel and Schnorr saw magnetic treatment not as a cure but as part of an entire aesthetic experience. Schlegel was fascinated by the laying on of hands, done by an artist as well as a doctor, and his re-telling of that magnetic treatment and Lesniowska's uncanny symptoms that re-enact what could be termed her "performance of illness." In explaining his use of that phrase, Alan Radley has argued that "we find the aesthetic where we least expect to find it—grounded in matters reported as horrific by the sick and feared by the healthy."[125] But it is also Schlegel's ceaselessly repetitive re-representation of Lesniowska's sick performance in his treatment diary that aestheticizes her illness.

Magnetic therapy as well as Schlegel's representations of it in the protocols uncannily magnify the patient's problems. Psychoanalytic treatment resembles in this sense the magnetic treatments intended to elicit more and stronger hallucinatory visions in the process of "magnetic sleep," since psychoanalytic therapy aims to make the patient relive earlier conflicts and replay earlier anxiety. Schlegel's magnetism misses the component, essential to psychoanalysis, of using the analyst's office to work through and hence move beyond past experiences and present symptoms. And yet Schlegel and the Countess felt that her clairvoyant episodes and feelings of illness and frailty were indeed stages along the way to a better and more beautiful future.

Despite Schlegel's frame, we can perceive how the Countess was used at the time and partially correct that misuse by enacting yet another re-representation of the symptoms she repeatedly experienced for such a long time. Hélène Cixous explains and mirrors this simultaneously positive and negative domination of the Other inherent in the act of representation when she describes the hysteric:

> The hysteric is a divine spirit that is always at the edge, the turning point, of making. She is one who does not make herself...she does not make herself but she does make the other. It is said that the hysteric "makes-believe" the father, plays the father, "makes-believe" the master. Plays, makes up, makes-believe: she makes-believe she is a woman, unmakes-believe too...plays at desire, plays the father...turns herself into him, unmakes him at the same time. Anyway, without the hysteric, there's no father... without the hysteric, no master, no analyst, no analysis! She's the *unorganizable* feminine construct, whose power of producing the other is a power that never returns to her. She is really a wellspring nourishing the other for eternity, yet not drawing back from the other...not recognizing herself in the images the other may or may not give her. She is given images that don't belong to her, and she forces herself, as we've all done, to resemble them.[126]

---

125 Alan Radley, "The Aesthetics of Illness: Narrative, Horror, and the Sublime," *Sociology of Health and Illness* 21.6 (1999) 780.

126 Hélène Cixous, "Fiction and its Phantoms: A Reading of Freud's *Das Unheimliche*" (*New Literary History* 7 [1976]) 548.

By representing her traumatic past and melancholy present in physical symptoms and nightmares, Lesniowska produced and nourished the men around her and "played at desire" in one of the acceptable ways available to her. By re-representing her dreams as clairvoyant and her psychosomata as mystical, Schlegel produced images that indeed did not really belong to Lesniowska herself. However, he also depended on her continued participation in the treatments: without the hysteric, no master, no analyst, no analysis. But like the master or the analyst whom Cixous envisions, Schlegel was unable to "organize" Lesniowska or her symptoms into anything like a unified whole. His protocols of her treatments, like his fragments on magnetism, remain partial and jumbled. When we read and thus represent to ourselves those incomplete re-representations, we are to a certain extent free to resist an authoritarian and paternalistic assessment of a sick woman. This freedom, however, comes with a price—we will never know, and thus never master, Franziska Lesniowska. Making and unmaking herself and her masters, Lesniowska remains an unfixable point far back on the historical horizon.

Despite his encouragement of the Countess's convent ambitions, and perhaps because his late-in-life interest in esoterica did not realize the project of "philosophical psychology" any more fully than critical philosophy or faculty psychology had done, Schlegel remained well aware that the body betrays the transcendental agenda. In the *Ideas on History* (*Ideen zur Geschichte*), Schlegel writes: "The gap stands desolate and monstrous before us: man is torn, art and life are separated" ("Trostlos und ungeheuer steht die Lücke vor uns: der Mensch ist zerrissen, die Kunst und das Leben sind getrennt").[127] This "gap" was symptomatic of the modern disease that Schlegel's later Romanticism, with its aim of integrating and "mixing" art and life into increasingly perfect aesthetic forms, aimed to heal but could not. Instead, like the Countess's magnetic visions, Schlegel's late and increasingly esoteric and incomplete texts threw the insolubility of the body-mind problem and of the divide between flesh and reason into uncanny and anxious relief.

Conclusion

Moritz's *Journal of Empirical Psychology* and Schlegel's *Protocol* can be read as part of a literature of treatment—not necessarily a healing-oriented treatment, but rather treatment in the sense of examination and dissection. These texts are products of the mainstream and margins of psychology and psychiatry in the early years of those disciplines. When the

---

[127] Schlegel, KA 22: 3.

attention of the "experts" (here: Moritz, Schlegel, and other philosophers and physicians involved in the production of the *Journal of Empirical Psychology* and in the therapy of animal magnetism) turns to sufferings characterized by an intense, repetitive, frightening dissociation of mind and body, of affect and sensation, of thinking and feeling, and ultimately also a disconnect between reality and appearance, then the experts' representations of those uncanny sufferings take two forms. The representations can in the first instance be read as over-clinical and super-descriptive; the fact that Moritz and Schlegel themselves refrain almost completely from any prescriptive statements concerning what is happening with and to the sufferers lends these documents a scientific gloss. But something else is going on, something that can be called an aestheticization of anxiety, and specifically of uncanny symptoms, that itself becomes uncanny. In both the *Journal* and the *Protocol*, therapy and its representations magnify and repeat, yet again, the already uncanny experience of the subject or patient.

Neither the *Journal* nor the *Protocol* promises narrative completion or aesthetic unity. Rather, like the disjointed and uncanny symptoms they represent, both texts are examples of what Helen Deutsch has called "anatomy's textual equivalent…a plethora of anecdotes." Deutsch explains that the anecdote arose "at the crossroads of history and science" in the eighteenth century, and that it disrupts "the relation between aesthetic immediacy and clinical objectivity."[128] Despite the supposed pure descriptiveness of the empirical psychology cases and the magnetic treatments, despite the lack of analysis and hence of any kind of personal prescriptive intervention by the authors, the ultimately anecdotal style of Moritz's and Schlegel's work means that their relative anonymity and supposed clinical objectivity is "haunted" by particularity and the subjective claims of the aesthetic.

Moritz and Schlegel choose "marginal" examples of psychosomatic disturbances—hallucinations, nervous disabilities, epilepsy-like symptoms, and anxiety attacks occurring in little-known or unknown people between 1780 and 1830. But in empirical psychology as well as in Romantic medicine, the distance from the margin to the center is not vast. By the time German psychiatry has reached a preliminary apex in the 1820s, the sick *is* the mainstream—by understanding psychiatric disorders better, practitioners attempt to better understand modern humanity. Romanticism has not enacted and does not consist of a *return* to the past; rather, Romanticism itself is a highly modern phenomenon. For instance, while animal magnetism can be read as representing the persistence of the primitive in the modern, it can also

---

[128] Helen Deutsch, "Doctor Johnson's Autopsy, or Anecdotal Immortality," *The Eighteenth Century: Theory and Interpretation* 40.2 (1999) 113-114. Deutsch relies on Joel Fineman's "The History of the Anecdote: Fiction and Fiction," in H. Aram Veeser, ed., *The New Historicism* (New York, 1989).

be seen as a symptom of at least the incipient re-involvement of the modern subject with his or her surroundings—a symptom of a modernity *as* newly "involved," non-detached, as abandoning even the pretense of objectivity.

Magnetism was on its way out almost as soon as it began. The time between Mesmer's peak of popularity and the time in which magnetism became a social diversion is short-lived; everyone knew it had no credible scientific basis. When Schlegel refers earnestly to an esoteric tradition, he is intentionally playing with a virtual reality in order to unite the revelations and aims of empirical and deductive psychology and of transcendental philosophy, and not only on an abstract conceptual level.

In his latest and most esoteric career phase, Schlegel returns to the interests evident in Kant's precritical writings, and attempts to "re-involve" philosophy with its objects by building the bridge between philosophy and psychology that Kant never completed. Schlegel's magnetism, with its references to and stylized yearning for a medieval mysticism, a medieval past that he knew never existed, is a modern magnetism. The Countess's symptoms were actually highly explicable and understandable in the context of her life circumstances, even in the era of pre-Freudian psychology, and Schlegel knew it. What interested him was not the relationship between her psychosomatic symptoms and past trauma, but rather the same "principle of the past" to which Schelling refers, a principle that can be mobilized in the modern present in the interest of re-involving a modernity in danger of being buried alive.

The uncanny, then, signals a kind of re-involvement with the object of analysis, not in the sense of a *return* to primitive or archaic ways of thinking, but as an involvement anew, when the only direction left to go is outwards. Already in the first decades of the psychological view of the subject, that view is experiencing a kind of secular afterlife. The death-like trance of magnetic sleep (in which the patient resembles something dead but unburied), the unparalleled terror of live burial, the inevitable decay of the mortal and transient, the ruin represented by the Romantic fragment[129]—all signal an end to the inward turn of psychology just as that turn is beginning, but this end is at the same time a *new* beginning. The men and women featured in Moritz's and Schlegel's case studies undergo real, attached, involved, material sufferings—sufferings not demonic but logically explicable.

Schlegel's aestheticization of the Countess into a modern mystic and his esoteric fragments on animal magnetism are hardly examples of an

[129] Philippe Lacoue-Labarthe and Jean-Luc Nancy show that the Romantic fragment is related to the concept of the ruin thusly: "Ruin and fragment conjoin the functions of the monument and of evocation; what is thereby both remembered as lost and presented in a sort of sketch (or blueprint) is always the living unity of a great individuality, author, or work." *The Literary Absolute: The Theory of Literature in German Romanticism*, trans. Philip Barnard and Cheryl Lester (Albany: State University of New York Press, 1988) 42.

Enlightened approach to uncanny disorders, at least as such an approach might be typically understood. But the uncanny psychosomatic disorders that Schlegel and Moritz document are nevertheless psychiatric predecessors to what Paul Gilroy will call in our century the attitude of the "cosmopolitan attached."[130] The apparent turn inward towards one's own sensations and symptoms, documented by Moritz's *Journal* in the 1780s and Schlegel's protocols in the 1820s—decades that bookend the French Revolution and the highly reactionary regimes that followed—this turn inward, this obsessive focus on the self, depends upon the participation of other selves, and upon intersubjective recognition. That recognition, which is also a sense of community enabled by the focus on the self and its perception of disorienting dissociation between mind and body, helps shape the sense of "estranged community" so characteristic of Western modernity and so prevalent in texts by authors and filmmakers from Kleist to Lang, to whom I turn in Chapter Five.

The act of reading these texts, of early psychology and Romantic pseudopsychology, is also an intersubjective act in that this reading transforms us into uncanny observers: that is, the exercise of perception and of observation, as a type of force, upon texts containing descriptions of psychosomatic disorders, transmits the experience of the uncanny. As Nicholas Royle puts it: "The uncanny can be felt in response to witnessing epileptic or similar fits, manifestations of insanity or other forms of what might appear merely mechanical or automatic life, such as one might associate with trance or hypnosis."[131] Samuel Weber expands on Freud's own contention that psychoanalysis itself is uncanny when he asks:

> Can psychoanalytic thinking itself escape the effects of what it endeavors to think? Can the disruptive distortions of unconscious processes be simply recognized, theoretically, as an object, or must they not leave their imprint on the process of theoretical objectification itself? Must not psychoanalytical thinking itself partake of - repeat - the dislocations it seeks to describe?[132]

Like psychoanalytic thinking, the psychology of Moritz and Schlegel is also changed by the objects it observes; in turn, readers of those observations partake of and are imbricated in their repetitive, dislocated, uncanny re-representations of psychosomatic disorders.

The next chapter returns to the idea that anxiety, occasioned by loss, creates a melancholy state that presupposes as well as continues a state of intersubjective relatedness—a state in which the players are aware of and attempting to sustain loss; acutely aware of death, and desirous of protection against that awareness. The main characters in the texts analyzed, "secret-

---

[130] Paul Gilroy, *Postcolonial Melancholia* (New York: Columbia University Press, 2005) 70-71.
[131] Royle, *The Uncanny: An Introduction* 1-2.
[132] Samuel Weber, *The Legend of Freud* (Stanford: Stanford University Press, 2000) xiv.

society" novels ("Geheimbundromane") by Ludwig Tieck and Friedrich Schiller, experience uncanny disorders that simultaneously remind of and disguise the reality of loss. These characters choose, whether consciously or not, to participate in a process similar to the one Sheldon Bach describes when he explains what happens at the termination of therapy, when the patient is about to lose his love object, the analyst:

> Faced with the catastrophic possibility of the loss of the mirroring-analyst, the patient conjures up inspiration, ghosts, ghouls and vampires, that is, he seeks refuge in an *alter ego* doubling process as a kind of 'life insurance' against ego dissolution. Thus he peoples another world in which the instinctual forces are both embodied and controlled.[133]

When they experience doubling and déjà vu, protagonists such as Tieck's William Lovell and Schiller's Prince, are holding the threat of dissolution at bay by creating and peopling an uncanny, melancholy, virtual reality.

---

[133] Sheldon Bach, "Narcissism, Continuity and the Uncanny," *The International Journal of Psycho-Analysis* 56 (1975) 78.

Chapter 4

Conspiracy Theories: The Melancholy and Manipulated Male Subject

We can also speak of a living person as uncanny, and we do so when we ascribe evil intentions to him. But that is not all; in addition to this we must feel that his intentions to harm us are going to be carried out with the help of special powers.
[Wir heissen auch einen lebenden Menschen unheimlich, und zwar dann, wenn wir ihm böse Absichten zutrauen. Aber das reicht nicht hin, wir müssen noch hinzutun, daß diese seine Absichten, uns zu schaden, sich mit Hilfe besonderer Kräfte verwirklichen werden.]
Freud, *The Uncanny [Das Unheimliche]*

1. The Curse of Enthusiasm

The latest edition of the standard diagnostic manual for psychiatrists, the *DSM-IV* (first published in 1994), states that depression is characterized by a lack of feeling and affect.[1] Abnormal behaviors strongly associated with depression, such as cutting one's own flesh, stem from a sense of deadness or what might be called a lack of enthusiasm; the sufferer wants to feel more alive, if only briefly and violently. Against the backdrop of today's psychiatry, then, it may seem surprising to read that the protagonist of Jean Paul's sprawling novel *Titan* (1800-1803), Albano, cuts himself when he feels especially excited—when he feels too full of life, feeling, and love.

In a "fever" of "youthful health" ("jenes Fieber der jungen Gesundheit") and overwhelmed simultaneously by the desire to die together with his sick father and by recurring memories of his dead mother, Albano "helps himself" by making himself bleed.[2] This self-inflicted damage, committed when he feels that his "lungs and heart are heavy and full of blood" ("die Lunge und das Herz von Blute schwer und voll")[3] progresses over time from habitual small cuts to a climactic "beautiful arm wound" ("schöne Armwunde") that bleeds enough to make Albano faint and mildly hallucinatory. Swooning, Albano

> thinks of the vanished mother, whose love now remains forever unreturned—oh, he would gladly have shed this blood for her—; and now love for his ill father sprung up

[1] *Diagnostic and Statistical Manual of Mental Disorders, Fourth Edition (DSM-IV)* (Washington, D.C.: American Psychiatric Association, 1994) 320-327, 345-349, 383-384.
[2] Jean Paul, *Titan* (Frankfurt am Main: Insel Taschenbuch, 1983) 33.
[3] Ibid, 33.

> hotter than ever in his breast: O come soon, said his heart, I want to love you unspeakably, beloved father!
> [Er dachte an die verschwundne Mutter, deren Liebe nun ewig unvergolten blieb—ach er hätte dieses Blut gern für sie vergossen—; und nun quoll heißer als je in seiner Brust die Liebe für den kränklichen Vater auf: o komme bald, sagte sein Herz, ich will dich so unaussprechlich lieben, du lieber Vater!][4]

In this uncanny twilight state occasioned by feeling too much (his life has become "too warm and too active" ["zu warm und zu treibend"][5]), Albano thinks about his own past, his own parents—but simultaneously about the spirit of antiquity and about the past of Western culture. As he searches his own memory at the entrance to a grotto "full of inscriptions of the past" ("voll Inschriften der vorigen Zeit"), he feels that that cultural past will become his future ("Da wurde in Albano die fremde Vergangenheit zur eigenen Zukunft").[6] These peregrinations through the mythic and individual past, combined with youth and three glasses of wine, contribute to Albano's repetitive bloodletting.

Jean Paul's characterization of self-cutting as not just a reaction to memory, but also as prompting a productive acknowledgment of the past's ongoing presence in Albano's adult life, is related indirectly to the belief, dating back to Galen's second-century codification of earlier biomedicine and still persistent around 1800, that bleeding is basically healthy. Blood signifies youth and health, and its periodic expulsion is the therapeutic release of excess fluid.[7] But Albano's "self-help" also reflects the incursion of a mentalistic view of disease into the world of traditional biological medicine. While such a view has been at least an intermittent factor in medical writings

---

[4] Jean Paul, *Titan* 36.
[5] Ibid, 35.
[6] Ibid, 35.
[7] Roy Porter, *Flesh in the Age of Reason* (New York and London: W.W. Norton, 2003) 45-46. Werner Leibbrand and Annemarie Wettley summarize the significance of blood and blood-letting in ancient mythology: referring specifically to the *Iliad*, they note: "Blut bedeutet gewiß Leben, Erinnerung, Bewußtsein, aber vergossenes Blut besitzt eine eigene Dämonie. Sie treibt den Mörder außer Landes....Das vergossene Blut verbindet sich mit der Erde, und so steht dann das ganze Land unter der Macht des Dämons....Das Blut wird noch mehr als der Leichnam zum Agens des Wahnsinns. Blut ist Befleckung, die die Krankheit auslöst....Vergossenes Blut is krankheitbringendes Miasma." *Der Wahnsinn. Geschichte der abendländischen Psychopathologie* (Freiburg and Munich: Alber, 1961) 14.

since antiquity,[8] it is modern psychology, as it develops after 1700,[9] that will render truly multivalent the ancient understanding of bleeding and of the release of bodily fluids as a response to disordered states of mind. By the late eighteenth century, in texts that evince a facility with the latest psychology, the release of fluids and other aberrant behaviors will be linked to new understandings of psychological maladies.

Jean Paul modeled the character of Albano in part on the protagonist of just such a psychologically informed text,[10] a novel with an excessively emotional and even violent hero: Ludwig Tieck's *Geschichte des Herrn William Lovell* (1795-1796[11]). One of William Lovell's essential problems is that he feels too much; he is, at the novel's outset, a classic eighteenth-century enthusiast (or "Schwärmer"). Like Albano, William rids himself of excess feeling by engaging in neurotic behaviors, but in William's case these behaviors do not "help" him. Compulsive sex, non-stop travel, duelling, drinking, and gambling are William's attempts to flee an individual and social past that refuses to release him.

There are different contexts for thinking about the problem of enthusiasm, of feeling too much, and about the disordered behaviors associated with it. In the late eighteenth century, enthusiasm was seen as an excess of an essentially laudable, positive quality, a quality of interest and creativity, almost exclusively in young men. This positive force could become unhealthy if the young man read too much or read the wrong thing—in particular, if he internalized negative role models by reading too many

---

[8] Theodore M. Brown notes: "Even in the unmistakably biological-reductionist Hippocratic Corpus,...certain mentalistic aetiological elements show through....In the 'Sacred Disease', even epilepsy - the paradigmatic example of naturalistic, biological disease in the Corpus - is said in certain circumstances to be 'caused by fear of the mysterious.'" *Companion Encyclopedia of the History of Medicine* Vol. 1, eds. W.F. Bynum and Roy Porter (London and New York: Routledge, 1997) 439-440.

[9] Matthew Bell reminds us that in the eighteenth and early nineteenth centuries, psychology in Germany "grew from a minor branch of philosophical doctrine into one of the central pillars of intellectual culture;" in this period, "psychology's evidential basis, theoretical structure, forms of articulation, and status both as a scientific discipline and as a cultural phenomenon took on a recognisably modern form." *The German Tradition of Psychology in Literature and Thought, 1700-1840* (Cambridge: Cambridge University Press, 2005) 1.

[10] Tieck's interest in contemporary psychology is evident in his correspondence; several examples are his letters to Moritz and to William Solger, some of which are cited later in this chapter. See Percy Matenko's collections *Letters to and from Ludwig Tieck and His Circle* (Chapel Hill: University of North Carolina Press, 1967) and *Tieck and Solger: The Complete Correspondence* (New York and Berlin: B. Westermann, 1933). For the influence of Tieck on Jean Paul and more on the relationship between these two novels, see F.J. Schneider, "Tiecks *William Lovell* and Jean Pauls *Titan*," *Zeitschrift für deutsche Philologie* 61 (1936) 58-75.

[11] The novel was revised and shortened in two subsequent editions, published in 1821 and 1828.

novels.[12] And William, who is that kind of enthusiast, is also, as a character, just such a negative model. But during this same period, enthusiasm also was understood, in the context of the new faculty psychology, as an organically based and mentally exacerbated problem: as the separation of imagination from sensation.[13] While this is not precisely the same phenomenon that Freud will much later call anxiety (understood, again, as a possible expression of the dissociation of emotion from affect),[14] the experience of enthusiasm is one of disorientation, and of estrangement from the overly-heavy body and overly-fast blood that make the experience possible.[15]

In the experience of enthusiasm as well as of its eighteenth-century companion state, melancholy (discussed in more detail below), physical phenomena point to something that ultimately cannot be explained materially or mechanistically. That is, if it were possible to open a person up and to see his blood circulating too quickly, an understanding of pathological behavior would still be elusive—in William's case, an understanding of why he is addicted to sex, or feels as if he is disintegrating, or sees frightening uncanny hallucinations. Organic problems such as an overly rapid blood flow instead serve as partial explanations for something perhaps best described as an excess of self, which meant at the same time an excess of the past of the self, and of physically encoded traces of the past within the self. The hysterical or hypochondriac symptoms that could result from this problem, especially in men, were considered manifestations of that psychosomatic excess.

Like enthusiasm, melancholy is defined, by around 1800, as an organically based mood state whose behavioral manifestations signify a desire to remember and to forget. These manifestations, or symptoms, are uncanny in that they nearly always represent a dissociation of affect (as observable in the symptom: shaking, numbness, fainting, etc.) from the earlier emotional state and the combination of physical characteristics (such as rapid blood flow or excited nerves) and experience (including loss of love or financial ruin) that contributed to that emotional state. Like the bizarre behaviors and "clairvoyant" hallucinations recorded by Moritz and Schlegel, the mood states of melancholy and enthusiasm and their hysterical or

---

[12] For a more detailed discussion of enthusiasm in the context of excessive reading, see Claire Baldwin, *The Emergence of the Modern German Novel: Christoph Martin Wieland, Sophe von La Roche, and Maria Anna Sagar* (Columbia, SC: Camden House, 2002) 9.

[13] Matthew Bell, *The German Tradition of Psychology in Literature and Thought, 1700-1840* 51.

[14] As presented in the essay on "The Uncanny," and explicated in Chapter One of this study.

[15] The origin of the emphasis on blood circulation as a probable contributor to mood and behavior lies in the seventeenth-century work of William Harvey, whose mechanistically oriented *Exercitation Anatomica de Motu Cordis et Sanguinis in Animalibus* (*An Anatomical Disquisition Concerning the Motion of the Heart and the Blood in Animals*) of 1628 influenced what Roy Porter calls Thomas Willis's later "rethinking of physiology at large" and the creation of the science of "neurologie," or study of the nerves, that figures prominently in eighteenth-century psychology and literature. See Porter, *Flesh in the Age of Reason* 52-56.

hypochondriac consequences are uncanny, but that uncanniness signals something more and different than the intrusion of the "night side" of nature into an otherwise sunny rationalistic universe. Uncanny border experiences, represented in novels around 1800 as resulting from insufficient integration of past with present, stand out from these texts as moments of sharp focus in otherwise meandering, allusive, and dense narratives. Live burial (or the fear of it), passages with intense descriptions of depersonalization, and horrific encounters with uncanny doubles function as painful but relieving "cuts" in texts that are literally overweight and too full of feeling.

Men of melancholy or enthusiastic temperament, as represented in late eighteenth- and nineteenth-century literature and psychology, were prone to feel themselves at the mercy of other, uncanny men with "special powers" akin to those to which Freud refers in his essay on "The Uncanny:" we think of others as uncanny not only when we think of their intentions as evil, but when we believe that they have special powers.[16] These powers, however, are nothing supernatural and in fact only exist in the mind of the melancholy man, who lives in a liminal uncanny lack-of-home. In contrast to Friedrich Schlegel's Countess Lesniowska and Karl Philipp Moritz's case studies of female patients in the *Journal of Empirical Psychology*, the male protagonists of the novels treated in this chapter, all of whom exhibit "hysterical" symptoms, are convinced that they are victims of conspiracies. To be sure, they are handicapped by nature; they suffer from an excess of sentiment (or of "Gemüt"). But their psychological and social doom is sealed by their perceived victimization at the hands of others—lovers, friends, brothers, fathers, and secret societies. This paranoia is a characteristic of "male hysteria" around 1800 (hysteria is discussed in more detail in Section 2.1 below); these characters' life-defining experiences as well as their hysterical maladies are uncanny. That is, the uncanny once again permits us to discern connections between the psychological and the social, between an individual and a culture gone awry—collectively victimized, as it were, by modernity as a grand conspiracy.

Melancholy predates modernity; like enthusiasm, it is a changeable phenomenon occurring in a wide variety of contexts. Like the uncanny, it proliferates in the mid- to late eighteenth century at the peak of the Enlightenment. But this period was populated by melancholics of a different sort than those referred to in the seminal *Saturn and Melancholy* (Raymond Klibansky, Erwin Panofsky, and Fritz Saxl; 1964), a work that relies heavily on Renaissance theories of melancholy and their famous re-envisioning by Walter Benjamin in *The Origins of German Tragedy* (1928), which recast

---

[16] Sigmund Freud, "Das Unheimliche," *Gesammelte Werke* 12 (Frankfurt am Main: Fischer, 1999) 256. This edition is abbreviated henceforth as GW. The translation is James Strachey's in "The Uncanny," *The Standard Edition of the Complete Psychological Works of Sigmund Freud*, vol. 17 (London: Hogarth, 1953-1974) 243. This edition is abbreviated henceforth as SE.

cultural production in the seventeenth century as driven by a melancholy signifying spiritual and metaphysical crisis.

In 1968, Gert Mattenklott applies Benjamin's thinking on the German drama to the later eighteenth century (in *Melancholie in der Dramatik des Sturm und Drang*), but also considers the prevalence of melancholy during that period in the rapidly developing field of psychology, which considered melancholy to be a disorder with physical and spiritual components. This conception is related to but also revises the tradition of thinking about melancholy dating back to Hippocrates, Aristotle, and the pseudo-Aristotelian *Problemata*, in which the melancholic's "black bile" contributes to his philosophical, political, or artistic exceptionalism.[17] By the late eighteenth and early nineteenth centuries, as indicated in the research on melancholy done by Wolf Lepenies, Hans-Jürgen Schings, and Matthew Bell, among others, the melancholic can be a victim of his specific psychophysical "type," a type that may well doom him to artistic failure rather than enabling him to achieve poetic greatness.[18] By 1800, the singular and "holy disease" ("heilige Krankheit") of epilepsy referred to in the *Problemata* has been refigured as hypochondriasis and as hysteria, which are biospiritual disruptions marked by uncanny repetition, as we will see in the readings below.

This general view of melancholy in the context of the philosophical psychology and the "mental physicalism"[19] of the late eighteenth and early nineteenth centuries can be read together with more contemporary understandings of melancholy, and particularly with those that emphasize melancholy not as merely a looking inwards and backwards, but as a form of connection with others—of a relatedness dictated by the fact that we are "stuck" in a present filled with re-presentations of lost love objects. In *Antigone's Claim* (2000), Judith Butler re-envisions older definitions of melancholy by going back to the plays of Sophocles. Butler contends that the crimes committed by Oedipus without conscious knowledge condemn Antigone to a "strange place between life and death"; "she is already living in

---

[17] Hans-Jürgen Schings quotes the *Problemata* on this point: "Warum erweisen sich alle außergewöhnlichen Männer in Philosophie oder Politik oder Dichtung oder in den Künsten als Melancholiker; und zwar ein Teil von ihnen so stark, daß sie sogar von krankhaften Erscheinungen, die von der schwarzen Galle ausgehen, ergriffen werden, wie man z.B. berichtet, was unter den Heroen dem Herakles widerfuhr?" *Melancholie und Aufklärung. Melancholiker und ihre Kritiker in Erfahrungsseelenkunde und Literatur des 18. Jahrhunderts* (Stuttgart: Metzler, 1977) 1.

[18] Matthew Bell cites Goethe's revision of *Die Leiden des jungen Werther*, in which a shifted understanding of melancholy reveals "not the artistic genius that the tradition of pseudo-Aristotle and the Renaissance imagined; the melancholic is more likely to be a failed artist. Melancholy might, in fact, be the result of artistic impotence. Hence Werther's failure as a creative artist could be behind his melancholy." *The German Tradition of Psychology in Literature and Thought, 1700-1840* 132.

[19] Ibid, 59.

the tomb prior to any banishment there."[20] This liminality is characterized for Butler by "melancholia": a state in which the displaced (here: Antigone) tries to claim a place by asserting a relatedness with others that is already ruled out by past crime—the incest taboo prevents Antigone from "any life and love she might have had."[21] Antigone asserts a claim to love, but since that claim has already been invalidated, her assertion remains a "shadowy form of signification."[22] This melancholia, this persistent and "stuck" state, is still revolutionary: "the unspeakable nevertheless makes itself heard through borrowing and exploiting the very terms that are meant to enforce its silence."[23] Antigone ultimately exploits her own position between life and death by imposing a burial law that both acknowledges the decay of the dead and prevents that decay from being witnessed.

By going back to a story that precedes all of the modern melancholy men whose mood states are the subject of so much literary and scientific scrutiny, Butler restores to melancholy the connotation of being buried alive, condemned to a state the German Romantics thought of as lifedeath.[24] Antigone is the template for future melancholics who are, at least symbolically, neither fully alive nor fully dead, due not merely to their organic temperaments, but to the intersection of those temperaments with their social and blood relationships. Imprisonment in uncanny melancholy comes through imbrication with others and with the unconscious guilt of others, as well as with one's own guilt. Attempting to speak even in the face of horror that renders one speechless and attempting to represent frightening experience even when paralyzed by anxiety are the acts that make bearable the return of repressed memory; these acts, of course, would not be possible without the traumatic past and its intervening repression.

In literary texts in particular, uncanny repetition of long-forgotten memory acts to assert a claim; this type of claim is similar to Hegel's understanding of a claim of entitlement, which is always based in guilt. As I

---

[20] Judith Butler, *Antigone's Claim: Kinship Between Life and Death* (New York: Columbia University Press, 2000) 77-78.

[21] Ibid, 78.

[22] Ibid, 78.

[23] Ibid, 78. Judith Butler's retelling of the story of Antigone here bears comparison to Karl Philipp Moritz's retelling of the story of Philomela, from the *Metamorphoses*: for Moritz, Philomela's weaving of the story of past trauma represents the same kind of "shadowy form of signification" and of speaking the unspeakable, from a position of liminality; Philomela is symbolically buried alive by her rapists, who have cut out her tongue, but she nevertheless re-represents that crime outside of conventional signification. See Moritz, "Die Signatur des Schönen," in *Beiträge zur Ästhetik*, ed. Hans Joachim Schrimpf and Hans Adler (Mainz: Dieterich'sche Verlagsbuchhandlung, 1989).

[24] David Farell Krell explains that the Jena Romantics and Idealists, in particular Novalis, Schelling, and Hegel, strove to show that this state of "*lifedeath*" is not exceptional but the norm, and they base this conviction in their philosophies of nature as "simultaneously life-giving and death-dealing." *Contagion: Sexuality, Disease, and Death in German Idealism and Romanticism* (Bloomington and Indianapolis: Indiana University Press, 1998) 2.

stated in Chapter Two, Hegel shows that when a claim of entitlement is made, one's guilt is simultaneously revealed—even though this guilt is unconscious (or, as Hegel says, "nonexisting"). Albano's self-cutting in *Titan*, like Nathanael's feverish dream of dismemberment in *The Sandman*, is a result of his "enthusiastic" and "melancholy" psychophysical temperament. But both men also respond to being haunted by their kin. Albano and Nathanael are paying for the past that their fathers represent, reacting in their present behavior to their fathers' past desire (*Verlangen*): for continuation, for life after death, for a son. By self-mutilating, and by dreaming of images that consciousness would find unthinkable, Albano and Nathanael sustain—or maintain, keep present—the past loss of their parents. By hurting themselves, these melancholy men bring their memories beyond the realm of the mind, and thereby "speak" a desire, as Albano says, to "love…unspeakably."[25] Jacques Derrida contends that in addition to what we conceive of as the binary spaces of the demonic (which he associates with enthusiasm, a confusion of limits, or a "fervor for fusion" with another) and the instrumental (which he thinks of as the space of extreme rationality and separation from others—the space of too much difference), there is a "third space" of the religious (which is not irrational, but rather an integrative space of responsibility and freedom in which similarity to others, and love for others, can be recognized without the collapse of boundaries or the erection of instrumental barriers).[26] It is one argument of this chapter that novels written around 1800 in which the uncanny plays a prominent role explore the persistence of the demonic realm in modern life, in an age in which, as Novalis put it, the lack of gods leads to the reign of demons.[27] However, these texts also indicate, even if negatively, spaces in which the demonic is confronted, and not by instrumental rationality. Although the characters in these novels who suffer from enthusiasm and melancholy do not achieve an integrated state of relatedness and recognition with others until it is too late, or not at all, their uncanny encounters with others and with their own bodies mark the beginning of a painful process of integration and assumption of responsibility.

This chapter, however, takes a closer look at men in trouble: men manipulated—ultimately by themselves, by their own choices, conscious or unconscious—into uncanny existences, and trapped in endless melancholy in

---

[25] Jean Paul, *Titan* 36.

[26] See Jacques Derrida, *The Gift of Death*, trans. David Wills (Chicago and London: The University of Chicago Press, 1995).

[27] Novalis locates the "death of gods" and the advent of modernity at the transition from pantheism to monotheism: "Wo keine Götter sind, walten Gespenster, und die eigentliche Entstehungszeit der europäischen Gespenster, die auch ihre Gestalt ziemlich vollständig erklärt, ist die Periode des Übergangs der griechischen Götterlehre in das Christentum." *Die Christenheit oder Europa, Werke*, ed. Gerhard Schulz (Munich: Beck, 1969) 499.

part also by their uncanny experiences. However, the overall positive epistemological function of the uncanny dynamic that I have championed in the previous two chapters remains: the uncanny could, were these characters gifted with more insight, point to a way of living with and through their dilemmas. And to a certain extent it does just that, by presenting readers with an early version of what will much later be known as existential dread and awareness, and hence with an emphasis on the need to live with repetitive psychological and social dilemmas via insight and thus to live more authentically—with others, but also with the persistence of the past in the present, a persistence represented by others (and, in the novels examined in this chapter, by their uncanny appearances and disappearances). The face of the father in Tieck's *Lovell* and the face of the Armenian behind the mask in Friedrich Schiller's *Ghost-Seer* all represent "the face of the other"[28] who is related to but different from the self, and who must be acknowledged if any kind of life outside the world of the self-positing subject is to be possible.

2. Male Hysteria and the Uncanny in Tieck and Schiller

Tieck's *William Lovell* and Schiller's *The Ghost-Seer* are not among the most frequently analyzed or read works of German literature.[29] Both can be considered unfinished—Tieck's revisions to *Lovell* of 1821 and 1828 shortened the novel (published initially in 1795-1796), but did not address all of its original plot inconsistencies or eliminate all of its redundancy; *The Ghost-Seer* (first published in 1787), Schiller's only novel, is a fragment. But while Tieck's "Bildungsroman" *Franz Sternbalds Wanderungen* and Schiller's dramas and aesthetic theory command far more attention, *Lovell* and *Ghost-Seer* are arguably their most psychologically compelling texts. This has directly to do with their uncanniness, which in turn motivates and

---

28 Emmanuel Levinas, *Outside the Subject*, trans. Michael B. Smith (Stanford: Stanford University Press, 1993).

29 This is in contrast to the fact that both novels were popular in their own time, and despite the influence of both on their contemporaries (Tieck took direct inspiration from Schiller's novel). Mathias Mayer points out that "die Wissenschaft mit dem *Geisterseher* eher schwer [tat]…zu wenig paßte die Schauergeschichte ins Klischee von Schiller als dem gefeierten oder gerügten angeblichen 'Moraltrompeter' (Nietzsche)," "Nachwort" in Friedrich Schiller, *Der Geisterseher* (Stuttgart: Philipp Reclam, 2003) 231. *William Lovell*, says Walter Münz, "zählt zu den am zwiespältigsten beurteilten - und in ihrer […] Originalfassung am wenigsten gekannten - Erzählwerken der deutschen Literatur;" he cites Friedrich Schlegel's review in the *Athenäum* (vol. 1.2 of 1798; in Friedrich Schlegel, *Kritische Ausgabe* II [Munich: Schöningh, 1967] 244f) in which Schlegel calls *Lovell* "ein[] Kampf der Prosa und der Poesie, wo die Prosa mit Füßen getreten wird und die Poesie über sich selbst den Hals bricht," and notes the general lack of response to the novel in Germanist circles. See Münz's "Nachwort" in Ludwig Tieck, *William Lovell* (Stuttgart: Reclam, 1999) 725-726 and the complete Schlegel review on pp. 709-710 of the same volume.

reveals a high level of anxiety in both works. In these novels, the difficulty or even impossibility of containing various kinds of emotional and physical excess is represented in compulsively repetitive ways, and all of the factors Freud eventually identifies as the constitutive elements of the uncanny are present in multiple settings: "animism, magic and sorcery, the omnipotence of thoughts, man's attitude to death, involuntary repetition and the castration complex" ("...Animismus, der Magie und Zauberei, der Allmacht der Gedanken, der Beziehung zum Tode, der unbeabsichtigten Wiederholung und dem Kastrationskomplex").[30] As in contemporary psychological literature, including the case studies of Moritz and Schlegel, these uncanny elements surface during the experience of psychic disorder occasioned either from within the self or from the community without, and have an impact on both the self and others.

William Lovell and *The Ghost-Seer*'s Prince in particular—but other men in these texts as well—endure emotional states resembling both the enthusiasm and melancholic lifedeath described in Section 1 above, but it is during uncanny encounters that those mood states are thrown into extreme focus. In the most uncanny moments in these novels, the characters' underlying and constant melancholy mutates into a kind of male hysteria. Hysterical symptoms, divorced from their origins in these characters' pasts, often occur in the literal face of aesthetic re-representation: while viewing a portrait or participating in an elaborately staged séance. The male protagonists' hysterical symptoms reveal a particularly uncanny form of melancholy which, while destructive within the novels themselves, actually points to one way of living with and through the tensions of Enlightened modernity. That is, the dissociated, uncanny experiences in these texts have an epistemological value beyond their destructiveness for the characters, who lack the insight to interpret the experiences.

To some extent, this argument runs counter to the popular understanding of the eighteenth-century uncanny worked out by Terry Castle and Elisabeth Bronfen (and introduced in Chapter One of this study).[31] Bronfen envisions a retreat into uncanny repetition as something that happens at the advent of Romanticism, a time in philosophical and social history when the world outside the self, and all the people in that world, are reduced to specters in the mind of the self-positing transcendental subject.[32] I want to say almost the opposite: that in these novels uncanny repetition (occurring in the context of hysteria caused by an organically based enthusiasm) that takes the form of neurotic symptoms with an enormous amount of accompanying

---

[30] Freud, GW 12: 256/SE 17: 243.

[31] Terry Castle calls the uncanny "the toxic side effect of the Enlightenment's rationalist project" in *The Female Thermometer: Eighteenth-Century Culture and the Invention of the Uncanny* (Oxford: Oxford University Press, 1995) 8.

[32] Elisabeth Bronfen, *The Knotted Subject: Hysteria and its Discontents* (Princeton: Princeton University Press, 1998) 140.

anxiety reminds us of the inescapability of others and of the inevitability of Enlightenment (literally, of the past coming to light) even as we try to escape it into a Romantic phantom world. Viewing enthusiastic excess, melancholic *lifedeath*, and their hysterical consequences against the backdrop of faculty psychology allows us to shift our understanding of subjectivity and violence around 1800, and not necessarily only inward. A psychological viewpoint is not restricted to introspection. It also can signify the medicalization and objectification of the self, which in turn expands the subject outward; the world then becomes what Victoria Nelson (in *The Secret Life of Puppets*) calls a "psychotopography" in which "interior psychic regions" are "projected onto an outer landscape."[33] *William Lovell*, which although written in 1795-1796 has many affinities with psychological realism, is one such psychotopography. William's hysterical symptoms thrust his psychic distress outwards, and in the process he is converted into a kind of object.

The psychic landscapes of *William Lovell* and *The Ghost-Seer* resist spectralization; the projection of interior domains onto external landscapes is different from the reduction of the world to a mental effect. Uncanny repetition is a way of resisting modern alienation and reification, though it does not and cannot bring about the actual return of the real. Rather, it stands as a reminder of what is lost. In William Lovell's case, uncanny encounters are occasioned primarily by his relationship with and rebellion against his dying father; as his rebellion acts itself out against other societal structures, the potential of the uncanny to both trap and liberate is revealed. Before proceeding with readings of uncanny symptoms in these two novels, I will explicate my understanding of male hysteria and demonstrate its relation to the phenomena of enthusiasm and melancholy so often seen in the men of eighteenth- and early nineteenth-century German fiction.

The use of the word "hysteria" may initially call to mind its deployment in the late nineteenth century as a catch-all description of a malady that was usually female and commonly attributed to sexual dissatisfaction, though Freud's description of a "Severe Case of Hemi-Anaesthesia in a Hysterical Male" of 1886 notes that male hysteria is also very ordinary, if often overlooked.[34] However, while the association of "hysteria" with its origin in the Greek "hystera," or uterus, is indeed reactivated around 1900, eighteenth-century hysteria often was dissociated from the uterus. This dissociation happens right around the time that the concept of the uncanny is "invented" and appears regularly in literature and aesthetic theory.[35] Hysteria indeed was diagnosed in the eighteenth century

---

33 Victoria Nelson, *The Secret Life of Puppets* (Cambridge and London: Harvard University Press, 2001) 110.

34 Freud, SE 1: 25.

35 I describe the emergence of the term "uncanny" in the 1770s and 1780s in Chapter Two.

with greater frequency in women than in men,[36] for whom the term "hypochondriasis" often was the preferred diagnosis.

Hypochondriasis was understood in varying ways in the eighteenth century—as manifesting merely in periodic spurts of irritability, or as a sign of "existential uncertainty"—but it often could be cured, at least in its more benign sporadic form, with the relatively simple steps of mental hygiene.[37] Both hypochondriasis and its equivalent among women in the eighteenth century, the vapors (vapeurs), were upper-class afflictions, and while men sought relief in mental hygiene, women pursued "fashionable" magnetic or electric treatments.[38] Hysteria, as it appears in late eighteenth-century psychological and literary discourse, was not as simple to address. It defied mental hygiene, resisted easy classification into mechanistic or materialist categories, and was in men, I contend, a form of Romantic rebellion against the more rationally explicable and curable Enlightened disorders of hypochondriasis and vapors.

Both hysteria and hypochondriasis mean, in Philipp Slavney's and Elaine Showalter's formulations, "behavior that produces the *appearance* of disease, although the patient is unconscious of the motives for feeling sick."[39] Stavros Mentzos provides a succinct description of the three main categories of hysteria, in the context of a definition that includes but is not limited to psychoanalytic understandings of the term. Mentzos intends these features as the broadest applicable characteristics of "hysteria" as it has been understood in modernity, whether in male or female patients:

> First, disruptions of physical functioning (conversion symptoms); secondly, disruptions of psychic functioning (primarily dissociative manifestations); and finally, thirdly, hysterical behavior patterns and character traits.
> (Erstens körperliche Funktionsstörungen [Konversionssymptome], zweitens psychische Funktionsstörungen [vorwiegend dissoziative Erscheinungen] und schließlich drittens hysterische Verhaltensmuster und Charakterzüge.)[40]

---

[36] Phillip R. Slavney, *Perspectives on "Hysteria"* (Baltimore and London: The Johns Hopkins University Press, 1990) 16.

[37] Henri F. Ellenberger discusses hypochondriasis in *The Discovery of the Unconscious: The History and Evolution of Dynamic Psychiatry* (New York: Basic Books, 1970) 187, 197. Carl Niekerk points out that hypochondria has its own conceptual "archeology" and that it was understood in different ways in different periods. He cites Georg Christoph Lichtenberg's association of hypochondria with "existentielle[r] Verunsicherung" in *Zwischen Naturgeschichte und Anthropologie. Lichtenbert im Kontext der Spätaufklärung* (Tübingen: Niemeyer, 2005) 129.

[38] Ellenberger, *The Discovery of the Unconscious: The History and Evolution of Dynamic Psychiatry* 187.

[39] Elaine Showalter, *Hystories: Hysterical Epidemics and Modern Media* (New York: Columbia University Press, 1997) 14.

[40] Stavros Mentzos, *Hysterie. Zur Psychodynamik unbewußter Inszenierungen* (Frankfurt am Main: Fischer Taschenbuch Verlag, 1989) 13.

The moment in which the hysterical symptom appears is a moment of dissociation between the symptom's original cause and the symptom itself. Freud describes it as a form of "splitting of the mind" ("Geistesspaltung").[41] This dissociation is mirrored in the history of hysteria itself, specifically in its divorce from supposedly uterine origins.

Scholars including Elaine Showalter (*Hystories: Hysterical Epidemics and Modern Media*, 1997), Elisabeth Bronfen (*The Knotted Subject: Hysteria and its Discontents*, 1998), and Paul Lerner (*Hysterical Men: War, Psychiatry, and the Politics of Trauma in Germany*, 1890-1930, 2003) make at least some use of Freud's conviction, in his early writings on anxiety, that "hysteria simply takes a number of its symptoms from the anxiety neurosis, and that there is an intimate relationship between anxiety neurosis and hysteria" ("die Hysterie eine Anzahl von Symptomen einfach der Angstneurose entlehnt und daß es eine innige Beziehung der Angstneurose zur Hysterie gibt").[42] Most scholars also refer at least glancingly to Freud's seduction theory of hysteria, which he himself eventually abandoned, and they adopt a much broader understanding of it as something akin to Showalter and Slavney's definition above. In pre-Freudian texts in which the uncanny plays a prominent role, the male subject's hysterical attacks are unleashed by an experience of frightening verisimilitude. That experience in turn inevitably has a strong libidinal component.

There is support for this contention historically but also more plastically across eras. In the *Classifications of Mental Disorders* (*Versuch über die Krankheiten des Kopfes*) of 1764, Kant says that hysteria happens when the otherwise normal imagination produces pictures "of things not actually present" ("Die Seele eines jeden Menschen ist, selbst in dem gesundesten Zustande geschäftig, allerlei Bilder von Dingen, die nicht gegenwärtig sein, zu malen"); in the hysteric, this type of hallucination ("Hirngespenst") is so "deep and lasting, as if caused by an externally stimulated sensation" ("eben so tief und zugleich eben so richtig...als eine sinnliche Empfindung nur machen kann").[43] In Tieck's *Phantasus* (published in 1812 and 1816), the character Ernst concludes similarly that all of the

---

41 Josef Breuer and Sigmund Freud, *Studies on Hysteria*, SE 2: 253.

42 Freud, "Über die Berechtigung von der Neurasthenie einen bestimmten Symptomenkomplex als 'Angst-Neurose' abzutrennen," GW 1: 342/ "On the Grounds for Detaching a Particular Syndrome From Neurasthenia Under the Description 'Anxiety Neurosis,'" SE 3: 103.

43 Immanuel Kant, *Versuch über die Krankheiten des Kopfes*, *Vorkritische Schriften bis 1768*, in *Werke in zwölf Bänden*, ed. Wilhelm Weischedel, volume 2 (Frankfurt am Main: Suhrkamp, 1996) 825-829. The translation is John Manolesco's in *Dreams of a Spirit-Seer by Immanuel Kant and Other Related Writings* (New York: Vantage Press, 1969) 163.

"ghosts" ("Gespenster") of our imaginations have their source in nature—our minds take material from nature and convert it into hallucination.[44]

Although the intersection of imperialism and modern psychiatry that Paul Lerner demonstrates is crucial for the popularization of the category of "male hysteria" in the later nineteenth century is yet to be reached, many of the social and cultural conditions that prodded psychiatrists to diagnose hysteria in men around 1900 are present in 1800 as well. A century before psychoanalysis emerges, hysteria is a way of maintaining and holding onto complexity, when so much of modernizing society, already before the period of classical modernism, is moving toward offering "solutions" to complexity, such as war.[45] Ernst Kretschmer points out that modern mobility and urbanization in particular provoke hysterical symptoms that "appear in the prehistoric forms of our ancestral existence;"[46] such anxiety permeates the fractionalized German territories in the late eighteenth and early nineteenth centuries, and psychology can only provide partial explanations for the increase in nervous disorders around this time.[47] Nevertheless, faculty psychologists attempt to specify an understanding of hysteria that is no longer strictly associated with the uterus.

In a study of hysteria and mysticism, Cristina Mazzoni notes that the male hysteric in modern Europe inevitably has androgynous characteristics. Conversely, the androgyne has traits compatible with the sexual ambiguity associated with hysteria: the "image of the androgyne…represents, among other things, physical and moral ambiguity (as a hysteric, yet at the same time also a male, he is suspended between being and having the phallus)."[48] This reading presents a more expansive view of hysteria than Freud's early understanding of anxiety as linked to sexual neuroses, and yet works with that understanding's more interesting ramifications for gender identity. Mazzoni concludes that in narrative discourse in the nineteenth-century and in other eras, hysteria is "a mimetic modality, a manipulable representational strategy, rather than a univocally referential diagnostic term."[49] Texts that feature hysterical men convert those men from subjects into objects and feminize them, which is a move that essentially mutates a man from a desiring male

---

44 Ludwig Tieck, *Phantasus*, ed. Manfred Frank (Frankfurt am Main: Deutscher Klassiker Verlag, 1985) 112-113.

45 Paul Lerner calls war an "antidote to complexity" in *Hysterical Men: War, Psychiatry, and the Politics of Trauma in Germany, 1890-1930* (Ithaca and London: Cornell University Press, 2003) 9.

46 Ernst Kretschmer, "Hysterie," *Wissen und Leben: Neue schweizer Rundschau* 17 (1923) 148; cited here in Lerner, *Hysterical Men: War, Psychiatry, and the Politics of Trauma in Germany, 1890-1930* 15.

47 Roy Porter addresses the "'coming-out' of the hypochondriac and the hysteric" around 1800 in *Flesh in the Age of Reason* 401ff.

48 Cristina Mazzoni, *Saint Hysteria: Neurosis, Mysticism, and Gender in European Culture* (Ithaca and London: Cornell University Press, 1996) 134.

49 Ibid, 5.

subject into a feminized object of desire. This is a strange form of rebellion against modern complexity, but it can be read as a rebellion nonetheless; these texts' reliance on the "masculine" maladies of melancholy (an ongoing sense of loss) and enthusiasm (too much feeling) makes the hysterical men within them representative of an anxiety that is modern and ancient at once.

Regardless of the sufferer's gender, the term "hysteria" is vexed, and even psychiatric practitioners who have advocated keeping it as a diagnostic category have some trouble with its fluidity. Pierre Janet argued that the term hysteria "should be preserved, although its primitive meaning has much changed. Truly, it has so grand and so beautiful a history that it would be painful to give it up."[50] Janet here acknowledges an aesthetic component in the experience and treatment of hysteria—it has a beautiful history; it is a gorgeous concept. There is definitely something reactionary about hysteria in the conventional understanding of it as self-repudiating, as a punishment of the self by itself for being inadequate, when of course that self has in actuality been silenced by dominant power structures and discourses.

Freud's famous patient Dora was hysteric; her brother was a revolutionary. And along these lines, what I am calling the "male hysteria" in *William Lovell* and in *The Ghost-Seer* is in part also a reactionary move into illness as a response to victimization; these men (William, Balder, and Burton in *Lovell* in particular; the Prince in *Ghost-Seer*) are all "disempowered" by their (biological or social) fathers' old feuds as well as by their own "enthusiastic" or "melancholy" character "types." But these men are not victims in the way that Dora is; they are not disempowered or silenced in the same manner. In Schiller and Tieck, disease-like symptoms are provoked indeed by the disempowerment brought on by an ever-more instrumental rationality—a disempowerment that is a kind of emasculation, a kind of castration and feminization—but also by the bringing-to-light of dark knowledge long forgotten. These hysterical symptoms are simultaneously symptoms of a kind of rebellion that seeks to preserve that which is complicated and difficult—to preserve the enthusiastic, the melancholy, to bring the outside in and move the inside out, in a very modern acknowledgement (whether conscious or not) of relatedness and of vulnerability.

Viewing enthusiastic excess, melancholic *lifedeath*, and their hysterical consequences against the backdrop of faculty psychology allows us to shift our understanding of subjectivity and violence around 1800, and not necessarily only inward. A psychological viewpoint is not restricted to introspection. It also can signify the medicalization and objectification of the self, which in turn expands the subject outward; the world then becomes what Victoria Nelson (in *The Secret Life of Puppets*) calls a "psychotopography" in

---

[50] Bronfen, *The Knotted Subject: Hysteria and its Discontents* 101.

which "interior psychic regions" are "projected onto an outer landscape."[51] *William Lovell*, which although written in 1795-1796 resembles in many respects a work of psychological realism, is one such psychotopography. William's hysterical symptoms thrust his psychic distress outwards, and in the process he is converted into a kind of object.

A shift to the psychological context, or to a psychological stance towards at least certain works of literature around 1800, results in a view of emotional states such as enthusiasm and melancholy that does not only predate Freud's view that neurotic behaviors are violence turned inward, directed by the self against itself. The integration of elements of faculty or empirical psychology into literary texts and texts of aesthetic theory around 1800 also anticipates an "exterocentric" worldview.[52] In other words, neurotic violence against the self and against others, violence due to too much feeling, too much enthusiasm, does not merely anticipate the insights of later depth psychology and psychoanalysis but anticipates the state of "relatedness," of melancholic imbrication with others and their pasts, that characterizes uncanny memory.

The dissociation of symptom from its original cause (in this case, the dissociation of hysterical symptoms from the uterus) is analogous to the paranoia induced by the secret societies of the eighteenth and nineteenth centuries, groups whose reputation for exerting influence likely always exceeded their real power, but which nevertheless seemed to be everywhere; Schiller felt it necessary to disavow membership in order to lend his *Don Carlos* aesthetic independence and credibility (although the drama presents a utopian worldview compatible with that of the Illuminati).[53] The secret society is a kind of body writ large, a social outgrowth of psychosomatic problems whose previously materialist explanations no longer suffice. The uncanny dissociation of symptom from cause forces a reconsideration, though not necessarily a complete rejection, of the historical domination of explanations for mental disorders that reduced those disorders to organic causes.[54]

---

[51] Victoria Nelson, *The Secret Life of Puppets* (Cambridge and London: Harvard University Press, 2001) 110.

[52] Edward Casey, *Remembering: A Phenomenological Study* (Bloomington and Indianapolis: Indiana University Press, 1987) 287.

[53] In the tenth letter of the *Briefe über Don Carlos*, Schiller writes "Ich bin weder Illuminat noch Maurer"; Walter Müller-Seidel points out that it remains unclear whether the drama itself is consistent or at odds with this statement. See Müller-Seidel and Wolfgang Riedel, eds., *Die Weimarer Klassik und ihre Geheimbunde* (Würzburg: Königshausen & Neumann, 2002) 15.

[54] Porter and Bynum, eds., *Companion Encyclopedia of the History of Medicine* 1: 438.

2.1. Tieck, *William Lovell (Geschichte des Herrn William Lovell)*

Ludwig Tieck (1773-1853) was preoccupied with how issues prevalent in the psychological literature and practice of his time might intersect with aesthetic concepts. A desire to understand his own disordered moods doubtless underscored this preoccupation, but Tieck also was interested in how the biological and mentalistic explanations of disease and the concerns of a philosophically-oriented psychology could be worked together in the interest of more effective and better poetry. In 1790, he attempted to distinguish between emotional states that are useful for poets and those that are not. Each emotion manifests in three possible stages, in increasing order of intensity; for instance, an initial state of "goodwill" can progress from there to "tenderness" and ultimately to "love." "Melancholy" may intensify into "madness" and finally to "insanity." "Cowardice" moves on to "fear," and then to "anxiety." Tieck calls the final stage of each emotional state "sublime," meaning that a precarious balance between philosophical and psychological elements has been struck. However, once passion progresses beyond that third stage of expression, it is "for the poet completely useless, because it is completely physical and there is no illusion" ("ganz für den Dichter unbrauchbar, weil es ganz körperl. ist und hier gar keine Illusion").[55] A complete enslavement to the body prevents the poet from applying imagination.

William Lovell is a novel that is nothing if not concerned with emotional states, their relation to each other, and their level of dependence on the body. Tieck's contemporaries viewed his representation of such relationships with a mixture of skepticism and concern. Rudolf Haym, author of *The Romantic School* (*Die Romantische Schule*), saw in *Lovell* a "spirit of skeptical melancholy" ("Geist der skeptischen Melancholie"), but concluded that that skepticism never amounts to more than a repetition of the same questions about the extent to which the mind is at the mercy of the body's whims, a repetition that "return(ed) unanswered to the questioner in a long resounding, much broken echo" ("die in langnachhallendem, vielgebrochem Echo unbeantwortet zu dem Frager zurückkehrte").[56] The Dutch statesman Jan Rudolf Thorbecke also found a form of repetition in the novel troubling, but simultaneously promising, when he called *Lovell*

> a movement in the negative world of appearance, after one once has destroyed that which is most essential in oneself, and cannot find it again in the external world. Then a fluctuation and arbitrariness arise in which one would have to go under, if the ghost of something true, with which one is never finished, were not in ceaseless pursuit.

---

[55] Ludwig Tieck, *Schriften 1789-1793*, ed. Achim Hölter (Frankfurt am Main: Klassiker Verlag, 1991) 651.

[56] Rudolf Haym, *Die Romantische Schule* (Berlin: Weidmann, 1949) 49, 50; quoted here in Matenko, *Tieck and Solger: The Complete Correspondence* 143.

> (ein sich Bewegen in der nichtigen Welt der Erscheinung, nachdem man einmahl das Wesentliche in sich selber zerstört hat, und es nun auch außer sich nicht wiederfinden kann. Dann entsteht ein Schwanken und eine Willkür, worin der Mensch geradezu untergehn müsste, wenn nicht ein Gespenst des Wahren, womit er nie fertig wird, ihn unablässig verfolgte und hielte.)[57]

A letter from Tieck to a close friend, the philosopher and aesthetic theorist Karl Wilhelm Ferdinand Solger, reveals that he also saw *Lovell* in ghostly but corporeal terms, and as engaging in an act of preservation if not of repetition. He compares the novel to a physical home for the dead, a "mausoleum of many closely kept and beloved passions and errors" ("Mausoleum vieler gehegten und geliebten Leiden und Irrthümer"). However, he goes on to say that once this mausoleum was constructed,

> the sketch artist and worker was already free of this suffering; I was almost always very cheerful when I was writing this book, but I just pleased myself when confused. Something of this mania certainly will always cling to me, and it has to do with my best qualities. Like Everything.
> (war der Zeichner und Arbeiter schon von diesen Leiden frei, ich war fast immer sehr heiter, als ich dies Buch schrieb, nur gefiel ich mir noch in der Verwirrung. Etwas von dieser Sucht wird mir gewiß immer anhängen bleiben, auch hängt es wohl mit meinem Besten wieder zusammen. Wie Alles.)[58]

By the time he had finished *Lovell*, Tieck believed he had reached a sort of compromise solution to a problem that had haunted him since adolescence: that of which personality type was best suited to live with and through agonizing and inevitable anxiety about the meaning of existence. The genius-poets of the Storm and Stress epoch displayed the "mania" ("Sucht") to which Tieck refers above—they were madly productive, or productively mad, but Tieck suspected that their passion was hyperbolic and in any event it could not be sustained. The alternative personality type found among artists and intellectuals of the time as Tieck saw it, was a type who the editor of his letters, Percy Matenko, calls the "calmer, colder, simpler, and truer people, who had definitely bidden farewell to all illusions and lived therefore in a narrow parochial world where none could envy their lot."[59] In *Lovell*, he presents both types, and they occur along a spectrum in the characters of Balder, William himself, Mortimer, Karl Wilmont, and Eduard Burton. He asserts that this exploration of character and of various psychosocial disorders has permitted him to reach a point at which the "mania" that will always be

---

[57] Letter from Jan Rudolf Thorbecke to Ludwig Tieck of December 7, 1821; quoted here in Matenko, *Letters To and From Ludwig Tieck and His Circle* 49.
[58] Letter from Ludwig Tieck to Karl Wilhelm Ferdinand Solger on March 31, 1815; quoted here in Matenko, *Tieck and Solger: The Complete Correspondence* 167-168.
[59] Matenko, *Tieck and Solger: The Complete Correspondence* 65.

part of him (and in fact helps make him successful) can be integrated with a more cheerful ("heiter") and balanced disposition.

Karl Solger was not quite persuaded by Tieck's insistence that, while *Lovell* indeed represented a difficult phase in his own life, he had used it successfully to represent and work through that phase and then to move on. Solger was troubled in particular by the text's lack of irony, which he held responsible for the reader's "uncanny" concern about the author's, rather than the characters', well-being. For Solger, the "fluctuation and arbitrariness" ("Schwanken und Willkür") of the "movement in the negative world of appearance" ("sich Bewegen in der nichtigen Welt der Erscheinung") identified by Thorbecke could well signal recurring problems from Tieck's own past. The lack of a leveling irony in the novel leads Solger to fear that Tieck may be stuck in a melancholy cycle. At the same time, he praises Tieck's poetic abilities, but does not make the connection that Tieck implies, in the poetic theory of 1790 referred to above, between melancholy emotion and aesthetic achievement. In a letter to Tieck, Solger writes:

> I read *Lovell* with great interest, primarily because it certainly represents an important period in your life. I know this condition, in which one finds oneself in certain youthful periods, and which later occasionally shows up again in weaker form. One sees that you yourself are caught up in these subjects and feelings, and therefore some of this appears almost arbitrary, because there is not enough irony. This is why I often had an uncanny feeling; not because the characters' situation made me fearful—I usually could understand how that was thought up by the author—but rather I feared for the author and his personal mood. Considering this, I must admire the power and composition of the presentation all the more, which could only belong to one destined to be a master.
> (Den *Lovell* habe ich mit großem Interesse gelesen vorzüglich weil er gewiß eine bedeutende Periode Ihres Lebens bezeichnet. Ich kenne diesen Zustand, in welchem man sich in gewissen Jugendperioden befindet, und welcher nach und nach schwächer sich auch späterhin wohl zuweilen wieder meldet. Man sieht, daß Sie selbst in den Gegenständen und Gefühlen befangen sind, und daher erscheint manches beinah willkürlich, weil es zu sehr an Ironie mangelt. Deshalb war mir oft unheimlich dabei zu Muthe, nicht gerade weil mich der Zustand der handelnden Personen ängstigte, denn diesen übersah ich dann am meisten, wie er von dem Verfasser gedacht war, sondern eben um des Verfassers und seiner persönlichen Stimmung willen. Wenn ich darauf sehe, so muß ich um so mehr die Kraft und Bildung der Darstellung bewundern, die nur dem so eigen sein konnte, der zum Meister bestimmt war.)[60]

Tieck's friends knew that he, like Karl Philipp Moritz, suffered intermittently but repeatedly from depressed moods as well as from an excess of emotion. *William Lovell* was, on the one hand, an attempt to imitate and improve upon English epistolary fiction; Richardson's *Clarissa* is the most commonly

---

[60] Letter from Karl Wilhelm Ferdinand Solger to Ludwig Tieck on March 18, 1815; quoted here in Matenko, *Tieck and Solger: The Complete Correspondence* 163.

mentioned model.[61] But it was simultaneously a working-through—a therapeutic replaying and repetition—of Tieck's own reading of and reactions to Carl Grosse's monumentally popular novel *The Genius* (*Der Genius*) of 1791. More successful among intellectuals of the period than either *Lovell* or Schiller's *Ghost-Seer* (1787/1789), *The Genius* was also powerful enough to send Tieck into delirium and then a temporary nervous collapse.[62] But although reading a novel was responsible for a neurotic outbreak, Tieck believed that he treated himself effectively by writing one in response. This confirmed his conviction that aesthetic creation ultimately rescued him from the potentially deadly dilemma of personality choice—specifically, the choice between overly enthusiastic genius and cold rationality.

Faculty psychologists of the late eighteenth century, including Tieck's friend Moritz, saw a close connection between the prevalence of certain psychosomatic disorders and psychophysical "types." Moritz asserts that melancholy, an excess of imagination, and enthusiastic fanaticism are interdependent problems, and quotes one Daniel Jenisch's assertion that these problems "kindle" one another "like electric sparks." Moritz's piece in the *Journal of Empirical Psychology* entitled "On Enthusiasm and its Sources in Our Times" ("Über die Schwärmerey und ihre Quellen in unseren Zeiten") is an attempt to explain why such behavior persists in an enlightened age, and includes the following testimony from Jenisch:

> I must also note, that (...) rapture, enthusiasm, phantastery and fanaticism hang together via a very fine organism, and like electric sparks, if more sober ideas do not intercede, will kindle one another.
> [Noch muß ich anmerken, daß {...} Schwärmerey, Enthusiasmus, Fantasterey und Fanatismus durch einen sehr feinen Organismus zusammenhängen, und wie electrische Funken, wenn leichtere Ideen nicht ins Mittel treten, sich eins an dem andern entzünden.][63]

When the character William Lovell spends too much time in what Tieck calls the "unnatural realms of fantasy,"[64] such experiences "kindle" one another within him as well, until he repeatedly experiences an uncanny anxiety: he

---

[61] In a letter to Solger, Tieck expresses a strong and searing criticism of the "undeutsches" German theater of the time, then immediately admits that his reactions are perhaps extreme and that something can be learned from other cultures. See Matenko, *Tieck and Solger: The Complete Correspondence* 168.

[62] Münz in *William Lovell* 727. Here Münz cites as evidence a letter of June 12, 1792 from Tieck to Wackenroder, saying that *Der Genius* had occasioned "Delirium und die wahrscheinlich schwerste Nervenkrise seines (Tiecks) Lebens."

[63] Karl Philipp Moritz, *Gnothi sauton oder Magazin zur Erfahrungsseelenkunde als ein Lesebuch für Gelehrte und Ungelehrte*, eds. Petra and Uwe Nettelbeck (Nördlingen: Franz Greno, 1986) 5: 219.

[64] Tieck, *William Lovell* 101.

feels that he is disintegrating or dissociating;[65] his unnatural imagination provokes a sick response in his physical nature.

In the novel, William's uncanny anxiety, provoked by enthusiasm, manifests as hysterical symptom, which is a violent affect. And in a sense the dissociation between the affect (the symptom) and the initial enthusiasm is what is uncanny. That is, the hysterical affect is the return of the repressed enthusiastic feeling, which is not welcome in the rapidly modernizing society in which William and his acquaintances find themselves. In this society, in England as well as on the continent, the landed gentry is clearly in an irrevocable process of decay—it is virtually being buried alive by urbanization and by a recently empowered middle class, whose assertion of power in finance and industry creates immense anxiety for the increasingly impotent aristocrats as well as for members of the middle class themselves.

Near the beginning of the novel, William leaves England for an ultimately deadly grand tour on the continent. He initially is accompanied by a fellow Englishman, Mortimer, but soon meets a cold Italian atheist named Rosa as well as a melancholic, romantic German, Balder. As he grows ever closer to Rosa, William begins to embark on love affairs, most notably with the gorgeous Louise, the Comtesse de Blainville (which means he is unfaithful to his supposed true love back home, Amalie) and to neglect his father back in England, his faithful old manservant Willy, as well as his former best friends and "good influences" Karl Wilmont (Amalie's brother) and Eduard Burton. With Rosa in Italy, and in the process of going from one one-night stand to the next, William is suddenly shocked and becomes ill when he spies Rosa together with a decrepit, elderly, frightening male figure. This apparition is uncanny in that it reminds William of a hated portrait hanging in the house of his father, a portrait William has tried to forget. The old man turns out to be Andrea Cosimo.

William enacts outwardly an uncanny repetition of the behavior of these men (Cosimo and Rosa), as, when he returns to England a hardened sensualist, he seduces Emilie, the sister of his childhood best friend Eduard and the girlfriend of Karl Wilmont. After he deserts her, she dies, and William decides to seek out his old girlfriend Amalie. He promises Amalie's ugly maid a night of sex if the maid will arrange a meeting with Amalie. The repulsive maid turns out to be none other than Louise, the Comtesse de Blainville, who has become horribly pockmarked, her body violently marked by contagious disease. Amalie's house goes up in flames, William saves her, but must flee from her brother, Karl Wilmont. Back on the continent, William becomes impoverished and ends up finding the melancholic German Balder

[65] The existential psychologist Leon Salzman aligns this kind of anxiety with the uncanny emotion "resulting from the abrupt appearance of intense anxiety in situations in which a person suddenly comes close to a realization of the dissociated components in his personality." See "Uncanny Feeling," *Psychiatry* 17 (1954) 100.

in an asylum. In Italy William discovers that the elderly Andrea Cosimo is indeed the subject of the hated portrait in William's (now-dead) father's home: Cosimo is none other than Waterloo, an unfaithful friend who caused Walter Lovell's (William's father's) financial ruin and deadly psychological stress. Finally, Karl Wilmont finds William and kills him in a duel. But not before William has become enlightened about what was really going on in his father's and his life; all that had been repressed comes to light.

William is not the only male character who evinces a potentially harmful enthusiasm with hysterical symptoms: he can be seen as occupying a position along a spectrum of men with varying degrees of symptoms, with his friend and eventual nemesis Eduard Burton positioned at one end and Balder at the other extreme. If we see William in the middle of this group, we can also see his male acquaintances and their symptomology as representing facets of William's own personality, or different possible courses that any male protagonist or reader could take. In any and every case, enthusiasm or excessive feeling, which itself is a response to an excess *of* feeling (which even Eduard Burton and Karl Wilmont eventually suffer), is acted out in compulsively repetitive ways in and on the external landscape; all of these behaviors are violent, or at least have a violent component. They include addictive sex, compulsive travel, fighting or duelling, and the frightening experiences of horrific uncanny visions.

All of this acting out is performed by this set of male characters who alternately occupy positions of victims and persecutors. Cosimo/Waterloo is perhaps the novel's only clear villain (that is, he is only a perpetrator and never a victim), and his appearances and disappearances in the novel are examples of the operation of revealing-and-withdrawing that Hélène Cixous has called *the* mechanism of the uncanny.[66] Cosimo represents the past coming back in a familiar but strange form, with violent consequences. This uncanny mechanism of revealing and withdrawing does not happen on a discursive level alone; it happens around 1800 in the context and course of psychological illness, with its physical symptoms that repetitively come and go.

In the following passages from the novel, at least one of the three hysterical behaviors or symptoms identified above occurs: dissociation (from oneself), phobia (specifically of women), and paranoia (fear of manipulation at the hands of secret societies or dark unseen forces)—all of these hysterical instances are uncanny, and all are the consequence of too much enthusiasm. And yet all can also be read as methods of living with loss—of moving forward while remembering, and of taking part in progress while resisting it.

---

[66] Hélène Cixous, "Fiction and its Phantoms: A Reading of Freud's *Das Unheimliche*," *New Literary History* 7 (1976) 525-548.

Near the end of the novel's first volume, William's friend Balder relates his experience of a classic neurotic anxiety attack with uncanny characteristics:

> I do not sleep, and I cannot wake up (…) I shudder and turn pale, when I raise my hand: who is this stranger, I ask, shocked, who reaches out his arm to me in greeting? - I grasp for it anxiously and grab, in horror, my own corpse-cold hand, like an estranged thing that does not belong to me.
> (Ich schlafe nicht und kann nicht erwachen […] ich fahre erbleichend zusammen, wenn ich meine Hand aufhebe: wer ist der Fremdling, frag' ich erschrocken, der mir den Arm zum Gruße entgegenstreckt? - Ich greife ängstlich darnach und ergreife schaudernd meine eigene, leichenkalte Hand, wie ein fremdartiges Stück, das mir nicht zugehört.)[67]

During these repeated attacks, the familiar is strange—Balder feels that he is observing his own body from a distance; he is alienated from himself. He repeatedly experiences what the existential psychologist Leon Salzman calls the uncanny emotion "resulting from the abrupt appearance of intense anxiety in situations in which a person suddenly comes close to a realization of the dissociated components in his personality."[68]

The above passage, and Salzman's description of the quintessentially uncanny emotion of anxiety created by dissociation, echo Tieck's narration of his own experience after he spent a night reading the first two parts of Carl Grosse's horror novel *The Genius* aloud to friends. In a much-cited letter to Wilhelm Heinrich Wackenroder, Tieck writes that, when trying to sleep in the early-morning hours,

> It was as if I were swimming in a stream, as if my head had detached itself and were swimming backwards, my body forwards, a sensation I had never had before; when I opened my eyes it was as if I were lying in a large vault, three coffins next to one another, I see the white gleaming bones clearly, everything stretched out to a horrible length, all of my limbs had become alien to me, and I started, when I reached for my face with my hand.
> (war mir als schwämme ich auf einem Strom, als löste sich mein Kopf ab und schwämme rückwärts, der Körper vorwärts, eine Empfindung die ich sonst noch nie gehabt habe, wenn ich die Augen aufmachte war mir's, als läg ich in einem weiten Totengewölbe, drei Särge nebeneinander, ich sehe deutlich die weißen, schimmernden Gebeine, alles dehnte sich in eine fürchterliche Länge, alle meine Glieder waren mir selbst fremd geworden, und ich erschrak, wenn ich mit der Hand nach meinem Gesicht faßte.)[69]

In the case of Balder's letter to William as well as in the context of Tieck's reading of *Genius* together with friends, an experience of horrifying

---

[67] Tieck, *William Lovell* 174.

[68] Salzman, "Uncanny Feeling" 100.

[69] Wilhelm Heinrich Wackenroder, *Werke und Briefe* (Heidelberg: Lambert Schneider, 1967) 325. Tieck's letter is from June 12, 1792.

dissociation and disorientation leads to a need to connect and communicate with others. For Balder, however, this attempt is ultimately hopeless; like his namesake, the Norse god Baldur,[70] he dies in a kind of exile, that of madness.

Balder's attacks, experienced in a kind of "twilight state," or "Dämmerzustand"[71] ("I do not sleep, and I cannot wake up"), also can be read as a response to his own enthusiastic excess and as the expression of a desire to die at least a little (this is reminiscent of Moritz, who documents a number of similar real-life cases in his *Journal of Empirical Psychology*, and who refers to this desire in himself as the wish to "be no more" ["nicht mehr seyn"]). The attacks also may be part of a related desire to, as Freud puts it, keep something out: "in alienation (or derealization) we are busy trying to shut something out of us" ("bei Entfremdung sind wir bemüht, etwas von uns auszuschließen").[72] It is in that state, however, in which we may achieve greatest clarity; or, in which the proximity between ease and disease is apparent: In a letter to Rosa, William writes of Balder: "In the midst of outbreaks of his insanity, Balder wrote me a letter in which many ideas are dark to me; he is either close to being healed, or more dangerously ill than ever" ("Balder hat mitten in den Ausbrüchen seines Wahnsinns einen Brief an mich geschrieben, in dem mir manche Ideen Dunkel sind, er ist entweder seiner Heilung nahe, oder gefährlicher krank, als je").[73]

But there is an equally uncanny experience of "fausse reconnaissance" or "déjà vu," in which, according to Freud, we want to bring in something that doesn't really belong ("we want to take something in as if it belonged to us" ["wir {wollen} etwas als zu unserem Ich gehörig annehmen"]).[74] And this phenomenon of "fausse reconnaissance" (false remembering) is what happens when William's object relations are most obviously distorted: in his exploitation of and re-encounters with the women he really despises.

---

70 Heather Sullivan notes and expands upon the reference to Norse mythology in *The Intercontextuality of Self and Nature in Ludwig Tieck's Early Works* (New York: Peter Lang 1997) 171-172n25.

71 Marianne Thalmann contends: "Tiecks Menschen leben mehr im Dämmerzustand als im Traum. Der Übergang vom Wachzustand in den traumhaften ist ein rascher und häufiger. Tieck selbst legte großen Wert auf seine eigenen Träume, deren Gequältheit sich ihm besonders einprägte. Er betrachtete den Traum an sich als Offenbarung verhemmter Tagesseiten der menschlicher Natur (Köpke, II, 126). Er wird ihm daher zum Ausdruck unserer höchsten Philosophie (*Lovell*, 348)." *Die Romantik des Trivialen. Von Grosses "Genius" bis Tiecks "William Lovell"* (Munich: Paul List, 1970) 47. Thalmann refers here to Rudolf Köpke's *Ludwig Tieck. Erinnerungen aus dem Leben eines Dichters* (Leipzig, 1855).

72 Freud, "Brief an Romain Rolland (Eine Erinnerungsstörung auf der Akropolis)," GW 16: 254-255/ "Letter to Romain Rolland (A Disturbance of Memory on the Acropolis," SE 22: 243. Freud explains the phenomenon of "false recognition" in more detail in "Über Fausse Reconnaissance ('Déjà Raconté') während der psychoanalytischen Arbeit," GW 10: 116-123/ "Fausse Reconnaissance ('Déjà Raconté') in Psycho-Analytic Treatment," SE 13: 201-207.

73 Tieck, *William Lovell* 213.

74 Freud, GW 16: 255/SE 22: 243.

The horribly disfigured Louise is a strange, yet familiar, reminder of the beautiful temptress she once was, as well as an uncanny replication or externalization of William's own desires. She is his desires' outward manifestation, their psychotopography, and her disfigurement reveals how degenerate his desires truly are, and therefore how degenerate he is. His increasingly wayward and abusive sexual life is the reality that her disfigured face and sexually repulsive body represent. Louise's face also is analogous to Freud's understanding of Medusa's head, which is (for Freud) apotropaic: it takes the place of a representation of the female genitals, which provokes horror and hysteria in "the enemy" (in this case, in William, who panics).[75] Louise is not unlike the uncanny dolls of nineteenth- and twentieth-century fiction and aesthetic theory, in that she fulfills what Wilhelm Stekel calls a "sexually aberrant" function.[76] When William agrees to have sex with her in exchange for the meeting with Amalie, he agrees to become Louise's object, to be used; his already decidedly ambiguous morality transmutes into the kind of physical ambiguity that Mazzoni contends characterizes the male hysteric. William possesses the phallus that Louise desires, but he must to an extent relinquish it in order to attain the object of his own desire. This act is not only symbolic; it carries with it the risk of real disease. In a letter to Rosa, William writes that Louise's husband, the Count Melun, died soon after their marriage; another lover, the Chevalier Valois, has shot himself.

In this same letter, William writes that Louise's disease has merely

> revealed the monster that already lay inside the beautiful woman I embraced—now, with every woman and girl I think: the old crone, who is limping by on a crutch, with gray hair, stooped, and with red eyes, she was once young and had suitors; she did not think then that she could change; it did not occur to her enraptured lover to laugh about himself, because he did not know the real figure to whom he addressed his declarations.—O, away from all of that!—But what are all the joys of this world? –It is a disgusting sight to me, when I see a pair being tender to one another. In childhood we wish for glassy beads, then love, then riches, then health, then only for life; in every phase we think we have come further, but we are going around in a circle…

---

[75] Freud writes: "Wenn das Medusenhaupt die Darstellung des weiblichen Genitales ersetzt, vielmehr dessen grauenerregende Wirkung von seiner lusterregenden isoliert, so kann man sich erinnern, dass die Zeigen der Genitalien auch sonst als apoptropaeische Handlung bekannt ist. Was einem selbst Grauen erregt, wird auch auf den abzuwehrenden Feind dieselbe Wirkung äussern. Noch bei Rabelais ergreift der Teufel die Flucht, nachdem ihm das Weib ihre Vulva gezeigt hat" ("If Medusa's head takes the place of a representation of the female genitals, or rather if it isolates their horrifying effects from the pleasure-giving ones, it may be recalled that displaying the genitals is familiar in other connections as an apotropaic act. What arouses horror in oneself will produce the same effect upon the enemy against whom one is seeking to defend oneself. We read in Rabelais of how the Devil took to flight when the woman showed him her vulva"), "Das Medusenhaupt," GW 17: 47-48/ "Medusa's Head," SE 18: 273.

[76] Wilhelm Stekel, *Sexual Aberrations* (New York: Liveright Publishing Corp., 1930) 54. Quoted here in Mike Kelley, *The Uncanny*, exhibit catalogue, with essays by Mike Kelley, John C. Welchman, and Christoph Grunenberg (Cologne: Verlag der Buchhandlung Walther König, 2004) 16.

> (dies Ungeheuer [lag] doch schon damals verlarvt in dem schönen Weibe..., das ich umarmte,
> —bei jedem Weibe und Mädchen fällt mir jetzt der Gedanke ein: Die Alte, die mit grauen Haaren, abgefallen, mit roten Augen und auf einer Krücke vorüberhinkt, war auch einmal jung und hatte ihre Anbeter, sie dachte damals nicht daran, daß sie sich ändern könne; ihrem begeisterten Liebhaber fiel es nicht ein, über sich selbst zu lachen, denn er kannte die Gestalt nicht, gegen die er seine Deklamationen richtete.—O hinweg davon!—Aber was sind alle Freuden dieser Welt? – Es ist mir ein widriger Anblick, wenn ich ein Paar gehn sehe, das zärtlich gegeneinander tut. In der Kindheit wünschen wir uns Glasperlen, dann Liebe, dann Reichtum, dann Gesundheit, dann nur noch das Leben; auf jeder Station glauben wir weitergekommen zu sein und fahren doch im Kreise herum...)[77]

William's description of the meaninglessness that accompanies transience echoes Balder's view of nature. In a letter to Eduard Burton written before William's own downward spiral begins, William recounts a conversation he has had with Balder while on a walk. William encourages Balder to enjoy himself: "Look at the beautiful creation all around us, I said to him, see how happy all of nature is!" ("Sieh die reizende Schöpfung umher, redete ich ihn wieder an, sieh wie sich die ganze Natur freut und glücklich ist!") But Balder answers: "And everything dies and decays; are you forgetting that we are walking over the bodies of millions of varied beings,—that nature's majesty takes its material from rot,—that it is nothing but disguised decomposition?" ("Und alles stirbt und verwes't; —vergissest du, daß wir über die Leichen von Millionen mannichfaltiger Geschöpfe gehn, —daß die Pracht der Natur ihren Stoff aus dem Moder nimmt, —daß sie nichts als eine verkleidete Verwesung ist?")[78] When William pleads with him to at least enjoy nature's beautiful disguise ("let us at least recognize that betrayal, which makes us happy, as true" ["so laß uns doch wenigstens den Betrug für wahr anerkennen, der uns glücklich macht"]), Balder refuses to relent: "Your deception does not make me happy; for me the colors are faded, the cloaking garment has fallen from nature, I see the white skeleton in its frightful nakedness" ("Deine Täuschung macht mich nicht glücklich, die Farben sind für mich verbleicht, das verhüllende Gewand von der Natur abgefallen, ich sehe das weiße Gerippe in seiner fürchterlichen Nacktheit").[79]

Unlike Freud, whose essay "On Transience" (examined at the beginning of Chapter Two) turns a similar walk through nature with a melancholy young friend into a meditation on resistance to mourning, William ultimately will not be able to intellectualize or to resist his companion's mood. Although in this early part of the novel, he is still able to condemn Balder's "terrible coldness" ("schreckliche Kalte") and to suggest that he surrender to cheerfulness, "so that your blood will flow faster in your

---

[77] Tieck, *William Lovell* 472-473.
[78] Ibid, 139.
[79] Ibid, 140.

veins" ("Überlaß dich der Heiterkeit, daß dein Blut schneller durch die Adern fließt"),[80] William will fall prey to the same types of psychic and physical disorders that plague Balder, and will come to the same conclusion about life's transience and about the permanence, the "real" truth, of death. Although other factors contribute to William's increasing neuroses and eventual downfall, his contact with Balder is crucial; here Tieck references contemporary faculty psychology's acknowledgment that mental disorders could be contagious.[81]

William's melancholy also is occasioned in part by a disrupted relation to his mother, who is portrayed in some letters as dead, in others as alive (probably due to Tieck's lack of revision), but always as absent. But while Oedipal conflicts are not absent from the novel, *William Lovell* is inspired by the existential dilemmas and disturbed object relations of the male subject, and not ultimately by the mother. That is, the mothers and female lovers are proximate factors rather than the real causes of William's problems.[82] In contrast to Louise, Amalie, William's first love (and his English, "heimliche Liebe") remains beautiful throughout the novel. But she never really is an object of desire; she functions as a means towards William's initial end, that is, to modify his overly enthusiastic and sentimental character in a rational direction, in the direction of his close male friend Eduard. But William's vulnerability to Rosa's manipulation, along with his own innate excess of sensuality, doom him to repetitive re-exploitations of woman after woman, and there really is no way out of this cycle. Louise is a horrifying uncanny apotropaic projection, and Amalie is not what he wants; by the time he does try to reunite with her, it is much too late.

Similarly, William's encounters with Cosimo/Waterloo, the man who reminds him of and in fact is the subject of the frightening painting in his childhood home, are uncanny and frightening, but the fact that the encounters

---

[80] Tieck, *William Lovell* 140.

[81] It is possible that Tieck's speculation about the contagious nature of mental disorders comes directly from his friend Karl Philipp Moritz, whose *Erfahrungsseelenkunde* includes this characteristic in an enumeration of the many facets of psychosomata; volume 4: 31 (also cited in Chapter Three).

[82] Here I rely on the premise of Martha Helfer's argument that, at least in several significant works of German Romantic literature, "the metaphysical ground of the Romantic project - presumed to be the maternal, eternal feminine embodied in the form of the beloved - proves to be the self-positing male subject." See "The Male Muses of Romanticism: The Poetics of Gender in Novalis, E.T.A. Hoffmann, and Eichendorff," *The German Quarterly* 78.3 (2005), 300. Helfer's work in no way excludes a psychoanalytic understanding of essential complexes and disorders, but it illuminates a competing and prevalent paradigm of the "male muse" in Romantic cultural production that challenges by-now standard readings of "woman (as) the idealized, unattainable 'other' against which the male poet defines himself in a gesture of wish fulfillment, (as) the priestess and source of enlightenment for the male poet…(as) 'the discursive production of the Mother as the source of discursive production.'" 299. The embedded quotation is from David Wellbery's "Foreword" in Friedrich A. Kittler: *Discourse Networks 1800/1900*, trans. Michael Metteer, with Chris Cullens (Stanford: Stanford University Press 1990) xxiii.

propel William into hysterical behavioral excesses (panic, insomnia, and nymphomanic episodes) is due to his growing sense of paranoia that secret, dark forces must be manipulating him. However, what is truly uncanny about the painting is the fact that ultimately it reveals that there is no supernatural force at work in William's downfall; his desire to believe that a hidden evil is at work results from his desire to deny his dependence on his own participation in a community of frail, finite beings.[83] The painting, placed in William's childhood home, brings the Other in—it is a rendering of a supposed foreigner whom William later comes to know, in Italy, as an Italian. The appearance of Cosimo in Italy later then brings the "inside," William's childhood past, out into the foreign environment. The painting functions as a kind of "ghost" in the novel—dead, but unburied. S. S. Prawer argues that the "uncanny portrait" in horror fiction and in film acts like an uncanny double, similar to the robot in *Metropolis* or the wooden doll Olympia in *Der Sandmann.* This double in turn has a ghostly function: "In the end the portrait seems to take (the protagonist) over altogether, marrying ancient fears of the dead 'possessing' the living with more modern fears on which the terror-film constantly plays: fears about the degree to which men can be manipulated, individually or collectively, by their fellow-men."[84]

William is attracted to and repelled by Rosa, who has a similar function to the Armenian in Schiller's *Geisterseher* or to father-like figures in other secret-society novels. William finds Rosa compelling precisely because Rosa's cold nature and the secret world he represents seem to offer strategies to contain and master the uncanny manifestations of William's hysterical excess. Secret societies offer a refuge from modernity, but they also entrap in further conspiracy and manipulation. The mysterious and threatening male figures William encounters, as well as his male friends (Karl and Eduard) who (justifiably) turn against him, can all be read as re-representations of his father, whose voice follows and haunts him in letters throughout his continental tour, the father against whom he could never successfully rebel—the person from whom he could never really differentiate himself and for whose past William ultimately ends up paying.

---

[83] As Heather Sullivan puts it: "Despite the deceptive usage of seemingly supernatural tricks, the only 'evil' present in *William Lovell* is the disturbing feelings arising with the realization of the necessary dependency on other human beings," *The Intercontextuality of Self and Nature in Ludwig Tieck's Early Works* 55. She points to William Lillyman's reading of *Lovell* as a novel that attests that there "is no penetrating, expansive view possible, no apprehension of the beyond, no extension of the boundaries of existence, no transformation of the world and the novel into a fairy tale; instead there is merely deceit and contrived illusion," *Reality's Dark Dream: The Narrative Fiction of Ludwig Tieck* (Berlin: Walter de Gruyter, 1979) 37-38. Quoted here in Sullivan 169-170n17.

[84] S.S. Prawer, *Caligari's Children: The Film as Tale of Terror* (Oxford: Oxford University Press, 1980) 57.

William and Balder, but also their seemingly rational counterparts Eduard and Karl, are all men in trouble: men manipulated—ultimately by themselves, by their own unconscious choices—into at least partly uncanny existences, and trapped in endless melancholy by their uncanny experiences. But the uncanny could, were these characters gifted with more insight, also point to the way out of their dilemmas. And to a certain extent it does just that, by presenting readers with an early version of what will much later be known as existential dread and awareness, and hence with an emphasis on the need to, if not escape, then acknowledge and live with repetitive psychological and social dilemmas via insight and thus to live more authentically.

In *William Lovell*, the nameless but implicitly present secret society re-represents the tension between regress and progress that is part of the uncanny, and this tension produces and is part of hysterical symptoms, manifested by male characters; these symptoms also have uncanny characteristics. By the later nineteenth century, the domination of secret societies in the literary and cultural imagination is over. Already by the time *Lovell* was first published, the role of the society as containing strategy is in serious question, as is the potential for the secret society to act as an antidote to the supposedly "toxic effects" of the Enlightenment-produced uncanny, and the ability of the society to function as a space for the experience of "fausse reconnaissance," in which the subject wants to take something in, make something external and potentially dark part of himself. William is certainly not a positive role model: he has become a victim of external forces as well as of his own uncanny perceptions. But, the novel *William Lovell*, the literary text, assumes in part the role the secret society can no longer play—it provides a set of codes for living with, if not mastering, what is essentially unmasterable—and ultimately for sustaining loss (and for maintaining complexity, darkness, and "enthusiasm") as well.

Like Schiller's *Ghost-Seer*, William *Lovell* is an epistolary novel; multiple character perspectives are represented via different letters. Perspectives on illness differ from character to character, as do the perspectives on friendship or on nature.[85] The fact that we can read the words of William's lovers renders William himself more of an object (whether of desire or of a dialogue), and makes the novel more a study of relations than of one individual's psychology.

But despite his epistolary (and therefore dialogical) narrative strategy and his clear condemnation of William's descent into hysteria (a

---

[85] Heather Sullivan notes that views of nature in particular in the novel are "[e]ntirely dependent upon the situation of the letter-writer and the expected recipient of the letter" and that "irony emerges in the incompatibility of these statements on nature with the characters' situation (for example, William's loss of property and wealth and his claim that all of nature is his *Eigentum*)." *The Intercontextuality of Self and Nature in Ludwig Tieck's Early Works* 77.

descent that can only lead to death); and, despite the fact that he proclaimed his own neuroses cured by the act of writing this novel, Tieck struggled with another problem—one which, in the post-psychoanalytic universe, can be discussed in language that Tieck did not know. Like his protagonist, Tieck wished to act transgressively, but his deployment of uncanny experience as a subversive force within narrative did not necessarily bring about real rebellion or real healing. He suffered within what Eric Santner has termed the "paradox of the *superego*." Referencing Kafka's *The Trial* (*Der Prozeß*), Santner explains:

> When we transgress the rule of law of a community, that is often when we are most fully in the thrall of the superego's power....The various forms of obscene, often sadomasochistic, sexual activity that transpire, for example, in the shadows of the courts in *The Trial* are, in the end, not so much spaces where the Law fails to reach but rather *the superegoic form of its reach*, the way in which a 'too much,' an excess of validity over meaning, achieves a certain degree of organization.[86]

True release from the superego would be manifested in an altogether different act, one not bound to any imperative to rebel against the Law by seeking out repetitive forms of enjoyment (for William: sex with a series of mistresses, for Tieck: constructions of lengthy novels). This release would take place not in the space of an enjoyment that purports to resist the Law but ultimately follows its mandates, but rather would happen in "the time and space of ethical encounter, a space where new possibilities of being-together, of responsiveness to the Other, can arise."[87]

That space is not reached within the text of *Lovell* itself. However, through an ethical encounter with this art, by exposing ourselves to aesthetic anxiety and to the anxiety depicted *within* this aesthetic form, we do reach or have the potential to reach something like that space of responsiveness. In other words, rather than divorcing Santner's notion of release from the pressures of the superego completely *from* uncanny repetition, I contend that repetition is a precondition for release, at least in this context—the context of reading *Lovell* and working our way back into history through fiction as well as other cultural products. An exposure to the kind of anxiety that drives *Lovell* can lead to a form of release.

In any event, in *Lovell* as in Jean Paul's *Titan*, inducements to the reader to "enjoy" the narrative occur repetitively, as the characters experience corporeal, mental, and temporal disruptions over and over again. In a passage from *Titan* that is perversely hopeful and that responds to the despair about transience articulated by William and Balder in *Lovell*, Jean Paul notes that the present is "the ape of the past" ("die Affe der Vergangenheit"). Like

---

[86] Eric Santner, *On the Psychotheology of Everyday Life: Reflections on Freud and Rosenzweig* (Chicago: The University of Chicago Press, 2001) 101-102, 103.
[87] Ibid, 103-104.

William, Albano "had to burn with desire" ("mußte brennen vor Verlangen") when he thinks of reuniting with his father—the father responsible for all of his troubles.[88] Like William, Albano's travels take him far from and then back to his father; both men are sent away from home *by* their fathers in the first place, but in a sense they never really leave—the trips that both men take through ever-changing spaces are filled with father figures who, even if in a profoundly sick way, ultimately direct them back home.

2.2. Schiller, *The Ghost-Seer (Der Geisterseher)*

First published in 1787, Friedrich Schiller's (1759-1805) only novel is representative of both the sharp focus and general chaos characteristic of a time of violent revolution.[89] *The Ghost-Seer* is the first famous German-language horror novel, but its influence extends beyond the burgeoning genre of gothic fiction around 1800. Tieck relied on it when writing *Lovell*; like William Lovell, *The Ghost-Seer*'s protagonist, the Prince, is both "melancholy" and "enthusiastic" (in fact, his character is marked by "enthusiastic melancholy" ["schwärmerische Melancholie"]);[90] the primary indicator of this at the novel's outset is that he reads too much. However, all the books and insight to which he has been exposed do him little good, and Count O—, in whose papers the account of the Prince's strange doings in Venice (a city that functions in the text as an externalized, "psychotopographic" representation of the decay and ruin that plague the Prince's mind) is found, notes that this is at least implicitly due to two factors: early socialization in the military, and lack of membership in the society of the Freemasons. The Prince's reading is "without discrimination. As his education had been neglected, and as he had early entered the career of arms, his understanding had never been fully matured. Hence the knowledge he afterwards acquired served but to increase the chaos of his ideas, because it was built on an unstable foundation" ("Er las viel, doch ohne Wahl; eine vernachlässigte Erziehung und frühe Kriegsdienste hatten seinen Geist nicht zur Reife kommen lassen. Alle Kenntnisse, die er nachher schöpfte, vermehrten nur die Verwirrung seiner Begriffe, weil sie auf keinen festen

---

[88] Jean Paul, *Titan* 13.

[89] In his biography of eighteenth-century philosopher, doctor, and author Marcus Herz, Martin L. Davies concisely describes the German Enlightenment as, on the one hand, extending a "dual promise of personal fulfillment and historical recognition" and, on the other, as an age rife with "squalor, parochialism, discrimination, philistinism, and dogmatism." Like Kant, Schelling, Moritz, Schlegel, and Tieck, Schiller helped to produce intellectual culture in this divided and contradictory climate. See Davies, *Identity or History? Marcus Herz and the End of Enlightenment* (Detroit: Wayne State University Press, 1995) 20-21.

[90] Schiller, *Der Geisterseher* 8, 9. The translation is Henry G. Bohn's in *The Ghost-Seer* (Columbia, SC: Camden House, 1992) 1, 2.

Grund gebaut waren").[91] Seduced by power and tormented by a sexual anxiety that he displaces eventually into a highly aesthetic experience (an encounter with a "Greek" woman in a Catholic church, to which "secret forces" have led him), the initially rational and insightful Prince succumbs to a combination of dissociation and paranoia.

The epistolary construction of the novel, which lends it the character of a dialogue, with multiple perspectives represented, consistently refuses to reveal what is really responsible for the Prince's eventual decline. He may actually be a victim of a Jesuit conspiracy to convert him to Catholicism (he is described at the novel's outset as a once-fervent but now-lapsed Protestant) and thus to surrender his power and possessions to the Catholics; his lack of proper education and overdose of reading may be the fundamental problem; or, his greatest handicap may be his melancholy character itself, something that no amount of education or proper social guidance can change. Schiller certainly raises the possibility that the secretive figures who are manipulating the Prince are mere con men. Although the "mysterious Armenian" who beckons the Prince and his companions to a frightening decapitation ritual in Venice is frightening, other figures of deception are demystified from the outset; a Sicilian "adventurer," for instance, likely represents one of the most famous scam artists of the day. Giuseppe Balsamo, otherwise known as Caliogstro,[92] inspired characters in secret-society novels by Goethe and Carl Grosse as well; in the letter of March 6, 1790 to Kant (mentioned in Chapter Two), Ludwig Ernst Borowski implicated Caliogstro's exploits in "the wave of hysteria that has been sweeping the country" ("diese Hysteriewelle, die das Land überwältigt").[93]

In one of the three most uncanny sequences in the novel, the anonymous Armenian, who seems to be able to predict events in the Prince's life and who appears and disappears continually in the Venetian streets, leads the Prince and Count O— indirectly to a coffeehouse where a card game is in progress. The Prince is only an onlooker, but he is told by the Venetian "who kept the bank" that his presence has disrupted the game. The Prince responds with a "cold" look and, when insulted further, throws the Venetian to the ground. The Count inadvertently calls out the Prince's name, meaning that he is now in danger in the Venetian's home territory. Suddenly, "officers of the

---

[91] Schiller, *Geisterseher* 9/*Ghost-Seer* 2.

[92] Caliogstro's most famous exploit was the so-called "Diamond Necklace Affair" at French court in 1785-1786, which the con man himself believed was one of the factors behind the French Revolution. See Jeffrey L. Sammons's introduction to *Ghost-Seer* vii.

[93] Letter from Ludwig Ernst Borowski to Immanuel Kant, March 6, 1790, with reference to Borowski's *Cagliostro, einer der merkwürdigsten Abenteurer seines Jahrhunderts, seine Geschichte, nebt raisonnement über ihn und den schwärmerischen Unfug unserer Zeit überhaupt* (Königsberg, 1790). Cited here in Immanuel Kant, *Dreams of a Spirit-Seer and Other Related Writings*, trans. John Manolesco (New York: Vantage Press, 1969) 159. This letter also was cited in Chapter Two.

Inquisition" ("einige Bedienten der Staatsinquisition") enter. The Prince and the Count are blindfolded and led to a hall in which there is "a circle of venerable old men, all dressed in black; the hall was hung round with black, and dimly lighted. A dead silence reigned in the assembly, which inspired us with a feeling of awe" ("Wir befanden uns in einem Kreise ehrwürdiger alter Männer, alle schwarz gekleidet, der ganze Saal mit schwarzen Tüchern behangen und sparsam erleuchtet, eine Totenstille in der ganzen Versammlung, welches einen schreckhaften Eindruck machte"). The circle of men opens to reveal the decapitated Venetian. The old man who seems to be the head Inquisitor asks the Prince whether he is "'content with this satisfaction'" ("'Sind Sie mit dieser Genugtuung zufrieden?'"), but the Prince has fainted. At this the Inquisitor addresses the Count: "'Go; and in future judge less hastily of the administration of justice in Venice'" ("'Gehen Sie nun...und urteilen Sie künftig weniger vorschnell von der Gerechtigkeit in Venedig'").[94] The visiting noblemen are left "filled with terror" ("starr von Schrecken")[95] about the seemingly omniscient Armenian who has instigated the entire sequence of events as well as about the Inquisitors who seem to be really in control of Venice, and perhaps much more. As the Prince remarks soon thereafter: "'A superior power attends me. Omniscience surrounds me. An invisible Being, whom I cannot escape, watches over my steps'" ("'Eine höhere Gewalt verfolgt mich. Allwissenheit schwebt um mich. Ein unsichtbares Wesen, dem ich nicht entfliehen kann, bewacht alle meine Schritte'").[96] The Prince remains in Venice to try to track down the mysterious Armenian.

During a visit to a "pleasure house" ("Lusthause") where he relates his strange adventures to date and becomes embroiled in a discussion about the "occult sciences" ("diese geheimen Künste")[97] in which a Russian officer also takes part, the Prince believes he sees the Armenian's image in a looking-glass that a cloaked Sicilian places in front of him. In sudden fright and shock, the Prince agrees to attend a séance at which, the Sicilian (the Caliogstro figure) promises, a ghost will be contacted who can give him more information about the secret world manipulating his actions and perceptions. The Count reports that "a fondness for the marvellous had always been (the Prince's) prevailing weakness" ("Mit der Geisterwelt in Verbindung zu stehen, war ehedem seine Lieblingsschwärmerei gewesen") and although rationality has long since defeated his beliefs in paranormal occurrences, "the appearance of the Armenian had revived them" ("seit jener ersten Erscheinung des Armeniers hatten sich alle Ideen wieder bei ihm gemeldet,

---

[94] Schiller, *Geisterseher* 14, 15/*Ghost-Seer* 5.

[95] Ibid, 15/5.

[96] Ibid, 19/8.

[97] Ibid, 19/9.

die seine reifere Vernunft so lange abgewiesen hatte").[98] The noblemen leave for the séance, and the Count reports that

> [at] almost two o'clock in the morning…the sorcerer came, and announced that all was prepared. Before we entered the room, he desired us to take off our shoes, and to appear in our shirts, stockings, and under garments. He bolted the doors after us…
> We found in the middle of the room a large black circle, drawn with charcoal, the space within which was capable of containing us all very easily.…An altar, covered with black cloth, was placed in the centre upon a carpet of red satin. A Chaldee Bible was laid open, together with a skull; and a silver crucifix was fastened upon the altar. …A thick smoke of frankincense darkened the room, and almost extinguished the lights.
> (Es war beinahe zwei uhr, als der Magier…erschien und uns ankündigte, daß es Zeit wäre. Ehe wir hineintraten, ward uns befohlen, die Schuhe auszuziehen und im bloßen Hemde, Strümpfen und Unterkleidern zu erscheinen. Hinter uns wurde…verriegelt.
> Wir fanden, als wir in den Saal zurückkamen, mit einer Kohle einen weiten Kreis beschrieben, der uns alle zehn bequem fassen konnte.…Ein Altar, mit schwarzem Tuch behangen, stand mitten im Kreis errichtet, unter welchen ein Teppich von rotem Atlas gebreitet war. Eine chaldäische Bibel lag bei einem Totenkopf aufgeschlagen auf dem Altar, und ein silbernes Kruzifix war darauf festgemacht.…Ein dicker Rauch von Olibanum verfinsterte den Saal, davon das Licht beinahe erstickte.[99]

The sorcerer proceeds to enact an elaborate ritual with this collection of Christian and pagan objects; finally, he conjures two "ghosts," both bloody and pale figures who move toward the half-dressed men. Although the sorcerer exclaims "I did not want thee" to the second figure, and appears to shoot it with a pistol, the ghost keeps walking, inspiring "terror and amazement" ("Schrecken und Erstaunen") in most of the spectators. The Prince, however, remains "fearless and tranquil, his eyes riveted on the second apparition" ("furchtlos und ruhig, die Augen starr auf die Erscheinung gerichtet").[100]

> "Yes, I know thee," said (the Prince) at length, with emotion; "Thou art *Lanoy*; thou art my friend. Whence comest thou?" "Eternity is mute. Ask me concerning my past life." "Who is it that lives in the convent which thou mentionedst to me in thy last moments?" "My daughter." "How? Hast thou been a father?" "Woe is me that I was not!" "Art thou not happy, *Lanoy*?" "God has judged." "Can I render thee any further service in this world?" "None, but to think of thyself." "How must I do that?"
> "Thou wilt learn at Rome."
> ("Ja! Ich erkenne dich", rief [der Prinz] endlich voll Rührung aus, "du bist Lanoy, du bist mein Freud—Woher kommst du?" "Die Ewigkeit ist stumm. Frage mich aus dem vergangnen Leben." "Wer lebt in dem Kloster, das du mir bezeichnet hast?" "Meine Tochter." "Wie? Du bist Vater gewesen?" "Weh mir, daß ich es zu wenig war!" "Bist du nicht glücklich, Lanoy?" "Gott hat gerichtet." "Kann ich dir auf dieser Welt noch

---

[98] Schiller, *Geisterseher* 22/*Ghost-Seer* 10.
[99] Ibid, 27/13.
[100] Ibid, 29/15.

> einen Dienst erzeigen?" "Keinen, als an dich selbst zu denken." "Wie muß ich das?" "In Rom wirst du es erfahren.")[101]

Lanoy's "ghost" places the emphasis in this conversation on recollections of the past, a past of which the Prince was unaware—Lanoy's past as a failed father and his loss of his daughter. The eternity of the future is silent, he says, but the past can speak, and can advise the Prince to turn inward, to think first and foremost of himself in his own future. But this "friend" is no friend at all. Shortly after the séance ends, the Russian officer is revealed to be the Armenian in disguise. He confronts the "sorcerer," who turns out to be the Sicilian (the Caliogstro figure). The group of noblemen, still half-dressed, discover in anger that the entire ceremony has been a sham.

Schiller then devotes a page to explaining precisely how the "sorcerer" created the special effects involved in the appearance of the "ghosts." The group of noblemen takes apart the altar and several floorboards, and discovers a secret vault, into which they descend. In the vault they find

> an electrical machine, a clock, and a little silver bell, which, as well as the electrical machine, was in communication with the altar and the crucifix that was fastened upon it. A hole had been made in the window shutter, opposite the chimney, which opened and shut with a slide. In this hole, as we learnt afterwards, was fixed a magic lanthorn from which the figure of the ghost had been reflected on the opposite wall, over the chimney.
> (eine Elektrisiermaschine, eine Uhr und eine kleine silberne Glocke, welche letztere, so wie die Elektrisiermaschine, mit dem Altar und dem darauf befestigten Kruzifixe Kommunikation hatte. Ein Fensterladen, der dem kamine gerade gegenüber stand, war durchbrochen und mit einem Schieber versehen, um, wie wir nachher erfuhren, eine magische Laterne in seine Öffnung einzupassen, aus welcher die verlangte Gestalt auf die Wand über dem Kamin gefallen war.)[102]

As Tzvetan Todorov says when he defines the uncanny, all of the seemingly paranormal, supernatural, fantastic, and frightening events here are completely explicable, and Schiller's text explicates them in considerable detail. However, even though the readers learn together with the Prince just how everything works, the effect of the fear that was inspired in the séance remains. The Prince will become increasingly divorced from reality from this point forward; he knows perfectly well that the appearance of his dead friend and the revelation of that friend's regrets as a failed father is a scam, but he falls victim to it nonetheless. Like the Sicilian/sorcerer's looking-glass, the electric machine that concocts the ghostly images is the height of artifice—technology and science used to create illusions and false perceptions. Shortly before the séance, however, the Prince has fallen ill with a fever for eight

[101] Schiller, *Geisterseher* 30/*Ghost-Seer* 15.
[102] Ibid, 33/17.

days, and this feverish (and therefore contagious) illness is part of the reason he must remain in Venice and therefore is able to attend the séance in the first place. The Prince's willingness, at least symbolically, to go to Rome (to convert) and his concomitant mental demise is apparently due to a juxtaposition of natural and artificial factors.

Convinced that secret forces are not only manipulating him, but are in fact all-powerful, and that, while the séance was a scam, the greater truthfulness of magic and sorcery is nevertheless prevalent in his life, the Prince enters a church, where he falls not into religious devotion but rather in love, with a beautiful young "Greek" woman who could just as well be an apparition, given her complete existence in and as appearance. The woman eventually is revealed to be a German, of noble but illegitimate birth, and it is clear from the letters exchanged between Count O— and a young baron that her appearance in the Prince's life has been engineered by the master manipulator Civitella (whose exploits are recounted in the letters of Part Two of the novel). However, the "Greek" woman's appearance, together with what Jeffrey Sammons calls the Prince's "slumbering, truly unconscious attraction to power,"[103] is enough to redirect (and misdirect) the Prince's life. The powerlessness that began for the Prince with the beheading of the Venetian he accused (which could be read as a symbolic castration) is replaced by a sensation of power when he observes the Greek woman and converts to Catholicism. But this restoration of power is an illusion; the Prince's disintegration is irrevocable. He really has fallen prey to spirit-seeing after all. Although the Prince's enlightenment about the reality of the séance could have lead to reflection about his real lost friend and thus to a form of mourning that friend, it does not. Ultimately, too many forces are conspiring against the Prince: The combination of the Jesuits' manipulation and his own melancholy, feverish character defeats his Enlightened side.

Rolf-Peter Janz, Fabian Stoermer, and Andreas Hiepko note the etymological and thematic connection in German between the "Schwindel" that means dizziness or vertigo and the "Schwindel" that means betrayal or trickery (English: "swindle").[104] During the scam séance, the noblemen experience a betrayal that, even though obvious, is still vertiginous, and has vertiginous consequences as well, particularly for the Prince. Although everyone knows that the "ghostly" materialization is a mere virtual reality, it has the power to change actual reality. The Prince's eventual flight into a life of dissipation much like William Lovell's is steered by Civitella and the Jesuits, but it cannot succeed without his participation; like a child who spins to make himself dizzy (or engages in "Drehschwindel"), the Prince deceives

---

[103] Schiller, *Ghost-Seer* xi.

[104] Rolf-Peter Janz, Fabian Stoermer, and Andreas Hiepko, eds, *Schwindelerfahrungen: Zur kulturhistorischen Diagnose eines vieldeutigen Symptoms* (Amsterdam and New York: Rodopi, 2003) 10.

himself through his own subjective projections.[105] The "Greek" woman is one such projection; in one of the novel's last letters, the baron quotes Civitella's account of peering through a looking-glass (here, a "Tubus") and seeing a woman similar to the "Greek" who is so beautiful that he asks himself: "Was it illusion, or the magic effect of the beautiful light? I thought I beheld a supernatural being" ("War es das Spiel meiner Einbildung, war es die Magie der Beleuchtung? Ich glaubte, ein überirdisches Wesen zu sehen").[106]

Civitella ultimately knows that the "magical" beautiful appearance of the woman seen through his glass is an illusion, and he uses the experience to manipulate the Prince, who on some level also knows he is living in an illusory world but who, like William Lovell, has given himself over to that world. He insists to the baron:

> Everybody naturally wishes to be what he is in perfection; in short, the whole aim of a prince's existence is to APPEAR HAPPY.…If we cannot drink of joy pure from the fountainhead, can there be any reason why we should not beguile ourselves with artificial pleasure—nay, even be content to accept a sorry substitute from the very hand that robs us of the higher boon?…Oh! how came we to fall on this subject? Why did you revive these recollections in me?
> (Jeder will doch gern ganz sein, was er ist, und unsre Existenz ist nun einmal, glücklich scheinen. …Wenn wir die Freude aus ihrem reinen Quell unmittelbar nicht mehr schöpfen dürfen, sollen wir uns auch nicht mit einem künstlichen Genuß hintergehen, nicht von eben der Hand, die uns beraubte, eine schwache Entschädigung empfangen dürfen?…O wie kommen wir darauf? Warum mußten Sie diese Erinnerungen in mir aufwecken?)[107]

In turning to dissolute pleasures and a decaying Church, the Prince attempts to flee his memories of a real and more reasonable past. The "appearance" of Lanoy at the séance, of the illusory "Greek," and of the murdered Venetian in an aestheticized context—within the dark circle of masked Inquisitors—each of these uncanny experiences points to the real manipulation and corruption that is exploiting the Prince's natural tendency to "enthusiasm" and "melancholy" for its own purposes.

Secret societies, in this and other novels of the period, also reveal, or bring to light, hidden knowledge. The labyrinthine and conspiratorial self-deceptions practiced by secret societies are simulations of reality whose deceptive character is known to all. The uncanniness of these rituals and deceptions is not in the appearance of the weird yet logically explicable things themselves, but in the feeling they evoke. Uncanniness is in the dissociation between what we sense in the present and the intimations that sensation evokes of our past, and in the feeling of "false remembering" that

---

[105] Janz, Stoermer, and Hiepko, *Schwindelerfahrungen: Zur kulturhistorischen Diagnose eines vieldeutigen Symptoms* 11.
[106] Schiller, *Geisterseher* 140/*Ghost-Seer* 78.
[107] Ibid, 113/62.

ensues. The recollection that the uncanny provokes is "false," yet can (though it does not always) function as enlightening. Like William Lovell, the Prince is enlightened, exposed to reality, but he nevertheless is an exemplar of failure; he is stuck.

The ritual, whether it is a secret-society ceremony, a decapitation in a shadow-court, a fake séance, or a magnetic therapy session, promises on some level to heal past wounds: to render justice, to soothe through repetition, to elicit visions and thus clarify truths about existence. The uncanny experience has the potential to be a healing experience, one much older than Freudian psychotherapy. The séances, materializations, and mesmeristic therapies of the eighteenth and nineteenth centuries were not unlike the ancient pseudomedicinal rites that Henri F. Ellenberger describes as performing

> (h)ealing through the *re-enactment of the initial trauma*...The medicine man consults with the family to find out what the patient was doing when he first became ill, and together they speculate as to the probable nature of the spirit. The medicine man then decides to reproduce the vision as closely as he can. He may dress up as a ghost or build a model of a monster. A realistic setting is devised, and the scene is suddenly revealed to the patient. If he reacts with great fear, the guess is considered to be correct. Ordinary treatments are used to bring the patient out of the state of collapse which follows this ordeal. The medicine man then takes off his ghost costume or destroys the model before the patient's eyes to relieve his mind of fear. Recovery is said to be rapid.[108]

Secret societies such as the Illuminati (to which Goethe and Schiller belonged), the Freemasons (where Moritz was a member), and the Rosicrucians were characterized by repetition and ritual. Members participated in rituals that everyone knew were "just" symbolic, but they had a real function in the lives of the societies. Hans-Jürgen Schings writes that the societies were part of the "signature" of the decade preceding the French Revolution.[109] *The Ghost-Seer* and *William Lovell*, like Goethe's *Meister*, thus document the end of the pre-revolutionary era. However, the birth of Enlightenment is also marked by myth—the myth *of* Enlightenment—and the age of dark forces is hardly over with the end of the dominance of the secret societies.

Schiller was both a member of a secret society, with its archaic rituals, and a student of modern medicine. He was fascinated by a fellow student, Grammont, who suffered from "hypochondriasis" and became

---

108 Ellenberger, *The Discovery of the Unconscious: The History and Evolution of Dynamic Psychiatry* 29.

109 See Hans-Jürgen Schings, "Die Zeit Wilhelm Meisters ist das vorrevolutionäre Jahrzehnt. Zur Signatur dieser Zeit gehört das Geheimbundwesen," in Walter Müller-Seidel and Wolfgang Riedel, eds, *Die Weimarer Klassik und ihre Geheimbünde* (Würzburg: Königshausen & Neumann, 2002) 178.

suicidally depressed. In his detailed "case study" of Grammont, Schiller noted that all illness could be considered a form of hypochondria, since illness in every instance signals a split between body and soul.[110] In his second medical dissertation (*Essay on the Connection of the Animal and Spiritual Natures of Man* [*Versuch über den Zusammenhang der tierischen Natur des Menschen mit seiner geistigen*]), Schiller devotes a section to the topic "Spiritual pain undermines the well-being of the machine" ("Geistiger Schmerz untergräbt das Wohl der Maschine"). When a person's "vital powers" are in "discordancy," he can question even obvious common sense; his perceptions *of* sense and of sensation are dissociated. Grammont suffered from just such a dissociation, and his character and problems provided Schiller with material for the Prince's "enthusiastic melancholy." But neither the Prince's nor Grammont's illness is due to disrupted body-mind interactions alone. The culture around them is culpable as well.[111]

Conclusion

In novels by Tieck and Schiller, secret societies or mysterious noble clans offer spaces and strategies for containing and instrumentalizing the uncanny, and thus for managing other people. These strategies are not merely authoritarian or regressive. Secret societies replicate the tension between regress and progress that Goethe, in a poem entitled "Secrets" ("Die Geheimnisse," published in two versions, in 1784 and 1785), says is part of secular humanism.[112] They ideally were supposed to function as a very real alternative space for the expression of ideas undistorted by too much reason and unclouded by too much feeling. But by the early nineteenth century, the domination of the secret societies, and their hold over the literary and cultural imagination, were waning.

In the texts examined in the next chapter, the countermeasures that secret societies offer, in an age in which men are plagued by instrumental rationality on the one hand and rampant emotions on the other, no longer obtain; the protagonists of these texts are at the mercy of the uncanny. Again, though, this very helplessness leads to the recognition that others are inescapable. In Karl Marx's formulation, it is the instability and unreliability

---

110 Friedrich Schiller, *Werke und Briefe in zwölf Bänden*, eds. Otto Dann, et al., vol. 8: *Theoretische Schriften* (Frankfurt am Main: Deutscher Klassiker Verlag, 2002) 59-72.

111 Bell, *The German Tradition of Psychology in Literature and Thought, 1700-1840* 62.

112 Hartmut Reinhardt analyzes the poem in the context of the historical phenomenon of secret societies in the late eighteenth century, in "Geheime Wege der Aufklärung. Goethe, der Illuminatenorden und das Epos-Fragment 'Die Geheimnisse,'" *Die Weimarer Klassik und ihre Geheimbünde*, eds. Walter Müller-Seidel and Wolfgang Riedel (Würzburg: Königshausen & Neumann, 2002) 165.

of the past, the modern lack of confidence in tradition, that force us to confront our real relations in the present: in the modern, "bourgeois epoch... all that is solid melts into air, all that is holy is profaned, and men at last are forced to face...the real conditions of their lives and their relations with fellow men."[113]

Uncanny experiences in the texts examined above have a double function: they bring the inside out (as illustrated in the experience of depersonalization, in the desire to die at least a little) *and* the outside in (as in "fausse reconnaissance," which is an attempt to live more expansively by internalizing something that does not belong to oneself). This double move is represented in mental disorders (such as in the case studies of Moritz's *Journal of Empirical Psychology* and in the ill Balder in *William Lovell*) and in social expression, in interactions with others: when "ghosts" (who are not actually mental projections, but real people) are seen walking *out* in the world, and in the trope of live burial, which represents a fantasy of return, of getting as far *in* as possible.

In the texts read in the next chapter, this double move of pushing-out and bringing-in continues, although I argue that it characterizes a modern, uncanny kind of love rather than psychosomatic illness. However, the unsettling figure of possible madness still lurks in texts that stretch into the early twentieth century, from the Romantic to the Neoromantic movements, work exemplified in the next chapter by Kleist, Hoffmann, Lang, and Schnitzler. The uncanny symptoms in these texts still reflect the problem of modernity that Foucault describes below. Here he envisions the modern not so much as the rise of the new as the moment *after* death, after the catastrophic decay created by plague and earthquake and pestilence. The modern is, in a sense, the walking dead:

> Thus the Renaissance, after the great terror of death, the fear of the apocalypses, and the threats of the other world, experienced a new danger in this world: that of a silent invasion from within, a secret gap in the earth, as it were. This invasion is that of the Insane, which places the Other world on the same level as this one, and on ground level, as it were. As a result, one no longer knows whether it is our world that is duplicated in a fantastic mirage; whether, on the contrary, it is the other world that takes possession of this world; or whether the secret of *our* world was to be already, without our knowing, the *other* world. This uncertain, ambiguous experience that allows strangeness to reside at the very heart of the familiar assumes with Hieronymus Bosch the style of the visible: the world is peopled in all its shells, in each of its herbs, with tiny disturbing, pitiful monsters that are at once truth and lies, illusion and secret, the Same and the Other.[114]

---

[113] Karl Marx and Friedrich Engels, *The Communist Manifesto*, trans. Gareth Stedman Jones (London and New York: Penguin, 2002) 7.

[114] Michel Foucault, *Mental Illness and Psychology* (Berkeley: University of California Press, 1976) 77.

Long after the Renaissance, this kind of "uncertain, ambiguous" experience, an experience undergirded by the intimate knowledge of death and decay, continues to define modern cultural products. And the "strangeness…at the very heart of the familiar" is in fact what makes the modern subject capable of love, even when it is displaced, misdirected, disoriented, and uncanny.

Chapter 5

Too Much Memory: Uncanny Love

...fiction presents more opportunities for creating uncanny feelings than are possible in real life.
[...die Fiktion {erschafft} neue Möglichkeiten des unheimlichen Gefühls..., die im Erleben wegfallen würden.]
Freud, *The Uncanny [Das Unheimliche]*

1. The Anxious Revolution Continues

The "long nineteenth century" is an apt term for the periods spanning a wide range of political, psychological, and aesthetic cultures in the German-speaking territories from roughly 1780 to 1930.[1] Texts of the late nineteenth century in particular represent a huge variety of approaches to topics from the decay of aristocratic culture to the rise of urban centers, but it is precisely this period that often goes underrepresented in German studies, whose literary histories tentatively give the name "Realism" or "Naturalism" to a period full of ghost stories and uncanny encounters with alter egos and demonic antagonists. The rapid spread of industry and technology in Bismarck's Germany is accompanied by a radical increase in séances held in upper-middle-class parlors, sightings of the Virgin Mary, and diagnoses of hysteria in men as well as in women.[2] The displacement of anxiety into the external world makes that rapidly urbanizing world into a space that Anthony Vidler has called a "psychometropolis."[3] In this world, the distinction between the real and the virtual, between action and thought, and between man and machine is blurred continually in life and in art.

Already in the early nineteenth century, authors such as E.T.A. Hoffmann thematize an uncomfortable yet pleasurable fear of puppets, or of

---

[1] This is also the title of David Blackbourn's book on the period: *The Long Nineteenth Century: A History of Germany, 1780-1918* (New York and Oxford: Oxford University Press, 1998).

[2] David Blackbourn traces the relationships between the rise of visionaries and socioeconomic changes in late nineteenth-century Germany in *Marpingen: Apparitions of the Virgin Mary in Bismarckian Germany* (Oxford: Clarendon Press, 1993). Paul Lerner's *Hysterical Men: War, Psychiatry, and the Politics of Trauma in Germany, 1890-1930* (Ithaca and London: Cornell University Press, 2003) focuses on diagnoses of hysteria in soldiers in particular. Cristina Mazzoni cites Jean-Martin Charcot's contention that he has "discovered" male hysteria around 1900, but then only in lower-class men (a turnabout from the prevalence of diagnoses of neurotic disorders such as hypochondriasis and the vapors, a century earlier, in primarily upper-class men and women). See *Saint Hysteria: Neurosis, Mysticism, and Gender in European Culture* (Ithaca and London: Cornell University Press, 1996) 5.

[3] Anthony Vidler, *The Architectural Uncanny: Essays in the Modern Unhomely* (Cambridge, MA: MIT Press, 1992).

human-like machines. Olimpia, the life-sized doll of Hoffmann's narrative *The Sandman* (*Der Sandmann*, 1816-1817), who is neither quite alive nor quite dead, is derived from La Mettrie's "machine man" (from his novel *L'homme machine*, 1750). However, Olimpia also anticipates the popular literary figure of the automaton, or "Scheintoter."

Fears about and fascinations with similarities between man and machine were prevalent centuries earlier, partially as a result of Cartesian dualism and its implication that the body was a mere shell for an autonomous mind. Throughout the nineteenth century and into the twentieth, the figure of the man-like machine as a being who is neither dead nor alive continues and combines the figure of the person who is buried alive (that is, not quite dead) and the ghost who is not buried at all (that is, not quite alive). This figure is not only represented by puppets and robots in literary texts and eventually in films, but by seemingly human characters whose autonomy ultimately is in question. By the end of Hoffmann's *Sandman*, for instance, the student Nathanael has become automaton- or doll-like himself. Gerhart Hauptmann's lineman Thiel and eventually Franz Kafka's terrified protagonists bear occasional resemblance to Heinrich von Kleist's marionette or Fritz Lang's robot (in the 1927 film *Metropolis*).

My aim in this chapter is to show that several of these uncanny figures—whether man or machine—represent a particularly modern problem: an excess of memory; so much memory, in fact, that the temptation of forgetting looms as both menace and solace. This excess of memory in turn signals a surfeit of desire, rather than a dead, zombie-like lack thereof. The prevalence of the automaton in texts from Kleist to Lang points to a modern, excessive, and uncanny form of love.

The texts examined here demonstrate the difficulty of heeding (or also, perhaps, what happens when we attempt to heed) Friedrich Nietzsche's call for active forgetting in the face of too much memory.[4] The obsession with historiography and archives that Nietzsche lamented in the nineteenth century arguably has mutated into a fixation on monuments and museums, or on a "museal culture," today. This culture resembles Nietzsche's "dyspeptic" whose capacity to forget has been damaged and who therefore "can't be done with anything."[5] Theorists from Andreas Huyssen to James Young and Christoph Grunenberg document the current omnipresence of "urban palimpsests," or the insistence by modern architects on barely concealing ideas of older forms (which could be understood as manifesting a desire to evoke the "principle of the past" rather than some actual past structure), in

---

[4] Friedrich Nietzsche, *Zur Genealogie der Moral*, in the *Kritische Studienausgabe*, eds. Gieorgio Colli and Mazzimo Montinari (Munich: Deutscher Taschenbuch Verlag 1999). The English translation is Francis Golffing's in Nietzsche, *The Birth of Tragedy and the Geneaology of Morals* (New York: Doubleday, 1956) 189.

[5] Ibid, 189.

urban spaces that reflect, says Huyssen, an obsession with remembering right at the heart of what is otherwise a "culture of amnesia."[6] Even when we try actively to forget, due to the overload of memories flooding our increasingly ahistorical culture, we risk returning to meaning through its opposite: Nietzsche calls nihilism — which can come of the "power, a form of strong health" that is oblivion — the "uncanniest of all guests" in modern Europe.[7]

The set of readings that follow focuses on the implications of the modern memory surfeit made visible by the uncanny, and on what that excess of memory reveals: an "uncanny love" that I contend is present in reworkings of ancient relationships in the "long nineteenth century:" relationships between fathers and sons, lovers, and husbands and wives. Two authors of the nineteenth century (Kleist and Hoffmann) and two of the early twentieth (Lang and Schnitzler) produce reworkings of mythical tales of foundational mistakes, errors that provide a necessary but unstable ground for modern love. What I am calling the surplus of memory and love in these texts is made uncanny by the intervention of technology, which is essentially the intervention of the modern and the enlightened, into the often nostalgic, metaphorical, irrational world of Romantic fiction and the Romantic worldview. It is not only technology but the advent of the truly psychological worldview that makes this confluence of Enlightened and Romantic thought possible and manifestable as uncanny symptomology. This was the ideal space for Freud's essay on "The Uncanny," to which I also devote attention below.

The texts examined in this chapter—from Kleist in the post-Napoleonic and reactionary environment of the early nineteenth century to Lang in the "nervous" age of the ultra-democratic and imminently authoritarian 1920s—are all composed in a modern era in which, as Claude Lévesque puts it, nearly "everything (written) is terribly autobiographical."[8] Certainly Franz Kafka's texts fit this description, with strangely anonymous figures that nevertheless re-represent Kafka's own relationship with his father again and again.

One potential and serious objection to this way of envisioning modern writing is that literary critics, and Germanist critics in particular, have relied too heavily on the Oedipal paradigm; on the other hand, a purely sociohistorical or political reading of Romantic and neo-Romantic works risks trivializing or overlooking the significance of psychoanalysis for those

---

[6] See Andreas Huyssen, *Twilight Memories: Marking Time in a Culture of Amnesia* (New York and London: Routledge, 1995), and *Present Pasts: Urban Palimpsests and the Politics of Memory* (Stanford: Stanford University Press, 2003).

[7] Friedrich Nietzsche, NL, KGW VIII 1: 123, quoted here in Gillespie, *Nihilism Before Nietzsche* (1995) xi. "Nihilism stands at the door…Whence comes this uncanniest of all guests?"

[8] From Claude Levesque's introduction to Jacques Derrida, *The Ear of the Other: Otobiography, Transference, Translation*, trans. Peggy Kamuf (Lincoln and London: University of Nebraska Press, 1988) 72.

works' context and content. It is possible to avoid both interpretive traps, but it is impossible to avoid discussing fathers and sons in these texts, for these are modern reworkings of ancient love relationships that are still of central importance for some of the twentieth century's most seminal authors. As Victor Turner puts it:

> one of the most effective defense mechanisms utilized by the ego against… unconscious fear is to identify with the terrifying object. In this way it is felt to be robbed of its power; and perhaps power may even be drained from it….identification also means replacement…identification…
> may indicate the potential fatherhood of the initiand and hence his capacity to replace structurally his own father.[9]

This mechanism of identification and replacement stands at the heart of uncanny love. Repeating, reiterating, restaging, and representing these gestures of identification and replacement intensify the uncanniness of the relationship, but also permit insight into the "age of nervousness" that Joachim Radkau views as characterizing the period following the Enlightenment, which Peter Gay describes as being marked by the "recovery of nerve."[10]

2. Disturbers of Love: Uncanny Displacement in Kleist and Hoffmann

Romantic fiction is full of what is often termed a nostalgic yearning for an earlier form of society characterized by meaningful and reliable community and communion with others. Novels such as Novalis's *Heinrich von Ofterdingen* or Kleist's *The Marquise of O…* do seem to present modernity as the problem. We are always resisting the new and always "going home," Novalis insists.[11] But there is another way of reading this yearning, at least within the framework of uncanny experience. Experiences of estrangement and uncanny anxiety express a yearning for community and relatedness that is different from the yearning expressed in visions of collapsed unity or in totalizing homogeneity. The extent to which Romantic texts really do privilege the primitive is questionable—the argument has been

---

[9] Victor Turner, *The Ritual Process: Structure and Anti-Structure* (New York: Aldine Publishing Company, 1969) 174.

[10] Joachim Radkau, *Das Zeitalter der Nervosität: Deutschland zwischen Bismarck und Hitler* (Munich: Carl Hanser, 1998). Peter Gay's description of the Enlightenment as the age of the "recovery of nerve" is taken from *The Enlightenment: An Interpretation.* Vol. 2: *The Science of Freedom.* New York and London: W.W. Norton, 1969.

[11] "Wo gehen wir denn hin? Immer nach Hause," Novalis, *Schriften. Die Werke Friedrich von Hardenbergs*, eds. Paul Kluckhohn and Richard Samuel, vol. 1 (Stuttgart: W. Kohlhammer, 1960) 373.

made repeatedly and compellingly that the German Romantics used fragmentation, hyperbole, and other strategies to criticize and ironize their own nostalgia for a glorified past that never truly existed.[12]

The narrator who launches Mary Shelley's *Frankenstein*, Captain Walton, writes to his faraway sister of his loneliness and desire for

> the company of a man who could sympathise with me; whose eyes would reply to mine. You may deem me romantic, my dear sister, but I bitterly feel the want of a friend....Now I am twenty-eight and am in reality more illiterate than many schoolboys of fifteen. It is true that I have thought more, and that my day-dreams are more extended and magnificent, but they want (as the painters call it) *keeping*; and I greatly need a friend who would have sense enough not to despise me as romantic, and affection enough for me to endeavour to regulate my mind.[13]

In the desolation of the pole, on his way to "discover the wondrous power which attracts the needle" and to unearth "the secret of the magnet," Walton finds his friend in the figure of Dr. Frankenstein, whose attempt to discover scientific secrets while creating a "friend" has resulted in a monster who is at once doppelganger and alter ego, who replaces his fiancée and the son he will never have, who terrifies and excites—the uncanniest of figures. Walton's own longing and his recognition of a similar, if disastrous, longing in Frankenstein leads him to embrace this uncanny "father" as his friend. Shelley privileges this friendship and the act of "keeping" (which in this context refers to aesthetic theory's concept of the "maintenance of the proper relation between the representations of nearer and more distant objects in a picture"[14]) while acknowledging its enormous mistakes and costs.

The urge for the "keeping" friend is an urge to share memory beyond one's own mind, and a longing for difference within community. The impulse is right, but in the modern age it goes wrong: Frankenstein avoids his fiancée, avoids real sex with a real woman, and creates a monster of his own gender with electricity and other technological arts. In Hoffmann's *The Sandman*, the scientist Spalanzani and alchemist Coppelius create Olimpia, a wooden doll who is child-like but no child; Nathanael, after himself experiencing an "electrical shock" ("elektrischen Schlag"), is increasingly unsure of his own humanity and ultimately falls in love with the silent Olimpia, a far better "friend" than his annoyingly reasonable and talkative

---

[12] Manfred Frank and Alice Kuzniar both make this argument in ways informed by very different theoretical frameworks: Frank in *Das Problem 'Zeit' in der deutschen Romantik. Zeitbewußtsein und Bewußtsein von Zeitlichkeit in der frühromantischen Philosophie und in Tiecks Dichtung* (Paderborn: Winkler 1990) and in *"Unendliche Annäherung." Die Anfänge der philosophischen Frühromantik* (Frankfurt am Main: Suhrkamp, 1997), and Kuzniar in *Delayed Endings: Nonclosure in Novalis and Hölderlin* (Athens: University of Georgia Press, 1987).

[13] Mary Shelley, *Frankenstein, or the Modern Prometheus*, ed. Maurice Hindle (London: Penguin Books, 1985) 19, 20.

[14] From Maurice Hindle's notes to Shelley's *Frankenstein* 267n1.

fiancée Klara. In the novel and film *Metropolis*, the scientist Rotwang tries to re-create his lost love, Hel; however, his creation ends up being true to the mythological origins of her name (in Norse mythology, Hel is the goddess of death) when she is misused to imitate yet another woman, Maria, in a plot to quell a workers' rebellion. Although doppelganger creation in every single text results in shocking, singular crimes, the desire that produces these creations is enduring and completely understandable. It is true that the desire to create is indeed related to a desire to get rid of or to efface the woman and the womb, and to employ an electrical shock as a kind of phallic power. But the desire to create is also related to the desire for a friendship that is love between two different yet similar minds. The creation of monstrous doppelganger is the result and embodiment of a kind of "uncanny love" that is completely modern, but also ancient, and the mistakes within these texts can point us toward an expanded view of relatedness.

The authors of the texts referred to in this section explore more than the implications of man misusing technology or of man becoming machine. They also help to develop an alternative tradition within Western thought: When they portray machines becoming men, they portray inanimate objects as forms of men, as things with something like souls.[15] Although Freud's interpretation of *The Sandman* rejects the idea that "intellectual uncertainty" about Olimpia's "reality" is at the heart of the story's uncanniness, it is nevertheless the case that the ability of the automaton to express what seem like feelings and to reflect the feelings of her observer is highly unsettling.[16] Certainly the supernatural figures large in Hoffmann's work, and scholars have analyzed the parapsychological and occult and contextualized it within the literary production of the early nineteenth century, and within the Gothic tradition in particular.[17] The "ego disturbances" ("Ich-Störungen") that Freud views as being at least "partly responsible for the impression of uncanniness" ("Ich glaube, daß diese Motive den Eindruck des Unheimlichen mitverschulden") in Hoffmann's texts is not incompatible with attributing sensation and emotion to an automaton, or with a confusion about the boundaries between reality and hallucination. The "ego-disturbances" that Freud locates in Hoffmann include the act of "harking back to particular phases in the evolution of the self-regarding feeling, a regression to a time

[15] Ulrich Weinzierl emphasizes the same tradition in the contemporary writing of Christoph Ransmayr, whose "technique…shows ensouled things, a cosmos without people" ("Seine Technik […] zeigt beseelte Dinge, einen Kosmos ohne Menschen"), in "Halbnomade. Christoph Ransmayrs Reflexionen," *Die Welt* March 21, 2004).

[16] Christoph Grunenberg's article in the exhibit catalogue for Mike Kelley's show "The Uncanny," entitled "Life in a Dead Circus: The Spectacle of the Real" addresses the relationship between feeling and unreality in the "dead" exhibited objects in depth. See Mike Kelley, *The Uncanny* (Cologne: Verlag der Buchhandlung Walther König, 2004) 57-64.

[17] Lee Jennings is one such scholar; see for instance "ETA Hoffmann's Hauntings. Notes Toward a Parapsychological Approach to Literature," *JEGP* 75 (1976) 559-567.

when the ego had not yet marked itself off sharply from the external world and from other people" ("ein Rückgreifen auf einzelne Phasen in der Entwicklungsgeschichte des Ich-Gefühls, um eine Regression in Zeiten, da das Ich sich noch nicht scharf von der Außenwelt und vom Anderem abgegrenzt hatte").[18] This lack of distinction between self and other and this "harking back" to a more primitive phase of development are phenomena that are compatible with believing in puppets as ensouled and in machines as animate.

In a reading of the uncanny in Joseph Eichendorff's work, Paola Mayer argues for a more comprehensive definition of the uncanny than that provided by either Jentsch or Freud—for an understanding that will re-include supernatural encounters and involvement with nature as an autonomous and even animate force.[19] But while this argument applies well to analyses of Eichendorff and other nineteenth-century naturalist texts with Gothic features, in the modern texts that I wish to examine, the experience of the uncanny is essentially a psychic event, a feeling of frightening, yet simultaneously dulling repetition of something not quite remembered. It usually is accompanied by physical symptoms associated with neuroses (the anxiety attack is the uncanny made visible, for instance) and is definitely not just of psychic, but of intrapsychic origin—the uncanny arises from encounters between different yet similar minds. Uncanny experiences in these texts are crucial, not for a reawakening or maintenance of the primitive within modernity (which may indeed be the case when nature is animated in Eichendorff's work, for instance), but rather for a fundamentally modern experience.

The emergence, enabled by modernity (and its prevalence of the Enlightened over the primitive), of a "third space" beyond the conventional bounds of reality and unreality, a space analogous to that of religion or belief but which resists any kind of totalizing system,[20] can bind us to the law and keep us in the state of "enjoyment" that Eric Santner identifies (and to which I referred in Chapter Four) as the "paradox of the superego."[21] The very attempt to live beyond the bounds of law ends up reinforcing our state of belonging to a community of law. But encounters with these texts can also

---

[18] Sigmund Freud, "Das Unheimliche," *Gesammelte Werke* 12 (Frankfurt am Main: Fischer, 1999) 249. This edition is abbreviated henceforth as GW. The translation is James Strachey's in "The Uncanny," *The Standard Edition of the Complete Psychological Works of Sigmund Freud*, 17 (London: Hogarth, 1953-1974) 236. This edition is abbreviated henceforth as SE.

[19] Paola Mayer, "Die unheimliche Landschaft. Ein Aspekt von Eichendorffs lyrischer Dichtung," *Athenäum* 5 (1995) 170-174.

[20] In Chapter One I outlined this idea of a "third space" as a realm of understanding and an attitude that is neither wholly irrational nor merely instrumental, and which demands an attitude of responsibility toward the other.

[21] Eric Santner, *On the Psychotheology of Everyday Life: Reflections on Freud and Rosenzweig* (Chicago: The University of Chicago Press, 2001) 101-102, 103.

help transform that repetitive, almost "mind-less" state of enjoyment represented in the texts into another space entirely. As I argued in Chapter One, the portrayals of different, yet strangely familiar others in these texts point the way toward liberation from the repetitive "enjoyment" inherent in modern relationships and toward the ability to envision a different kind of repetition, within more just relationships, as a kind of freedom.[22] This freeing repetition can only take place, however, after exposure to some form of what Freud calls a "disturber of love" ("Störer der Liebe").[23] Such figures, who are often also sought-after love objects, ideal "friends," or replacements for either parents or children, always actually separate the protagonists from their real loves and destroy key elements of the protagonists' lives.

In *The Secret Life of Puppets*, Victoria Nelson describes two traditions of thinking about the human and the machine (or: the simulacrum, the automaton, the puppet), and subsumes them under the two authors Heinrich von Kleist and Ernst Theodor Amadeus Hoffmann. Kleist ensouls puppets, while Hoffmann, in the more progressive tradition of the two, shows the automaton-like nature of man. But, Nelson argues, these two views are not really so far apart. Both "ensoul[...] the inanimate."[24] The uncanniness and anxiety inherent in these traditions, and the depiction of man-like machines and machine-like men, are a manifestation and externalization of guilt, debt, and obligation. The relationship between man and machine also depends on context, and in Kleist's works in particular there exists a clear contrast between two contexts for and understandings of the aestheticized anxiety that manifests in uncanny phenomena: in Kleist, history and the people who are more or less its victims are presented as mechanical, automaton-like, puppetesque; this is good in aesthetic theory and in the puppet itself, but bad in fiction and for people. Hoffmann is far less severe; his works bend more generously towards the modern. This clash of contexts is also to an extent a clash of cultures—a culture that valorizes the primitive or archaic (Kleist), and one that chooses modernity, despite its perils.

---

[22] Søren Kierkegaard imagines such a form of repetition as freedom in *The Concept of Anxiety: A Simple Psychologically Orienting Deliberation on the Dogmatic Issue of Hereditary Sin*, ed. and trans. Reidar Thomte and Albert B. Anderson (Princeton: Princeton University Press, 1980). As Julian Roberts explains, for Kierkegaard: "Repetition is action that does not sustain continuity, or build tamely on what is there already, but which leaps joyously into another frame altogether," *German Philosophy: An Introduction* (Atlantic Highlands, NJ: Humanities Press International, Inc., 1988) 289.

[23] Freud, GW 12: 244/SE 17: 231.

[24] Victoria Nelson, *The Secret Life of Puppets* (Cambridge: Harvard University Press, 2002) 67.

2.1. Kleist, *The Family Schroffenstein (Die Familie Schroffenstein)*

Heinrich von Kleist's (1777-1811) writings, like his life, are saturated with uncertainty. This may seem odd, given that his texts contain clear embodiments of patriarchal authority (Piachi in *The Foundling* [*Der Findling*], or the Commandant in *The Marquise of O...* [*Die Marquise von O...*]), or considering the extremely definitive gesture of the double-suicide of Kleist and Henriette Vogel. But in Kleist's œuvre, it is precisely the extremes of character and experience that imperfectly mask a deep insecurity about what is being defended and maintained. His texts seem to espouse two different agendas: In his famous aesthetic treatise, *On the Marionette Theater* (*Über das Marionettentheater*), Kleist apparently advocates repetition and duplication, even when overtly uncanny, as being of aesthetic and possibly ethical value. Yet fictional pieces including *The Foundling* and the drama *The Family Schroffenstein* (*Die Familie Schroffenstein*), seem anxious to assert the necessity of adhering to some sort of authentic identity, whether that identity is expressed in geographical home or in family name and on family property. Attempts to revise or remake oneself and to progress through uncanny replication (through replacing a lost son with an adopted one, for instance, or a dead wife with a new one) are lethal.

In an essay on architectural space, James Risser states: "An uncanny space is...first of all a space of a place of displacement."[25] In the architectonics of Kleist's texts, geographical and psychic displacements represent (although they are not wholly reducible to) "ego disturbances" externalized onto the landscape. These disturbances, in turn, are forms of psychotopographication similar to that found in Tieck's *William Lovell*, and with similarly deadly consequences. *The Foundling* and *The Family Schroffenstein* consist of series of uncanny repetitions and displacements that almost no one survives. For Kleist, uncanny repetition is acceptable in aesthetic form and to illustrate a point of aesthetic theory, as is the case with the puppet in the *Marionette Theater*. But when it comes to the possibility of using the puppet to discern something more fundamental about human nature —that is, when uncanny experience occurs in Kleist's fiction, where he does explore issues relevant to human nature—then uncanny love equals the wrong kind of knowledge, and that wrong knowledge in turn equals death.

Kleist's view of the person emerges most profoundly from the "mental physicalism" of his time, a view that, as explained in Chapter Two of this study, perceives the mind as embodied but also avows a difference (in space and time) between a physical sensation and its mental perception (or

---

25 James Risser, "Siting Order at the Limits of Construction: Deconstructing Architectural Space," *Research in Phenomenology* 22 (1992) 70.

apperception).[26] Kleist also anticipates Darwin's collapse of what Margot Norris calls

> the cardinal traditional difference between humans and animals by suggesting that the mind is not a fixed spiritual entity but a heuristic form as protean as the body....the mind consists of myriad conscious and unconscious, rational and irrational heuristic behaviors (emotions, curiosity, imagination, memory, reason, self-consciousness, among others) that take their forms not from ideal entities but from the forces, needs, and desires that propel the body in its relation to the world.[27]

When Kleist's essay *On the Marionette Theater* articulates what Victoria Nelson calls the Neoplatonic, Romantic ideal of the ensouled puppet (who nevertheless does not suffer from the "soul sicknesses" that plague humans),[28] it seems to advocate the technological progress that can break down boundaries between man and machine, to envision the body (whether natural or artificial) as a physical expression of mental desire, and to embrace the potentially uncanny consequences of this melding. In the essay, Kleist says the puppet would "never be affected" by illness or mental trouble, which can also be read as meaning "would have no affect." That is, the puppet will never suffer the dissociation between affect and impulse that marks the uncanny. However, the doll's lack of affect can be understood as itself a dissociation, as a sign of something disoriented and wrong, or as something displaced. Kleist's standpoint is similar to Goethe's as described by Karl Philipp Moritz, whose reference in *Anton Reiser* to Werther's comparison of life with a puppet play concludes that we are most self-conscious when we are aware of our puppet-like nature, and that we are most body-conscious when we view the bodies of others and are estranged from our own. The doppelganger-creating technology that contributes to an aesthetics of fear in Hoffmann (and the sensation of one's own body as that of a wooden puppet, which is the source of anxiety in Moritz) is, in Kleist's essay, the departure point for an aesthetics of grace; like Goethe, Kleist uses a puppet play as an analogy for the beautiful expression of self-consciousness. In the *Marionette Theater*, technology enables dolls to repeat and improve upon the movements of humans in a manner that is graceful, but "not affected."

Kleist also seems anything but uncertain in *The Foundling*, although its characters are nothing but "affected" by all the things that the puppet lacks

---

[26] Matthew Bell describes "mental physicalism" more fully in *The German Tradition of Psychology in Literature and Thought, 1700-1840* (Cambridge: Cambridge University Press, 2005) 59.

[27] Margot Norris, *Beasts of the Modern Imagination: Darwin, Nietzsche, Kafka, Ernst, and Lawrence* (Baltimore: Johns Hopkins University Press, 1985) 47. Quoted here in Akira Mizuta Lippit, *Electric Animal: Toward a Rhetoric of Wildlife* (Minneapolis: University of Minnesota Press, 2000) 225n58.

[28] Nelson, *The Secret Life of Puppets* 30ff. Puppets resemble gods in that they are considered either to have infinite consciousness or no consciousness at all.

—history, consciousness, and disease. In this text, leaving home, denying paternity, or asserting the wrong paternity (the wrong history) are all deadly. Piachi wants to save Nicolo, ends up killing his own son and setting in motion a deadly Oedipal dynamic. Nicolo replaces Paolo, but also Colino, Elvira's love; Piachi also has replaced Colino. As a father, whether biological or adoptive, Piachi is a figure of longing, the one whose desire for love (even when indicated negatively, for instance in Elvira's "nervous" disease, which is marked by fever and thus likely contagious and sexually transmitted) impels the narrative; when Piachi dies, the text ends. But the story's most uncanny scenes are ones in which modernity and technology help reveal an age-old and deadly dynamic between father and son. *The Foundling*'s displacements (the fatal adoption of Nicolo as a replacement for Paolo, for instance) and deaths (Paolo's, due to a "plague-like illness") are in part consequences of too much modern mobility. In this sense, the entire narrative can be read as an argument to stay home and respect the Prussian property law of 1794, which codified patriarchal authority. However, the trouble and uncertainty in *The Foundling* go even deeper. Elvira's feverish illness begins shortly after her marriage to Piachi; even had Paolo lived, she would have this disease. Something is already wrong with the father figure, with Piachi; that is, something is already wrong at home, the "heimlich" is already "unheimlich." Uncanniness in *The Foundling* begins at home, which in Kleist is already, as Risser puts it, a "space of a place of displacement."

Kleist deploys the uncanny in a similarly dystopic way in *The Family Schroffenstein.* I focus here on this text due to the particularly drawn-out and emphasized series of uncanny spaces that are created through displacement and dissociation within it: dissociation between mind and body, between self and other, and between past and present. In *Schroffenstein*, the body's uncanny repetition (yet at a dissociated remove) of mental activity, the inability of characters to be anything but inauthentic simulations of family, friends, or lovers to one another, and the jarring yet recollective disconnect between past trauma and present tragedy combine to create an aesthetic effect that is different from the one that scholars commonly identify in Kleist's texts: a situation in which "all substance has become surface."[29] If that were the case, then readers would have an easier time with Kleist, for there would only be a world of illusions in which to traffic. Rather, *Schroffenstein* (and I would argue that this goes for several other works by Kleist as well) presents us, through its series of uncanny spaces created by the aforementioned displacements, with an aesthetic universe that is anxiety-inducing precisely because we uncomfortably suspect that there *is* plenty of substance beneath and prior to the visible surface. That substance, however, is part of a repressed past that returns only sporadically in uncanny repetition.

---

[29] See for instance Jürgen Schröder's argument about *Der Findling* in "Kleists Novelle 'Der Findling'. Ein Plädoyer für Nicolo," *Kleist-Jahrbuch* (1985) 115.

The notes written in the margin of an earlier version of *Schroffenstein*, a version located in Spain rather than Germany and entitled *Die Familie Ghonorez*, contain the much-quoted phrase: "Fate is a master of sleight-of-hand" ("Das Schicksal ist ein Taschenspieler").[30] At *Schroffenstein*'s end, Johann, the bastard son of the family's house of Rossitz, says to Ursula, the gravedigger's widow who has cut off the finger of the dead but legitimate Peter, son of the same house: "You are good at sleight-of-hand" ("Du spielst gut aus der Tasche").[31] This absurd casting of a superstitious old woman as the master of fate, but also as a sleight-of-hand magician, seems to seal the play's presentation of history as defined by error and accident. While the trajectory of history in *Schroffenstein* does have an origin and an end, contingency and discontinuity between present and past define that trajectory. Specifically, the inability of any character or collective to construct a consistently meaningful narrative of origin, loss, and recuperation is a dilemma behind many of the manifestations of uncanny displacement in the drama.

The Idealist and Early Romantic philosophy that directly preceded and was contemporary with Kleist's work on the various versions of his first drama is, as a philosophy of self-consciousness and its history, concerned with identifying the mind's originary moment. The "original act"—"Urhandlung"—or "Ursprung," a primal leap, is that moment, the split between subject and object, that Johann Gottlieb Fichte describes as the point at which "the incomprehensible One divides itself into these two (Subject and Object)" ("das unbegreifliche Eine sich in diese beide [Subject und Object] trennt"), hence enabling the existence of consciousness itself.[32] Unlike Fichte, Novalis contends that the "Ursprung" is not deducible on the basis of our present self-knowledge, saying: "*the first act*…obviously cannot exist in consciousness, but is, so to speak, the cause and effect of 'feeling'" ("*die erste Handlung* […] kann evidenterweise im Bewußtsein nicht vorkommen, ist aber, wie es heißt, dem 'Gefühl' als Ursache und Wirkung [gegeben]").[33] The feeling present before consciousness makes all future acts of consciousness into repetitions or re-enactments of earlier, pre-conscious sensations. This is why the "first act" cannot be located at a firm point in history—it is not present to consciousness, and all attempts to know it are only re-presentations. Uncanny events, in Kleist's drama, will be uncanny because they demonstrate the inability to ever fully get back to the past, while still repeating elements of the past—or, while recollecting what Schelling

[30] Heinrich von Kleist, *Sämtliche Werke und Briefe* vol. 1, ed. Helmut Sembdner (Munich: Deutscher Taschenbuch Verlag, 1994) 833. This edition is abbreviated as SW.

[31] Ibid, 156.

[32] Johann Gottlieb Fichte, *Werke* vol. 2, eds. Reinhard Lauth and Hans Jacob (Stuttgart: Frommann, 1964) 225.

[33] Novalis, *Schriften. Die Werke Friedrich von Hardenbergs* vol. 2, eds. Paul Kluckhohn and Richard Samuel (Stuttgart: Kohlhammer, 1960-1988) 115.

calls the "principle of the past," an idea of past-ness. Kleist's contemporaries Fichte and Novalis wish to repossess, through poetic recreation, a feeling, or sense, of the birth of consciousness in order to make history *make* sense. But Kleist shows this to be impossible, at least in *Schroffenstein* (and, I would say, in *The Foundling* as well).

Jessica Benjamin has recast the primal leap of Early Romanticism and Idealism in psychoanalytic terms by presenting it as a jump between body and mind, between meaning and speech, and between self and other; this is a move we reenact when we think we are attempting to "return" to something natural, unpolluted, even primitive or pre-modern, or when we are simply attempting to understand our own histories, our own narratives of loss and remembrance.[34] But without Novalis' confidence that the origin of subjectivity, and hence meaning, is present to intuition, the attempt to "leap back" can go very wrong—as it does in *Schroffenstein*, in which self-consciousness and the understanding of oneself, others, and one's community in time can be read as a sort of perversion of the primal leap into a primal accident, an error, repeated compulsively on multiple levels—in and through various bodies and minds and times and places.

The problem of displacement in *Schroffenstein* is a problem of disembodiment (which leads to misunderstanding of oneself, a kind of false self-consciousness) and of misrecognition (that is, of misunderstanding of another) within temporal discontinuity. "Displacement" is understood here not as opposed to an implicitly better stationary "place," and also not as synonymous with a privileging of contingency or coincidence as opposed to continuity, linearity, and stability. Michel Foucault defines the body, intersubjective recognition, and history as fundamentally displaced categories. He asks how we can say anything about these entities without falling into a trap of privileging a "place" or "meaning" where they do not reside.[35] This problem, the problem of saying these displaced entities, none of which has a clear point of origin let alone a stable residence, is for Foucault a problem of knowledge—and of who has that knowledge and how it is deployed.

Rather than thinking that we can use knowledge to understand the essence of or something intrinsic about the body (and its relationship to the mind), about each other, or about our place in time, Foucault argues that we can deploy knowledge to recreate relationships in and among those categories of meaning through various discursive practices. In a statement that could be read as a revision of one of Fichte's statements about knowing, that when we cut away everything from the "I" we have that which is "not I"—or, that our

---

[34] Jessica Benjamin, *Shadow of the Other: Intersubjectivity and Gender in Psychoanalysis* (New York and London: Routledge, 1998) 1-35.

[35] Michel Foucault, *The Foucault Reader*, ed. Paul Rabinow (New York: Pantheon Books, 1984) 87-88.

knowledge of what is "I" and what is "not I" comes not from understanding, but from a knowing that is a kind of instrumentalization—Foucault says: "Knowledge is not made for understanding, it is made for cutting."[36] In *Schroffenstein*, the knowledge that forcibly separates "I" from "not I," or self from other, is ostensible rather than veridical, simulated or pretended rather than real, and statements based on this pseudo-knowledge are indicative of disembodiment, of misrecognition, or of discontinuity. Such statements are occasionally signaled in the drama by phrases such as "as if," "like," or "it seems to me, as if I were..." ("als ob," "wie" or "mir kommt es vor, ich sei...").[37] As they render knowledge about a world of essences unstable, these phrases simultaneously emphasize the subject's role in creating the world of appearances. And the false or pseudo-knowledge in the text nearly always precedes a "cutting," in the sense of violence, of some sort.

Much has been made, and rightly so, of the difference between Kant's questioning about the conditions for the possibility of experience and Kleist's questioning about the legitimacy of experience itself, and especially in the research on *Schroffenstein*, whose various incarnations were penned at the same time that Kleist underwent arguably his most famous philosophical crisis (the so-called "Kant-Crisis"). Again, I would like to understand this philosophical difference at least partly in temporal terms. In *Schroffenstein* there is no stable, true originary place or identity that has been lost in the past, and Kleist offers no sense of there being something else in the future, out there, that evades all our past conventions and concepts—as does Kant's sublime—not even negatively. Self-alienation and misrecognition, even within the relationship between the heroic and rebellious lovers Agnes and Ottokar, prevent a meaningful object world from emerging, and hence also preclude even a negative vision of meaningful intersubjectivity. Kleist's gender construction, which is regressive more often than it hints at emancipation, as well as his presentation of blood ties as inescapable and the fact that Ottokar really carries out the will of the fathers (and dooms Agnes and himself in trying to save her), means that the children of *Schroffenstein* are the (usually malfunctioning) limbs of the patriarchal body rather than the constructors of a failed but legitimate, beautiful alternative community.

Several of Kleist's Romantic and Idealist contemporaries also questioned the existence of an alternative "place" of metaphysical meaning. And the very idea of missing something or of making a mistake implies that there is something to be missed, something to be done correctly, and hence could be understood as an evocation of meaning, if only negatively. But in the work of Fichte, or of Friedrich Schlegel or Novalis, there is a consistent insistence on identity and the meaningful recognition of another—even if this re-cognition is really the cognition, repeating itself, of an invariably male

[36] Foucault, *The Foucault Reader* 87-88.
[37] Kleist, SW 1: 73, 74, et al.

subject. The fact that Kleist does not evince a similar insistence does not mean, however, that he provides an emancipatory reading of relationships between meaning, language, institutions (such as the family or the military), and individuals. Jacques Lacan's famous statement that there is no way out but the way in would have, for Kleist, not been much of a suggestion; at least in *Schroffenstein*, the way in is also no way out, and all ends in a nightmare of collapsed identity in which there is no difference, no exit. Uncanny displacements only point the way to no way out.

In *Schroffenstein*, the meaning that appears in representation is false, and this thorough-going falsity is played out in the narrative's presented temporality. Instead of leading us to a trajectory of origin and loss and the option of either repetition or recovery, fate plays cheap sleight-of-hand tricks. As the psychoanalyst Irvin D. Yalom has put it, "a life never goes wrong because of a false trail; it goes wrong because the main trail is false,"[38] and this is the problem—or at least part of the problem—in *Schroffenstein.*

Moments in *Schroffenstein* (as in other texts by Kleist, including *The Marquise of O...* or *The Foundling*) in which body and mind function, or rather malfunction, in synchrony is when both give up and fainting (or "powerlessness," "Ohnmacht") ensues. After Sylvester, the head of the Schroffensteins' house of Warwand, recovers from a fainting spell incurred by Jeronimus's accusation that he is a murderer, he says "A mind is indeed/a miserable thing" ("Ein Geist ist doch/Ein elend Ding"); and, a few lines later, "My body is to blame for everything" ("Mein Leib ist doch an allem schuld").[39] Significant parts of the play can be read in light of Kleist's giving up of the notion that splitting body and mind could lead to rational happiness.[40] Rather than seeking a philosophy of embodied mind, or attempting to unite mind and body conceptually in a harmonious dialectic (as Novalis, for instance, occasionally did in his response to Idealist philosophy as well as to hedonistic trends of the period), Kleist demonstrates various ways in which a mind-body relationship still conceived of as dualistic goes violently awry. While men and women struggle with similar feelings of disembodiment, self-alienation and anxiety, these experiences are nonetheless presented in a gendered fashion. Specifically, male experiences of disembodiment can all be read as failed but active efforts to rewrite history by returning to the moment just before the "primal leap" ("Ursprung"), while female, and particularly Agnes's, self-alienation expresses itself not as an active attempt to change the course of events but as a confusion about one's own identity and mistrust of others.

---

38 Irvin D. Yalom, *Love's Executioner and Other Tales of Psychotherapy* (New York: HarperCollins, 1989) 227.

39 Kleist, SW 1: 92.

40 Theodore Ziolkowski, *German Romanticism and its Institutions* (Princeton: Princeton University Press, 1990) 342.

Ottokar's leap from the tower in order to save Agnes from Rupert's revenge is not so much a recreation of a primal leap as it is an attempt to get back to a pre-leap circumstance. If he can save Agnes, in a move that might eradicate his own consciousness, he can erase the family's false consciousness and false, uncanny history. Of course this action does not ultimately save Agnes, nor, as far as we know, does Ottokar even lose consciousness as a result of his fifty-foot leap to a stone pavement. Like Sylvester, Johann *does* lose consciousness, but this also provides no release or salvation. Johann goes mad without emerging from the prison of self-consciousness—he knows of the crimes transpiring around him, and narrates their real story. In this case the voice of knowledge emanates from the body of the supposedly insane bastard son, and it is indeed Johann who comes closest to articulating a vision of a unified body and mind, though only by evoking an image of extreme pain, as he promises to cut his own chest open and to keep the wound open with needles in order to remember his anger at Ottokar.[41] But none of these men's attempts to revise history by losing consciousness or by hurting themselves actually succeed, and their failures are to an extent reproduced on the intersubjective level, which is defined in the play by misrecognition, or uncanny displacement between self and other, and particularly between man and woman whose "uncanny love" reveals their possession of the wrong kind of knowledge.

Gerhard Neumann has argued that in Kleist's *On the Gradual Development of Thoughts While Speaking* (*Über die allmähliche Verfertigung der Gedanken beim Reden*, 1804), a relationship constituted in gender difference permits speech: "Language develops, according to Kleist's theory, in the field of gender difference simultaneously as a spark...that ignites between the male and female poles, and as the release of energy in a Kleistian bottle" ("Sprache entsteht, so Kleists Theorie, im Spannungsfeld der Geschlechterdifferenz, gleichsam als Funke...der zwischen den Polen des Männlichen und des Weiblichen zündet, als Entladung der Energie in der Kleistschen Flasche").[42] And the fact that Agnes, in contrast to the deceptive Gertrude and even to Eustache (who belies her allegiance to her house and her complicity in its pursuit of revenge with assertions that she is a fundamentally innocent, "oppressed woman" ["unterdrücktes Weib"]),[43] may seem to communicate in a direct manner (she says to Sylvius: "Then look,/as I must laugh, when someone/acts ridiculous,/so must I cry,/when someone dies" ["Denn sieh,/Wie ich muß lachen, eh ich will, wenn einer/sich lächerlich bezeigt,/so muß ich weinen,/Wenn einer stirbt"])[44] would seem to

---

[41] Kleist, SW 1: 90.

[42] Gerhard Neumann, "Das Stocken der Sprache und das Straucheln des Körpers," *Heinrich von Kleist. Kriegsfall - Rechtsfall - Sündenfall*, ed. Gerhard Neumann (Freiburg im Breisgau: Rombach, 1994) 14.

[43] Kleist, SW 1: 123.

[44] Kleist, SW 1: 76.

promise the development of a similar state of relatedness, a state similar to that which *Frankenstein*'s Captain Walton called the "keeping tension" of friendship, between herself and Ottokar. But Agnes demonstrates a lack of connection to others, in the form of distrust, at crucial points in the drama. She is skeptical of the priest (saying "I almost believe he does not say it as he thinks it" ["Doch glaub ich fast, er sagts nicht, wie ers denkt"]) as well as of Ottokar.[45] Her attempts to escape physically the growing tangle of misunderstandings between the houses of Warwand and Rossitz by walking far into the countryside and by entering a relationship with Ottokar fail. While her dialogues with Ottokar function as sites where, as Neumann says, language "sparks" between male and female "poles," they neither free the pair from their fathers nor free Agnes from being, to a certain extent, a creature of Ottokar's fantasy.[46] The question of who Agnes is remains fundamentally a question of who she is for Ottokar, for her father, and for Ottokar's father. And the question of who she is for these men is not answered conclusively. This lack of an answer is due in part to the fact that on the discursive level the play makes a disembodied impression. Agnes's body, for instance, is symbolized by her veil (over which Ottokar and Johann quarrel); cloth stands in for bodies most famously in the scene in which Agnes and Ottokar exchange clothes.

Moira Gatens has shown that the Idealist repression of the term "body" echoes the aestheticization and abstraction of what the Idealists themselves considered to be thought's corporeal origins.[47] *Schroffenstein* demonstrates how unstable the construction of a dichotomous opposition between body and mind is. Conceiving of the mind as separate from nature, as Rupert does in the first act when he denies Eustache's efforts to avoid participating in the revenge-swearing ritual ("I know, Eustache, men are the avengers - /You are the complaining women of nature./But now nothing more of nature" ["Ich weiß, Eustache, Männer sind die Rächer - /Ihr seid die Klageweiber der Natur./Doch nichts mehr von Natur"]),[48] requires conceiving a split between thought and bodily perception. Yet inconsistencies in

---

[45] Ibid, 76, 78, 88, 89.

[46] See also Joachim Pfeiffer, *Die zerbrochenen Bilder. Gestörte Ordnungen im Werk Heinrich von Kleists* (Würzburg: Königshausen & Neumann, 1989) 77-80. Gayatri Chakravorty Spivak's assertion that Western literature and philosophy reveal "how, unobtrusively but crucially, a certain metaphor of woman has produced (rather than merely illustrated) a discourse that we are obliged 'historically' to call the discourse of man...the discourse of man is in the metaphor of woman" is consistent with Pfeiffer's psychoanalytic interpretation of the relationship between Ottokar and Agnes as shaped by powerful and primitive male fantasies expressed in metaphor. See Spivak, "Displacement and the Discourse of Woman," *Displacement: Derrida and After*, ed. Mark Krupnick (Bloomington: Indiana University Press, 1983) 169.

[47] Moira Gatens, "Toward a Feminist Philosophy of the Body," *Crossing Boundaries: Feminisms and the Critique of Knowledges*, eds. Barbara Caine, E.A. Grosz, and Marie de Lepervanche (Sydney: Allen & Unwin, 1988) 35.

[48] Kleist, SW 1: 65.

consciousness in the play are attributed to the body's ability to influence the mind, as in Sylvester's fainting episode, in which body and mind indeed communicate, but in a nonsynthetic, crippling manner. While nature is associated with the female, and the body is figured as a feminine garment (Agnes's veil), *Schroffenstein*'s male characters, by fainting, going mad, or acting irrationally, destabilize that association in order to release themselves from self-consciousness, to achieve corporeal substance and to occupy the physical space that the female body otherwise might command. This displacement is reflected in the relationship between self and other as well as in the relationship between body and mind.

Adam Müller, with whom Kleist worked closely, implicitly addresses the self-other relationship in his critique of Fichte, which reads in part: "A subject with no object opposing it, is absolutely nothing" ("Ein Subjekt, dem kein Objekt entgegenstände, ist absolut nichts").[49] There must be borders between a recognizable subject and object, borders not just projected by the absolute subject-ego, in order for that subject to have any meaning. But the cave where Agnes and Ottokar meet, the very place in which the most potentially plausible alternative to the blood-feud world of the fathers is created, has unclear boundaries (it is "an area in the mountains" ["eine Gegend im Gebirge"]); in this vaguely denoted place, statements of boundless and excessive love are made. Agnes says Ottokar can call her his, "in the most boundless sense" ("in der grenzenlosesten Bedeutung").[50] In *Schroffenstein,* Kleist may well be responding to Fichte's theory of alterity, but this response is formulated not as a construction of an alternative, but rather as a vision of what might happen if Fichte is right: if the thing in itself can be reduced to a wholly immanent interpretation within consciousness, and if the meaning of the interpersonal other resides wholly in its being represented by the subject.[51]

Not only the lack of clear distinction between self and other but a recurring pattern of uncanny misrecognition contributes to another troubling form of displacement in the drama. The fact that no just and durable self-other relationship coalesces—or rather, the revelation that such a relationship perhaps cannot exist in the first place—has not been linked in the scholarship

---

49 Curt Hohoff, *Heinrich von Kleist in Selbstzeugnissen und Bilddokumenten* (Hamburg: Rowohlt, 1958) 94. For more of Kleist's critique of Fichte, see Hohoff, 97. In the introduction to the first issue of the journal *Phöbus*, of January 1808, while defending the idea of a truly accessible art, editors Kleist and Adam Müller write: "Eine weltumphassende Idee populär vorzutragen, kann nichts anderes heißen, als sie in jedem noch so untergeordneten Kreise des Lebens wiederfinden...Darum ist Fichten und so vielen andern der redlichste Vorsatz der Popularität nie gelungen, weil sie nicht vor allen Dingen die begriffen, welche begreifen sollten."

50 Kleist, SW 1: 108.

51 Robert R. Williams, "The Question of the Other in Fichte's Thought," *Fichte: Historical Contexts, Contemporary Controversies*, eds. Daniel Breazeale and Tom Rockmore (Atlantic Highlands, NJ: Humanities Press International, 1994) 142.

on *Schroffenstein* to Kleist's skepticism about a unified self and a history with a stable origin and goal. There is a largely unarticulated longing in the play for a "true other," for a love object neither created nor controlled by the self.

The Early Romantics have, at least from this angle, less of a struggle with alterity than does Kleist. In Friedrich Schlegel's *Lucinde* (1799), Julius conceives of his relationship to his lover in terms of mystical correspondences between microcosm and macrocosm, saying "They were the universe to one another" ("Sie waren einer dem anderen das Universum").[52] Novalis echoes this when he writes: "My beloved is the abbreviation of the universe, the universe the elongation of my beloved" ("Meine Geliebte ist die Abbreviatur des Universums, das Universum die Elongatur meiner Geliebten").[53] But in Kleist's drama, there is no Romantic apperception or direct knowledge of another and even mediated knowledge is mistaken, based on misreadings of attempts at communication. In *Schroffenstein* people think they know people whom they do not, and think they are experiencing things they are not. This is fundamentally a problem of losing a grounding in history, of having no reliable origin or goal, as well as of losing others, or love objects. The problem for an interpretation that wishes to see Kleist as ultimately critical of such a stance, and as therefore advocating an enlightened and progressive philosophy, is that this inevitable loss is not maintained, or sustained, in any form in the play—at the end, the main players are dead.

After a contentious meeting with Agnes in the grotto, in which if anything it is clear it is that he does not know her, Ottokar says to Johann: "Everyone has two values: one of which/one only learns from himself, the other/one must inquire about" ("Zwei Werte hat ein jeder Mensch: den einen/ Lernt man nur kennen aus sich selbst, den andern/Muß man erfragen").[54] This implies a need for someone, or something, outside oneself. Indeed, the scenes between Agnes and Ottokar have often been read as a fulfillment of just such a need, and as a working-out of what Kleist himself was experiencing, or idealizing, at the time in his own relationships. But it is rather in the simultaneous existence of misunderstandings (which are kinds of separations) and lack of boundaries between the lovers that this relationship primarily

---

52 Friedrich Schlegel, *Kritische-Friedrich-Schlegel-Ausgabe* vol. 5, ed. Ernst Behler (Munich/ Paderborn/Vienna: Schöningh, 1967) 67.

53 Novalis, *Schriften* 2: 441. See also Leibniz, who writes in the "Prinzipien der Natur und Gnade," "In der Natur ist alles angefüllt. (...) Und da wegen der Erfülltheit der Welt alles verknüpft ist, und jeder Körper auf jeden anderen Körper je nach Entfernung mehr oder weniger stark einwirkt und von ihm durch Gegenwirkung betroffen wird, so folgt daraus, daß jede Monade ein lebendiger Spiegel oder mit innerer Handlung ausgestattet ist, daß sie das Weltall gemäß ihrem Gesichtspunkt darstellt und ebenso geregelt ist wie das All selbst" (*Kleine Schriften zur Metaphysik. Philosophische Schriften*, vol. 1, ed. Hans Heinz Holz [Frankfurt am Main: Suhrkamp, 1996] 417).

54 Kleist, SW 1: 89.

resides. Although in the end the fact that they are from the same family, rather than from truly separate worlds, damns them, their own failed attempts to create a new history for themselves and to belong to each other "in the most boundless sense" certainly contribute to their death.

When Ottokar tries to posit a new origin, a new history, by renaming and "baptizing" Agnes as "Maria," he also tries to remove her from her family, and from society; in fact, though, the foundation of this new history is a much older story.[55] But Agnes of course isn't really Maria, the original, she is a resemblance: "the one who is similar to the mother of God" ("Die Ähnliche der Mutter Gottes"), as Ottokar puts it.[56] Ottokar is disappointed when he and Agnes cannot recapture what he fantasizes as a perfect past moment when he says: "How it was then/Completely different, so completely different. Your soul/lay open before me, like a beautiful book,/…Now you are/a closed letter" ("Wie war es damals/Ganz anders, so ganz anders. Deine Seele/Lag offen vor mir, wie ein schönes Buch,/[…] Nun bist/Du ein verschloßner Brief").[57] But in the grotto where this reminiscence takes place, set like the rest of the play in a simulation of the Middle Ages,[58] Agnes doesn't recognize her lover, who says: "am I not Ottokar?" ("bin ich nicht Ottokar?") She replies: "Everything is/so strange and suspicious to me today,/ The strange message, then your late appearance,/Now this question" ("Es ist/ So seltsam alles heute mir verdächtig,/Der fremde Bote, dann dein spät Erscheinen,/Nun diese Frage").[59]

Agnes does take a risk and cross the border of misunderstanding when she drinks the water Ottokar offers her, water she mistakes for poison, but she is not fundamentally mistaken—neither she nor Ottokar has really escaped their fathers or their fathers' desires. Physical escape does not equal mental escape, so that the love grotto becomes another site of separation between body and mind. In fact, the lovers are further displaced within this

---

[55] Wolf Kittler, *Die Geburt des Partisanen aus dem Geist der Poesie. Heinrich von Kleist und die Strategie der Befreiungskriege* (Freiburg im Breisgau: Rombach, 1987) 47.

[56] Kleist, SW 1: 74.

[57] Ibid, 105.

[58] This setting was Wieland's advice to Kleist. See Hohoff, *Heinrich von Kleist in Selbstzeugnissen und Bilddokumenten* 33.

[59] Kleist, SW 1: 144.

site of displacement.[60] The grotto is also a site of concealment; Ottokar predicts that on his wedding night with Agnes, darkness will weave "the veil around the holy love,/Like now" ("den Schleier um die heilge Liebe,/Wie jetzt").[61] While feeling seems to be elevated over knowledge in the grotto, whenAgnes expresses this sentiment ("There is something, that exists higher than all delusion,/And knowledge - feeling" ["Denn etwas gibts, das über alles Wähnen,/Und Wissen hoch erhaben - das Gefühl"]), she and Ottokar do not agree; they argue about the truth behind Peter's murder. Ottokar: "O Agnes, is it possible? Must I/reprimand you so soon? Did you not promise,/to hide none of your most secret feelings from me?... Are you your father?" ("O Agnes, ist es möglich? Muß ich dich/So früh schon mahnen? Hast du nicht versprochen,/Mir deiner heimlichsten Gedanken keinen/zu bergen? [...] Bist du dein Vater denn?") Agnes replies: "As little,/as you are your (father)" ("So wenig,/Wie du der deinige").[62] Finally, Agnes suspects Ottokar of trying to poison her after he tells her he is Johann's friend. She says: "He brings water, brings/me poison, all the same, I drink it all,/he must/do the most monstrous deed to me" ("Er bringe Wasser, bringe/Mir Gift, gleichviel, ich trink es aus,/ er soll/Das Ungeheuerste an mir vollenden").[63] Ottokar responds: "You seem to me so strangely changed" ("Du scheinst so seltsam mir verändert").[64] The uncanny change that both have gone through really is more of a return to what was always there—their fathers' demands, desires, and identities.

Anthony Stephens states that while Kleist may be attempting, through the relationship between Agnes and Ottokar, to pose "the question of the equality of the sexes and of the possibility of an emancipatory discourse," discourse is fundamentally linguistic, and, Stephens says, "all language is a repository of customary codes and meanings."[65] Even in the "locus amoenus" of the grotto, Agnes and Ottokar are not just two—the others, the collective, the culture, and the past are with them, and the grotto is not a way out. Stephens also points out: "Ritual enactments of the ascertaining of truth by

---

[60] Pfeiffer offers a psychoanalytic reading of the grotto scenes that comes to a similar interpretive conclusion. Referring in part to previous analyses by Hinrich Seeba (see note 57 below) and Lilian Hoverland (*Heinrich von Kleist und das Prinzip der Gestaltung* [Königstein: Scriptor, 1978]), Pfeiffer writes: "In der *Familie Schroffenstein* ist die Liebesnacht in der Höhle eine Inszenierung, eine Art 'Mysterienspiel', das von Ottokar imaginiert und inszeniert wird. Die Vereinigung der Liebenden findet nur in der Phantasie statt.[...] All dies geschieht nur als Traumspiel, im Inneren einer mütterlich-bergenden Höhle - also jenseits familiärer Destruktion. Das Spiel im Spiel ermöglicht in einer uterinen Phantasie die Verflüssigung fester Strukturen, eine 'Regung ohne Maß und Ordnung' (V. 2483), das phantasmatische Durchbrechen geschlechtlicher Identitäten - ein Spiel mit primärprozeßhaften Bildwelten," *Die zerbrochenen Bilder. Gestörte Ordnungen im Werk Heinrich von Kleists* 78.

[61] Kleist, SW 1: 147.

[62] Ibid, 108.

[63] Ibid, 106.

[64] Ibid, 107.

[65] Anthony Stephens, *Heinrich von Kleist: The Dramas and Stories* (Oxford and Providence: Berg, 1994) 25.

language…an interrogation (such as Ottokar's of Agnes) may reveal most when its ostensible object is already known."[66] If we go a step further, we see that the ostensible object is only ostensibly known, and that therefore the ritual enactment of possessing that ostensible knowledge through language constitutes yet another displacement—not necessarily away from any real, essential, intrinsic, privileged past place of meaning, but certainly away from a principle of the past that has been insufficiently remembered and therefore also betrayed.

But all attempts to know, recognize, or experience an interpersonal other in this drama are based in a false notion of alterity in the first place. The houses of Rossitz and Warwand are one family, divided, rather than two families. Hence misrecognition occurs more in the context of a monad misknowing himself, or of one body, one blood, divided against itself, rather than in the context of a real self-other encounter. The family is not only the institution or the community, but the ego, the repository and constructor of the knowledge that counts and the knowledge that cuts. And that knowledge is wrong; the trail is false, as is also apparent in the uncanny displacements in the drama between past and present time.

The revenge that Rupert forces the others in his house to swear on the house of Warwand calls for what they believe to be the continuation of a blood feud, a "hunt (…) as if for snakes" ("Jagd […] wie nach Schlangen")[67] —the violent paying of a debt owed to one's own side of the family. The revenge is called for due to the contract of inheritance, which invokes a notion of community-based (or family-based) debt to the future, and specifically to the future family, whom Kleist describes as "survivors" ("Überlebenden"). When Peter's body is found with a finger cut off (and here we have once more the sign of the amputated digit surfacing, Freud would say, as an apotropaic displacement of the phallus), the debt invoked in the contract also becomes a debt to the past (to right a past wrong). The contract and the swearing of revenge symbolize this notion of debt. Wolf Kittler positions Kleist's usage of contract in the context of the "General Landlaw for the Prussian States" ("Allgemeines Landrecht für die Preußischen Staaten," or ALR) of 1794. The ALR encodes notions of political community in notions of family, thereby continuing an older tradition. Specifically, the contract of inheritance stipulated in the ALR denotes the tying of family property to male lineage; Kittler reminds us that this type of contract became common in German-speaking territories in the seventeenth century.[68] Hinrich Seeba states that, in *Schroffenstein*, the "enmity of the related families…is a timeless institution, which encompasses the consciousness of its members so completely, that they no longer perceive it as

66 Stephens, 2.
67 Kleist, SW 1: 66.
68 Kittler, 40-41.

destructive. The enmity has become their consciousness" ("Feindschaft der verwandten Familien [...] eine zeitlose Institution [ist], die das Bewußtsein der Mitglieder so sehr ausfüllt, daß sie von ihnen nicht mehr als Zerrissenheit durchschaut wird. Die Feindschaft ist ihr Bewußtsein selbst geworden").[69] This understanding of the contract of inheritance and of the family seems to establish a continuous view of community over time, albeit a negative one.

But in the play this apparent continuity breaks down numerous times, notably when Agnes and Ottokar refuse to act in accordance with the contract; the dissociative gap between children and parents symbolizes a gap between present and past. But while a new continuity seems to be established —or, rather, perhaps, an old one re-established—when Rupert and Sylvester reconcile after murdering their own children, it is due to a sense of guilt and debt rather than to a rejection thereof. The future, it is implied, can only be secured if a debt, the debt of guilt, continues to be paid. The uneasy alliance between the two family heads at the play's end constitutes part of such a debt-paying. Kleist's presentation of guilt as debt illuminates a disjointed but still mutually dependent view of community and its history.

Anthony Stephens contrasts Kleist's philosophy of history with that of contemporaries such as Novalis, Hegel, and Hölderlin who, Stephens claims, "all managed to fix a coherent mythical vision of their age...What distinguishes Kleist from his Romantic contemporaries is not any reluctance to experiment with myth, but his unwillingness to allow such experiments to produce coherent results."[70] Again, a conceptual movement—in this case, one of discontinuity—on a metalevel of poetic creation is mirrored in the play itself. The possibility of discontinuity in a community through time is first expressed explicitly in the play by Jeronimus, who in the first scene questions the Kirchenvogt as to what all the present trouble has to do with the contract, which was created in the past. The Kirchenvogt insists on continuity in the much-quoted lines: "Ah, sir, the will is part of the business./Because it is exactly as you said, the apple/is not part of the fall" ("Ei, Herr, der Erbvertrag gehört zur Sache./Denn das ist just als sagtest du, der Apfel/Gehöre nicht zum Sündenfall").[71] But this apparent seamlessness is phony; Peter's death is due to drowning rather than to murder, and the contract therefore does not apply. In fact, as the play proceeds, the contract itself plays an increasingly smaller role, as revenge and the concomitant notions of guilt and debt take over.[72] Any true continuity between past and present is horrific; Ottokar says: "One

---

[69] Hinrich C. Seeba, "Der Sündenfall des Verdachts: Identitätskrise und Sprachskepsis in Kleists 'Familie Schroffenstein,'" *Kleists Aktualität. Neue Aufsätze und Essays 1966-1978*, ed. Walter Müller-Seidel (Darmstadt: Wissenschaftliche Buchgesellschaft, 1981) 115.

[70] Stephens, 29.

[71] Kleist, SW 1: 69.

[72] Stephens, 28.

is still terrified/of things he was taught as a child" ("Denn es schauert stets/ Der Mensch, wo man als Kind es ihm gelehrt").[73]

The questions prompted by the fundamentally disjointed and alienated view in *Schroffenstein* of the relationship between children and parents, and between present and past, are potentially very broad, and are not only relevant in the context of Kleist's response to Enlightenment philosophies of history. They include the question of how a community (here of a family, but potentially also of other types of institutions, such as those that appear in Kleist's later works) can assert and understand the *presence* of the past. How can we speak of a community of memories, of the memories of a family? How can we assert a debt or duty to the past that is collective rather than personal? Conflicts in *Schroffenstein* arise in part when individuals assert a need to create a timeline or a history, an identity for themselves that is outside of or counter to the collective.

Ottokar and Agnes want to form a new community, but cannot. And despite Ottokar's attempt to create a new future history by forming new memories (reminiscing about his "baptism" of Agnes as "Maria," he says "I want to remember you with this name/On this beautiful day, when I baptized you" ["Erinnern will ich Dich mit diesem Namen/An jenen schönen Tag, wo ich Dich taufte"][74]), when he and Agnes die, it is the memory of the fathers that prevails. In *Schroffenstein* memory, and hence the nature of collective identity over time, is subsumed into the code of revenge and is all based on a mistake. The debt owed is very specific—revenge for a specific wrong, in a specific family (Kleist is not necessarily saying that all communities must owe similar debts for all crimes at all times, everywhere), but again, it is based on a misunderstanding that repeats itself throughout the play, and hence is generalized to some degree. Could we perhaps read here a possible alternative vision in an argument against the past (since the past cannot be recreated and is inevitably misremembered, rendering continuity between past and present impossible) as a legitimate constituent of collective identity? That is, could we read in *Schroffenstein* a sort of negatively articulated hope for a notion of community based on something else, perhaps on citizens' rights, that is, on a state-based notion of identity rather than one that is blood-based? The fact that Kleist allegorizes the family *to* the state, and particularly to post-1792 France,[75] makes this doubtful.

With the reconciliation between the houses of Warwand and Rossitz houses at the play's end, Kleist at least indirectly implies that the old order will perhaps be better because it has learned from the past—though the reconciliation is also ambiguous. But the implied new order is still defined by old blood. Any hope for a different kind of community, one based, for

---

[73] Kleist, SW 1: 146.
[74] Kleist, SW 1: 104.
[75] Stephens, 33.

instance, on rationality and revisability or even on beauty rather than on unrevisable blood ties, would have to be ahistorical—not exclusive, but elective, and not homogenous, but diverse, at least potentially. Memory—as debt, a sense of obligation between present and past, between children and parents—would not be central or even relevant to such a community. The only hope for continuity and community is in returning to the fathers' voices of authority—voices that speak a language unlikely to escape or to reshape fate, which will likely remain a "Taschenspieler." The only voice that provides an alternative vision at the play's conclusion is Johann's, and he is indeed tied to the fractured family timeline by blood—and precisely *not* in a legal or rational sense. And Johann is alone. No one responds to his statements, intersubjective learning does not happen, and the relationship of this community (the family) to the past remains an instrumental one—a primitive relationship of debt-paying, of revenge. Merely forgetting the family's incorrect memories would also not ensure a just future, though such a forgetting might promise to form the basis for a new, less barbaric and absurd, type of community. In a sense Ottokar and Agnes try too hard to get away—or, rather, the possibility for a just community lies not in forgetting, nor in an evocation of the beautiful or of the sublime, of something that ultimately evades language, but in a discursively shaped setting that includes the very will to power that it tries to escape, and knows it.

Since such a possibility is not present in *Schroffenstein*, neither is any reliable sense of identity, whether one based on belonging to a different type of community, to a new order (perhaps a to community of lovers, or to one of elective rather than blood membership, or to an order of aesthetic experience), or one created by taking the "way in" and focusing on the community's smallest part, on the individual. None of these means of constructing identity is even the negatively implied way out. In *The Foundling* and in *The Family Schroffenstein*, actions that initially seem aesthetically pleasing or ethically valid ultimately prove to be neither aesthetically nor ethically viable. Kleist also found no way out in life; he killed himself in a double-suicide with his friend Henriette Vogel. Kleist's love for his apparently platonic friend Vogel, a love marked by "ego disturbances" and confused boundaries, was an uncanny love at its most destructive, a love marked by simultaneous excess and weariness of life (Moritz's "Lebensüberdruß," synonymous with the desire to "be no more" ["nicht mehr seyn"]).[76]

---

[76] Karl Philipp Moritz, *Gnothi sauton oder Magazin zur Erfahrungsseelenkunde als ėin Lesebuch für Gelehrte und Ungelehrte*, eds. Petra and Uwe Nettelbeck, vol. 4 (Nördlingen: Franz Greno, 1986) 1, 24. This passage was cited in Chapter Three.

2.2. Hoffmann, *The Sandman* (*Der Sandmann*)

In *Modernism and Time* (2000), Ronald Schleifer asserts that there were two Industrial Revolutions: the first occurs in the late eighteenth century; the second, in the late nineteenth century, repeats the basic characteristics of the first, but with new technology, such as the steam engine and the assembly line, that shapes modes of urban existence in new ways.[77] The works of Kleist and of E.T.A. Hoffmann can be read as responding to the first revolution (as does Hegel when he conceives of modern time as dialectical[78]), while "Realist" texts such as those by Gerhart Hauptmann respond to the second. Hoffmann's *The Sandman* (*Der Sandmann*, which appeared in the collection entitled *Nachtstücke* of 1816-1817), however, displays a mode of response to an industrialization and modernization perceived increasingly *as* uncanny, as contributing to alienation via spectralization, that is not unlike the response formulated by much later texts. He deploys uncanny scenarios to respond *to* the perceived problem *of* uncanniness. The effect of *The Sandman* is deeply disorienting, and yet it is exactly through the depiction and generation of anxiety about the revolutionary aspects of modernity that Hoffmann communicates a nineteenth-century revival of an ancient yearning for friendship, community, and love.

In "The Uncanny," Freud states that the figure of the Sandman in Hoffmann's tale is always "a disturber of love" ("Störer der Liebe").[79] He means this primarily in the context of the love between Nathanael and his father[80]: By (in Nathanael's hallucination, at any rate) removing Nathanael's eyes and thus symbolically castrating him, the Sandman (or the alchemist Coppelius) fundamentally disturbs any present or possible future love for Nathanael. Like Frankenstein, Nathanael leaves his fiancée Klara, thus postponing his wedding and, ostensibly, sexual relations, in order to pursue university studies. That choice, which is in a sense a choice to separate mind and body (for Klara promises Nathanael not only physical union, but a "clear" path to reason), and is also an attempt to flee his past, leads Nathanael not to enlightenment but to the wrong kind of knowledge, which must in turn lead to death. Each substitute father whom Nathanael then meets at the university is a bad father. The professor Spalanzani has created the doll

---

[77] Ronald Schleifer, *Modernism and Time: The Logic of Abundance in Literature, Science, and Culture, 1880-1930* (Cambridge: Cambridge University Press, 2000) 4-6.

[78] Ibid, 4.

[79] Freud, GW 12: 244/SE 17: 231.

[80] Freud notes that Hoffmann had an unhappy relationship with his own father:
"E.T.A. Hoffmann war das Kind einer unglücklichen Ehe. Als er drei Jahre war, trennte sich der Vater von seiner kleinen Familie und lebte nie wieder mit ihr vereint. Nach den Belegen, die E. Grisebach in der biographischen Einleitung zu Hoffmanns Werken beibringt, war die Beziehung zum Vater immer eine der wundesten Stellen in des Dichters Gefühlsleben." GW 12: 245n1.

Olimpia, with whom Nathanael initially falls in love, but who ends up contributing to his death by confusing him further about the nature of the relationship between reality and representation. And, in encountering Coppola (or re-encountering Coppelius, and thus the Sandman), Nathanael is never able to escape the false knowledge of the alchemical experiments that killed his father.

Victoria Nelson describes alchemy as a "classic union of *gnosis* and *episteme*,…both an experimental science and a religious practice."[81] It is a practice reflective of the desire, dating at least as far back as ancient Egypt, to achieve immortality by animating matter. *The Sandman*, like *Frankenstein*, is in part a cautionary tale about what can go wrong when this is attempted, and particularly when man attempts to play god via science, to circumvent the woman and the womb and to create life in a laboratory. But Hoffmann's agenda, unlike Kleist's, is neither anti-progressive nor anti-modern.

David Ellison criticizes what he calls the "rigid and self-justifying interpretive framework" in Freud's "Uncanny" essay, which he says focuses on Nathanael to the point of excluding the other characters in the text. In particular, says Ellison, Olimpia's uncanny repetition of characteristics of Nathanael himself is significant: "The resemblance between a young poet and an automaton is not the least of the story's ironically turned uncanny effects."[82] As a refiguring and parody of the Romantic ideal of the young genius-poet, Nathanael represents the height of creativity, and the automaton displays a total lack of creativity. Yet both ultimately receive the same treatment: they are dismembered (Nathanael in his hallucination of what the Sandman does to him, and then in his suicidal fall; Olimpia by Spalanzani) and displaced (Nathanael by Klara's eventual husband, Olimpia by Klara). Hoffmann uses characters such as Klara (which, as with Schelling's Clara, can mean "clear-sighted") and Lothar to counteract the threat not so much of technology per se as of an encroaching mechanistic worldview. This threat helps determine the story's end, as Nathanael first accuses Klara of being a doll herself, then pitches himself to the ground from the top of a tower, ending all reason and all hallucination.

As in Kleist's *Schroffenstein*, the uncanny spaces in Hoffmann's *Sandman* are spaces of displacement. Coppola substitutes for Coppelius, who substitutes for the Sandman of the horrifying tales related to Nathanael by his sister's nanny at bedtime. Olimpia replaces Klara, who then re-replaces Olimpia at the story's end, when Nathanael confuses Klara with a "wooden automaton." The pocket telescope through which Nathanael sees Klara substitutes for the eyeglasses sold by Coppelius and which in turn reminded Nathanael of the glass eyes of Coppola's laboratory. Klara's husband replaces

---

[81] Nelson, *The Secret Life of Puppets* 37.

[82] David R. Ellison, *Ethics and Aesthetics in European Modernist Literature: From the Sublime to the Uncanny* (Cambridge and New York: Cambridge University Press, 2001) 61.

Nathanael. Nothing is where it belongs in the tale; or, nothing remains without a substitute, nothing is not simulated or the subject of uncanny repetition, and all of the substitutions are also repetitions or echoes of the things they replace. The supposedly peaceful ending is, upon closer reading, anything but: Klara is living calmly with her new husband and children, and an eerie quiet of forgetting has descended; all anxiety has vanished, and with it all sense of needing to sustain elements of a lost past—all need to remember.

Like William Lovell and Balder, like Freud's poet friend in the essay on "Transience," and to a certain extent like Schelling's Clara as well, Nathanael is sick, a victim of his own unconscious choices. And yet the texts in which each of these figures appears depict death and decay (the deformity of the once-beautiful Comtesse, the corpses and rot underneath nature's shimmering surface, Nathanael's descent into madness and finally suicide) as restorative of a larger truthfulness. In the case of *The Sandman*, death restores the love "disturbed" and destroyed by Coppelius. It is in this context appropriate to cite Ernst Jentsch's essay on the uncanny, the piece that precedes Freud's reading and in which *The Sandman* is also explicated. As Stanley Cavell explains,

> Jentsch attributes the sense of the uncanny to the recognition of an uncertainty in our ability to distinguish the animate from the inanimate. Hoffmann's story features the beautiful automaton Olimpia with whom the hero falls in love...At first this love serves for the amusement of others who are certain they see right through the inanimateness of the machine; but then the memory of the love serves to feed their own anxiety that they may be making the same error with their beloveds.[83]

Cavell also re-reads the end scene of *The Sandman*, saying that, contra Freud, Nathanael's "desire" at the end is *for* his father—a father-figure does not obstruct the looking-glass, rather: "the leap from the tower is to the father, in accusation and appeal."[84]

Throughout the tale, Nathanael increasingly becomes more puppet-like himself; he feels that he is manipulated by "a dark hostile power which traitorously fixes a thread in our hearts." But this thread can also be understood as a form of umbilical cord, or of community connecting us with others. There is no other choice in the rapidly modernizing and industrializing era that Hoffmann is partaking in and responding to—we simply are pulled along, always slightly out of synch with our own present, but Hoffmann's text points us in the direction of insight, in particular into the natures of our own minds.

---

[83] Stanley Cavell, *In Quest of the Ordinary: Lines of Skepticism and Romanticism* (Chicago: University of Chicago Press, 1988) 155.

[84] Ibid, 157.

In a note that appeared in 1919 in the *International Journal of Psychoanalysis*, entitled "E.T.A. Hoffmann on the Function of Consciousness" ("E.T.A. Hoffmann über die Bewußtseinsfunktion"), Freud asserts that Hoffmann has already discovered something that operates much like the unconscious:

> In the novel *The Devil's Elixir* (Part II, Hesse's edition, p. 210), rich in masterly depictions of pathological mental states, Schönfeld comforts the temporarily mentally disturbed hero with the following words: "What do you gain from this! I mean from the particular mental function that one calls consciousness and which is nothing other than the damnable activity of a condemned gatekeeper—an official—an assistant, who has opened his unholy office in the parlor and says to all exports: hey...hey... transport is forbidden...in the country, in the country is where it stays."
> (In dem an meisterhaften Schilderungen pathologischer Geisteszustände reichen Roman *Die Elixiere des Teufels* (II. Teil, Hesses Ausgabe, S. 210) tröstet Schönfeld den vorübergehend bewußtseinsgestörten Helden mit folgenden Worten: "Was haben Sie denn nun davon! ich meine von der besonderen Geistesfunktion, die man Bewußtsein nennt und die nichts anderes ist als die verfluchte Tätigkeit eines verdammten Toreinnehmers—Akzieseoffizianten—Oberkontrollassistenten, der sein heilloses Komptoir im Oberstübchen aufgeschlagen hat und zu aller Ware, die hinaus will, sagt: hei... hei... die Ausfuhr ist verboten... im Lande, im Lande bleibt's.")[85]

The "exports" that Nathanael's "gatekeeper" forbids could have permitted him to live and to form truly intersubjective relationships; only the uncanny dynamic in the text (the dynamic identified by Freud as well as by Jentzsch) permits us to see this.

In *The Sandman*, the "twilight state" ("Dämmerzustand") that is a kind of catatonia and is not unlike the "magnetic sleep" of clairvoyance, is a response, as it is in Tieck's *William Lovell*, to too much life, to excess; it is hence indicative of a desire to avoid excessive feelings and desires by dying, by "being no more" ("nicht mehr seyn"). This is an expression of a fundamental "ego disturbance" in each text. But all of these characters also long for home. In Kleist this longing is phrased in terms compatible with conservative Romantic nationalism—home is where we belong, and mobility means death. In Hoffmann and texts of the later nineteenth and early twentieth centuries, the longing is less reactionary; these authors acknowledge more openly that displacement is a universal characteristic of modernity, that all citizens of the modern globe are trapped in a world of uncanny strangeness, and that nostalgia can be a progressive force. As Svetlana Boym writes: "The nostalgic is never a native but a displaced person who mediates between the local and the universal."[86] That form of mediation is what the text of *The Sandman* accomplishes as well—between Nathanael and Klara, feeling and reason, home and university, between alchemy and the

---

[85] Freud, GW Nachtragsband (Texte aus den Jahren 1885-1938): 769. The note appeared originally in the *Internationale Zeitschrift für Psychoanalyse* vol. 5 (1919) 308.

[86] Svetlana Boym, *The Future of Nostalgia* (New York: Basic Books, 2001) 12.

modern science that creates prosthetic devices, and between the child whose world is structured by the reassuringly consistent, if frightening, world of fantasy and folklore and the adult whose life is determined by the unpredictable return of real memory.

3. Uncanny Love and the Aesthetics of Healing in Lang and Schnitzler

Psychoanalysis claims that insight into the nature of the self, gained through the excavation of memories, is what heals; this insight emerges from the "keeping" love of the therapy relationship, a love that in turn happens when the mind is made other to itself—when the world of the unconscious is conjured in the therapy setting. But it is also in the conjuring of that world that the patient is prone to uncanny feelings, as memories with a highly mediated relationship to the real past are excavated, and as the patient engages in resistance. Uncanny anxiety surfaces when we are repressing, when we are idealizing—in other words, when we attempt the Romantic attitude, but when we are nevertheless confronted with the rational, the ultimately explicable, and with the facts of loss and of death. The following works present, in aestheticized form, the uncanny characteristics of involuntary repetition, and of the omnipotence of thoughts in particular.[87] These characteristics appear most prominently in the love relationships that are central to both pieces, and mark those relationships as uncanny. The result, in Fritz Lang's 1927 film *Metropolis*, and in Arthur Schnitzler's 1926 narrative *Dream Story*, is not merely the depiction of alternate worlds—a science-fiction future in which robots replicate humans, or a dreamscape Vienna in which an irrevocable estrangement from one's own mind and body can happen in one night. The protagonists of the film and the novella experience uncanny traumas while in love, and depict modern love *as* uncanny, as marked by a surfeit of a past that keeps coming back in strangely familiar form.

3.1. Lang, *Metropolis*

The historian Joachim Radkau has labeled the entire period from 1880 to 1933 in Germany the "age of nervousness,"[88] and he means this quite literally. He points out that diagnoses of anxiety-related disorders rose sharply in Germany around 1880 and persisted through the rise of fascism. Radkau applies the insights of psychoanalysis, another characteristic development of

[87] Freud, GW 12: 256/SE 17: 243.
[88] Radkau, *Das Zeitalter der Nervosität: Deutschland zwischen Bismarck und Hitler.*

this anxious era, in order to diagnose an entire culture and its political as well as individual physical ailments. This same period was also an age of gadgets and gizmos. In the late 1920s, at the apotheosis of the "age of nervousness," a device appeared alongside the newest eyeglasses, cameras, breathing and hearing aids, and alongside the newest psychoanalytic treatments as well. This device, known as the "Wunderblock" ("Mystic Writing-Pad"), was never widely used but it prompted Freud to diverge topically from essays he wrote during the 1920s—essays on the practice of psychoanalysis, on neurotic disorders, and on religion—and to examine instead the seemingly new, or renewed, relationship between technology, remembering, and forgetting.

In the essay entitled "Notes Upon a Mystic Writing-Pad" ("Notiz über den Wunderblock," 1925), Freud notes the congruity between the prosthetic devices that improve the functioning of our senses and sensory organs. For instance, he says, spectacles, cameras, and hearing aids are all fitted onto or against the physical body.[89] Freud goes on to describe the "Mystic Writing-Pad" as a mnemonic aid that he speculates is, in form and function, similar to our faculty of perception ("Wahrnehmungsapparat"), which is intimately linked to the faculty of memory. He describes the device as follows:

> The Mystic Pad is a slab of dark brown resin or wax with a paper edging; over the slab is laid a thin transparent sheet, the top end of which is firmly secured to the slab while its bottom end rests on it without being fixed to it. This transparent sheet is the more interesting part of the little device. It itself consists of two layers, which can be detached from each other except at their two ends. The upper layer is a transparent piece of celluloid; the lower layer is made of thin translucent waxed paper.... To make use of the Mystic Pad, one writes upon the celluloid portion of the covering-sheet which rests on the wax slab. For this purpose no pencil or chalk is necessary, since the writing does not depend on material being deposited on the receptive surface. It is a return to the ancient method of writing on tablets of clay or wax: a pointed stilus scratches the surface, the depressions upon which constitute the "writing."...If one wishes to destroy what has been written, all that is necessary is to raise the double covering-sheet from the wax slab by a light pull, starting from the free lower end....The Mystic Pad is now clear of writing and ready to receive fresh notes.
> (Der Wunderblock ist eine in einen Papierrand gefaßte Tafel aus dunkelbräunlicher Harz- oder Wachsmasse, über welche ein dünnes, durchscheinendes Blatt gelegt ist, am oberen Ende an der Wachstafel fest haftend, am unteren ihr frei anliegend. Dieses Blatt ist der interessantere Anteil dese kleinen Apparats. Es besteht selbst aus zwei Schichten, die außer an den beiden queren Rändern voneinander abgehoben werden können. Die obere Schichte ist eine durchsichtige Zelluloidplatte, die untere ein dünnes, also durchscheinendes Wachspapier....Man gebraucht diesen Wunderblock, indem man die Aufschreibung auf der Zelluloidplatte des die Wachstafel deckenden Blattes ausführt. Dazu bedarf es keines Bleistifts oder einer Kreide, denn das Schreiben beruht nicht darauf, daß Material an die aufnehmende Fläche abgegeben wird. Es ist eine Rückkehr zur Art, wie die Alten auf Ton- und Wachstäfelchen schrieben. Ein spitzer Stilus ritzt die oberfläche, deren Vertiefungen die 'Schrift' ergeben....Will man die Aufschreibung

[89] Freud, "Notiz über den Wunderblock," GW 14: 4/ "A Note Upon the 'Mystic Writing-Pad,'" SE 19: 228-229.

> zerstören, so genügt es, das zusammengesetzte Deckblatt von seinem freien, unteren Rand her mit leichtem Griff von der Wachstafel abzuheben....Der Wunderblock ist nun schriftfrei und bereit, neue Aufzeichnungen aufzunehmen.)[90]

The Mystic Pad is both very new—constructed partly out of celluloid, a relatively recent material—and very old—a return to an ancient form of writing. The operation of the Pad also recalls Plato's analogy of the memory faculty to a wax tablet upon which impressions are made (often extremely painfully, as Nietzsche adds in *The Genealogy of Morals*). And, Freud notes: "The celluloid is a 'protective shield against stimuli'; the layer which actually receives the stimuli is the paper" ("Das Zelluloid ist ein 'Reizschutz'; die eigentlich reizaufnehmende Schicht ist das Papier").[91] This two-tiered system enables something previously not possible: an artificial imitation of how our memory actually works. The Pad is, like our memory faculty, capable of recording an unlimited amount of new data while at the same time capable of preserving traces of that data ("Erinnerungsspuren") into the future—although those traces are prone to alterations.[92] These memory traces are the ground of consciousness itself—they are where consciousness arises, according to Freud.[93] The Pad fascinates because it offers a successful technological simulation of this process; here technology duplicates memory's paradoxical attributes of preservation and decay, or alteration.

The Pad records real memories (or: real representations of memories), and duplicates, or re-presents, the functioning of our memory faculty. The practice of psychoanalytic healing is meant to enact real change and also to duplicate, to serve as a representation, of real encounters and conflicts in the world. Freud understands the interaction between doctor and patient as a replay of conflict, in a way as a sort of theater where real change happens and a representation of that change occurs. The process of transference is crucial in this representation, or duplication, that then enables real change. Representation, in the form of the practice-conflict in the psychiatrist's office, precedes reality. The doctor's notes—Freud's meticulously written-up case records, for instance—serve as artificial memory aids, or as forms of memory traces.

While Freud's focus in the "Mystic Writing-Pad" essay is on analyzing the similarity between this new technology and the memory faculty in order to show more clearly how memory works, an aesthetic component can also be read into the piece—or, the piece can also be read as a contribution to aesthetic theory. While Freud in general does not focus much on theories of beauty or taste (although he does devote some space in his writings to the problem of symbolic knowledge, and he acknowledges the

---

[90] Freud, GW 14: 5/SE 19: 229.

[91] Ibid, 6/230.

[92] Ibid, 4/228.

[93] Ibid, 4-5/228-229. This is a paraphrase of an argument from "Jenseits des Lustprinzips."

growing interest in applying insights from psychoanalysis to humanistic disciplines[94]), he enters this realm in interpreting E.T.A. Hoffmann's *The Sandman* in "The Uncanny." *The Sandman* has significant plot-element similarities to Fritz Lang's science-fiction film of 1927, *Metropolis*. This film was released only two years after Freud wrote his essay on the Mystic Pad.

Metropolis is a cultural artifact in which the mechanical reproduction (re-representation) of the female human form—a type of reproduction that exemplifies what Freud would term "uncanny doubling"—signifies an understanding of gender and a mode of transference that together aestheticize the traditional (and at that point quite recently developed) psychoanalytic model. The model already contains a component we can potentially understand as aesthetic, as noted above—if we want to understand the process of representation and duplication (which is also a kind of remembering and repetition) that happens during psychoanalytic treatment as having a potential aesthetic aspect. But the plot and dazzling spectacle of *Metropolis* unambiguously aestheticize reality. It is the technology of film, of celluloid—in *Metropolis* and in the "Mystic Writing-Pad"—that permits this simultaneity, this collapse of reality and representation, while promising to preserve the past better—to enable memory traces to persist, and thus to prevent us from falling into an eternal empty present, void of memory, numb and forgetful.

Studies of the intersections of aesthetics and power from the Frankfurt School to the present have explored the contradictions inherent in *Metropolis*' reliance on images of technology in critiquing mechanized modernity. However, few efforts have been made to demonstrate the film's use of psychoanalytic insights. In this section I show how traditional psychoanalytic elements of transference and gender identification can contribute to an analysis of a specifically modern and uncanny erotics of power, a nervous, anxious dynamic that could be still significant today for understandings of how technologies of art and reproduction impact the psyche.

Metropolis presents a humanity not merely in thrall to technology, but to an episteme of a doomed duality between subject and object, and ultimately to a dialectic of submission and domination. The parody of the abuse of power via sex enacted by the robot version of Maria in the film, who is, Andreas Huyssen concludes, both "vamp and machine,"[95] functions not simply as parody or social commentary, but on an aesthetic level as an uncanny repetition of the unjust object relations that ultimately persist in the film, although in altered form. That is, at the film's end it looks as if a new, potentially just relationship will obtain between workers and overlords—but

---

[94] See for instance Freud, GW 14: 305.

[95] Andreas Huyssen, "The Vamp and the Machine: Technology and Sexuality in Fritz Lang's *Metropolis*," *New German Critique* 24/25 (1981/82) 221-237.

this happens at the pacifist heroine Maria's expense (not just at the expense of the robot Maria who goes up in flames, but at the expense of the real woman who is replaced by Freder, the main overlord's son, at the film's conclusion). In fact, Maria is re-presented—replaced, actually—twice in the film: by her lifelike robot double and ultimately by Freder.

As the robot represents only Maria's aesthetic qualities—only her beautiful form—it simultaneously serves as an illustration of how technology can perform an uncanny "haunting," not only of "real" humans per se, but of the idea of gender itself. As Maria's body is copied in the form of a beautiful machine, her identification as female is transformed into a pure image-identification. It is this insubstantial image that ends up not only seducing the film's hero, but permitting him to adopt, through a process of transference, the substance of the "real" woman. The film's ultimate healing insight, that a heart must mediate between brain and muscle, or between mind and body, is therefore actually enabled by the abuse of power via technology.

With the creation and actions of the robot Maria, as in Freud's definition of the uncanny, concepts that seem opposed come together: the familiar and the comfortable ("das Heimliche") intersect with the hidden, the repressed ("das Unheimliche").[96] Freud's essay on the uncanny emphasizes the fact that "heimlich" and "unheimlich" often have the exact same definitions, in etymological, philosophical, and sociohistorical contexts. In *Metropolis*, it is the robot's resemblance to Maria, to the familiar and the comforting (the "heimlich"), that ingratiates her with the workers and permits her to lead them to destroy the machines and thus their own homes (again, that which is "heimlich"). The robot retains Maria's image by re-presenting it —the workers remember Maria by seeing the robot—but the machine simultaneously replaces Maria and causes the workers to forget her. The robot Maria—or rather, the robot Maria on film, in film—is a diabolical, sexed-up kind of "writing-pad," which also retains and erases.

The robot's erasure of Maria, though it will not last, is necessary for the film's second replacement to happen. The hero Freder eventually erases the real Maria, the real "heart" of the story—yet he retains what she represented. He joins brain and muscle together at the end of the film, standing in the center of the frame between the burly worker and his (Freder's) ruling-class father. But this replacement, which is also a remembering of Maria's past actions, is not merely a matter of an active male hero stepping in, a son fulfilling his patriarchically determined role as continuer of and improvement on his father's life trajectory.

Metropolis does not dissolve into a simplistic indictment of industrialization and modernization and does not unequivocally tout the value of "real" flesh and blood over machines.[97] But the film bears a message that

---

[96] Freud, GW 12: 235.
[97] See especially Huyssen, "The Vamp and the Machine."

is not only more complex, but more disturbing. The suspense that occurs between Maria's reproduction as a robot and the film's ending, in which the real hero and heroine and then the city's captains of industry (the city's "brain" or mind) and its slave-like workers (the city's "muscle" or body) are reconciled, can be read as an aestheticized analogy of the suspense of the psychoanalytic healing process, in which transformations that are not always beautiful lead to transference and eventually to insight into one's own psychic identifications, gender and otherwise. The film thus ends up advocating a kind of aestheticized psychoanalytic model or aestheticizing psychoanalytic healing into a world of beautiful simulations.

A transference dynamic—transference working exactly as it should, in Freud's theory—helps block the formation of more just intersubjective (as opposed to abusive subject-object) relationships in *Metropolis*. The doubling of Maria permits what Freud calls the development and projection of "tender emotions as well as emotions of enmity" ("Gefühlsbeziehungen zärtlicher wie feindseliger Natur") on Freder's part. In the middle phase of his career, Freud defines neurotic transference as follows:

> "Transference" is the name for the neurotic's obvious tendency to develop feelings of a tender but also hostile nature toward her doctor, feelings that are not founded in the real situation, but which rather come from the parental relationship (Oedipus complex) of the patient. Transference is proof that the adult has not overcome her prior childish dependence; transference meshes with the power of so-called "suggestion." When the doctor learns to handle it, transference alone can enable him to prompt the ill person to overcome her inner resistances and to release her repressions. The psychoanalytic treatment becomes in this manner a late form of education for the adult, a correction to the education of the child.
> ("Übertragung" nennt man die auffällige Eigentümlichkeit der Neurotiker, Gefühlsbeziehungen zärtlicher wie feindseliger Natur zu ihrem Arzt zu entwickeln, die nicht in der realen Situation begründet sind, sondern aus der Elternbeziehung [Ödipuskomplex] der Patienten stammen. Die Übertragung ist ein Beweis dafür, daß auch der Erwachsene seine einstige kindliche Abhängigkeit nicht überwunden hat, sie deckt sich mit der Macht, die man "Suggestion" genannt hat; ihre Handhabung, die der Arzt erlernen soll, setzt ihn allein in den Stand, den Kranken zur Überwindung seiner inneren Widerstände und zur Aufhebung seiner Verdrängungen zu bewegen. Die psychoanalytische Behandlung wird so zu einer Nacherziehung des Erwachsenen, einer Korrektur der Erziehung des Kindes.)[98]

Freder, the neurotic, has not mastered his previous childlike dependence (what Freud calls "seine einstige kindliche Abhängigkeit"); the process of transference is rooted in Oedipal constellations. Shortly after Freder moves symbolically out of his childhood (in the pleasure garden, in the above-ground city) and into preliminary adulthood by joining the workers, then falls for Maria, she is kidnapped and the evil scientist Rotwang constructs her robot double, a "machine man."

---

[98] Freud, "Psycho-Analyse," GW 14: 305.

The real impetus behind the creation of that machine was quite unclear until 2002, when the Friedrich-Wilhelm-Murnau Foundation, together with Transit Films, released a restored version of *Metropolis* on DVD in which several scenes deleted by the film's American distributor, Paramount, are re-inserted.[99] The new release includes the film's original orchestral score, photos of stills from lost scenes, a documentary on the making of the film in 1927, and scene-by-scene audio commentary. The restoration represents a collaboration of the Bundesarchiv-Filmarchiv, the Munich Filmmuseum, and the Deutsches Filminstitut in Wiesbaden, whose teams worked with all that does remain of *Metropolis*—an incomplete original negative and the various shortened editions released since 1927. The film of 2002 reveals definitively that the robot double of Maria is a reconstruction of Freder's dead mother, Hel, and we learn more about Joh Fredersen and the scientist Rotwang, past rivals for Hel's affections, as well.

In the restored scene entitled "Fredersen at Rotwang's House," we learn that Rotwang's house is "ancient"—overlooked by the urban technological progress surrounding it. But Rotwang, while he possesses qualities of a medieval alchemist, is not actually ancient nor is he the home's true owner. He stole the home by force and now uses it for his dubious inventive activities. During the creation of the machine-man, the robot that ultimately becomes Maria's double, Rotwang lost his right hand, and has replaced it with a prosthesis made of steel taken from the material used to produce the robot. Rotwang thus is partly himself a machine-man, and his human body is simultaneously always a reminder of loss, with the hand once more functioning as a signifier of castration anxiety.[100] Joh Fredersen has symbolically castrated Rotwang; or, Rotwang has castrated himself in the pursuit of forbidden knowledge. Ultimately we will see that *Metropolis* hardly bans knowledge per se. Rather, uncanny experiences stem not from primitivity coming back in the urban modern age, but from things one wishes one did not know asserting themselves in the midst of the desire to retreat to what Freud calls the "biological fetal situation" ("biologische Fötalsituation").[101]

When Joh Fredersen enters Rotwang's house to seek the scientist's aid in defeating the workers' rebellion, he stumbles upon a bust of his dead wife, placed upon a pedestal "as wide as a wall and as tall as a man." This monumental statue of Hel, as the audio commentary on the re-release of 2002

---

[99] Fritz Lang, dir., *Metropolis* (1927), restored authorized edition with the original 1927 orchestral score, licensed by Transit Films on behalf of the Friedrich-Wilhelm-Murnau-Stiftung (Wiesbaden: 2002). All references in the text to captions and to audio commentary are from this version of the film.

[100] Freud, "Fausse Reconnaissance (Déjà Raconté) in Psycho-Analysis," SE 13: 206. Also cited in Chapter Three.

[101] Freud, "Hemmung, Symptom und Angst" GW 14: 168-169.

reminds us, also memorializes the "Hel of the Nordic sagas (who) was the ruler of the underworld. Motherly goddess of death." The commentary also notes that Metropolis is "the mother city, city of all mothers, mother of all cities," which refers to the word's Greek roots (*metera* = mother; *polis* = city).

The inscription on the bust's pedestal reveals Rotwang's feelings about and relationship to Hel: "HEL/Born for my happiness and mankind's blessing/Lost/to Joh Fredersen/Died/Giving birth to Freder, Joh Fredersen's son." The names of Freder and Fredersen, son and father, are given more space on the inscription than the names of either Hel or Rotwang, the pair that has been displaced. However, although Hel's killers, Fredersen and Freder, now rule or will rule Metropolis, she represents the city itself—the ancient city in which Rotwang's house was built, the city in which the goddesses of Nordic saga still reigned. Joh Fredersen, however, wants nothing of this past. Although he is visibly moved by seeing Hel's likeness on a pedestal and by reading the damning inscription, he attacks the advancing Rotwang: "A brain like yours, Rotwang…should be able to forget…. Let the dead rest in peace, Rotwang…For you, as for me, she is dead…." Fredersen here appropriates the dead *for* the living, rhetorically repossessing and then disposing of Hel while ordering Rotwang to repress her.

Rotwang, in an angry outburst directed right into the camera, rejects this entirely and reappropriates Hel for himself: "For me, she is not dead, Joh Fredersen, - for me, she lives—!" Rotwang and Fredersen here each claim Hel for themselves, and Rotwang goes further than that. Holding up his prosthesis, he cries, "Do you think that losing a hand is too high a price to pay for re-creating Hel—?!" He hereby reveals that he has lost his hand in the act of reanimating the dead, and he invites Fredersen to his laboratory to see this recreation for himself: "Do you want to see her?"

The two men ascend a spiral staircase into Rotwang's laboratory, which is a re-presentation and adaptation of imaginings of laboratories ranging from the late-medieval site of Faust's alchemical experiments, through Frankenstein's chambers and the secret room in which Nathanael's father works together with the Sandman. The screenplay for *Metropolis* calls Rotwang's lab "half a quack's kitchen from the year 1500, and half experimental laboratory of a man from the year 2000," and the audio commentary on the 2002 re-release elaborates, saying that Rotwang himself represents "magic and modern in one entity." This mix of old and new is found throughout the film: Rotwang's old house amidst skyscrapers, the Moloch of the underground Worker's City surrounded by technology, Maria's transformation from a sort of socialist update of the Virgin Mary into a machine.

In each instance, the new is neither a simple repetition nor a complete abandonment of the old, but rather is a symbol dissociated in some way from its original referent. The existence of the symbol in each case, as well as its dissociation from the past, is enabled by technology of some kind. The robot Maria is no longer the exact reproduction of Hel that Rotwang had intended, but a figure related to yet dissociated from the dead woman, and mobilized for a new purpose: to defeat the workers' rebellion. The robot thus does end up enabling Rotwang to "forget," or repress, Hel—and yet simultaneously the robot is Hel's uncanny return. Rotwang's laboratory, the screenplay states, is "centuries behind, centuries ahead." Like the uncanny symbols in the film, the lab exists in a state of "eerie temporal discoordination" similar to that which Gregg Horowitz identifies in Freud's collection of ghostly objects[102]—the laboratory neither completely replicates past spaces of experimentation, nor is it fully modern; thus, it preserves a sense of the difference between past and present rather than precisely repeating elements of either period. The clock-like machine that Freder must manipulate when he takes over a shift from an exhausted worker in the underground city is visually an uncanny recurrence of the crucifix; both are forms of machinery that kill, with no obvious purpose beyond destruction. Fredersen's modern watch, a chronometron Movado, says the audio commentary, "is the epitome of 20s modernity," but it is juxtaposed with Rotwang's use of an ancient-looking compass as he plots a path through the labyrinthine spaces of the underground city. The city itself, with its skyscrapers and highways literally on top of the workers' city but also surrounding much older structures such as Rotwang's house, is an urban palimpsest, a visual urban parallel to the Mystic Writing-Pad.

All of these uncanny repetitions (uncanny in that they summon resemblances to past objects rather than replicate those objects precisely; they remind of things hidden) serve to heighten the spectator's sense of anxiety about what will happen to the lovers whose relationship forms the film's core: Freder and Maria. The "mother-city" Metropolis, which is an "unhomely home" ("unheimliche Heimat") for these lovers, functions within the film as what Freud terms the "psychic mother-object" for characters and spectators alike. In his late-career theory of anxiety, Freud describes the purpose of this object as follows:

> (Anxiety reveals itself) to be the product of the psychic helplessness of the nursling, which is obviously the counterpart of his biological helplessness. The striking coincidence, that the condition of birth anxiety as well as nursling anxiety is the separation from the mother, needs no psychological interpretation.... The psychic mother-object substitutes for the child's biological fetal situation.
> ([Die Angst zeigt sich] als Produkt der psychischen Hilflosigkeit des Säuglings, welche das selbstverständliche Gegenstück seiner biologischen Hilflosigkeit ist. Das auffällige Zusammentreffen, daß sowohl die Geburtsangst wie die Säuglingsangst die

[102] Gregg Horowitz, *Sustaining Loss: Art and Mournful Life* (Stanford: Stanford University Press, 2001) 130. In Chapter One, I interpreted this argument to mean that Freud's collection of artifacts from various periods and cultures preserved a sense of difference between past and present; Rotwang's laboratory arguably functions in a similar way within the narrative of the film.

> Bedingung der Trennung von der Mutter anerkennt, bedarf keiner psychologischen Deutung.... Das psychische Mutterobjekt ersetzt dem Kinde die biologische Fötalsituation.)[103]

The Oedipal nature of the film's relationships is revealed further when Freder confronts Rotwang, demanding "Where is Maria?" Rotwang replies: "She is with your father." Freder then rushes to his father, Johann Fredersen's, office, only to find Fredersen with Maria in a seductive pose. This prompts a filmically interesting sequence in which images flash rapidly to signify Freder's nervous collapse—scenes from his tumultuous recent experiences in the workers' city, along with images of Maria's face.

Freder's stamina and nerves are tested during his adventure in the workers' city; he cries out while suspended in a crucifix-like position on the huge clock-like structure: "Father, I did not know ten hours could be torture!" But it is the moment when he believes he has lost his lover to his father that prompts his breakdown and ultimate move into full symbolic adulthood. At the climax of the film, the real Maria escapes from Rotwang's lair and embraces Freder, who says "Yes, you are the real Maria" after looking into her eyes as they stand in the midst of the flood created by the aroused workers' attempt to destroy the machines that power the city. Although hero and heroine are encircled by the children of the workers, who are pleading for help in escaping the underground city, it is here in the moment of real danger that Freder's anxiety attack finally ends (the attack or breakdown visually represented by the rapidly flashing images mentioned above). Surrounded by water, by children in water, and tightly embraced by the real Maria (who it is now clear loves Freder, not his father), Freder is right in the middle of a representation of the "biological fetal situation." Freud makes clear that anxiety occurs when subject and object separate, or actually when the object world is created. In re-joining with Maria in the flood, the frightening subject-object separation has ended for Freder, but it has ended in a literally watery, melting-together, in a blurring of boundaries rather than in a clearly demarcated intersubjectivity.

At the film's end, after Maria says (and this is the third time this phrase occurs in the film) "There can be no understanding between the hands and the brain unless the heart acts as mediator," Freder becomes Maria, or rather he substitutes for her—he replaces her. The transference is then complete. None of this would have been possible without technology, or without the uncanny double.

Maria the robot is creepy because she appears as Maria the madonna, but acts like Maria the whore—thereby activating the long-familiar, repressed erotic feelings that Freder and the other members of the all-male worker corps, and possibly the viewers, have toward the real Maria. In the

---

[103] Freud, "Hemmung, Symptom und Angst," GW 14: 168-169.

process of the film's plot, this uncanny dynamic activates, via aesthetic representation, an erotics of power that recalls and reveals the aesthetic aspects of the psychoanalytic process, part of a healing science (a science that heals "modern" neuroses). Modern technology enables the aesthetic representation of mediation and healing that takes place in the film. We are reassured by and through the same technology that created all the problems in the first place. At the same time, technology enables endless remembering—which is not that different from forgetting. The celluloid sheet, the film, of the Mystic Writing-Pad is, Freud says, a "protective shield" ("Reizschutz"). One of the questions raised by both Freud's essay on the Pad and Lang's film is whether we technologically enabled and enhanced beings exist, now, not in the permanent-impression-space of the wax tablet (the space in which a lasting impression can be made, but once filled, there no room for anything else), but rather in the space of the protective celluloid covering, that which can be erased and refilled, and erased and refilled, indefinitely.

Thea von Harbou's 1926 novel *Metropolis*, first published in Frankfurt's *Illustriertes Blatt* and the basis for Lang's film, famously asserts that the "mediator between head and hands must be the heart." However, as the audio commentary on the 2002 video release of *Metropolis* points out, Fritz Lang did not subscribe to this motto—his real interest was the machinery within and of the film. Yet Lang's film is a repetition and revision of Harbou's novel that simultaneously enacts a shifting of its content. Their collaboration and relationship ended when the Third Reich began. Fritz Lang emigrated to Hollywood, and Thea von Harbou remained in Germany.

3.2. Schnitzler, *Dream Story* (*Traumnovelle*)

In *Civilization and its Discontents* (*Das Unbehagen in der Kultur*, 1930), Freud addresses an often-overlooked consequence of technological progress. In an era focused on the experience of speed and shock occasioned by the photograph and the film, a focus displayed famously in Walter Benjamin's theses on art in the age of mechanical reproducibility, Freud reminds us that technology also slows things down. In particular, the magnifying glass and the lens can "hold fleeting visual impressions fast" ("die flüchtigen Seheindrücke festhalten") and therefore function as "materializations of the…memory" ("Materialisationen des…Vermögens der Erinnerung, des Gedächtnisses").[104] The ability of the lens to materialize memory and hold it fast is part of its prosthetic function. This argument recalls Karl Philipp Moritz's aesthetic theory of the late eighteenth century, in

[104] Sigmund Freud, *Das Unbehagen in der Kultur und andere kulturtheoretische Schriften* (Frankfurt am Main: Fischer, 2004) 57.

which he notes that artists give "duration to one of the fleeting moments... which therefore shake the soul most strongly, because in everything that presents itself to the eye, always the one through the other, just as the whole through itself, *speaks* and becomes *meaningful*" ("einem der fliehenden Momente Dauer...welcher deswegen am stärksten die Seel' erschütterte, weil in allem, was in ihm auf einmal sich dem Auge darstellt, immer eines durch das andre, so wie das Ganze durch sich selber, *redend* und *bedeutend* wird").[105]

In Arthur Schnitzler's *Dream Story* (*Traumnovelle*, 1926) as well as in the film version directed by Stanley Kubrick entitled *Eyes Wide Shut* (1999), uncanny repetition enabled by prosthetic technology holds moments fast, slows time down, and renders memory material. In the case of *Eyes Wide Shut*, the film itself acts to slow down perception, with its continual repetitions of various visual motifs (from women's red hair and similarly proportioned bodies to nearly-identical Christmas trees in apartments all over the city) and lengthy dream-like sequences. However, these "fixings" and materializations of memory, enabled by and constituted in technology, do not necessarily inspire confidence in memory's stability or reliability. The embodiments of memory that happen in and through the film function to render the story's content both progressive and regressive, in part due to *what* is being preserved (for instance, the arguably pornographic renderings of women's bodies as nearly identical and therefore as replaceable) but also due to *how* and in *what setting* (dream, hallucination, parties; doctor's office, interactions with patients) this preservation (or holding-fast, sustaining) of particular memories occurs.

Dream Story's protagonist, the physician Fridolin, experiences an uncanny sensation similar to the one Freud has during the walk described in "The Uncanny." The moment of guilt-inspired derealization that Freud experienced on the Acropolis in 1904, which he described and analyzed in detail in the letter to Romain Rolland of 1936, was not his only experience of repetition-driven uncanniness. In "The Uncanny," Freud describes his anxiety when

> walking, one hot summer afternoon, through the deserted streets of a provincial town in Italy which was unknown to me....Nothing but painted women were to be seen at the windows of the small houses, and I hastened to leave the narrow street at the next turning.
>
> (Als ich einst an einem heißen Sommernachmittag die mir unbekannten, menschenleeren Straßen einer italienischen Kleinstadt durchstreifte, geriet ich in eine Gegend, über deren Charakter ich nicht lange in Zweifel bleiben konnte. Es waren nur geschminkte Frauen an den Fenstern der kleinen Häuser zu sehen, und ich beeilte mich, die enge Straße durch die nächste Einbiegung zu verlassen.)[106]

---

[105] Karl Philipp Moritz, *Die Signatur des Schönen, oder inwiefern Kunstwerke beschrieben werden können?* in *Beiträge zur Ästhetik*, eds. Hans Joachim Schrimpf and Hans Adler (Mainz: Dieterischsche Verlagsbuchhandlung, 1989) 81-82.

[106] Freud, GW 12: 249/SE 17: 237.

Although he tries to leave, Freud ends up in this same hot, claustrophobic prostitute quarter three times; his repeated presence starts to attract attention and, he says, "a feeling overcame me which I can only describe as uncanny" ("Dann aber erfaßte mich ein Gefühl, das ich nur als unheimlich bezeichnen kann").[107] While this experience of repeatedly getting lost in the same place, a place defined by commercialized lust, is not the same thing as the "art attack" Freud had on the Acropolis in the presence of overwhelming beauty, both uncanny moments occur during travel. Both resemble in some respects the description in the Hippocratic corpus of the fifth to third centuries B.C. of a disease that "usually attacks abroad, if a person is travelling a lonely road somewhere, and fear seizes him."[108] Freud's account of disorientation while walking also is reminiscent of Emanuel Swedenborg's eighteenth-century account of being "mentally taken to another place" in the *Arcana Coelestia.*[109] Although Swedenborg attributes his out-of-body experience to divine intervention, this form of uncanny displacement can be actually a very modern kind of problem—in Freud's case, the disorientation he feels is occasioned by modern travel, by the ability to be mobile, to be "estranged" in the first place. In this experience, as in Freud's in Greece, the unconscious mind reminds us of our strangeness to ourselves, and of our estrangement from ourselves.

As Fridolin perambulates through Vienna during his dream-like night, it seems that, as for Freud, "nothing but painted women" confront him. The prostitute Domino, a costume-shop girl who is completely instrumentalized for her father's gain, and prostitutes at a strange party with elements reminiscent of both the séance and Inquisition ritual in Schiller's *Ghost-Seer*—all serve as externalizations of his own memory and his own dreams. These dreams, or fantasies ("Träume"), Frederic Raphael points out, are etymologically proximitous in German to the notion of trauma ("Trauma"); in fact, Raphael says, *Traum* and *Trauma* "were almost indistinguishable in the Vienna which was at home to both."[110] Fridolin's "Traum" sequence is instigated by the "Trauma" of hearing about his wife's sexual fantasies and therefore also of acknowledging that neither he nor Albertine is precisely who they seem to be. When he returns, after his "dream"-filled night, to Albertine and their daughter, his home has become unhomely—he sees wife and daughter as repetitions of the painted women

---

[107] Freud, GW 12: 249/SE 17: 237.

[108] Cited in Theodore M. Brown's entry on "Mental Diseases" in the *Companion Encyclopedia of the History of Medicine*, eds. Roy Porter and W.F. Bynum, vol. 1 (London and New York: Routledge, 1997) 439. Brown quotes Hippocrates, *Works*, ed. and trans. W.H.S. Jones, E.T. Withington and Paul Potter, vol. 6 (London: Loeb Classical Library/Heinemann, 1923-88), 235.

[109] From the excerpts from Swedenborg's *Arcana Coelestia* in Kant, *Träume eines Geistersehers, erläutert durch Träume der Metaphysik* 98. This passage was cited in Chapter Two.

[110] From Frederic Raphael's introduction to Arthur Schnitzler, *Dream Story*, trans. J.M.Q. Davies (New York: Penguin Books, 1999) vi.

without, but now they are within. Fridolin's feeling of disorientation from his walk through and adventures in the city persists inside his now unhomely (or, uncanny) home.

The depiction of the objects that perpetuate the protagonist's uncanny anxiety in the film version of *Dream Story*, *Eyes Wide Shut* (1999), transmits a similar uncanny feeling to the viewer, who accompanies Bill (Fridolin) throughout the entire film and thus must adopt his perspective—the film is an imagological rendering of Schnitzler's inner monologue. Bill's (Fridolin's) wife, Alice (Albertine) has in the film the same hair and body as the prostitute Domino as well as the prostitutes at the mysterious orgy organized by a group reminiscent of a secret society. Most unsettlingly, Bill's daughter has the same red hair as well, and will likely look just like not only Alice but the prostitutes when she is older.

The uncanny repetition of women's bodies in the film is reminiscent of Joris-Karl Huysmans' description of a Paris boutique in 1883 (which is the correct temporal context for both *Dream Story* and *Eyes Wide Shut*, as I explain below):

> At the sight of these (realistic, often repulsive) ranks of bosoms (mannequin busts arranged in a boutique "on the rue Legendre in the Batignolles district of Paris"), the Curtius museum of the bust, we are vaguely reminded of the pigeon-holes containing the antique sculpture at the Louvre where the same torso, repeated ad infinitum, is to the acquired taste of those who yawn while contemplating it on rainy days.
> But what a great difference there is between such inhuman pieces of marble and the stuffed percaline of these terrifying objects! The Greek breasts correspond to a pattern laid down by centuries-old taste and are now lifeless; nothing we could find suggestive will ever again emanate from these conventional figures sculpted in a cold substance of which our eyes have grown tired. And let's admit it. How distasteful it would be if a Parisienne undressed to reveal such impeccable charms and if, at our every lapse, we were obliged to fondle monotonous throats and breasts that were all alike.
> How vastly superior to these sad statues of Venus are our dressmaker's dummies that are so full of life. How much more insinuative our upholstered busts, the mere sight of which makes us dream.[111]

The monotonous perfection of the bodies in *Eyes Wide Shut* and the variety of the amputated bosoms in the dress shop are both uncanny, in different ways whose inversion of one another recalls the relationship between the dead-but-unburied "ghosts" of Freud's collection the live-but-buried "victims" of the psychological studies and psychological fiction discussed in Chapters Three and Four. The figure of the naked female body is here the figure of the substitute and of displacement; she/they occupy what James Risser calls *the* space of the uncanny: "a space of a place of displacement."[112]

---

[111] From Joris-Karl Huysmans' review of a Paris boutique in 1883 in *L'Art Moderne*, cited here in Mike Kelley, *The Uncanny* 20.

[112] Risser, "Siting Order at the Limits of Construction: Deconstructing Architectural Space" 70.

The repetition of perfection and its eternal availability in *Eyes* echoes the Marquis de Sade's insistence on repeating the same scenarios, and on brandishing them brutally at the reader via seemingly endless versions of what are fundamentally the same savage sexual routines enacted by similar bodies. The busts in the shop are uncanny in their realism, but the repeated nature of their amputation actually contributes to a sense of "superior" singularity. They are not actually real, but they are more realistic, and thus more terrifying than the bland repetition of beauty in Greek sculpture. For Fridolin and Bill as well as for the reader of Schnitzler's novella and the viewer of Kubrick's film, real bodies seem unrealistic due to their perfection and uncanny repetition.

Women are not the only objects of exchange value in the novella and film, however. Fridolin/Bill is a doctor, comfortable but not rich. His wealthy and secretive clients invite him to their parties, but he does not truly belong—Fridolin and Albertine know no one at the party at the novella's beginning, for instance, with the exception of Nachtigall, a friend from Fridolin's past who is also essentially a servant to the affluent (he plays the piano at the party). The novella also emphasizes Fridolin's Jewishness—he is a figure of displacement from the beginning, not quite inside the circle of the powerful and not quite outside it. This displaced status is stressed all the more when Fridolin sneaks into the orgy and, in a scene reminiscent of the beheading of the Venetian in Schiller's *Ghost-Seer*, finds himself encircled by masked and cloaked figures, all of whom know something he does not. The novella and the film employ disorientation and repetition to underscore the characters' mutual instrumentalization and utilization (the prostitutes and by extension all women in the novella and film are objects of exchange value; Fridolin/Bill's societal and therefore personal worth is equal only to the service he provides his rich clients), but the impression made by the film in particular is also a highly aestheticized one. The film indulges the viewer's desire for these perfect bodies in a way that the mannequin shop does not—the realistic, amputated mannequin busts repel rather than attract.

The repetition of women's bodies inspires more uncanny sensation in Fridolin and in the reader, a kind of anxiety similar to that inspired by Hoffmann's *Sandman*, at first about who Fridolin's loved one really is, and ultimately about his own identity. Fridolin's disorientation and uncertainty about the orgy—about who these people (who, in the film, all wear highly similar costumes and masks) really are and about where he has actually been—extends back into his relationship with Albertine, a relationship revealed as never having been quite what he thought it was. As Fridolin begins to see Albertine as an uncanny repetition who herself is uncannily repeated, their entire relationship takes on uncanny, simulative qualities. The disoriented, uncanny love between Fridolin and Albertine in their unhomely-home extends hypostatically to other relationships and other places in the novella:

all forms of relating become dream-like, disoriented, and unhinged; all cafes resemble one another, and any one domicile could just as well be another.

Fridolin's musings about his own memories, musings that take place primarily during his wanderings through the city over a long night, through time and space, form a monologue of extended estrangement. Like Tieck's William, Schiller's Prince, Hoffmann's Nathanael, and Kleist's Piachi, Fridolin is nostalgic and melancholy: his memory retains (or keeps *in*) what he wants to get rid of (keep *out*), and he experiences this "false remembering" during highly aestheticized moments—the staged drama of the orgy, the masquerade of a ball. But Fridolin's uncanny melancholy, though miserable, is also deeply enjoyable and ultimately does lead him to a form of enlightenment and healing. In a discussion of a foreigner's nostalgic and melancholy longing, while he is not at home, *for* home, Julia Kristeva postulates that perhaps this melancholic estranged person is actually happy, as

> even he who, seemingly, flees the slimy poison of depression, does not hold back, as he lies in bed, during those glaucous moments between waking and sleeping. For in the intervening period of nostalgia, saturated with fragrances and sounds to which he no longer belongs and which, because of that, wound him less than those of the here and now, the foreigner is a dreamer making love with absence, one exquisitely depressed. Happy?[113]

Fridolin and Albertine are of course also incredibly self-absorbed, and everything in the dream-worlds around them seems only to reflect their inner lives. However, what nevertheless makes their experiences related, intersubjective, and "exterocentric" (that is, externalizations of their own minds outwards rather than flights into inwardness and solipsism) is the estrangement that both characters feel. In this, they are again not unlike the foreigners of Kristeva's theory, who are characterized by

> Deep-seated narcissism? Blank psychosis beneath the swirl of existential conflicts? In crossing a border (…or two) the foreigner has changed his discomforts into a base of resistance, a citadel of life. Moreover, had he stayed home, he might perhaps have become a dropout, an invalid, an outlaw…Without a home, he disseminates on the contrary the actor's paradox: multiplying masks and 'false selves' he is never completely true nor completely false, as he is able to tune in to loves and aversions the superficial antennae of a basaltic heart.…This means that, settled within himself, the foreigner has no self.…I do what *they* want *me* to, but it is not 'me'—'me' is elsewhere, 'me' belongs to no one, 'me' does not belong to 'me,'…does 'me' exist?[114]

When Albertine finds Fridolin's mask, she confronts him with it—and yet she also does not, merely leaving it on his pillow where it need not be discussed but also cannot be avoided. With this act, Albertine consciously expresses the

---

113 Julia Kristeva, *Strangers to Ourselves*, trans. Leon S. Roudiez (New York: Columbia University Press, 1991) 10.

114 Ibid, 8.

realization that her dreams have already unconsciously revealed: when masked, whether in an actual costume or in their everyday interactions, Albertine and Fridolin are neither fully themselves nor anyone else.

The film *Eyes Wide Shut* is a repetition, yet also a shifting, of *Dream Story*, and it contains a visual tribute to the novella's narrative uncanniness in nearly every frame. The similar bodies and hair of the women and girls, but also the similarities between the Christmas trees that are found in nearly every interior space in the film, among holiday decorations, the repeated use of red and blue, all coalesce to form an imbrication of images that are and are not quite the same. The film's setting in New York City around the year 2000 is also a recollection of Vienna in 1900; the culture of cafes and Old-World apartments is emphasized, and contemporary technology is downplayed. Frederic Raphael's introduction to the English translation of *Dream Story* notes that although the narrative was not published until 1926, "it shows no signs of taking place in a post-1918, post-Hapsburg world. Its characters and atmosphere are as dated as its traffic: there are no cars or buses, no hint of Austria's final reduction to a post-imperial republic."[115] And, although it seems to Bill in the course of his wanderings that he has met everyone before, he cannot be sure that his memory is not deceiving him.

At the film's end, Alice and Bill are shopping for Christmas presents with their daughter, Helen. Helen spots a baby buggy, and Alice responds: "It's old-fashioned." This observation, which is not in the novella, is something new (added to the film) that nonetheless repeats the novella's sentiment. Indeed, the buggy is old-fashioned, but it is not actually old. The characters surround themselves, in novella and film, with "old-fashioned" things that represent a longing for a past to which they cannot return and which perhaps never really existed. The buggy is analogous to the novella itself, which is also "old-fashioned," but it also represents the novella's uncanny echo, the film *Eyes Wide Shut*, which portrays New York City in the "old-fashioned" style of Vienna. The novella portrays a likeness of Vienna before the First World War, although it does not represent the real past. The film portrays a New York before September 11, 2001—a time in which the city and the world were, to a degree, still "old-fashioned."

In his description of the Paris boutique in 1883, Huysmans writes that the perfect breasts of the abbreviated torsos on display, which he calls "this nascent puberty," "arouses" in the spectator "the libertine concern for things begun since we surmise what follows."[116] What follows, to be precise, is decay. The transience about which Freud reassures us after his walk with his anxious poet friend in the essay "On Transience" is indeed frightening and repulsive, but also cyclical, or revolutionary. In *The Future of Nostalgia*

---

[115] From Raphael's introduction in Schnitzler, *Dream Story* xiii.
[116] From Huysmans in Kelley, *The Uncanny* 19.

(2001), Svetlana Boym notes that "tradition" and "revolution" are not really opposites, conceptually or etymologically:

> Tradition means both delivery—handing down or passing on a doctrine—and surrender or betrayal. *Traduttore, traditore, translator, traitor*. The word revolution, similarly, means both cyclical repetition and the radical break. Hence tradition and revolution incorporate each other and rely on their opposition.[117]

Revolution contains the meaning of a cycle and of a rebellion. The poet, Fridolin/Bill, and the reader/viewer are all anxious about what will never come again. However, Freud is right—it will come again, it will all come back, even though it has died—not in the sense of a literal resurrection or spirit-vision, but in memory, the memory of ghosts dead but unburied. This revolutionary (cyclical), repetitive transience is a link to memory beyond mind; it shows us how we can survive our own deaths after we are no more, through ghosts in the "secular afterlife" of modern art—in this case, in the uncanny love that maintains loss and dies, over and over again, in Schnitzler's novella and Kubrick's film.

Conclusion

In his early work, Freud insists that anxiety emanates from excess desire: "what finds discharge in the generating of anxiety is precisely the surplus of unutilized libido."[118] Anxiety is the release of excess, and specifically of too much wanting, of excessive energy. The inexorable and inescapable companion of this excessive desire is guilt, which in turn represents an excess of memory. What Nietzsche refers to as the burden of the past, of too much past, of guilt about debts ("Schuld" about "Schulden") undischarged and hence anxiety-inducing, Kierkegaard understands as the consequence of original sin.[119] In either of these related views, the uncanny expands beyond the return of the repressed into a modern memory model.

The modern, industrialized, urban memory is a memory held down, or fixed, with the help of technology—but the technological fix does not render memory more reliable. The modern subject, and specifically the subject from the beginning of the "long nineteenth century" onwards, as we have encountered him in texts from Kleist to Lang, exists in an uncanny liminal zone between a highly constructed kind of narrative coherence and a lack thereof. And he needs, wants, craves love, though this love and the

[117] Svetlana Boym, *The Future of Nostalgia* 19.
[118] Freud, letter to Fliess of November 14, 1897; cited here in *Inhibitions, Symptoms, and Anxiety* (New York: W.W. Norton & Company, 1959) 5.
[119] Søren Kierkegaard, *The Concept of Anxiety: A Simple Psychologically Orienting Deliberation on the Dogmatic Issue of Hereditary Sin.*

excessive desire for it also often takes uncanny forms: between the desirous father and the son who mirrors him without compensating for his losses, between the creator and the machine who duplicates lost love without ever quite replacing it, between the lovers whose misunderstandings function as a kind of negative impetus to continue to reach for one another, and between the husband whose loss of his wife (to a re-membered fantasy) makes him seek her replica in countless other mirror-image bodies.

The anxiety that impels these characters to act sometimes leads them in very wrong directions, and sometimes seems to only force them back into their own minds. But the way in can also be a way out, or at least a way around. The experience of displaced uncanny anxiety and of uncanny forms of love (such as the love between man and machine) can be seen as a way of compensating for what Heinrich Schirmbeck calls the "social-ethical deficit of modernity."[120] He contends that Oedipus' fear, and Oedipal fear, can be taken out of the context of the father-son dyad and seen as motivating a very old and ongoing attempt to mobilize excessive desire in a never-ending, but very productive and necessary, attempt to repay the victims of modernity and the debt owed by modernity by constructing relationships of "relatedness" with real, yet inevitably different and estranged others. Sometimes, as is the case with modernity itself, the consequences of the movement of the uncanny and of the anxiety to which it responds and which it simultaneously generates are profoundly ethical, and sometimes they are profoundly amoral. But these consequences are always finite, always transient, always repetitive, and always remind us of loss and of the incompleteness of any compensation.

In texts by Schnitzler and Lang in particular, a progressive, revelatory potential of the uncanny is realized, if only briefly, in spaces of ancient-yet-modern love between subjects who desire relatedness to the point of illness. And, as Schelling already pointed out in the *Philosophy of Mythology*, the object of desire for these subjects—in the case of these texts, for the son, for the creator, for the lover—is not really the father, or the machine, or the beloved. The object of desire is the father's desire (as Schelling reminds us, the Hebrew "word that…means 'father' is derived from a verb that means 'to desire, to long for;' that is, which contains the concept of need"[121]), which is the desire to compensate for what the father lacks, and to replace the father's loss. On the Acropolis, Freud has an uncanny feeling that what he sees is not real, and when he analyzes the experience much later, he realizes that he wishes his father had wished for something different, and feels guilty because he also knows that his desires are *not* his father's. This

---

[120] This phrase is also the subtitle of Heinrich Schirmbeck's *Die Angst des Ödipus. Zum sozial-ethischen Defizit der Moderne* (Frankfurt am Main: Peter Lang, 1996).

[121] Friedrich Schelling, *Philosophie der Mythologie*, in *Schellingiana* 6, eds. Andreas Roser and Holger Schulten (Stuttgart-Bad Cannstatt: Frommann-Holzboog, 1996) 55. This passage was cited in Chapter One.

desire to possess and fulfill the desire of others in general is transient, but repeated; the desiring father in particular—who is still the primary figure in quests for and about relatedness in Western culture, since the myth of Oedipus is still with us—is omnipresent yet lost, but also fallible, mortal, uncannily re-membered, and loved.

Chapter 6

Conclusion - Childish Anxiety, Wish, Belief

We remember that in their early games children do not distinguish at all sharply between living and inanimate objects, and that they are especially fond of treating their dolls like live people.... [C]hildren have no fear of their dolls coming to life, they may even desire it. The source of uncanny feelings would not, therefore, be an infantile fear in this case, but rather an infantile wish or even merely an infantile belief.
[Wir erinnern uns, daß das Kind im frühen Alter des Spielens überhaupt nicht scharf zwischen Belebtem und Leblosem unterscheidet und daß es besonders gern seine Puppe wie ein lebendes Wesen behandelt.... [D]as Kind hat sich vor dem Beleben seiner Puppen nicht gefürchtet, vielleicht es sogar gewünscht. Die Quelle des unheimlichen Gefühls wäre also hier nicht eine Kinderangst, sondern ein Kinderwunsch oder auch nur ein Kinderglaube.]
Freud, *The Uncanny [Das Unheimliche]*

In his essay on "The Uncanny," Freud states that fear is not necessarily at the basis of uncanny feelings. Instead, these feelings may stem from "an infantile wish or even merely an infantile belief" ("ein Kinderwunsch oder auch nur ein Kinderglaube"). The perfectly normal, but also transgressive, desire for a doll to come to life is one way of expressing and living in the "senseless anxiety" that Freud describes in *The Future of an Illusion*, when he says that "life and the universe must be robbed of their terrors...then we can breathe freely, can feel at home in the uncanny and can deal by psychical means with our senseless anxiety" ("der Welt und dem Leben sollen ihre Schrecken genommen werden...dann atmet man auf, fühlt sich heimisch im Unheimlichen, kann seine sinnlose Angst psychisch bearbeiten").[1] The wish to animate a doll is a desirous way of acknowledging and even eliciting uncanny sensations; a way of making anxiety make sense.

In 1913-1914, Rainer Maria Rilke wrote an essay entitled "Dolls: On the Wax Dolls of Lotte Pritzel" ("Puppen: Zu den Wachs-Puppen der Lotte Pritzel"); it was inspired by his visit to an exhibit of life-sized adult dolls in Munich, by Kleist's essay *On the Marionette Theater*, and possibly also by Hoffmann's *Sandman* and essay on "Automata" (1814). Rilke's piece brings these earlier texts into dialogue with some of the major insights of psychoanalysis, as it concurs with Freud's view that childish wishes are at the foundation of interest in the uncanny—and specifically in dolls that are

[1] Sigmund Freud, *Die Zukunft einer Illusion*, in *Gesammelte Werke*, vol. 14 (Frankfurt am Main: Fischer, 1999) 338. This edition is abbreviated henceforth as GW. The translation is James Strachey's in *The Future of an Illusion, The Standard Edition of the Complete Psychological Works of Sigmund Freud*, vol. 21 (London: Hogarth, 1953-1974) 16, 17. This edition is abbreviated henceforth as SE.

uncanny because they reflect the child's developing, individuating ego. When the child realizes that the doll will never become an independent, real other with whom the child can really interact, however, then

> the world of children is over. The doll has finally outgrown the inspection, the participation, the desire and the concern of the child; it is independent, it has grown up, has aged early, it has entered all of the unrealities of its own existence.
> ([ist] die Welt der Kinder vorbei.... [Die] Puppe [ist] endlich dem Einsehen, der Teilnehmung, der Lust und dem Kummer des Kindes entwachsen, sie ist selbständig, sie ist groß geworden, frühalt, sie hat alle Unwirklichkeiten ihres eigenen Lebens angetreten.)[2]

Children's dolls are themselves "unchangeable" ("unveränderlich"); they accompany the child through changes physical and mental, and occupy spaces in the child's developing memory. They are "dragged along into cribs, in the heavy folds of illnesses, they appear in dreams, entangled in the dramas of feverish nights: such were these dolls" ("mitgezogen in die Gitterbetten, verschleppt in die schweren Falten der Krankheiten, in den Träumen vorkommend, verwickelt in die Verhängnisse der Fiebernächte: so waren jene Puppen").[3] Marionettes differ from dolls in that they can still inspire the fantasy of the adult and can in fact become a vessel for the adult's already-developed "soul"; they are dolls for grown-ups.[4] An animated marionette makes us uncannily aware of our proximity to puppets or to machines, and forces us to remember that we have, as Moritz says about the puppets in Goethe's *Werther*,

> a body subject to all of the laws of destruction in the corporeal universe, like a piece of wood that we saw or cut, and that one must move according to the exact same laws that govern man-made machines.—We are only occasionally aware of this destructibility and physicality of our body, and we shock ourselves when we suddenly feel that we believe ourselves to be something we are not, and are instead something that we fear.
> ([ein] Körper...der ebensowohl allen Gesetzen der Zerstörung in der Körperwelt unterworfen ist, als ein Stück Holz, das wir zersägen oder zerschneiden, und daß er sich nach eben den Gesetzen, wie jede andere von Menschen zusammengesetzte körperliche Maschine bewegt. Diese Zerstörbarkeit und Körperlichkeit unsers Körpers wird uns nur bei gewissen Anlässen lebhaft—und macht daß wir vor uns selbst erschrecken, indem wir plötzlich fühlen, daß wir etwas zu sein glaubten, was wir wirklich nicht sind, und statt dessen etwas sind, was wir zu sein uns fürchten.)[5]

Lotte Pritzel's wax dolls are also uncanny and do involve the use of fantasy and imagination—they are "animated during the day with strange and tireless

---

[2] Rainer Maria Rilke, *Schriften*, ed. Horst Nalewski (Frankfurt am Main: Insel, 1996) 685.
[3] Ibid, 686.
[4] Ibid, 689.
[5] Moritz, *Anton Reiser. Ein psychologischer Roman* (Stuttgart: Reclam, 1990) 293. This passage was cited in Chapter Three.

powers" ("am Tag mit fremden Kräften unermüdlich gelebt")[6]—but they only live through the life of the child, a life breathed into them artificially, and the child is not the adult puppeteer who, like an "angel," sets marionettes in motion and enables them to enact adult fantasies and fears.

The marionette can shock us by making us experience the uncanny sensation that we are marionette-like; the marionette transgresses boundaries. The child's doll, on the other hand, is a temporary mechanism used to erect boundaries in an invasive, excessive world. The child, who is not ready for intersubjective love, uses the doll as follows:

> The simplest act of love transcended our (childish) understanding, we could not live and act with a person who *was* something; at most we could push ourselves upon such a person and get lost in him. With the doll, in contrast, we were forced to realize that when we gave ourselves over to it, no one was left at all. The doll said nothing, so we began to assume responsibilities for it, to divide our gradually growing selves into part and counterpart. To a certain extent we used the doll to keep the world, which transgressed our boundaries and invaded us, away from our bodies.
> (Der einfachste Verkehr der Liebe ging schon über unsere Begriffe hinaus, mit einer Person, die etwas *war*, konnten wir unmöglich leben und handeln, wir konnten uns höchstens in sie hineindrücken und in ihr verlorengehen. Der Puppe gegenüber waren wir gezwungen, uns zu behaupten, denn wenn wir uns an sie aufgaben, so war überhaupt niemand mehr da. Sie erwiderte nichts, so kamen wir in die Lage, für sie Leistungen zu übernehmen, unser allmählich breiteres Wesen zu spalten in Teil und Gegenteil, uns gewissermaßen durch sie die Welt, die unabgegrenzt in uns überging, vom Leibe zu halten.)[7]

Dolls help the child's ego to develop, but Rilke emphasizes their frightening and disturbing aspects as well: their verisimilitude, but also their lifelessness, the fact that they require the memory and imagination of people to "ensoul" them, and specifically the minds of children whose very existence *as* children is temporary. During childhood, in

> a time in which everyone was still concerned with always answering us quickly and completely, the doll was the first who met us with a silence larger than life, a silence that later always followed us, whenever we found ourselves somewhere at the border of existence.
> (einer Zeit, wo noch alle bemüht waren, uns immer rasch und beschwichtigend zu antworten, war sie, die Puppe, die erste, die uns jenes überlebensgroße Schweigen antat, das uns später immer wieder aus dem Raum anhauchte, wenn wir irgendwo an die Grenze unseres Daseins traten.)

Childhood ends but this silence will persist, especially in border moments when one is confronted with one's own finitude and essential solitude. The doll that never ages and is, when kept by an adult at all, usually part of a collection (and is usually found at home; the doll is the uncanny

[6] Rilke, *Schriften* 686.
[7] Ibid, 687-688.

[*Unheimliche*] at the heart of the home [*Heimliche*]), will forever be a silent "ghost," dead but unburied, an empty vessel, but also a preserver of the loss of childhood.

The doll can continue to "act" even after the "world of children is over," however, particularly in the minds of melancholy adults who search endlessly for solace in similitude:

> Does the doll not continue to produce an unholy effect in the person who chases after vague satisfactions, merely out of protest against the dissatisfaction that has ruined his disposition? —I remember seeing, in the hands of the children in the main house of an isolated Russian estate, an old, heirloom doll that looked like the entire family.
> (Ob nicht in dem und jenem seine Puppe heillos weiterwirkt, so daß er hinter vagen Befriedigungen her ist, einfach aus Widerspruch gegen das Unbefriedigtsein, mit dem sie sein Gemüt verdorben hat? —Ich entsinne mich, auf dem Herrenhaus eines abgelegenen russischen Gutes, in den Händen der Kinder, eine alte ererbte Puppe gesehen zu haben, der die ganze Familie ähnlich sah.)[8]

The searching, anxious child confronted by the doll's silence is, in this case, confronted as well with a doll that replicates not only the child himself, but the entire family, and thus the family's past; this child, Rilke implies, will become a searching, anxious adult. In the doll, which is "less than a thing" (but it is precisely that lack of substance that gives it so much significance[9]), we experience an absence of love that remains with us into adulthood and in part is responsible for making us search for a love that is always elusive.

Freud dismisses the doll Olimpia as the main source of uncanny feeling in Hoffmann's *Sandman*, in part because she is too obviously an aesthetic recreation of a woman, and not frightening in the manner of the castrating Coppelius/Coppola. However, Freud dismisses the doll in the context of an interpretation of a literary text, a text that takes its substance from mythical tales, and Freud's psychoanalysis draws some of its substance from those tales as well. The dead fathers that haunt the child (and will, Rilke implies, haunt the adult) in the form of a doll (a doll that looks like an entire family) haunt psychoanalysis as well. In an important sense Freud does represent the return of Enlightenment after the long nineteenth century of Romanticism, but he also inherits the Romantic tendency to aestheticize anxiety. Psychoanalysis, which merges the tools of literary and artistic criticism with the interpretation of symptoms, was also an aesthetic endeavor.

In writings ranging from studies of "neurotic" religious ceremonials, to descriptions of demonic possession in the modern age, to investigations of patients' fantasies about children being beaten, Freud draws out the sensual and aesthetic components of each experience—aspects having to do with

[8] Rilke, *Schriften* 689.
[9] Ibid, 689.

judgments of taste as well as with "aesthetics" in its earlier sense, the study of sensation. Such experiential components, in his patients and in himself, are part of his data. This data is compiled and re-presented in order to, in most instances, arrive at some conclusion about what a present sensation says about the patient's (or Freud's) ability to live with his past. Most interesting for Freud, as for Kant, Schelling, Moritz, Schlegel, Tieck, Schiller, and also for the "neo-Romantics" Lang and Schnitzler, were those present sensations that indicated a clear dissociation within the mind or between mind and body. The anxiety discharged by a present experience that is not always, but is often, an explicitly aesthetic experience (seeing the Acropolis, viewing a painting or portrait, dreaming, encountering a doll) is linked to something past, but is no longer explicitly bound to that past.

In the preface I argued that uncanny memories, which are anxious recollections in the present of a vague past and which keep in what we try to push out, actually force us outward and towards others. Through dissociation between mind and body, exemplified in the image of the disembodied hand, the fingers falling off, the wooden hand of the puppet reaching out, or the silence of the doll, in that dissociation and disembodiment we are forced to recognize that anything that attempts to sustain life and deny loss is an illusion. The truly modern is the dead and decaying, the unburied dead and the buried alive, the thoroughly transient. And it is in this aesthetic anxiety that we experience what Gregg Horowitz has called the "secular afterlife" of modernity's own finitude.[10] Like artistic modernism, the uncanny is the "secular afterlife of the dead."[11] And, conversely, uncanny memories, which present and embody the "afterlife" of the past in the secular present, are the quintessence of the artistic modern.

The desire to get back to a past that we also fear reflects in part an anxiety about the persistence *of* the past in the present—an anxiety about the persistence of childish wishes and childish beliefs (the child's dreams, *Träume*) as well as about any childhood trauma (*Trauma*). But the desire represented in the return of disconnected images and sensations of things long hidden also reflects the very modern fear that, along with the no-longer-needed doll, childhood could be gotten rid of altogether. Hoffmann's *Sandmann*, like Mary Shelley's *Frankenstein* and Lang's *Metropolis* and any number of other narratives about uncanny automata, presents the possibility that artificially created beings may replace natural ones, thus erasing not only the child but the process of development and individuation that animates psychoanalysis, cultural inquiry, aesthetic theory, and our memories. Uncanny sensations, by re-involving us with the "principle of the past," preserve that principle against its impending destruction.

---

[10] Gregg Horowitz, *Sustaining Loss: Art and Mournful Life* (Stanford: Stanford University Press, 2001) 198.

[11] Ibid, 198.

In this book I have attempted to present uncanny repetition, in modern German texts that span the "long" nineteenth century, as a model for modern memory and desire. This involves a conception of repetition as a form of freedom, of acknowledging that we must go in and go back in order to go out and go forward. This is not a reactionary stance but rather a mournful one: uncanny figures, whether they appear as traditional doppelgänger, as the neuroses suffered by a panoply of protagonists, as strange but familiar portraits, or as hallucinations—all speak desire from the anxious modern spaces of loss and of ruin. The cases in Moritz's *Journal*, Schlegel's recording of Lesniowska's magnetic treatments, and the sufferings of the protagonists in eighteenth- and nineteenth-century secret-society novels would not seem examples of freedom. But we can look beyond this and recognize the epistemological value of insight into uncanny repetition. We, the readers and re-representers of these texts, are to an extent liberated by the repetitive act of reading and re-reading these texts, all of which represent some form of "alternative" to the mainstream tradition of Western and specifically German thought.

If a characteristic of the "modern" is the concrete and the observable (as Carsten Zelle argues within the context of eighteenth-century psychology), then the uncanny—which arises in modernity—is the persistent presence of the anti-modern, or so the understanding has gone.[12] But the uncanny only shows up in the form of concrete phenomena, and in observable experience. Tzvetan Todorov reminds us that the uncanny is distinguished from, for instance, the fantastic because it is ultimately explicable and observable. Victor Turner's work on ritual asserts that the liminal moment in ritual, which is an uncanny moment, serves to reintegrate participants into reality, albeit into a reality different from the one they left.[13]

In *Flesh in the Age of Reason*, Roy Porter's comments on the history of the relationship between body and mind as part of the history of the "self":

> The history of the self is commonly told as the rise of modern individualism, the maturing self-consciousness of the self-determining individual.... In this triumphalist telling, the secret of selfhood is located in authenticity and individuality, and the story presented is one of the surmounting of intractable obstacles in the achievement of autonomy. This great labour of inner character-building typically involves breaking free from religious persecution, political tyranny and the shackles of hidebound convention.[14]

The story I have told here is counter to this history, while not precisely opposite to it. The history *of* the uncanny as well as the history that uncanny

[12] Carsten Zelle, "Experiment, Experience and Observation in Eighteenth-Century Anthropology and Psychology - The Examples of Krüger's *Experimentalseelenlehre* and Moritz' *Erfahrungsseelenkunde*," *Orbis Litterarum* 56.2 (2001) 93.

[13] Victor Turner, *The Ritual Process: Structure and Anti-Structure* (Chicago: Aldine, 1969).

[14] Roy Porter, *Flesh in the Age of Reason* (New York and London: W.W. Norton, 2003) 3.

experiences tell is a history of the self different from the "triumphalist" narrative Porter describes. It is a history of repetition rather than of incessant forward movement, a history of the awareness of the lack of authenticity and the surrender of individuality; and yet, the history of the uncanny still represents a kind of liberation and revolution (in Svetlana Boym's sense of cycle and rebellion).[15] When we, the readers and interpreters of these texts, play the role that Hélène Cixous attributes to the hysteric—when we incorporate others into ourselves and play for real—we sustain loss via relatedness. At about the same time of the ascendancy of modern cultural products such as the self-portrait and the autobiography,[16] uncanny repetition, often of mistakes made by the oldest, most archaic myths, surfaces within and in the discourse around exactly those types of products (the portrait is a terrifying double, the autobiography is the place to explore one's own psychic instability); uncanny repetition thus resists the Western triumphalist self-history that Porter describes. The anxiety that comes of realizing that that history may be wrong is a powerful incentive to keep us related to others and grounded in the present rather than escaping into the future and a metaphysical notion of self. The achievements of humanism and Enlightenment cannot be undone—the Cartesian ego is still "the spring of human self-understanding," and the mind is still "a unique storeroom of consciousness, a personal new world, ripe for discovery,"[17] but the uncanny counterhistory cannot be discarded or erased either.

This study has focused on texts written in the modern age, and during the period of classical European modernity (approximately 1780 to 1930); it reflects a desire to move thinking about the uncanny beyond the paradigm of the dialectic of Enlightenment. This desire is prompted by the fact that we now inhabit what Paul Gilroy, quoting Enrique Dussel, terms "trans-modernity": "a geopolitical project with a longer reach and more profound consequences than is customarily appreciated."[18] If we rethink the uncanny for the trans-modern era, we will move the thesis on the dialectic of Enlightenment beyond its own time and update it in a way that is productive for understanding the uncanny *during* the period of classical modernity as well.

In his study of the concept "uncanny," Nicholas Royle contends: "The uncanny is a crisis of the proper: it entails a critical disturbance of what is proper (from the Latin proprius, 'own'), a disturbance of the very idea of personal or private property;"[19] then, later, he states: "The world is

---

[15] Svetlana Boym, *The Future of Nostalgia* (New York: Basic Books, 2001) 19. I referenced Boym's thinking on tradition, repetition, and revolution in Chapter Five.
[16] Porter, *Flesh in the Age of Reason* 5.
[17] Ibid, 6-7.
[18] Paul Gilroy, *Postcolonial Melancholia* (New York: Columbia University Press, 2005) 44.
[19] Nicholas Royle, *The Uncanny: An Introduction* (New York and London: Routledge, 2003) 1.

uncanny."[20] The entire world has become "improper" and "unhomely," unwelcoming, to itself. Quoting an article about the millennium in the *Guardian* of January 1, 2000, Royle says that the

> central uncanny paradox has to do with what "has led us to understand ourselves so profoundly and yet still organise our world so badly". On the one hand we appear to be moving increasingly close to 'know[ing] the innermost secrets of human existence'; on the other we are rendering increasingly uninhabitable the very planet that is our home.[21]

However, Royle goes on to say that the *Guardian* piece "remains bound up within a Christian discourse and thinking, implicitly subordinating its evocations of the uncanny within this religious framework." We may not be able to dispense with this framework entirely, but we can attempt to develop "possibilities for construing the uncanny differently....[T]he uncanny can perhaps provide ways of beginning to think in less dogmatic terms about the nature of the world, ourselves and a politics of the future."[22] What would a possible form of such future politics look like? It would likely not resemble the politics of the patriarchal community of Kleist's narratives, in which blood determines property relations and identity is overdetermined, nor would it re-enact Freud's or Schnitzler's dreamscapes, in which no identity is certain. It might, however, resemble the new cosmopolitanism that Paul Gilroy calls for in *Postcolonial Melancholia*, a sensibility of community which, he says, has "estrangement" as a primary feature.[23] This would require acknowledging and accepting the presence of the uncanny in our modern and finite lives. Such a community would be analogous to Freud's healthy person, the person who can love and work. The ability to love and work does not require that we decipher every memory (live in absolute clarity) or that we subscribe to a belief system (live in ignorance). The best we can do, in the absence of absolute knowledge about the real past and in the absence of a metaphysical belief system, is to interrogate the uncanny and the anxiety behind it when and where we can. The contemporary, transmodern uncanny articulates an intuition of something more without succumbing to religion, and reminds us of the evanescence, and permanence, of memory.

---

[20] Ibid, 3.
[21] Ibid, 3.
[22] Ibid, 3.
[23] Gilroy, *Postcolonial Melancholia* 68.

Bibliography

Primary Sources

Aeschylus. *Prometheus*. In *Aeschylus in Two Volumes*. Trans. Herbert Weir Smyth. London: William Heinemann Ltd., 1930.

—. *The Oresteia*. Trans. Richmond Lattimore. Chicago: University of Chicago Press, 1953.

Aristotle. *De anima (On the Soul)*. Trans. Hugh Lawson-Tancred. London: Penguin, 1986.

Baumgarten, Alexander Gottlieb. *Texte zur Grundlegung der Ästhetik*. Trans. and ed. Hans Rudolf Schweizer. Hamburg: F. Meiner, 1983.

Brandis, Joachim Dietrich. *Über psychische Heilmittel und Magnetismus*. Copenhagen: Glydendalische Buchhandlung, 1818.

Brentano, Franz. *Psychologie vom empirischen Standpunkte*. Leipzig: Duncker & Humblot, 1874.

Burke, Edmund. *A Philosophical Enquiry Into the Origins of Our Ideas of the Sublime and Beautiful*. 1757. Oxford: Oxford University Press, 1990.

—. *A Philosophical Enquiry Into the Origins of Our Ideas of the Sublime and Beautiful*. Second edition, 1759. New York: Garland Publishing, 1971.

Carus, Carl Gustav. *Versuch einer Darstellung des Nervensystems und insbesondere des Gehirns nach ihrer Bedeutung*. Leipzig: Breitkopf and Härtel, 1814.

—. *Vorlesungen über Psychologie gehalten im Winter 1829/30 zu Dresden*. Leipzig, 1831. Eds. Friedrich Arnold and Edgar Michaëlis. Darmstadt: Hermann Gentner, 1958.

Carus, Friedrich August. *Geschichte der Psychologie*. 1808. Berlin: Springer, 1990.

Dessoir, Max. *Vom Jenseits der Seele. Die Geheimwissenschaften in kritischer Betrachtung*. 4. und 5. Auflage. Stuttgart: Enke, 1920.

Freud, Sigmund. *Gesammelte Werke*. Eds. Anna Freud, et al. Frankfurt am Main: Fischer, 1999.

—. *The Standard Edition of the Complete Psychological Works*. Ed. James Strachey. 23 vols. London: Hogarth, 1953-1974.

Fries, Jakob Friedrich. *Handbuch der Psychischen Anthropologie oder der Lehre von der Natur des menschlichen Geistes*. 2 vols. Jena: Croker, 1820-21.

Goethe, Johann Wolfgang von. *Werke*. Vol. 2. Ed. Erich Trunz. Munich: C.H. Beck, 1981.

Grosse, Carl. *Der Genius. Aus den Papieren des Marquis C* von G***. Frankfurt am Main: Zweitausendeins, 1982.

—. *Helim, oder Über die Seelenwanderung*. Zittau und Leipzig: Johann David Schöps, 1789.

—. *Ueber das Erhabene. Mit einer Einleitung und einem Anhang mit Briefen Bodmers, Langes und Pyras*. Ed. Carsten Zelle. Frankfurt am Main and New York: Peter Lang, 1991.

Harbou, Thea von. *Metropolis*. Ed. Herbert W. Franke. Frankfurt am Main: Ullstein, 1984.

Hartmann, Eduard von. *Philosophie des Unbewussten*. Seventh edition. Berlin: Carl Duncker, 1876.

—. *Sämtliche Werke*. Vol. 6. Ed. Hans-Egon Hass. Berlin: Propyläen, 1962-1974.

Hawthorne, Nathaniel. *The House of the Seven Gables*. Ed. Allan Lloyd Smith. London: Everyman, 1995.

Hegel, Georg Wilhelm Friedrich. *Theorie-Werkausgabe*. Eds. Eva Moldenhauer and Karl Markus Michel. Volume 3. Frankfurt am Main: Suhrkamp, 1969.

—. *Phenomenology of Spirit*. Trans. A.V. Miller. Oxford: Oxford University Press, 1977.

Heidegger, Martin. *Gesamtausgabe*. Vol. 20. *Prolegomena zur Geschichte des Zeitbegriffs*. Frankfurt am Main: Vittorio Klostermann, 1979.

Herz, Marcus. Grundriß aller medicinischen Wissenschaften. Berlin: Christian Friedrich Voß und Sohn, 1782.

—. *Über die frühe Beerdigung der Juden. Zweyte verbesserte und vermehrte Auflage. Berlin: Christian Friedrich Voß und Sohn, 1788.*

Hoffmann, E.T.A. *Der Sandmann. Das öde Haus*. Ed. Manfred Wacker. Stuttgart: Philipp Reclam, 1984.

—. *Poetische Werke in Sechs Bänden*. Berlin: Aufbau, 1958.

Jentsch, Ernst. "Zur Psychologie des Unheimlichen." *Psychiatrisch-Neurologische Wochenschrift* 22 (1906) 196-198 and 23 (1906) 203-205.

Kafka, Franz. *Sämtliche Erzählungen*. Ed. Paul Raabe. Frankfurt am Main: Fischer, 1970.

Kant, Immanuel. *Critique of Judgment*. Trans. Werner S. Pluhar. Indianapolis: Hackett Publishing, 1987.

—. *Dreams of a Spirit-Seer and Other Related Writings*. Trans. John Manolesco. New York: Vantage Press, 1969.

—. *Schriften zur Ästhetik und Naturphilosophie*. Eds. Manfred Frank and Véronique Zanetti. Frankfurt am Main : Deutscher Klassiker Verlag, 1996.

—. *Träume eines Geistersehers, erläutert durch Träume der Metaphysik*. Stuttgart: Philipp Reclam, 1976.

—. *Werke in zwölf Bänden*. Ed. Wilhelm Weischedel. 8. Auflage. Frankfurt am Main: Suhrkamp, 1996.

Kelley, Mike. *The Uncanny*. Exhibit catalogue, with essays by Mike Kelley, John C. Welchman, and Christoph Grunenberg. Cologne: Verlag der Buchhandlung Walther König, 2004.

Kierkegaard, Søren. *The Concept of Anxiety: A Simple Psychologically Orienting Deliberation on the Dogmatic Issue of Hereditary Sin*. Ed. and trans. Reidar Thomte and Albert B. Anderson. Princeton: Princeton University Press, 1980.

—. "Verzweiflung als Krankheit im Geist, im Selbst." *Selbstbewusstseinstheorien von Fichte bis Sartre*, ed. Manfred Frank. Frankfurt am Main: Suhrkamp, 1991.

Kleist, Heinrich von. *Sämtliche Werke und Briefe*. 2 vols. Ed. Helmut Sembdner. Munich: Deutscher Taschenbuch Verlag, 1994.

Krüger, Johann Gottlob. *Neue Lehre von den Gemüthsbewegungen / mit einer Vorrede vom Gelde; begleitet von Herrn Johann Gottlob Krügern, Der Weitweisheit und Arzneygelähtrheit Doctorn und Professorn auf der Königl. Preuszl. Friedrichs Universität*. Halle: C.H. Hemmerde, 1746.

—. *Gedanken von Erziehung der Kinder*. Halle: Carl Hermann Hemmerde, 1760.

—. *Träume*. 3. verm. Aufl. Halle: C.H. Hemmerde, 1765.

Kubrick, Stanley. *Eyes Wide Shut. A Screenplay by Stanley Kubrick and Frederic Raphael*. New York: Warner Books, 1999.

Lang, Fritz, Dir. *Metropolis*. 1927. Restored authorized edition with the original 1927 orchestral score. Licensed by Transit Films on behalf of the Friedrich-Wilhelm-Murnau-Stiftung, Wiesbaden, 2002.

Leibniz, Gottfried Wilhelm. *Kleine Schriften zur Metaphysik. Opuscules metaphysiques*. Ed. and trans. Hans Heinz Holz. Frankfurt am Main: Insel, 1965.

Locke, John. *An Essay Concerning Human Understanding*. Ed. A. D. Woozley. London: Collins, 1964.

Marx, Karl, and Friedrich Engels. *The Communist Manifesto*. Trans. Gareth Stedman Jones. London and New York: Penguin, 2002.

Mesmer, Franz Anton. *Mesmerism. The Discovery of Animal Magnetism*. Trans. Joseph Bouleur. Edmonds, WA: Holmes Publishing Group, 1998.

—. *Mesmerismus. Oder System der Wechselwirkungen, Theorie und Anwendung des tierischen Magnestismus als allgemeine Heilkunde zur Erhaltung des Menschen*. Ed. Karl Christian Wolfart. Berlin: Nicolaische Buchhandlung, 1814.

Moritz, Karl Philipp. *Anton Reiser. Ein psychologischer Roman*. Stuttgart: Philipp Reclam, 1990.

—. *Beiträge zur Ästhetik*. Eds. Hans Joachim Schrimpf and Hans Adler. Mainz: Dieterischsche Verlagsbuchhandlung, 1989.

—. *Gnothi sauton oder Magazin zur Erfahrungsseelenkunde als ein Lesebuch für Gelehrte und Ungelehrte.* Eds. Petra and Uwe Nettelbeck. Nördlingen: Franz Greno, 1986.

—. *Werke.* Ed. Horst Günther. Frankfurt am Main: Insel, 1981.

Muratori, Lodovico Antonio. *On the Power of the Human Imagination (Della Forza della Fantasia Umana).* Venice: Giambatista Pasaquale, 1745.

Nietzsche, Friedrich. *Kritische Studienausgabe.* Eds. Gieorgio Colli and Mazzimo Montinari. Munich: Deutscher Taschenbuch Verlag 1999.

Novalis. *Heinrich von Ofterdingen.* Munich: Wilhelm Goldmann, 1983.

—. *Schriften. Die Werke Friedrich von Hardenbergs.* Eds. Paul Kluckhohn and Richard Samuel. Stuttgart: W. Kohlhammer, 1960-1988.

—. *Werke.* Ed. Gerhard Schulz. Munich: Beck, 1969.

Otto, Rudolf. *Das Heilige. Über das Irrationale in der Idee des Göttlichen und Sein Verhältnis zum Rationalen.* Munich: C.H. Beck, 1963.

Platner, Ernst. *Neue Anthropologie für Ärzte und Weltweise. Mit besonderer Rücksicht auf Physiologie, Pathologie, Moralphilosophie und Ästhetik.* Erster Theil. Leipzig, 1772, 1790.

Rilke, Rainer Maria. *Schriften.* Ed. Horst Nalewski. Frankfurg am Main: Insel, 1996.

Ritter, Joachim Wilhelm. *Beweis, daß ein beständiger Galvanismus den Lebensprozeß in dem Thierreich begleite. Nebst neuen Versuchen und Bemerkungen über den Galvanismus.* Weimar: Verlag des Industrie-Comptoirs, 1798.

Schelling, Friedrich Joseph Wilhelm von. *Ausgewählte Schriften.* Ed. Manfred Frank. Frankfurt am Main: Suhrkamp, 1985.

—. *Briefe und Dokumente.* Ed. Horst Furhmans. Bonn: , 1962-1975.

—. *Clara: Or, On Nature's Connection to the Spirit World.* Trans. Fiona Steinkamp. Albany: State University of New York Press, 2002.

—. *First Outline of a System of the Philosophy of Nature.* Trans. Keith R. Peterson. Albany: State University of New York Press, 2004.

—. *Philosophie der Mythologie. Nachschrift der letzten Münchener Vorlesungen 1841. Schellingiana.* Eds. Andreas Roser and Holger Schulten. Stuttgart-Bad Cannstatt: Frommann-Holzboog, 1996.

—. *Sämmtliche Werke.* Ed. K.F.A. Schelling. Neunter Band. 1816-1832. Stuttgart and Augsburg: Cotta, 1861. Reprinted 1957.

—. *Von der Weltseele. Eine Hypothese der höheren Physik zur Erklärung des allgemeinen Organismus.* Hamburg: Friedrich Perther, 1798.

—. *Die Weltalter. Fragmente.* Ed. Manfred Schröter. Munich, 1979.

—. *Werke.* Ed. Manfred Schröter. Vol. 4: Schriften zur Philosophie der Freiheit, 1804-1815. Munich, 1927.

—. *Zur Geschichte der neueren Philosophie.* Münchener Vorlesungen. Darmstadt: Wissenschaftliche Buchgesellschaft, 1953.

Schelling, Karl Eberhard. *Werke.* Ed. Manfred Schröter. Munich: C.H. Beck, 1965.

Schiller, Friedrich. *Werke und Briefe in Zwölf Bänden*. Eds. Otto Dann, et al. Frankfurt am Main: Deutscher Klassiker Verlag, 2002.
Schlegel, Friedrich. *Kritische Ausgabe*. Ed. Ernst Behler. Munich: Schöningh, 1958-.
Schnitzler, Arthur. *Ausgewählte Werke in Acht Bänden*. Ed. Heinz Ludwig Arnold. Frankfurt am Main: Fischer, 1999.
Schubert, Gotthilf Heinrich von. *Krankheiten und Störungen der menschlichen Seele*. Stuttgart: Cotta, 1845.
—-. *Die Symbolik des Traumes*. 1814. Heidelberg: Lambert Schneider, 1968.
Sulzer, Johann Georg. *Kurzer Begriff aller Wißenschaften*. Leipzig, 1759.
Tieck, Ludwig. *Schriften in zwölf Bänden*. Ed. Manfred Frank. Frankfurt am Main: Deutscher Klassiker Verlag, 1985.
—-. *William Lovell*. Ed. Walter Münz. Stuttgart: Philipp Reclam, 1999.
Vischer, Friedrich Theodor. *Ästhetik oder Wissenschaft des Schönen*. Reutlingen and Leipzig: Carl Mäcken, 1848.
Wackenroder, Wilhelm Heinrich. *Werke und Briefe*. Heidelberg: Lambert Schneider, 1967.

Secondary Sources

Adler, Hans. "Fundus Animae—der Grund der Seele. Zur Gnoseologie des Dunklen in der Aufklärung." *Deutsche Vierteljahrsschrift für Literaturwissenschaft und Geistesgeschichte* 62 (1988) 197-220.
Adorno, Theodor, and Max Horkheimer. *Dialektik der Aufklärung*. Frankfurt am Main: Fischer, 1988.
Albrecht, Wolfgang. *Das Angenehme und das Nützliche. Fallstudien zur literarischen Spätaufklärung in Deutschland.* Berlin: Walter de Gruyter, 1997.
Andriopoulos, Stefan. "Die Laterna magica der Philosophie. Gespenster bei Kant, Hegel und Schopenhauer." *Deutsche Vierteljahrsschrift für Literaturwissenschaft und Geistesgeschichte* 80 (2006) 173-211.
—-. "Occult Conspiracies: Spirits and Secret Societies in Schiller's *Ghost Seer*." *New German Critique* 35.1 (2008) 65-81.
Angerer, Marie-Luise. "The Uncanny Pleasure of Repetition." *Basics in Ambigua*. Austellungskatalog Galerie der Jenoptik AG. Trans. Nick Grindell. Jena, 2003.
Arens, Katherine. *Structures of Knowing: Psychologies of the Nineteenth Century*. Dordrecht, Boston, and London: Kluwer Academic Publishers, 1989.
Arnzen, Michael. "The Return of the Uncanny." *Paradoxa: Studies in World Literary Genres* 3.3-4 (1997) 315-320.
Bach, Sheldon. "Narcissism, Continuity and the Uncanny." *The International Journal of Psycho-Analysis* 56 (1975) 77-86.

Balke, Friedrich, Harun Maye, and Leander Scholz, eds. *Ästhetische Regime um 1800.* Munich: Fink, 2009.

Ballantyne, Andrew. Review of *The Architectural Uncanny: Essays in the Modern Unhomely. The British Journal of Aesthetics* 34.2 (1994) 193-194.

Baudrillard, Jean. *Simulations*. Trans. Paul Foss, Paul Patton, and Philip Beitchman. New York: Semiotext(e) Inc., 1983.

—-. "Two Essays." Trans. Arthur B. Evans. *Science-Fiction Studies* 18 (1991) 309-313.

Baucom, Ian. *Specters of the Atlantic: Finance Capital, Slavery, and the Philosophy of History*. Durham: Duke University Press, 2005.

Behler, Ernst. "Philosophie in Notizheften. Friedrich Schlegels Lehrjahre - Rechenschaft vor der Nachwelt." *Rheinischer Merkur* 9.1 (March 1963) 13.

Bell, Matthew. *The German Tradition of Psychology in Literature and Thought, 1700-1840*. Cambridge: Cambridge University Press, 2005.

Benjamin, Jessica. *The Bonds of Love: Psychoanalysis, Feminism, and the Problem of Domination*. New York: Pantheon Books, 1988.

—-. *Like Subjects, Love Objects: Essays on Recognition and Sexual Difference*. New Haven and London: Yale University Press, 1995.

—-. *Shadow of the Other: Intersubjectivity and Gender in Psychoanalysis*. New York and London: Routledge, 1998.

Bennholdt-Thomsen, Anke, and Alredo Guzzoni. "Vorläufer der Tiefenpsychologie. Der psychologische Ansatz des Karl Philipp Moritz - Zwischen Selbsterkenntnis und Selbsttäuschung." *Jahrbuch für Verstehende Tiefenpsychologie und Kulturanalyse* 1 (1981) 197-212.

Bergler, Edmund. "The Psycho-analysis of the Uncanny." *The International Journal of Psycho-Analysis* 15.2/3 (1934) 215-244.

Berlin, Isaiah. *The Roots of Romanticism*. Ed. Henry Hardy. Princeton: Princeton University Press, 1999.

Berrios, German E., and Roy Porter, eds. *A History of Clinical Psychiatry: The Origin and History of Psychiatric Disorders*. London: The Athlone Press, 1995.

Bezold, Raimund. *Popularphilosophie und Erfahrungsseelenkunde im Werk von Karl Philipp Moritz*. Würzburg, 1984.

Blackbourn, David. *The Long Nineteenth Century: A History of Germany, 1780-1918*. New York and Oxford: Oxford University Press, 1998.

—-. *Marpingen: Apparitions of the Virgin Mary in Bismarckian Germany*. Oxford: Clarendon Press, 1993.

Blackbourn, David, and Geoff Eley. *The Peculiarities of German History: Bourgeois Society and Politics in Nineteenth-Century Germany*. Oxford: Oxford University Press, 1984.

Blankenburg, Martin. "Der 'thierische' Magnetismus in Deutschland." *Der Mesmerismus und das Ende der Aufklärung in Frankreich*, by Robert Darnton. Frankfurt am Main: Ullstein, 1986. 191-231.

Blasberg, Cornelia. "Geschichte als Palimpsest. Schreiben und Lesen über die 'Kinder der Täter.'" *Deutsche Vierteljahrsschrift für Literaturwissenschaft und Geistesgeschichte* (2003) 464-495.

Bondeson, Jan. *Buried Alive: The Terrifying History of Our Most Primal Fear*. New York and London: W.W. Norton & Company, 2001.

Botting, Fred, ed. *Frankenstein: Contemporary Critical Essays*. London: Macmillan, 1995.

Bowlby, John. *Attachment and Loss*. New York: Basic Books, 1980.

Boym, Svetlana. *The Future of Nostalgia*. New York: Basic Books, 2001.

Braungart, Georg. "'Intransitive Zeichen': 'Die Signatur des Schönen' im menschlichen Körper bei Karl Philipp Moritz." *Rhetorik*. Vol. 13. Eds. Joachim Dyck, Walter Jens, and Gert Ueding. Tübingen: Niemeyer, 1994.

—-. *Leibhafter Sinn. Der andere Diskurs der Moderne*. Tübingen: Niemeyer, 1995.

Breazeale, Daniel, and Tom Rockmore, eds. *Fichte: Historical Contexts, Contemporary Controversies*. Atlantic Highlands, NJ: Humanities Press International, 1994.

Bresnick, Adam. "Prosopoetic Compulsion: Reading the Uncanny in Freud and Hoffmann." *The Germanic Review* 71.2 (1996) 114-32.

Brod, Max. "Kafka: Father and Son." (1938) *The Literary Imagination: Psychoanalysis and the Genius of the Writer*. Ed. Hendrik M. Ruitenbeek. Chicago: Quadrangle Books, 1965. 81-96.

Bronfen, Elisabeth. *The Knotted Subject: Hysteria and its Discontents*. Princeton: Princeton University Press, 1998.

Bächtold-Stäubli, Hanns, ed. *Handwörterbuch des Deutschen Aberglaubens*. Berlin and Leipzig: Walter de Gruyter, 1934-1935.

Behler, Ernst. *Friedrich Schlegel*. Hamburg: Rowohlt, 1988.

—-. *"Philosophie in Notizheften. Friedrich Schlegels Lehrjahre—Rechenschaft vor der Nachwelt."* Rheinischer Merkur *9.1 (March 1963) 13.*

Borchardt, Edith. "Arthur Schnitzler's *Traumnovelle* and Stanley Kubrick's *Eyes Wide Shut*: The Structure of Fantasy." *Journal of the Fantastic in the Arts* 12.1 (2001) 4-17.

Breger, Claudia, and Tobias Döring, eds. *Figuren der/des Dritten. Erkundungen kultureller Zwischenräume*. Amsterdam and Atlanta: Rodopi, 1998.

Butler, Judith. *Antigone's Claim: Kinship Between Life and Death*. New York: Columbia University Press, 2000.

—-. *The Psychic Life of Power: Theories in Subjection*. Stanford: Stanford University Press, 1997.

Caine, Barbara, E.A. Grosz, and Marie de Lepervanche, eds. *Crossing Boundaries: Feminisms and the Critique of Knowledges*. Sydney: Allen & Unwin, 1988.
Casey, Edward S. *Remembering: A Phenomenological Study*. Bloomington and Indianapolis: Indiana University Press, 1987.
Cassirer, Ernst. *The Philosophy of the Enlightenment*. Trans. Fritz C.A. Koelln and James P. Pettegrove. Boston: Beacon Press, 1951.
Castello, Maria Leonarda. *Schwärmertum und Gewalt in Goethes "Werther," Tiecks "William Lovell" und Büchners "Lenz."* Würzburg: Matthias Hauck, 1993.
Castle, Terry. *The Female Thermometer: Eighteenth-Century Culture and the Invention of the Uncanny*. Oxford: Oxford University Press, 1995.
—-. "*Paradoxa* Interview." Conducted by Michael Arnzen. *Paradoxa: Studies in World Literary Genres* 3.3-4 (1997) 521-526.
Cavell, Stanley. *In Quest of the Ordinary: Lines of Skepticism and Romanticism*. Chicago: University of Chicago Press, 1988.
Cersowsky, Peter. *Phantastische Literatur im ersten Viertel des 20. Jahrhunderts*. Munich 1983.
Cixous, Hélène. "Fiction and its Phantoms: A Reading of Freud's *Das Unheimliche*." *New Literary History* 7 (1976) 525-548.
Coates, Paul. *The Double and the Other: Identity as Ideology in Post-Romantic Fiction*. New York: St. Martin's Press, 1988.
Cohn, Jan, and Thomas H. Miles. "The Sublime: In Alchemy, Aesthetics and Psychoanalysis." *Modern Philology* 74 (1977) 289-304.
Cooper, Arnold M. "The Unconscious Core of Perversion." *Perversions and Near-Perversions in Clinical Practice: New Psychoanalytic Perspectives*. New Haven: Yale University Press, 1991.
Corkhill, Alan. "Tiecks *William Lovell* und Wildes *The Picture of Dorian Gray*: Eine kontinuierliche Tradition." *Archiv für das Studium der neueren Sprachen und Literatur* 224.2 (1987) 346-352.
Costazza, Alessandro. *Schönheit und Nützlichkeit. Karl Philipp Moritz und die Ästhetik des 18. Jahrhunderts*. Bern: Peter Lang, 1996.
Cresap, Steven. "Sublime Politics: On the Uses of an Aesthetics of Terror." *Clio* 19.2 (1990) 111-125.
D'Alessandro, August J. "A Historical Review of *Die Symbolik des Traumes*." *Psychiatric Quarterly Supplement* 42.2 (1968) 337-343.
Damasio, Antonio. *The Feeling of What Happens: Body and Emotion in the Making of Consciousness*. San Diego, New York, and London: Harcourt, 1999.
Darnton, Robert. *Mesmerism and the End of the Enlightenment in France*. Cambridge: Harvard University Press, 1968.
Davies, Martin L. *Identity or History? Marcus Herz and the End of the Enlightenment*. Detroit: Wayne State University Press, 1995.

—. "Karl Philipp Moritz's *Erfahrungsseelenkunde*: Its Social and Intellectual Origins." *Oxford German Studies* 16 (1985) 13-35.

David-Menard, Monique, and Alison Ross. "Kant's 'An Essay on the Maladies of the Mind' and Observations on the Feeling of the Beautiful and the Sublime." *Hypatia* 15.4 (2000) 82-98.

Deleuze, Gilles. *The Logic of Sense*. Trans. March Lester and Charles Stivale, ed. Constantin V. Boundas. New York: Columbia University Press, 1990.

Derrida, Jacques. *Archive Fever: A Freudian Impression*. Trans. Eric Prenowitz. Chicago and London: The University of Chicago Press, 1995.

—. *The Ear of the Other: Otobiography, Transference, Translation*. Trans. Peggy Kamuf. Lincoln and London: University of Nebraska Press, 1988.

—. *The Gift of Death*. Trans. David Wills. Chicago and London: The University of Chicago Press, 1995.

Diagnostic and Statistical Manual of Mental Disorders, Fourth Edition (DSM-IV). Washington, D.C.: American Psychiatric Association, 1994.

Dessoir, Max. *Geschichte der neueren deutschen Psychologie*. Berlin: Duncker, 1897.

Deutsch, Helen. "Doctor Johnson's Autopsy, or Anecdotal Immortality." *The Eighteenth Century: Theory and Interpretation* 40.2 (1999) 113-127.

Duenwald, Mary. "A New Era in Treating Imaginary Ills." *The New York Times* March 30, 2004. D1, D6.

Durham, Scott. *Phantom Communities: The Simulacrum and the Limits of Postmodernism*. Stanford: Stanford University Press, 1998.

Dutoit, Thomas. "Ghost Stories, the Sublime and Fantastic Thirds in Kant and Kleist." *Colloquia Germanica* 27.3 (1994) 225-254.

Dyck, Joachim. "Zur Psychoanalyse der Melancholie. Karl Philipp Moritz' *Anton Reiser*. *Kontroversen, alte und neue*. Ed. Albrecht Schöne. Volume 6, 175-182.

Eagleton, Terry. *The Ideology of the Aesthetic*. Oxford: Blackwell Publishers, 1997.

Eibl, Karl. "Abgrund mit Geländer. Bemerkungen zur Soziologie des 'angenehmen Grauens' im 18. Jahrhundert." *Aufklärung* 8.1 (1994) 3-14.

Ego, Anneliese. *Animalischer Magnetismus oder Aufklärung. Eine mentalitätsgeschichtliche Studie zum Konflikt um ein Heilkonzept im 18. Jahrhundert*. Würzburg: Königshausen und Neumann, 1991.

Eliade, Mircea. *Shamanism: Archaic Techniques of Ecstacy*. Trans. Willard R. Trask. New York: Pantheon Books, 1964.

Elias, Norbert. *Involvement and Detachment*. Trans. Edmund Jephcott. Oxford: Basil Blackwell, 1987.

Ellenberger, Henri F. *The Discovery of the Unconscious: The History and Evolution of Dynamic Psychiatry*. New York: Basic Books, 1970.
Ellison, David R. *Ethics and Aesthetics in European Modern Literature: From the Sublime to the Uncanny*. Cambridge and New York: Cambridge University Press, 2001.
Elsaesser, Thomas. *Metropolis*. London: British Film Institute, 2000.
Engelstein, Stefani. *Anxious Anatomy: The Conception of the Human Form in Literary and Naturalist Discourse*. Albany: State University of New York Press, 2008.
—. "Reproductive Machines in E. T. A. Hoffmann." *Body Dialectics in the Age of Goethe*. Eds. Marianne Henn and Holger A. Pausch. Amsterdam and New York: Rodopi, 2003.
Enterline, Lynn. *The Tears of Narcissus: Melancholia and Masculinity in Early Modern Writing*. Stanford: Stanford University Press, 1995.
Falkenberg, Marc. *Rethinking the Uncanny in Hoffmann and Tieck*. Berlin: Lang, 2005.
Feigelson, Carolyn. "Personality Death, Object Loss, and the Uncanny." *International Journal of Psycho-Analysis* 74.2 (1993) 331-345.
Feuerzeig, Lisa. "Heroines in Perversity: Marie Schmith, Animal Magnetism, and the Schubert Circle." *19th-Century Music* 21 (1997) 223-243.
Finke, Michael, and Carl Niekerk, eds. *One Hundred Years of Masochism: Literary Contexts,* Amsterdam and Atlanta: Rodopi, 2000.
Fisher, Philip. *The Vehement Passions*. Princeton and Oxford: Princeton University Press, 2002.
Fischer-Hornberger, Esther. *Hypochondrie. Melancholie bis Neurose: Krankheiten und Zustandsbilder*. Bern: Huber, 1970.
Forssmann, Juliane. *Intimations of Ambiguity: The Narrative Treatment of the Uncanny in Selected Texts of Romantic English and German Prose Fiction*. Stuttgart: Hans-Dieter Heinz, 1998.
Foucault, Michel. *The Birth of the Clinic: An Archaeology of Medical Perception*. Trans. A.M. Sheridan Smith. New York: Vintage Books, 1994.
—. *Language, Counter-Memory, Practice. Selected Essays and Interviews*. Ed. Donald F. Bouchard. Trans. Donald F. Bouchard and Sherry Simon. Ithaca: Cornell University Press, 1993.
—. *Mental Illness and Psychology*. Trans. Alan Sheridan. Berkeley: University of California Press, 1987.
Frank, Manfred, ed. *Selbstbewusstseinstheorien von Fichte bis Sartre*. Frankfurt am Main: Suhrkamp, 1991.
—. *Selbstgefühl. Eine historisch-systematische Erkundung*. Frankfurt am Main: Suhrkamp, 2002.
Frank, Manfred, and Gerhard Kurz, eds. *Materialien zu Schellings philosophischen Anfängen*. Frankfurt am Main: Suhrkamp, 1975.

Franzel, Sean. "'Welches Gesetz ist der Mensch in seiner Wirksamkeit?' Pedagogy and Media in Fichte's Encounter with Mesmerism." *The Germanic Review* (2009) 3-25.

Frickmann, Sybille. "'Jeder Mensch nach dem ihm eignen Maaß'—Karl Philipp Moritz' Konzept einer 'Seelenkrankheitskunde.'" *The German Quarterly* 61.3 (1988) 387-402.

Friedrich, Hans-Edwin. "'Die innerste Tiefe der Zerstörung'. Die Dialektik von Zerstörung und Bildung im Werk von Karl Philipp Moritz." *Aufklärung* 8.1 (1994) 69-90.

Frisch, Shelley L. "Poetics of the Uncanny: E. T. A. Hoffmann's 'Sandman.'" *The Scope of the Fantastic: Theory, Technique, Major Authors*. Eds. Robert A. Collins, Howard D. Pearce, and Eric S. Rabin. Westport, CT: Greenwood, 1985. 49-55.

Fry, Paul H. "The Possession of the Sublime." *Studies in Romanticism* 26.2 (1987) 187-207.

Gaderer, Rupert. "Liebe im Zeitalter der Elektrizität. E.T.A. Hoffmanns Homines electrificati." *Liebe: Diskurse und Praktiken*. Eds. Reinhard Sieder, Franz X. Eder, and Daniela Hammer-Tugendhat. Vienna: Studien Verlag, 2008. 43-61.

Gampel, Yolanda. "The Interminable Uncanniness." *Psychoanalysis at the Political Border: Essays in Honor of Rafael Moses*. Madison, CT: International Universities Press, 1996. 85-98.

Gardner, Sebastian. *Irrationality and the Philosophy of Psychoanalysis*. Cambridge: Cambridge University Press, 1993.

Garmann, Gerburg. *Die Traumlandschaften Ludwig Tiecks. Traumreise und Individuationsprozeß aus romantischer Perspektive*. Opladen: Westdeutscher Verlag, 1989.

Gay, Peter. *The Enlightenment: An Interpretation*. Vol. 2: *The Science of Freedom*. New York and London: W.W. Norton, 1969.

Gelfand, Toby, and John Kerr, eds. *Freud and the History of Psychoanalysis*. Hillsdale: Analytic Press, Inc., 1992.

Gilman, Sander L. *The Case of Sigmund Freud: Medicine and Identity at the Fin de Siècle*. Baltimore: Johns Hopkins University Press, 1993.

Gilroy, Paul. *Postcolonial Melancholia*. New York: Columbia University Press, 2005.

Ginsburg, Ruth. "A Primal Scene of Reading: Freud and Hoffmann." *Literature and Psychology* 38.3 (1992) 24-46.

Görres, Hans-Joachim. "Hinter einer Mauer des Schweigens. Epilepsie – die Unheimliche Krankheit." *Universitas* 6 (1988) 659-667.

Goetschel, Willi. *Constituting Critique: Kant's Writing as Critical Praxis*. Durham: Duke University Press, 1994.

Goodall, J. R. "Theories of the Unheimliche and Rilke's Phantom Hand." *Religion and Literature* 21.2 (1989) 45.

Goodrick-Clarke, Nicholas. "The Esoteric Uses of Electricity: Theologies of Electricity From Swabian Pietism to Ariosophy." *Aries* 4.1 (2004) 69-90.

Graham, George. *Philosophy of Mind: An Introduction.* Malden, MA: Blackwell Publishers, 1998.

Grau, Alexander. "Clara. Über Schellings gleichnamiges Fragment." *Zeitschrift für philosophische Forschung* 51.4 (1997) 590-610.

Gray, Richard T. "The Hermeneut(r)ic(k) of the Psychic Narrative: Freud's 'Das Unheimliche' and Hofmannsthal's *Reitergeschichte*." *The German Quarterly* 62.4 (1989) 473-488.

Grene, David, and Richmond Lattimore, eds. *The Complete Greek Tragedies: Volume I, Aeschylus*. Chicago: The University of Chicago Press, 1959.

Grenville, Bruce, ed. *The Uncanny: Experiments in Cyborg Culture.* Arsenal Pulp Press, 2002.

Grotjahn, M. "Some Clinical Illustrations of Freud's Analysis of the Uncanny." *Bulletin of the Menninger Clinic* 12 (1948) 57-60.

Grotstein, James S. "The Alter Ego and Déjà vu Phenomena: Notes and Reflections." *The Plural Self: Multiplicity in Everyday Life*. Eds. John Rowan and Mick Cooper. London: Sage Publications, 1999. 28-50.

Gunning, Tom. *The Films of Fritz Lang: Allegories of Vision and Modernity.* London: British Film Institute, 2000.

—-. "Phantom Images and Modern Manifestations: Spirit Photography, Magic Theater, Trick Films, and Photography's Uncanny." *Fugitive Images: From Photography to Video*, ed. Patrice Petro. Bloomington: Indiana University Press, 1995. 42-71.

Guratzsch, Dankwart. "Dreister als irgendein Apostel. Friedrich Schlegel gibt auch an seinem 200. Geburtstag seinen Biographen und Kritikern noch immer Rätsel auf," *Die Welt* 60 (March 11, 1972) IV.

Habermas, Jürgen. *Der philosophische Diskurs der Moderne. Zwölf Vorlesungen.* Frankfurt am Main: Suhrkamp, 1985.

Hacking, Ian. *Mad Travelers: Reflections on the Reality of Transient Mental Illnesses.* Charlottesville and London: University Press of Virginia, 1998.

Hahn, Torsten, Erich Kleinschmidt, and Nicolas Pethes, eds. *Kontingenz und Steuerung. Literatur als Gesellschaftsexperiment 1750-1830.* Würzburg: Königshausen & Neumann, 2004.

Hammermeister, Kai. *The German Aesthetic Tradition.* Cambridge: Cambridge University Press, 2002.

Haym, Rudolf. *Die romantische Schule.* Ed. Edwin Redslob. Berlin: Weidmann, 1949.

Heilmann, Markus. *Die Krise der Aufklärung als Krise des Erzählens. Tiecks "William Lovell" und der europäische Brieffroman.* Stuttgart: Metzler, 1992.

Heim, Michael. *The Metaphysics of Virtual Reality*. New York and Oxford: Oxford University Press, 1993.

Helfer, Martha B. "The Male Muses of Romanticism: The Poetics of Gender in Novalis, E.T.A. Hoffmann, and Eichendorff." *The German Quarterly* 78.3 (2005) 299-319.

Helmetag, Charles H. "Dream Odysseys: Schnitzler's *Traumnovelle* and Kubrick's *Eyes Wide Shut*." *Literature/Film Quarterly* 31.4 (2003) 276-286.

Hertz, Neil. *The End of the Line: Essays on Psychoanalysis and the Sublime.* New York: Columbia University Press, 1985.

Hohoff, Curt. *Heinrich von Kleist in Selbstzeugnissen und Bilddokumenten.* Hamburg: Rowohlt, 1958.

Hollmer, Heide. "Das Leiden an der Kunst. Ein Moritz-Thema und seine Folgen für die *Herzensergießungen eines kunstliebenden Klosterbruders*." *Text + Kritik* 118/119 (1993) 107-117.

Homann, Renate. "Gewalt der Aufklärung - Aufklärung der Gewalt. Zum Erhabenen in Heinrich von Kleists Erzählungen." *Aufklärung* 8.1 (1994) 33-62.

Hoppe, Birgit. *Das andere Gesicht. Grenzen und Potentiale der Hysterie.* Pfaffenweiler: Centaurus Verlagsgesellschaft, 1986.

Horowitz, Gregg M. *Sustaining Loss: Art and Mournful Life*. Stanford: Stanford University Press, 2001.

Huhn, Thomas. "The Kantian Sublime and the Nostalgia for Violence." *The Journal of Aesthetics and Art Criticism* 53.3 (1995) 269-275.

Hundert, Edward M. *Philosophy, Psychiatry and Neuroscience: Three Approaches to the Mind.* Oxford and New York: Oxford University Press, 1989.

Huyssen, Andreas. *Present Pasts: Urban Palimpsests and the Politics of Memory*. Stanford: Stanford University Press, 2003.

—-. *Twilight Memories: Marking Time in a Culture of Amnesia.* New York and London: Routledge, 1995.

—-. "The Vamp and the Machine: Technology and Sexuality in Fritz Lang's *Metropolis*." *New German Critique* 24/25 (1981/82) 221-237.

Irwin, Harvey J. *An Introduction to Parapsychology, Third Edition.* New York: McFarland, 2003.

Jackson, Rosemary. *Fantasy: The Literature of Subversion*. London: Methuen, 1981.

Jähnig, Dieter. *Schelling. Die Kunst in der Philosophie.* Erster Band. *Schellings Begründung von Natur und Geschichte*. Pfüllingen: Günther Neske, 1966.

Janz, Rolf-Peter. "Die ästhetische Bewältigung des Schreckens. Zu Schillers Theorie des Erhabenen." *Geschichte als Literatur. Formen und Grenzen der Repräsentation von Vergangenheit*, eds. Hartmut Eggert, Ulrich Profitlich, and Klaus R. Scherpe. Stuttgart: Metzler, 1990.

Janz, Rolf-Peter, Fabian Stoermer, and Andreas Hiepko, eds. *Schwindelerfahrungen: Zur kulturhistorischen Diagnose eines vieldeutigen Symptoms*. Amsterdam and New York: Rodopi, 2003.

Jennings, Lee B. "ETA Hoffmann's Hauntings. Notes Toward a Parapsychological Approach to Literature," *JEGP* 75 (1976) 559-567.

Johnson, Laurie. *The Art of Recollection in Jena Romanticism: Memory, History, Fiction, and Fragmentation in Texts by Friedrich Schlegel and Novalis*. Tübingen: Niemeyer, 2002.

Jones, Ernest. *Sigmund Freud: Life and Work*. London: Hogarth Press, 1953.

Jones, Malcom V. "*Der Sandmann* and *The Uncanny*: A Sketch for an Alternative Approach." *Paragraph: A Journal of Modern Critical Theory* 7 (1986) 77-101.

Jung, Werner. "Das Unheimliche ist nur des Heimlichen Ende. Die Literatur und das Unheimliche." *Literatur für Leser* 1 (2004).

—. *Schöner Schein der Häßlichkeit oder Häßlichkeit des schönen Scheins*. Frankfurt am Main: Athenäum, 1987.

Kaufmann, Doris. *Aufklärung, bürgerliche Selbsterfahrung und die "Erfindung" der Psychiatrie in Deutschland, 1770-1850*. Göttingen: Vandenhoeck & Ruprecht, 1995.

Kelso, Sylvia. "The Postmodern Uncanny: Or Establishing Uncertainty." *Paradoxa* 3.3-4 (1997) 456-470.

Kershner, Sybille. "'Aus Furcht, zu zerspringen'. Grenzen der Selbsterkenntnis, Krankheit und Geschlecht in popularphilosophischen Texten von Weikard, Pockels und Moritz." *Das achtzehnte Jahrhundert. Mitteilungen der deutschen Gesellschaft für Erforschung des achtzehnten Jahrhunderts* 16.2 (1992) 120-136.

—. *Karl Philipp Moritz und die "Erfahrungsseelenkunde." Literatur und Psychologie im 18. Jahrhundert*. Herne: Verlag für Wissenschaft und Kunst, 1991.

Kilcher, Andreas B. "Ästhetik des Magnets. Zu einem physikalischen Modell der Kunst in der Frühromantik." *Deutsche Vierteljahrsschrift für Literaturwissenschaft und Geistesgeschichte* 72.3 (1998) 463-511.

Klibansky, Raymond, Erwin Panofsky, and Fritz Saxl. *Saturn and Melancholy: Studies in the History of Natural Philosophy, Religion, and Art*. London, 1964.

Kleinschmidt, Erich. *Die Entdeckung der Intensität. Geschichte einer Denkfigur im 18. Jahrhundert*. Göttingen: Wallstein, 2004.

Koepnick, Lutz. *The Dark Mirror: German Cinema Between Hitler and Hollywood*. Berkeley: University of California Press, 2002.

Kolle, Kurt, ed. *Grosse Nervenärzte. 21 Lebensbilder*. 2 vols. Stuttgart: Georg Thieme, 1956.

Koslofsky, Craig M. *The Reformation of the Dead: Death and Ritual in Early Modern Germany, 1450-1700*. London and New York: MacMillan/ St. Martin's Press, 2000.

Kowalik, Jill Anne. "Pietist Grief, *Empfindsamkeit*, and Werther." *Goethe Yearbook* 9 (1999) 77-130.

Krapp, Peter. "'Screen Memory': Hypertext und Deckerinnerung." *Deutscher Vierteljahrsschrift für Literaturwissehschaft und Geistesgeschichte* 72 (1998) 279-296.

Kraft, Hartmut, ed. *Psychoanalyse und das Unheimliche. Die Entwicklung der analytischen Kunstpsychologie seit Freud*. Cologne, 1984.

Krasner, James. "Doubtful Arms and Phantom Limbs: Literary Portrayals of Embodied Grief." *PMLA* 119.2 (2004) 218-232.

Krell, David Farrell. *Contagion: Sexuality, Disease, and Death in German Idealism and Romanticism*. Bloomington and Indianapolis: Indiana University Press, 1998.

—. "Das Unheimliche: Architectural Section of Heidegger and Freud." *Research in Phenomenology* 22 (1992) 43-61.

Kristeva, Julia. *Strangers to Ourselves*. Trans. Leon S. Roudiez. New York: Columbia University Press, 1991.

Krotkoff, Hertha. "Zur geheimen Gesellschaft in Arthur Schnitzlers *Traumnovelle*." *The German Quarterly* 46.2 (1973) 202-209.

Krupnick, Mark, ed. *Displacement: Derrida and After*. Bloomington: Indiana University Press, 1983.

Kunkle, Sheila. "The Uncanny Effects of Cruelty." *Paradoxa: Studies in World Literary Genres* 3.3-4 (1997) 556-570.

Kuzniar, Alice. "A Higher Language: Novalis on Communication With Animals." *The German Quarterly* 76.4 (2003) 426-442.

Laing, R.D. *The Divided Self: An Existential Study in Sanity and Madness*. London: Penguin Books, 1990.

—. "An Examination of Tillich's Theory of Anxiety and Neurosis." *British Journal of Medical Psychology* 30 (1957) 88-91.

Lakoff, George and Mark Johnson. *Philosophy in the Flesh: The Embodied Mind and its Challenge to Western Thought*. New York: Basic Books, 1999.

Leder, Drew. *The Absent Body*. Chicago and London: University of Chicago Press, 1990.

Lehmann, Horst H. "Lob der Frechheit und des Müßiggangs," *Neues Deutschland* 58 (March 10, 1997) 12.

Leibbrand, Werner. *Die spekulative Medizin der Romantik*. Hamburg: Claassen, 1956.

Leibbrand, Werner, and Annemarie Wettley. *Der Wahnsinn. Geschichte der abendländischen Psychopathologie*. Freiburg and Munich: Alber, 1961.

Leibold, Tobias. *Enzyklopädische Anthropologien. Formierungen des Wissens vom Menschen im frühen 19. Jahrhundert bei G.H. Schubert, H. Steffens und G.E. Schulze*. Würzburg: Königshausen & Neumann, 2009.

Lepenies, Wolf. *Melancholie und Gesellschaft*. Frankfurt am Main: Suhrkamp, 1969.

Lerner, Paul. *Hysterical Men: War, Psychiatry, and the Politics of Trauma in Germany, 1890-1930*. Ithaca and London: Cornell University Press, 2003.

Lerner, Paul, and Michael Micale, eds. *Traumatic Pasts: History, Psychiatry, and Trauma in the Modern Age, 1870-1930*. Cambridge: Cambridge University Press, 2001.

Lesky, Erna. *The Vienna Medical School of the Nineteenth Century*. Baltimore and London: Johns Hopkins University Press, 1976.

Levinas, Emmanuel. *Outside the Subject*. Trans. Michael B. Smith. Stanford: Stanford University Press, 1993.

Levine, David. *The Body's Recollection of Being: Phenomenological Psychology and the Deconstruction of Nihilism*. London and Boston: Routledge & Kegan Paul, 1985.

Librett, Jeffrey S. *The Rhetoric of Cultural Dialogue: Jews and Germans from Moses Mendelssohn to Richard Wagner and Beyond*. Stanford: Stanford University Press, 2000.

Lippit, Akira Mizuta. *Electric Animal: Toward a Rhetoric of Wildlife*. Minneapolis: University of Minnesota Press, 2000.

Liverpool, Graham. *Freud's Literary Culture*. Cambridge: Cambridge University Press, 2000.

Lydenberg, Robin. "Freud's Uncanny Narratives." *PMLA* 112.5 (1997) 1072-1086.

Mack, Michael. "Freud's Other Enlightenment: Turning the Tables on Kant." *New German Critique* 85 (2002) 3-33.

Magherini, Graziella. *La sindrome di Stendhal*. Florence: Ponte alle Grazie, 1989.

—. "The Unconscious and Art: The Aesthetic Uncanny and the Function of the Selected Fact." Paper delivered at The Third New Style European Psychoanalytical Federation Annual Conference in Helsinki, Finland, 15-18 April, 2004.

Mahlendorf, Ursula. "E.T.A. Hoffmann's "The Sandmann": The Fictional Psycho-biography of a Romantic Poet." *American Imago* 32.3 (1975) 217-232.

—. "Die Psychologie der Romantik." *Romantik-Handbuch*. Ed. Helmut Schanze. Stuttgart: Kröner, 1994. 590-604.

Marx, Patricia. "Art Attack." *The New York Times Magazine*. August 20, 2000, pp. 69-72.

Maasschelein, Anneleen. "The Concept as Ghost: Conceptualization of the Uncanny in Late-Twentieth-Century Theory." *Mosaic: A Journal for the Interdisciplinary Study of Literature* 35.1 (2002) 53-68.

—. "Double Reading/Reading Double: Psychoanalytic Poetics at Work." *Paradoxa: Studies in World Literary Genres* 3.3-4 (1997) 395-406.

Matenko, Percy. *Tieck and Solger: The Complete Correspondence*. New York and Berlin: B. Westermann, 1933.

Matenko, Percy, Edwin H. Zeydel, and Bertha M. Masche, eds. *Letters To and From Ludwig Tieck and His Circle*. Chapel Hill: University of North Carolina Press, 1967.

May, Rollo. *The Meaning of Anxiety*. New York: W.W. Norton, 1996.

Mayer, Paola."Das Unheimliche als Strafe und Warnung. Zu einem Aspekt von E.T.A. Hoffmanns Kritik an der Frühromantik." *E.T.A. Hoffmann Jahrbuch* 8 (2000) 56-68.

—. "Die unheimliche Landschaft. Ein Aspekt von Eichendorffs lyrischer Dichtung." *Athenäum* 5 (1995) 169-196.

Mazzoni, Cristina. *Saint Hysteria: Neurosis, Mysticism, and Gender in European Culture*. Ithaca and London: Cornell University Press, 1996.

McCaffrey, Phillip. "Erasing the Body: Freud's Uncanny Father-Child." *American Imago* 49.4 (1992) 371-390.

—. "Freud's Uncanny Women." *Reading Freud's Reading*. Eds. Sander Gilman, et al. New York: New York University Press, 1994. 91-108.

Mentzos, Stavros. *Hysterie. Zur Psychodynamik unbewußter Inszenierungen*. Frankfurt am Main: Fischer Taschenbuch Verlag, 1989.

Micale, Mark. *Approaching Hysteria: Disease and Its Interpretations*. 1995.

Miller, Norbert. "Sehnsucht nach dem Unendlichen. Vor 150 Jahren starb Friedrich Schlegel." *Süddeutsche Zeitung* 10 (January 13-14, 1979) 138.

Mitchell, Juliet. *Mad Men and Medusas: Reclaiming Hysteria*. New York: Basic Books, 2000.

Muderlak, Astrid. *Das Magazin zur Erfahrungsseelenkunde und die Technik der Psychoanalyse*. Diss. University of Munich, 1990.

Müller-Braunschweig, Hans. "Der unheimliche Körper." *Psychotherapie, Psychosomatik, medizinische Psychologie* 42.1 (1992) 16-23.

Müller-Seidel, Walter, and Wolfgang Riedel, eds. *Die Weimarer Klassik und ihre Geheimbünde*. Würzburg: Königshausen & Neumann, 2002.

Müller-Sievers, Helmut. *Self-Generation: Biology, Philosophy, and Literature Around 1800*. Stanford: Stanford University Press, 1997.

Müller-Tamm, Pia, and Katharina Sykora, eds. *Puppen - Körper - Automata. Phantasmen der Moderne*. Anläßlich der Ausstellung Puppen - Körper - Automata. Phantasmen der Moderne, Kunstsammlung

Nordrhein-Westfalen, Düsseldorf vom 24. Juli bis 17. Oktober 1999. Cologne: Oktagon, 1999.

Nelson, Victoria. *The Secret Life of Puppets*. Cambridge: Harvard University Press, 2002.

Neu, Jerome, ed. *The Cambridge Companion to Freud.* Cambridge: Cambridge University Press, 1998.

Neumann, Gerhard, ed. *Heinrich von Kleist. Kriegsfall - Rechtsfall - Sündenfall.* Freiburg im Breisgau: Rombach, 1994.

Niekerk, Carl. "Men in Pain: Disease and Displacement in *Der Findling*." *Kleists Erzählungen und Dramen. Neue Studien.* Eds. Paul Michael Lützeler and David Pan. Würzburg: Königshausen & Neumann, 2001. 107-119.

—-. *Zwischen Naturgeschichte und Anthropologie. Lichtenberg im Kontext der Spätaufklärung*. Tübingen: Niemeyer, 2005.

Nobus, Dany. "De Artistieke Geheimenissen van het Unheimliche." *Psychoanalytische Perspektieven* 19/20 (1993) 127-141.

Norris, Margot. *Beasts of the Modern Imagination: Darwin, Nietzsche, Kafka, Ernst, and Lawrence*. Baltimore: Johns Hopkins University Press, 1985.

Oelkers, Jürgen. "Väter und Söhne: Über Anklage, Mißverständnis und den fehlenden Adressaten in der Erziehung." *Neue Sammlung* 38.4 (1998) 533-553.

Oswald, Ellen. *Figuren der Melancholie. Ludwig Tiecks "William Lovell" im Kontext von Erfahrungsseelenkunde und Pädagogik.* Bern: Peter Lang, 1991.

Peel, Ellen. "Psychoanalysis and the Uncanny in Literature." *Comparative Literature Studies* 17.4 (1980) 410-417.

Peters, Uwe Henrik. *Studies in German Romantic Psychiatry: Justinus Kerner as a Psychiatric Practitioner, E.T.A. Hoffmann as a Psychiatric Theorist*. London: Institute of Germanic Studies, University of London, 1990.

Pfeiffer, Joachim. *Die zerbrochenen Bilder. Gestörte Ordnungen im Werk Heinrich von Kleists*. Würzburg: Königshausen & Neumann, 1989.

Pfotenhauer, Helmut. "Karl Philipp Moritz: *Erfahrungsseelenkunde* als Literatur." *Literarische Anthropologie. Selbstbiographien und ihre Geschichte - am Leitfaden des Leibes*. Stuttgart, 1987. 93-115.

Piccolomini, Manfredi. "Going to Pieces in Florence." *Archaeology* 43.4 (1990) 64-67.

Pietzcker, Carl. "Die Literatur und das Unheimliche. Überlegungen anläßlich des Unheimlichen an der Realität von Völkervernichtungsmitteln." *fragmente* 11 (1984) 93-112.

Pizer, John. "Body and Soul: Lessing's Consistent Distinctions." *Lessing Yearbook* 26 (1994) 55-75.

Pocock, Judy. "Collaborative Dreaming: Schnitzler's *Traumnovelle*, Kubrick's *Eyes Wide Shut*, and the 'Paradox of the Ordinary.'" *Arachne* 7.1/2 (2000) 76-93.

Porter, Roy. *Flesh in the Age of Reason*. New York and London: W.W. Norton, 2003.

—-. *The Greatest Benefit to Mankind: A Medical History of Humanity*. New York and London: W.W. Norton, 1997.

Porter, Roy, and W.F. Bynum, eds. *Companion Encyclopedia of the History of Medicine*. Vol. 1. London and New York: Routledge, 1997.

Prager, Brad. *Aesthetic Vision and German Romanticism: Writing Images*. Rochester, NY: Camden House, 2007.

Prawer, S.S. *Caligari's Children: The Film as Tale of Terror*. Oxford: Oxford University Press, 1980.

—-. "Hoffmann's Uncanny Guest: A Reading of 'Der Sandmann.'" *German Life and Letters* 18 (1964/65) 297-308.

Preitz, Max. *Friedrich Schlegel und Novalis. Biographie einer Romantikerfreundschaft in ihren Briefen*. Darmstadt: H. Gentner, 1957.

Quackelbeen, Julien. "Het Unheimliche: Een Klinisch-Theoretische Verkenning." *Psychoanalytische Perspektieven* 19/20 (1993) 7-25.

Quackelbeen, Julien, and Dany Nobus. "Freud en *Der Sandmann* of de Psychoanalyticus en het Literair Werk." *Psychoanalytische Perspektieven* 19/20 (1993) 79-126.

Radkau, Johann. *Das Zeitalter der Nervosität. Deutschland zwischen Bismarck und Hitler*. Munich: Carl Hanser, 1998.

Radley, Alan. "The Aesthetics of Illness: Narrative, Horror and the Sublime." *Sociology of Health and Illness* 21.6 (1999) 778-796.

Rand, Nicholas, and Maria Torok. "'The Sandman' Looks at 'The Uncanny': The Return of the Repressed or of the Secret—Hoffmann's Question to Freud." *Speculations After Freud: Psychoanalysis, Philosophy and Culture*. Florence, KY: Taylor & Francis/Routledge, 1994. 185-203.

Reinalter, Helmut, ed. *Aufklärung und Geheimgesellschaften. Zur politischen Funktion und Sozialstruktur der Freimaurerlogen im 18. Jahrhundert*. Munich: R. Oldenbourg, 1989.

Risser, James. "Siting Order at the Limits of Construction: Deconstructing Architectural Space." *Research in Phenomenology* 22 (1992) 70.

Roback, Abraham Aaron. *History of Psychology and Psychiatry*. New York: Philosophical Library, 1961.

Roberts, Julian. *German Philosophy: An Introduction*. Atlantic Highlands, NJ: Humanities Press International, Inc., 1988.

Rothberg, Michael. *Traumatic Realism: The Demands of Holocaust Representation*. Minneapolis: University of Minnesota Press, 2000.

Rothfield, Lawrence. *Vital Signs: Medical Realism in Nineteenth-Century Fiction*. Princeton: Princeton University Press, 1992.
Rorty, Richard. *Philosophy and the Mirror of Nature*. Princeton: Princeton University Press, 1980.
Rose, Louis. *The Freudian Calling: Early Viennese Psychoanalysis and the Pursuit of Cultural Science*. Detroit: Wayne State University Press, 1998.
Ross, Daniel W. "Seeking a Way Home: The Uncanny in Wordsworth's 'Immortality Ode.'" *Studies in English Literature, 1500-1900* 32.4 (1992) 625-644.
Royle, Nicholas. *The Uncanny: An Introduction*. New York and London: Routledge, 2003.
Rushing, Robert. *Resisting Arrest: Detective Fiction and Popular Culture*. New York: Other Press, 2007.
Ryan, Judith. *The Vanishing Subject. Early Psychology and Literary Modernism*. Chicago and London: University of Chicago Press, 1991.
Salz-Hombach, Klaus. *Philosophische Psychologie im 19. Jahrhundert. Entstehung und Problemgeschichte*. Munich: Karl Alber Freiburg, 1993.
Salzman, Leon. "Uncanny Feeling." *Psychiatry* 17 (1954) 100-102.
Santner, Eric L. "On Masters, Slaves, and Other Seducers: Arthur Schnitzler's *Traumnovelle*." *Modern Austrian Literature* 19.3/4 (1986) 33-48.
—. *On the Psychotheology of Everyday Life: Reflections on Freud and Rosenzweig*. Chicago: The University of Chicago Press, 2001.
Sass, Louis A. *Madness and Modernism: Insanity in the Light of Modern Art, Literature, and Thought*. New York: Basic Books, 1992.
Scheuerbrandt, Heike. "Die Stimme der Natur. Dietrich Georg Kiesers Auffassung vom tierischen Magnetismus." *Athenäum. Jahrbuch für Romantik* (1999) 227-252.
Schings, Hans-Jürgen. *Der ganze Mensch. Anthropologie und Literatur im 18. Jahrhundert*. Stuttgart: Metzler, 1994.
—. *Melancholie und Aufklärung. Melancholiker und ihre Kritiker in Erfahrungsseelenkunde und Literatur des 18. Jahrhunderts*. Stuttgart: Metzler, 1977.
Schirmbeck, Heinrich. *Die Angst des Ödipus. Zum sozial-ethischen Defizit der Moderne*. Frankfurt am Main: Peter Lang, 1996.
Schleifer, Ronald. *Modernism and Time: The Logic of Abundance in Literature, Science, and Culture, 1880-1930*. Cambridge: Cambridge University Press, 2000.
Schmidt, Jochen. *Geschichte des Genie-Gedankens 1750-1945*.Vol. 1. *Von der Aufklärung bis zum Idealismus*. Darmstadt: Wissenschaftliche Buchgesellschaft, 1985.

Schneider, F. J. "Tiecks *William Lovell* and Jean Pauls *Titan.*" *Zeitschrift für deutsche Philologie* 61 (1936) 58-75.

Schrimpf, Hans Joachim. "Arthur Schnitzlers *Traumnovelle.*" *Zeitschrift für deutsche Philologie* 82 (1963) 172-192.

—. *Karl Philipp Moritz*. Stuttgart: Metzler, 1980.

—. "Das *Magazin zur Erfahrungsseelenkunde* und sein Herausgeber." *Zeitschrift für deutsche Philologie* 99.2 (1980) 161-187.

Schutjer, Karin. *Narrating Community After Kant: Schiller, Goethe, and Hölderlin*. Detroit: Wayne State University Press, 2001.

Schwarz, Anette. *Melancholie. Figuren und Orte einer Stimmung*. Vienna: Passagen, 1996.

—. "Social Subjects and Tragic Legacies: The Uncanny in Theodor Storm's *Der Schimmelreiter.*" *Germanic Review* 73.3 (1998) 251-266.

Schwarz, Egon. "A Puzzle and an Enigma: Stanley Kubrick's *Eyes Wide Shut* and Arthur Schnitzler's *Traumnovelle.*" *Modern Austrian Literature* 34.1/2 (2001) 103-111.

Scruton, Roger. *The Aesthetic Understanding: Essays in the Philosophy of Art and Culture*. South Bend: St. Augustine's Press, 1998.

Sebald, W.G. "Das Schrecknis der Liebe. Überlegungen zu Schnitzlers *Traumnovelle.*" *Merkur* 2 (1985) 120-131.

Segar, Kenneth. "Determinism and Character: Arthur Schnitzler's *Traumnovelle* and his Unpublished Critique of Psychoanalysis." *Oxford German Studies* 8 (1973) 114-127.

Selinsky, Herman. "On Depersonalization and Derealization." *Journal of the Hillside Hospital* 5 (1956) 402-415.

Setzer, Sharon M. "Wordsworth's Wanderer, the Epitaph, and the Uncanny." *Genre* 24.4 (1991) 361-380.

Shorter, Edward. *From Paralysis to Fatigue: A History of Psychosomatic Illness in the Modern Era*. New York: Macmillan, 1992.

—. *A History of Psychiatry: From the Era of the Asylum to the Age of Prozac*. New York: John Wiley & Sons, 1997.

Showalter, Elaine. *The Female Malady: Women, Madness, and English Culture, 1830-1980*. New York: Pantheon, 1985.

—. *Hystories: Hysterical Epidemics and Modern Media*. New York: Columbia University Press, 1997.

Siegel, Jeanne. "Uncanny Repetition." *Arts Magazine* 66.1 (1991) 31.

Simonis, Annette. "'Das Schöne ist eine höhere Sprache'. Karl Philipp Moritz' Ästhetik zwischen Ontologie und Transzendental-philosophie." *Deutschevierteljahrsschrift* 68.3 (1994) 490-505.

Simpson, David. "Commentary: Updating the Sublime." *Studies in Romanticism* 26.2 (1987) 245-259.

Sinn, Christian. "'Acht Jahre unter der Erde'. Geheime Gesellschaften des 18. Jahrhunderts und ihre Menschenexperimente in Jean Pauls *Die unsichtbare Loge* (1793)." *Jahrbuch der Jean-Paul Gesellschaft* 44 (2007).

Skura, M.A. *The Literary Use of the Psychoanalytic Process*. New Haven and London: Yale University Press, 1981.

Slater, Lauren. *Lying: A Metaphorical Memoir*. New York: Random House, 2000.

Slavney, Phillip R. *Perspectives on "Hysteria."* Baltimore and London: The Johns Hopkins University Press, 1990.

Smith, Andrew. *Gothic Radicalism: Literature, Philosophy and Psychoanalysis in the Nineteenth Century*. Houndmills, England and New York: Macmillan-St. Martin's, 2000.

Spector, Jack J. *The Aesthetics of Freud*. New York: Praeger, 1972.

Steig, Michael. "Defining the Grotesque: An Attempt at Synthesis." *Journal of Aesthetics and Art Criticism* 29.2 (1970) 253-260.

Steigerwald, Jörn, and Daniela Watzke, eds. *Reiz – Imagination – Aufmerksamkeit. Erregung und Steuerung von Einbildungskraft im klassischen Zeitalter (1680-1830)*. Würzburg: Königshausen & Neumann, 2003.

Stein, Howard F. "The Holocaust, the Uncanny, and the Jewish Sense of History." *Political Psychology* 5.1 (1984) 5-35.

Stewart, Susan. *On Longing: Narratives of the Miniature, the Gigantic, the Souvenir, the Collection*. Durham and London: Duke University Press, 1993.

Stoicea, Gabriela. "Re-Producing the Class and Gender Divide: Fritz Lang's *Metropolis*." *Women in German Yearbook* 22 (2006) 21-42.

Sullivan, Harry Stack. *The Interpersonal Theory of Psychiatry*. New York: W.W. Norton, 1953.

Sullivan, Heather. *The Intercontextuality of Self and Nature in Ludwig Tieck's Early Works*. New York: Peter Lang, 1997.

Svenaeus, Fredrik. "The Body Uncanny: Further Steps Toward a Phenomenology of Illness." *Medicine, Health Care & Philosophy* 3.2 (2000) 125-137.

—. "Freud's Philosophy of the Uncanny." *Scandinavian Psychoanalytic Review* 22 (1999) 239-254.

—. "Das Unheimliche: Towards a Phenomenology of Illness." *Medicine, Health Care & Philosophy* 3.1 (2000) 3-16.

Tatar, Maria. "The Politics of the Gaze: Mesmerism Before the French Revolution and After." *The French Revolution and the Age of Goethe*. Ed. Gerhard Hoffmeister. Hildesheim: Olms, 1989. 67-79.

—. *Spellbound: Studies on Mesmerism and Literature*. Princeton: Princeton University Press, 1978.

Tauber, Alfred I. "From Descartes' Dream to Husserl's Nightmare." *The Elusive Synthesis: Aesthetics and Science*, ed. A. I. Tauber. Dordrecht: Kluwer Academic, 1995.

Taylor, Charles. *Sources of the Self: The Making of Modern Identity*. Cambridge: Harvard University Press, 1989.

Terdiman, Richard. *Present Past: Modernity and the Memory Crisis*. Ithaca: Cornell University Press, 1993.

Thalmann, Marianne. *Probleme der Dämonie in Ludwig Tiecks Schriften*. Hildesheim: Gerstenberg, 1978.

—. *Die Romantik des Trivialen. Von Grosses "Genius" bis Tiecks "William Lovell."* Munich: Paul List, 1970.

Tholen, Georg Christoph. "Das Unheimliche an der Realität und die Realität des Unheimlichen." *fragmente* 11 (1984) 6-29.

Tiffany, Daniel. *Toy Medium: Materialism and Modern Lyric*. Berkeley: University of California Press, 2000.

Todorov, Tzvetan. *The Fantastic: A Structural Approach to a Literary Genre*. Trans. Richard Howard. Ithaca: Cornell University Press, 1975.

—. *Theories of the Symbol*. Trans. Catherine Porter. Ithaca: Cornell University Press, 1982.

Todd, Jane Marie. "The Veiled Woman in Freud's 'Das Unheimliche." *Signs: Journal of Women in Culture and Society* 11.3 (1986) 519-528.

Trainer, James. *Ludwig Tieck: From Gothic to Romantic*. The Hague: Mouton & Co., 1964.

Turner, Victor. *The Ritual Process: Structure and Anti-Structure*. Chicago: Aldine, 1969.

Ueding, Gert. "Die Wahrheit lebt in der Täuschung fort. Historische Aspekte der Vor-Schein-Ästhetik." *Literatur ist Utopie*, ed. Gert Ueding. Frankfurt am Main: Suhrkamp, 1978. 81-102.

Uexküll, Thure von. "Historische Überlegung zu dem Problem einer Medizin-Semiotik." *Zeitschrift für Semiotik* 6.1/2 (1984) 53-58.

Van Reijen, Willem, and Gunzelin Schmid Noerr, eds. *Vierzig Jahre Flaschenpost: 'Dialektik der Aufklärung' 1947 bis 1987*. Frankfurt am Main: Fischer Taschenbuch, 1987.

Verwey, Gerlof. *Psychiatry In An Anthropological and Biomedical Context : Philosophical Presuppositions and Implications of German Psychiatry, 1820-1870*. Trans. Lynne Richards, Philip Hyams, and Johan Staargaard. Dordrecht and Boston: D. Reidel Publishing Co., 1985.

Vidler, Anthony. *The Architectural Uncanny: Essays in the Modern Unhomely*. Cambridge, MA: MIT Press, 1992.

Vietta, Silvio, and Dirk Kemper, eds. *Ästhetische Moderne in Europa. Grundzüge und Problemzusammenhänge seit der Romantik*. Munich: Fink, 1998.

Vitek, Jack. "Another Squint at *Eyes Wide Shut*: A Postmodern Reading." *Modern Austrian Literature* 34.1/2 (2001) 113-124.

Von der Thüsen, Joachim. *Het verlangen naar huivering. Over het sublieme, het wrede en het unheimliche*. Amsterdam: Querido, 1997.

Wagenknecht, David. "Here's Looking at You, Peter Quint: *The Turn of the Screw*, Freud's *Dora*, and the Aesthetics of Hysteria." *American Imago* 55.4 (1998) 423-458.

Walter, Jürgen. "Das Unheimliche as Wirkungsfunktion. Eine rezeptionsästhetische Analyse von E.T.A. Hoffmanns Erzählung *Der Sandmann*." *Mitteilungen der E.T.A. Hoffmann-Gesellschaft e.V.* 30 (1984) 15-33.

Walzel, Oskar, ed. *Friedrich Schlegels Briefe an seinen Bruder August Wilhelm*. Berlin: Speyer & Peters, 1890.

Weber, Samuel. *The Legend of Freud*. Stanford: Stanford University Press, 2000.

Weinzierl, Ulrich. "Halbnomade. Christoph Ransmayrs Reflexionen." *Die Welt*. March 21, 2004.

Weiskel, Thomas. *The Romantic Sublime: Studies in the Structure and Psychology of Transcendence*. Baltimore: Johns Hopkins University Press, 1976.

Weissberg, Liliane. *Geistersprache. Philosophischer und literarischer Diskurs im späten achtzehnten Jahrhundert*. Würzburg: Königshausen & Neumann, 1990.

Wieckenberg, Ernst-Peter. "Die Schwindsucht, der Körper und die Aufklärung bei Karl Philipp Moritz." *Text + Kritik* 118/119 (1993) 15-23.

Williamson, Patricia. "La Petite Mort: Sex Equated to Death in Stanley Kubrick's *Eyes Wide Shut*." *Journal of Evolutionary Psychology* 8 (2001) 165-171.

Wilson, W. Daniel. *Unterirdische Gänge. Goethe, Freimaurerei und Politik*. Göttingen: Wallstein, 1999.

Wöbkemeier, Rita. *Erzählte Krankheit. Medizinische und literarische Phantasien um 1800*. Stuttgart: Metzler, 1990.

Wolters, Gereon, ed. *Franz Anton Mesmer und der Mesmerismus. Wissenschaft, Scharlatanerie, Poesie*. Konstanz: Universitätsverlag, 1988.

Worbs, Michael. *Nervenkunst. Literatur und Psychoanalyse im Wien der Jahrhundertwende*. Frankfurt am Main: Europäische Verlagsanstalt, 1983.

Yalom, Irvin D. *Love's Executioner and Other Tales of Psychotherapy*. New York: HarperCollins, 1989.

Yolton, John W. *Thinking Matter: Materialism in Eighteenth-Century Britain*. Minneapolis: University of Minnesota Press, 1984.

Young, James E. "Against Redemption: The Arts of Countermemory in Germany Today." *Symbolic Loss: The Ambiguity of Mourning and Memory at Century's End*. Ed. Peter Homans. Charlottesville: The University Press of Virginia, 2000. 126-144.

Zelle, Carsten. *Angenehmes Grauen. Literaturhistorische Beiträge zur Ästhetik des Schrecklichen im achtzehnten Jahrhundert*. Hamburg: F. Meiner, 1987.

—-. "Erhabenheit und Frühromantik. Zu Carl Grosses Buch *Über das Erhabene* von 1788." *Neohelicon* 17.2 (1990) 27-41.

—-. "Experiment, Experience and Observation in Eighteenth-Century Anthropology and Psychology—The Examples of Krüger's *Experimentalseelenlehre* and Moritz' *Erfahrungsseelenkunde*." *Orbis Litterarum* 56.2 (2001) 93-105.

—-. *Vernünftige Ärzte. Hallesche Psychomediziner und die Anfänge der Anthropologie in der deutschsprachigen Frühaufklärung*. Tübingen: Niemeyer, 2001.

Ziolkowski, Theodore. *German Romanticism and its Institutions*. Princeton: Princeton University Press, 1990.

Zizek, Slavoj. *The Abyss of Freedom/Ages of the World*. An essay by Slavoj Zizek with the text of Schelling's *Die Weltalter* (second draft, 1813) in English translation by Judith Norman. Ann Arbor: University of Michigan Press, 1997.

—-. *Welcome to the Desert of the Real! Five Essays on September 11 and Related Dates*. London and New York: Verso, 2002.

www.ingramcontent.com/pod-product-compliance
Lightning Source LLC
LaVergne TN
LVHW102227300926
849160LV00005B/49